UNMANNED AERIAL SYSTEMS
THE DEFINITIVE GUIDE

BY MICHAEL LEASURE

UNMANNED AERIAL SYSTEMS: THE DEFINITIVE GUIDE

Unmanned Aviation Systems: The Definite Guide
ISBN-13: 978-1-941144-43-5
by Michael Leasure

Copyright © 2016 Michael Leasure. All rights reserved.
Printed in the United States of America

All rights reserved. No part of the materials protected by this copyright may be reproduced or utilized in any form, electronic or mechanical, including photocopying, recording, or by any information storage and retrieval system, without written permission from the copyright owner.

The content, statements, views, and opinions herein are the sole expression of the respective authors and not that of Aircraft Technical Book Company, LLC. References to any specific commercial product, process, or service by trade name, trademark, manufacturer, or otherwise does not constitute or imply its endorsement or recommendation by the author nor Aircraft Technical Book Company, LLC, and such reference shall not be used for advertising or product endorsement purposes. All trademarks cited are the property of their respective owners. This copyrighted work is an independent publication and has not been authorized, sponsored, or otherwise approved by the owners of the trademarks or service marks reference in this product.

There may be images in this booth that feature models; these models do not necessarily endorse, represent, or participate in the activities represented in the images. Any screenshots in this product are for educational and instructive purposes only.

The author(s) and publisher have made every effort in the preparation of this book to ensure the accuracy of the information. However, the information contained in this book is sold without warranty, either express or implied. Neither the author(s) or Aircraft Technical Book Company, LLC will be held liable for any damages caused or alleged to be caused either directly or indirectly by this book.

Distributed by:

Aircraft Technical Book Company, LLC
PO Box 270
Tabernash, CO 80478
970.726.5111
www.actechbooks.com
orders@actechbooks.com

Author: Michael Leasure

Trademarks
All terms and references that are know to be trademarks to the author(s) and the publisher have been capitalized and acknowledged. However, Aircraft Technical Book Company, LLC cannot guarantee the accuracy of these trademarks.

ABOUT THE AUTHOR

MICHAEL LEASURE

Michael Leasure has been involved in the aviation community for over 44 years. His interest in aviation began at an early age. He first published an original design model aircraft in 1984 while attending Purdue University in Aviation Technology. Over the subsequent years, he achieved many more milestones in his aviation career, including a private pilot's license with experience in aerobatics, complex aircraft, and tailwheel operations. He also earned an airframe and powerplant license with inspection authorization. The last decade of his aviation activities have been devoted primarily to unmanned aircraft design, construction, pilotage, and development. He has over 10 years' experience in field deployment of precision agricultural aircraft where he served as operator, observer, and technician. He is currently an associate professor at Purdue University in the Aviation Technology department. His ongoing efforts include research, teaching, and flying for recreation, fixed wing and multirotor autonomous aircraft.

DEDICATION

The author of this text has spent years teaching in the aviation program at Purdue University. As autonomous aircraft operations have become more prominent, they decided that a definitive text was needed for both serious hobbyists as well as those seeking to work in this new and growing industry. That provided the basis for writing this text.

I would like to thank all the people that have contributed over the years to our UAS knowledge as well as my family and co-workers that have had to "tolerate" this obsession! It was, and is, much appreciated.

Michael Leasure

TABLE OF CONTENTS

Unmanned Aerial Systems: The Definitive Guide 2
About the Author 3
Dedication 4
Acknowledgments 4

Chapter 1
Introduction to Unmanned Aerial Systems 9

Chapter 2
Unmanned Aerial Vehicle Design and Construction 13
    Introduction to Designs 13
        Mission Driven Design 13
    Platform Selection 14
    Specific Platform Advantages and Disadvantages 14
    Rotorcraft Advantages and Disadvantages 15
    Hybrid Designs and Airships 16
    Powerplant Selection 17
    Build, Modify or Readymade 18
    Aerodynamics and Flight Controls 18
    Forces Acting On an Aircraft 18
    Airfoils and Lift 19
    Airfoil Shapes 20
        Wing Configurations 21
        Propellers and Rotorcraft 22
    Axes of Motion of an Aircraft 23
    Aircraft Stability and Control 24
        Unique Forces Acting on the Helicopter 24
        Torque Compensation 25
        Unmanned Multirotor Aerodynamics 26
        Multirotor Stability 27
    Flight Controller 27
    Aircraft Loads and Stress 28
        Multiple Stresses 29
        Stress Considerations in Repair 29
    Fuselage 30
        Truss Type 30
        Monocoque Type 30
            Semimonocoque Type 31
            Wing Spars 31
        Wing Ribs 31
        Wing Skin 32

Chapter 3
Aircraft Structures, Materials, and Repair 33
    Aircraft Structural Concepts 33
    Stresses in Structural Repairs 34
        Tension 35
        Compression 35
        Shear 35
        Compound Stresses 35
    Aerospace Materials and their Properties 35
        Wooden Structures 35
        Adhesives 36
        Preparation for the Application of Adhesives 36
        Fabric Coverings 37
        Metallic Structural Materials 38
        Structural Fasteners 39
        Blind Rivets 40
    Metal Airframe Inspection 40
        Types of Metallic Damage and Defects 41
        Classification of Metal Damage 42
    Composite Structures 44
        Materials 44
    Laminates 44
        Types of Composite Fibrous Materials 45
        Carbon and/or Graphite Fiber 45
        Matrix Materials 45
        Pre-Impregnated Products 46
        Wet Layup Process 46
        Sandwich Structures 47
        Foam Core Structures 47
    Composite Structural Damage 48
        Inspection of Composite Materials 49
            Nondestructive Inspection, Composites 49
    Composite Repair Techniques 50
        Prepreg Composites 51
    Aircraft Structures, Damage and Repair 52
        Fuselage 52
        Wings 53
        Flight Control Surfaces 55
        Dual Purpose Flight Control Surfaces 56
        Fabric 56
        Landing Gear 56
        Helicopter Structure 57

Chapter 4
Electricity, Electrical, Communications and Navigation Systems . 59
    Basic Electricity 59
        Current 59
        Resistance 60

Contents

- Conductors and Insulators 60
- Power 61
- Electrical Energy Production 61
  - Pressure 61
  - Chemical 62
  - Fuel Cells 63
  - Thermal Electricity Generation 64
  - Solar Energy 64
  - Mechanical Generators 64
- Direct and Alternating Current 64
- Circuit Protection Devices 65
  - Switches 66
- Switch Types 66
- Motors 67
- Circuits 67
- Semiconductors 67
- Logic Circuits 68
- Instrument Systems 69
  - Instrument Components 69
  - Instrument Classifications 69
  - Instrument Operating Principles 69
  - Types of Pressure 71
  - Pressure Measuring Instruments 72
  - Pressure Switches 72
  - Pitot-Static Systems 73
  - Altimeters and Altitude 74
- Speed and Distance Measurements 76
  - Airspeed Indicators 76
  - Mechanical Motion Indicators 77
  - Accelerometers 78
  - Stall Warning and Angle of Attack Indicators 78
- Temperature Measuring Instruments 79
  - Non-Electric Temperature Indicators 79
  - Electrical Temperature Measuring Indicators 80
  - Direction Indicating Instruments 80
  - Solid State Magnetometers 80
  - Attitude Indicators 80
- Communication and Navigation Systems 81
  - Analog and Digital Signals 81
  - Radio Communication 82
- Radio Wave Creation and Transmission 83
- Commonly Used Unmanned Aircraft Antennas 85
  - Skew-Planar Wheel Antenna 86
  - Cloverleaf Antenna 86
  - Dipole Antenna 86
  - Patch Antenna 86
- Antenna Wiring 86
- Transceivers 87
- Internet Wi-Fi 87
- Mobile Phone Technology 88
- Bluetooth 89
- Aviation Navigation Systems 89
  - VOR 89
  - Tactical Air Navigation (TACAN) 89
  - Global Navigation Satellite System 90
  - Global Positioning System 90
  - GNSS Augmentation 90
  - Satellite Based Augmentation Systems 91
  - Ground-Based Augmentation System 91
  - ADS-B 92

Chapter 5
Powerplant Theory and Operation 93
- Internal Combustion-Reciprocating Engines 93
  - Reciprocating Engine Operation 93
  - Internal Combustion Engine Terminology 94
- Four-Stroke or Four-Cycle Engine 94
  - Intake Stroke 95
  - Valve Timing 95
  - Compression Stroke and Ignition 96
  - Power Stroke 96
  - Exhaust Valve 96
  - Exhaust Stroke 96
- Two-Stroke Engines 97
- Diesel Cycle Engines 97
- Diesel Engine Fuel 97
- Engine Power and Efficiency Calculations 98
  - Work 98
  - Horsepower 98
  - Piston Displacement 98
  - Area of a Circle 99
  - Compression Ratio 99
- Gas Turbine Engine Characteristics 100
- Gas Turbine Types and Operation 100
- Electric Motor Propulsion Characteristics 102
- Types of Electric Motors 102
- Electronic Speed Control (ESC) 102
  - Inrunner versus Outrunner Motors 103
- Electric Motor Power Ratings and Selection 104
  - Watt-Motor Comparison 104
  - KV or kV Motor Rating 104
- Powerplant Inspection and Maintenance 105
- Fueled Engine Maintenance 105

Chapter 6
Flight Control 107
    Control Systems 107
        Manual Flight Control 107
    Assisted Manual Control 108
    Autonomous Flight Control 109
    Telemetry 111
    Data Logging 111
    Failsafe Systems 112
    Firmware 112
    Autopilot Installation 113
    Autonomous Testing 114
    Test Flight and Flight Test 115
        First Person View (FPV) 115

Chapter 7
Sensors and Payloads 117
    Payload Installation 117
    Payload Integration 118
    Payload Mounting Systems 118
    Gyro Stabilization 119
    Air Sampling Payloads 119
    Acoustic Payloads 120
        Unconventional Payloads 120
    Weight and Balance 121
    Aircraft Weight 121
    Effects of Weight 121
    Weight Limitations 122
    Center of Gravity 122
        Center of Gravity Calculation 123
        Calculating an Aircraft's CG 123
        Stability and Balance 124
        Rotorcraft Stability 124
        Mechanical Balancing 125
    Special Stability Issues 125

Chapter 8
Airspace Operations 127
    Airspace 127
    Airspace Classes and Navigational Charts 128
    IFR Flight in Controlled Airspace (Class A, B, C, D, and E) 128
    UAS and VFR Flight in Controlled Airspace (Class A, B, C, D, and E) 128
    IFR Flight in Uncontrolled Airspace (Class G) 129
    UAS and VFR Flight in Uncontrolled Airspace (Class G) 129
    Aeronautical Charting 129
    Sectional Charts 129
    Instrument Charts 129
    Air Traffic Control Facilities 129
    Terminal Radar Approach Control (TRACON) 130
    Combined Radar Approach Control and Tower with Radar 131
    Enroute air traffic control 131
    Flight Service Stations 131
    ATC Services in Different Airspace Classes 131
        Class F and G Airspace 133
        Special Use Airspace 133
        Prohibited Areas 134
        Restricted Areas 134
        Temporary Flight Restrictions 134
        Special flight rules areas 135
        DC Flight Restricted Zone and Special Flight Rules Area 135
        Warning Area 135
        Military Operations Area 136
        Military Training Routes 136
        Alert Areas 136
        Controlled Firing Areas 136
    Communications Systems 137
        Radio Phraseology 137
        Standard Pronunciation 137
        Numbers 137
        Altitudes 137
        Time 138
        Altimeter Settings 139
        Wind Direction and Velocity 139
        Headings 139
        Aircraft Speeds 139
        Air Traffic Control Facilities 140
        Airways, Routes, and Navigation Aid Descriptions 140
        Aircraft Identification 140
        VHF Omnidirectional Range (VOR) 141
        DME Position Determination 142
        Tactical Air Navigation (TACAN) 142
        VORTAC 142
        Area Navigation 142
        Global Navigation Satellite System 142
            Global Positioning System 143
        GNSS Augmentation 143
        Satellite Based Augmentation Systems 143
        Ground-Based Augmentation System 144
    Airport Layout and Runway Numbering 144
    Weather 146
        Atmosphere 146
        Atmospheric Pressure 147
        Altitude and Flight Performance 147

Wind and Air Currents 148
Convective Air Currents 148
Effect of Obstructions on Wind 149
Wind and Pressure Representation on Surface
Weather Maps 149
Moisture and Temperature 150
Relative Humidity 151
Temperature/Dew Point Relationship 151
Dew, Frost and Fog 152
Clouds 152
Cloud Types 152
Cloud Coverage 154
Visibility 155
Precipitation 155
Air Masses 156
Fronts 157
Warm Front 157
Cold Front 157
Stationary Front 158
Occluded Front 158
Thunderstorms 158
Squall Line 159
Tornadoes 159
Hail 159
Observations 159
Surface Aviation Weather Observations 159
Aviation Routine Weather Report (METAR) 160
Radar Observations 161
Satellite Observations 161
Aviation Forecasts 161
Terminal Aerodrome Forecasts (TAF) 161
Area Forecasts 163
Weather Charts 164
Surface Analysis Chart 164
Weather Depiction Chart 164
Significant Weather Prognostic Charts 165

Chapter 9
Flight Operations 167
Location and Environment 167
Aircraft Launch and Recovery 167
Aircraft Retrieval 168
Operational Considerations 169
Auxiliary Equipment 169
Flight Profile and Payload Planning 171
Post Flight Analysis 171
Flight and Systems Training 171

Systems Training 173
Battery Management 174
Documents Relevant to Performance and Flight 174
Pilots (Operators) Operating Handbook 174
Type Certificate Data Sheets 175
Structural Repair Manual 175
Weight and Balance Forms 175
Airworthiness Directives 176
Operator's Logbook 176
Signal Spoofing 177
Encryption 177
Unmanned Systems Human Factors and Safety 177

Chapter 10
Regulations 181
Federal Aviation Regulations 181
Proposed New UAS Rules 184
Operational Requirements 184
Vehicle Requirements 184
Operator requirements 185
Operational Requirements 185
MicroDrone Option 185
Proposed FARs that relate to UAVs 186
State and Local Law 186

Chapter 11
Future Trends and Technology 199
Power Systems 199
Larger Aircraft 200
Collision Avoidance 200
Regulations 200
Future Applications and Deployment 201
Artificial Intelligence 201
Summary of Trends 201

Index 211
Workbook 215
Workbook Answer Key 293

CHAPTER 1

INTRODUCTION TO UNMANNED AERIAL SYSTEMS

Civilian unmanned aviation systems (UAS) are emerging as a significant new segment of aviation. An unmanned aerial vehicle (UAV) is a type of aircraft, which has no onboard crew. UAVs are sometimes known as both autonomous drones and remotely piloted vehicles (RPVs). The combination of a UAV and the systems needed to guide and control it are known as an unmanned aerial system.

Unmanned flight is not a new concept. Unmanned balloons were developed as military weapons in the mid-1800s. Further experimentation occurred after the turn of the century with the development of drones controlled by primitive autopilot and flight control systems. Other UAVs were built that were remotely flown from the ground through the use of radio equipment. As early as 1916 an unmanned, radio-controlled "torpedo" was being developed by the British company Sopwith. The craft spanned 14 feet and had a 35 horsepower engine.

Radio interference from the engine's magneto was a problem and required locating the control radio in the tail of the aircraft. The weight of the radio and flight control equipment, as well as radio and other technology limitations, were an impediment to the widespread use of these types of aircraft.

In 1917, less than 20 years after the Wright brothers first flew, and ten years before Lindbergh's historic flight, the Kettering Bug was developed for the U.S. Army (the Air Force did not yet exist). The "Bug" carried 300 pounds of explosives, flew by radio control to its target, then shed its wings, dropping straight down and exploding on or near its target. Both the British and the U.S. military continued

Figure 1-1. Kettering bug.

Unmanned Aerial Systems: The Definitive Guide

Figure 1-2. A restored RP-2 Dennyplane aerial gunnery drone.

Figure 1-3. German V1 buzz bomb pilotless aircraft.

Figure 1-4. U.S. Navy Firebee.

work on "pilotless" aircraft during the period between WWI and WWII. Designers believed that remotely piloted aircraft could be useful for training anti-aircraft gunners and fighter pilots. In 1935 Reginald Denny, a British transplant living in the U.S., demonstrated a radio controlled prototype target drone to the US Army. This aircraft, eventually known as the RP-2, was accepted by the Army and was subsequently modified and built in large numbers. By the end of World War II close to 20,000 drones had been built and used by the Army and Navy for target practice.

At about the same time, the Germans developed the V1. A rudimentary UAV used to fly explosives from Germany to London, the V1 was equipped with a dampened pendulum system that controlled the aircraft pitch. A crude gyrocompass provided stability and flight control, while power was provided by a large pulse jet engine. The V1 was essentially operated by pointing it towards the target, regulating flight time, speed, and altitude, to affect an impact at the chosen location.

While the military has developed ever larger and more sophisticated unmanned aircraft, rapid development has occurred in the smaller, more affordable, civilian unmanned aerial systems. As navigation and flight control systems have become smaller and less expensive to purchase, UAVs have become less costly and easier to operate than ever before. This has opened up the possibility of widespread civilian use. In recent years, UASs have declined in price such that quite capable platforms can be obtained for less than $1,000 that are easy to control, relatively simple to operate, and capable of flying at reasonable altitudes and airspeeds for up to an hour at a time. Intense development by modelers and hobbyists has contributed to commercial designs that let virtually anyone with the interest to fly UAVs to do so.

Figure 1-5. IAI Scout type reconnaissance aircraft.

None of these small UAVs would have been possible without advances in technology like the development of lightweight composite aircraft structures such as carbon fiber, fiberglass, and foam cores. Increased battery capacity, combined with lighter weight structures and the development of more powerful and efficient electric motors, has made the physical design and operations of UAVs much easier. But probably the most enabling development has been the miniaturization and technology advances in computer communications, control, and processing systems. The advances in navigation sensors, cameras, computer control chips, and software, as well as the commonplace use of Wi-Fi and Bluetooth communications devices have made it possible for the development and proliferation of UAVs.

For decades, aircraft operations over the U.S. were primarily separated into recreational model aircraft flight and manned aircraft operations (private, commercial and military). Further distinctions were made utilizing aircraft weight and speed with regulatory requirements increasing with each. Historically, the aviation community relied upon organizations such as the Academy of Model Aeronautics (AMA) to establish, and communicate, safety protocols for operating model aircraft. The FAA issued suggestions in 1981 for model aircraft operations in the form of Advisory Circular AC 91-57, Model Aircraft Operating Standards. This document outlined recommended guidelines and provided modelers with standards to follow regarding safe operations. The current weight limit of 55 pounds for recreational model aircraft, as well as the maximum operating altitude of 400 feet above ground level (AGL), can trace their origins to this document and the AMA. Manned aircraft operators are required to remain at least 500 feet away from persons, vessels, vehicles, and structures, except for the purpose of take-off and landing. The 100 feet separation provided a safety margin that proved effective for decades.

With the capability to virtually enter the cockpit of their model aircraft via a small video camera and radio connection, the first person viewer (FPV) capability allowed model aircraft to fly beyond the line of sight of the operator. Another technological advance in the form of autonomous flight, with a Global Positioning System (GPS) equipped autopilot, allows operations beyond a pilot's line of sight.

Figure 1-6. FPV allows operators a pilot's view from their aircraft.

Unmanned Aerial Systems: The Definitive Guide

Figure 1-7. Multirotor UAV.

As these aircraft proliferated, the burden for collision avoidance began to rest with the manned aircraft pilot who could not adequately see, nor avoid, these small unmanned aircraft. The unmanned pilot, in turn, cannot maintain adequate situational awareness with FPV due to the limited field of view of the camera. Even with a swiveling, gimbaled camera system, the speed difference between a hovering multirotor and fixed wing manned aircraft renders collision avoidance difficult if not impossible. The safety concerns were such that the FAA needed to begin the lengthy and difficult regulatory process.

There is no denying that unmanned civilian aircraft offer possibilities in areas of precision agriculture, air sampling, surveillance, mapping, recreation, and other area beyond our imagination. UASs are here to stay as a new and rapidly growing segment of the aviation industry. Their integration into the airspace system needs to be balanced between safety, privacy, and the need to not stifle innovation and progress. It is the purpose of this text to educate those individuals (designers and builders, operators, observers, and technicians) involved in this exciting new segment of aviation in an effort to provide that needed level of safety.

CHAPTER 2

UNMANNED AERIAL VEHICLE DESIGN AND CONSTRUCTION

INTRODUCTION TO DESIGNS

Current unmanned aircraft designs owe much of their performance and reliability to techniques developed in traditional manned and model aviation. Design elements that have been proven to function in model aircraft for decades are seen in today's small unmanned aerial systems (sUAS). Likewise, the design elements of larger and heavier unmanned aircraft can trace their origins to the successful application of technology derived from manned aircraft. From small aircraft to airliners; the materials, aerodynamics, and propulsion systems used in UASs are shared between the manned and unmanned segments of aviation.

MISSION DRIVEN DESIGN

The UAS, with few exceptions, is designed from concept, test flight, and deployment, to accomplish a fairly specific mission. A mission is defined as the expected use, or application, of the aircraft. It is the intended purpose for which the aircraft was created. It is the mission requirements that typically define almost every element of a given design. A design not created with a specific mission in mind is a design that may end up with a broad range of performance capabilities but will seldom perform any of them particularly well. For example, a user needs to determine if the mission requires vertical liftoff and/or hovering flight. If it does not, then a fixed-wing design might be a better alternative than a rotorcraft. But if vertical, or hovering, capabilities are a priority, than a rotorcraft of some sort will likely be needed. Other mission parameters that need to be defined include the flight stability attributes, mission duration, needed maneuverability, as well as the load carrying capacity of the aircraft. Each of these requirements will further refine the aircraft design selection.

Figure 2-1. Multirotor aircraft preparing for operation from unimproved field.

Unmanned Aerial Systems: The Definitive Guide

Figure 2-2. Fixed-wing hand launch for an agricultural imaging flight.

Figure 2-3. Some operating areas are more noise sensitive than others.

Figure 2-4. A catapult may be used in the absence of a suitable runway for takeoff.

For example, the need to operate from rural areas, without runways, is a common mission parameter in agricultural applications of unmanned aircraft. That requirement may dictate the use of a rotorcraft, or a fixed-wing design with capabilities such as catapult, or hand launch. The landing methods employed could include parachutes, slow flight into standing vegetation, or capture nets. The advantages of fixed-wing designs include low vibration, large payload capability, and lengthy duration. Those advantages must be weighed against the challenges inherent in using an aircraft that needs significant space for landing and takeoff.

PLATFORM SELECTION

The mission requirements primarily dictate the selection of either a fixed, or rotary wing design. There are advantages and disadvantages to each configuration, as well as personal preferences from operating experience. An experienced fixed-wing operator may be highly skilled, and well prepared, for flying safely and confidently with a conventional winged aircraft. When confronted with the differences in operating a rotorcraft, they may be less confident or skilled, and the risk of an operator error induced mishap rises. Likewise, a rotorcraft operator would face the same issues when operating a conventional fixed-wing design. Cross training can alleviate much of the risk, however most operators will still prefer piloting one type aircraft to another based upon personal experience.

SPECIFIC PLATFORM ADVANTAGES AND DISADVANTAGES

The traditional fixed-wing aircraft has many applications. They are relatively inexpensive to construct and repair compared to rotorcraft of comparable weight and capability. A fixed-wing aircraft uses natural stability in flight and is not dependent upon continuous propulsion to remain aloft. If anything goes wrong with the propulsion, or flight stability systems, a fixed-wing aircraft can often glide to a reasonably safe landing. Fixed-wing aircraft can usually carry more weight for a longer time than a comparable rotorcraft. Low vibration, as well as the ability to completely stop and restart the motors in flight, can assist in the use of cameras and other systems that are vibration sensitive. Fixed-wing, electric powered aircraft are also very quiet and may be desired for surveillance work or when flying in noise sensitive areas. These areas include neighborhoods, parks, and wildlife refuges to name a few.

Every aircraft design is a series of compromises. Fixed-wing aircraft cannot stop in flight or hover. They also require relatively smooth, lengthy surfaces for takeoff and landing. They can be difficult to transport to the operational site as they may be relatively large and time consuming to disassemble and reassemble on site. The use of fixed-wing aircraft in congested urban areas may be limited to higher altitudes due to their inability to easily avoid ground based obstacles and their limited maneuverability.

ROTORCRAFT ADVANTAGES AND DISADVANTAGES

The helicopter and other multirotor designs, have become common in small unmanned applications. Their primary advantages include the ability to stop in flight, or hover, as well as their vertical takeoff and landing capability. These flight characteristics make them ideally suited to congested urban operations as well as indoor use. Rotorcraft may be operated from small launch platforms as well as boats, providing access to areas that would otherwise be impossible to reach. Rotorcraft designs are extremely adaptable to increases in overall vehicle size and configuration. Rotorcraft with 1, 3, 4, 6, 8, or more motor driven propellers, providing both lift and flight control, are common.

Rotorcraft, as compared to fixed-wing designs, are relatively loud, high in vibration, and lack substantial duration and weight lifting capability. Multirotors are highly dependent upon flight control electronics for stability with tuning and adjusting required to achieve stable flight. An improperly

Figure 2-5. Common quadcopter type multirotor.

tuned multirotor can be difficult, if not impossible, to fly. A flight controller failure will usually result in a loss of stability and a resultant out of control crash with a possible loss of the aircraft. If battery capacity and condition are not monitored closely, the multirotor may fail to complete a flight with an off field landing being the inevitable outcome. A multirotor aircraft will not glide like a fixed-wing aircraft, nor can they auto-rotate to a safe landing like a helicopter. The rotors also present an obvious danger to personnel and safety procedures are required to be in place at all times. A safety shroud not only protects the rotors from damage, but more importantly, it protects nearby persons or property.

Figure 2-6. Osprey tilt rotor aircraft transitioning to forward flight.

Figure 2-7. Unmanned tilt rotor aircraft.

HYBRID DESIGNS AND AIRSHIPS

Some unmanned aircraft do not fit into either the conventional rotorcraft or fixed-wing categories. These aircraft designs attempt to minimize the disadvantages and optimize the advantages of both types. The manned V-22 Osprey operated by the U.S. military is an example of this concept using large rotors for vertical lift, small wings for forward flight, and equipped with large horsepower engines to accomplish both tasks.

There are similar unmanned aircraft designed to utilize rotors for vertical takeoff and landing, with high-speed forward flight capability. Aircraft of this type are challenging from a flight control standpoint as they must be stable and controllable in hover, then transition to forward flight, and back smoothly. The ability to hover, and fly in conventional forward flight, is easily achieved through electronic controlled stability. It is the transition between the two flight modes that has proven difficult.

The "tail-sitter" type aircraft is another hybrid design concept. With this aircraft, the propeller, or propellers, are positioned in the front as with any conventional aircraft. The difference is that the thrust provided

Figure 2-8. Takeoff and landing position of tail sitter unmanned aircraft.

Figure 2-9. Unmanned airship performing research of power requirements for maneuverability.

is sufficient to lift the aircraft vertically from this nose up position. Flight is accomplished by lifting the vehicle vertically, pitching it over for horizontal flight, and then transitioning back to the nose up attitude for the tail first descent and landing. Backing the aircraft down, tail first, to a soft landing is extremely difficult.

Rigid airships have been used as unmanned aircraft as well. They provide high lift and duration characteristics not obtainable with other designs. Their low vibration, quiet operation, and long flight duration must be weighed against their susceptibility to wind, however. An airship tethered to the ground, called an aerostat, is a common method to utilize the advantages of this type of aircraft while managing the winds effects.

POWERPLANT SELECTION

The selection of the means of propulsion for a UAV will be based upon the proposed mission of the aircraft. Small unmanned vehicles often utilize battery powered electric motors for their clean, quit, reliable operating

Figure 2-10. An aerostat type airship with tethering tower.

Unmanned Aerial Systems: The Definitive Guide

Figure 2-11. Large reciprocating, pusher engine aircraft with forward electronics bay.

characteristics. Internal combustion engines are used in larger UAVs where payload capacities, as well as flight endurance, are primary concerns. The placement of the engine exhaust plume to the rear of the aircraft, so as to not degrade camera image quality or inhibit other sensors, will often dictate a pusher engine configuration with the camera towards the front of the aircraft. This configuration has the added advantage of distancing the payload and autopilot from vibration and engine ignition interference.

BUILD, MODIFY OR READYMADE

The decision to purchase a readymade aircraft, or to design and build a unique system, will depend upon many factors. There are increasing numbers of aircraft available for purchase that may have the capabilities and features desired for specific missions. The advantages of this approach include: quick deployment, available parts supply, factory support, and a community of users to share information. Another advantage is that the software which accompanies many commercially available systems includes automated image processing, as well as data evaluation, tailored to specific user needs.

On the other hand, if the mission parameters are unique, the best choice may be to design and build an aircraft for a very specific set of performance requirements. An example might be a large fixed-wing aircraft that must be hand launched, carry a heavy sensor package, and land in unimproved areas such as standing vegetation, or dirt clearings, without damage to the aircraft, sensors, or vegetation. Another unique example would be a rotorcraft, operating over water, with the requirement for flotation and water proofing of sensitive data gathering equipment. It is highly unlikely that a commercial, off-the-shelf design, could handle these unique mission requirements without modification.

You might choose to design, build, and test your own aircraft. Without significant experience, it will likely be difficult to quickly, accurately, and safely design, test, and build such an aircraft in a short period of time. It might prove to be a better option to purchase a readymade aircraft and modify it for unique purposes. This approach is common with many operators tailoring their unique data gathering payload to a readily available commercial design. It should be noted, however, that if ultimate performance is the goal, an airframe, propulsion system, and payload created to complement each other from inception, will likely prove to be the best design.

AERODYNAMICS AND FLIGHT CONTROLS

Unmanned aircraft employ a range of methods to create lift with flight control systems tailored to provide the level of controllability and stability needed. Unlike most manned aircraft, it is common to see unmanned aircraft with no conventional rudder, ailerons, or even landing gear, if those items are deemed unnecessary to the mission requirements. Elevon control is common on unmanned flying wings. For the purposes of understanding the forces that act upon UAVs, the terms and theories explained in this chapter apply to both manned and unmanned flight vehicles.

FORCES ACTING ON AN AIRCRAFT

An aircraft in flight is the center of a continuous battle of forces. This conflict of forces is key to understanding how the aircraft performs the maneuvers required for it while in the air. There is nothing mysterious about these forces; they been known for centuries. It is the interaction of the forces that ultimately determine if, and how, the aircraft flies. Each force can be calculated, and the aircraft is designed to take advantage of each.

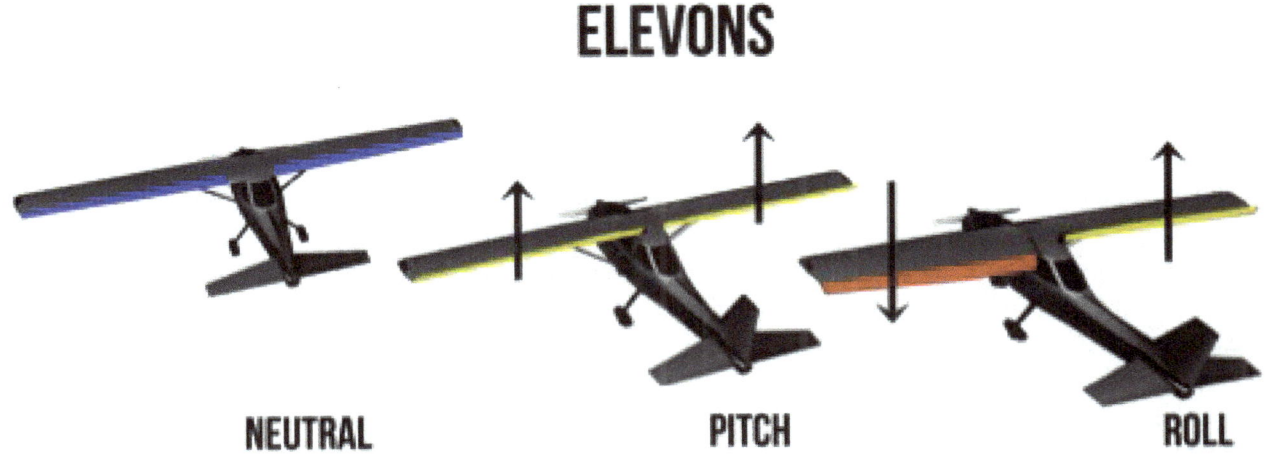

Figure 2-12. Elevons provide pitch and roll control.

While in flight, the ultimate path of the aircraft is based on the magnitude and direction of four fundamental forces: weight, lift, drag, and thrust. These four forces act upon the aircraft in unique and individual ways.

- Weight or gravity - is the force that wants to pull the aircraft down towards the earth. Weight is the force of gravity acting downward upon everything in the UAV, such as the aircraft itself, crew, fuel, systems and payload.
- Lift - is the force that pushes (or lifts) the aircraft upward. Lift acts vertically and generally counteracts the effect of weight.
- Thrust - is the force that propels the aircraft forward. Thrust is the forward force usually produced by the powerplant and overcomes drag.
- Drag - is the force that opposes thrust and generally exerts a braking action that tends to hold the aircraft back. Drag is caused by the disruption, or friction, of the airflow as it is impeded or passes over the wings, fuselage, and other protruding objects.

These four forces are in balance when the aircraft is in straight-and-level unaccelerated flight. The forces of lift and drag are the direct result of the relationship between the relative wind and the aircraft. Relative wind is the air that flows over the wings and around the rest of the aircraft. The lifting force always acts perpendicularly (upwards) to the relative wind. Drag always acts parallel to, and in the same direction as, the relative wind. Thrust normally operates in a forward direction, pulling the aircraft along. Weight is a downward force, towards the earth's surface.

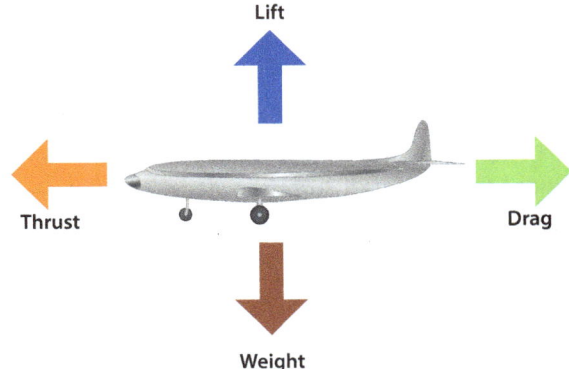

Figure 2-13. The balance of forces needed for flight.

AIRFOILS AND LIFT

An airfoil is any surface designed to convert forward motion through the air into a force that operates in a certain direction. Any part of the aircraft that converts airflow resistance into a force (pressure) is an airfoil. A conventional wing is an excellent example of an airfoil. In most cases, an airfoil is not symmetric; one surface has greater curvature than the other surface.

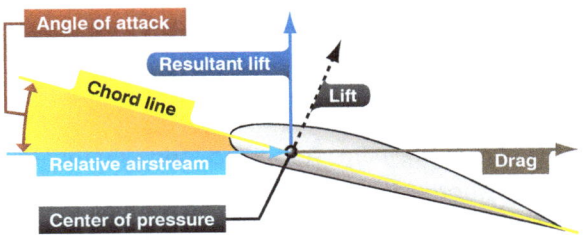

Figure 2-14. Lift and the center of pressure.

Unmanned Aerial Systems: The Definitive Guide

The difference in curvature of the upper and lower surfaces of the wing is what produces some of the lifting force. Air flowing over the top surface of the wing must reach the trailing edge of the wing in the same amount of time as the air flowing under the wing. To accomplish this, the air passing over the top surface must move at a greater velocity than the air passing below the wing because of the greater distance it must travel along the top surface. According to Bernoulli's principle, this increased velocity results in a corresponding decrease in pressure on the top surface of the wing. Thus, a pressure differential is created between the upper and lower surfaces of the wing, forcing the wing upward in the direction of the lower pressure.

Lift can be increased by increasing the angle of attack (AOA) of the wing. Angle of attack is the angle between the chord line of the wing (a straight line between the leading and trailing edge of the wing) and the relative wind. In general, if you increase this angle, the overall distance required for airflow over the top of the wing is increased, thereby increasing the lift produced by the wing. Newton's third law (which states that for every action there is an equal and opposite reaction) also contributes to lift in this situation. As the AOA is increased, the air leaving the wing is deflected downward, and as a result, additional lift is produced by the wing. Lift may also be increased by increasing the wing area, the velocity or density of the air, or by dynamically changing the shape of the airfoil (flaps).

In general, whenever the lift of an aircraft's wing equals the force of gravity, the aircraft maintains level flight. Increasing the lift will cause the aircraft to initiate a climb; decreasing the lift will cause the aircraft to begin a descent.

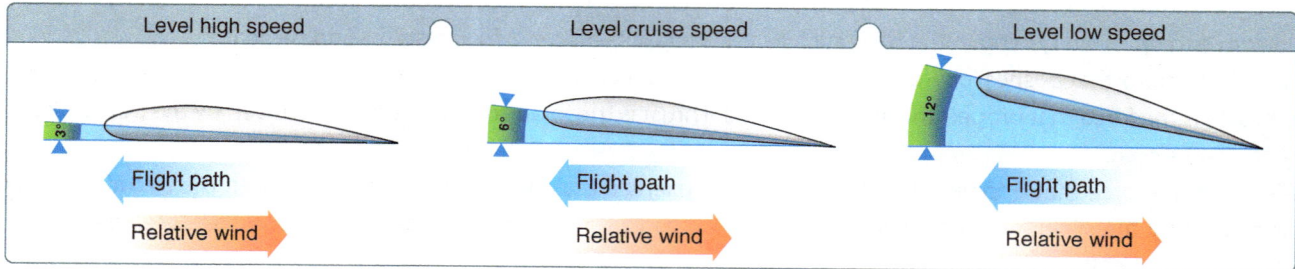

Figure 2-15. Increasing angle of attack increases lift.

Increasing the angle of attack of a wing typically increases the amount of lift produced, but only to a point. At high angles of attack, the airflow becomes turbulent and begins to separate from the upper surface of the wing. When the lift is sufficiently disrupted by this turbulent airflow and can no longer counteract the effects of gravity, the wing is said to "stall". The wing will continue to provide insufficient lift until the angle of attack is lowered. Most aircraft are designed such that if a wing stall occurs, the nose pitches down, the AOA is reduced, and lift is automatically restored.

AIRFOIL SHAPES

A longitudinal cross section of the wing taken at any point along the span of the wing is called an airfoil section. Wings can be designed such that the airfoil shape is consistent along the entire span of the wing, or the airfoil can change shape along the span. If constructed in such a manner, the individual airfoil sections can have properties that differ, yet create an overall advantageous design planform. A wing may have different airfoil sections along the span from root to tip, with taper, twist, and/or sweepback being employed to any section. The resultant aerodynamic properties of the wing will be determined by the action of each section along the span.

For example, the shape of the airfoil determines the amount of turbulence, or skin friction produced, consequently affecting the efficiency of the wing. Turbulence and skin friction are primarily affected by the fineness ratio, which is defined as the ratio of the chord of the airfoil to the maximum thickness. An aircraft with a thin wing has a high fineness ratio. A thick wing has a low fineness ratio. A wing with a high fineness ratio produces a large amount of skin friction. A wing with a low fineness ratio produces a large amount of turbulence. The best wing is a compromise between these two extremes to hold both turbulence and skin friction to a minimum at the airspeed most often flown by the aircraft. In general, thick wing sections with low aspect ratios (span/chord) are aircraft designed for low speed, high lift flight. Conversely, if a wing has a thin airfoil section and high aspect ratio, it is better suited to higher speed, efficient flight, at the expense of low speed lifting capability.

The overall efficiency of a wing is measured in terms of the lift to drag ratio (L/D). This ratio varies with angle of attack, but generally reaches a defined maximum value for a particular AOA. At this angle, the wing can be said to be operating at its maximum efficiency. The shape of the airfoil is the factor that most determines the AOA at which the wing is most efficient. It also determines the overall efficiency of the wing.

WING CONFIGURATIONS

Wing shapes vary, with each different shape providing certain desirable flight characteristics. Control at various operating speeds, the amount of lift generated, balance, and stability all change as the shape of a wing is altered. Both the leading edge and the trailing edge of the wing may be straight or curved, or one edge may be straight and the other curved. One or both edges may be tapered so that the wing is narrower at the tip than at the root where it joins the fuselage.

The wing tip may be square, rounded, or even pointed. The wings of an aircraft can be attached to the fuselage at the top, mid-fuselage, or at the bottom. They may extend perpendicular to the horizontal plane of the fuselage, or can angle up or down slightly. This angle is known as the wing dihedral. The dihedral angle affects the lateral stability of the aircraft. An unmanned aircraft with adequate dihedral may be flown without ailerons, utilizing the rudder control only for turning and banking flight control.

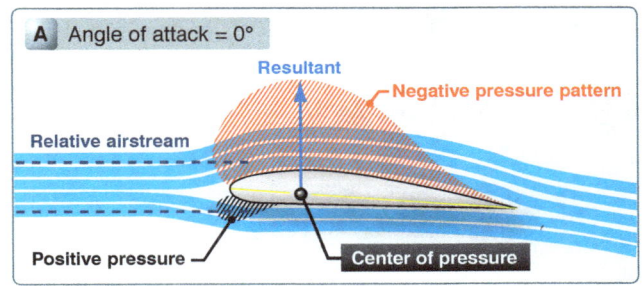
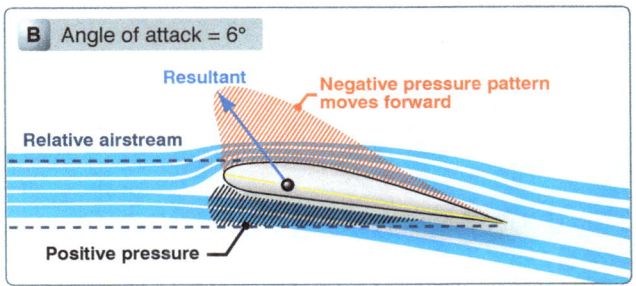
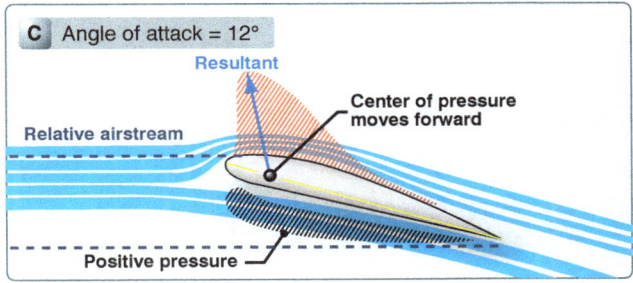
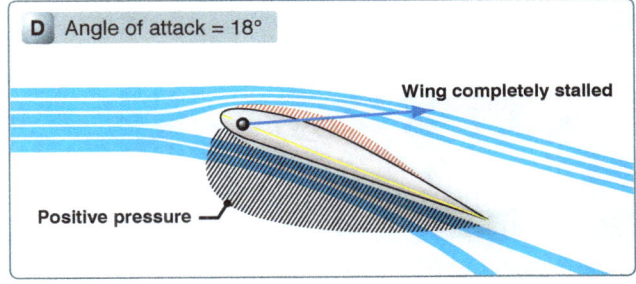

Figure 2-16. Wing stall.

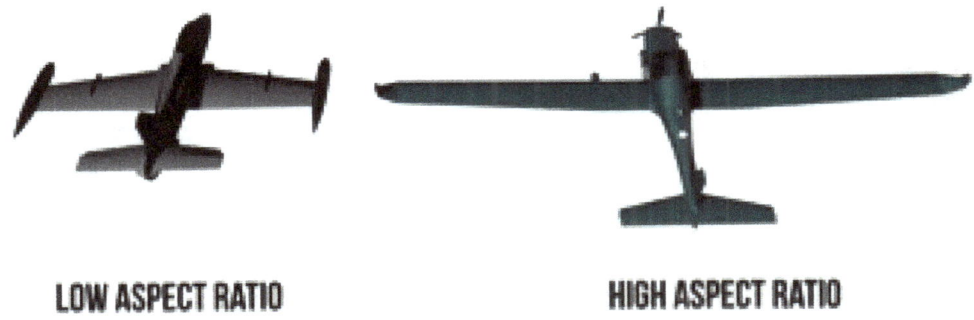

Figure 2-17. Aspect ratio: the relationship of span to chord of the wing.

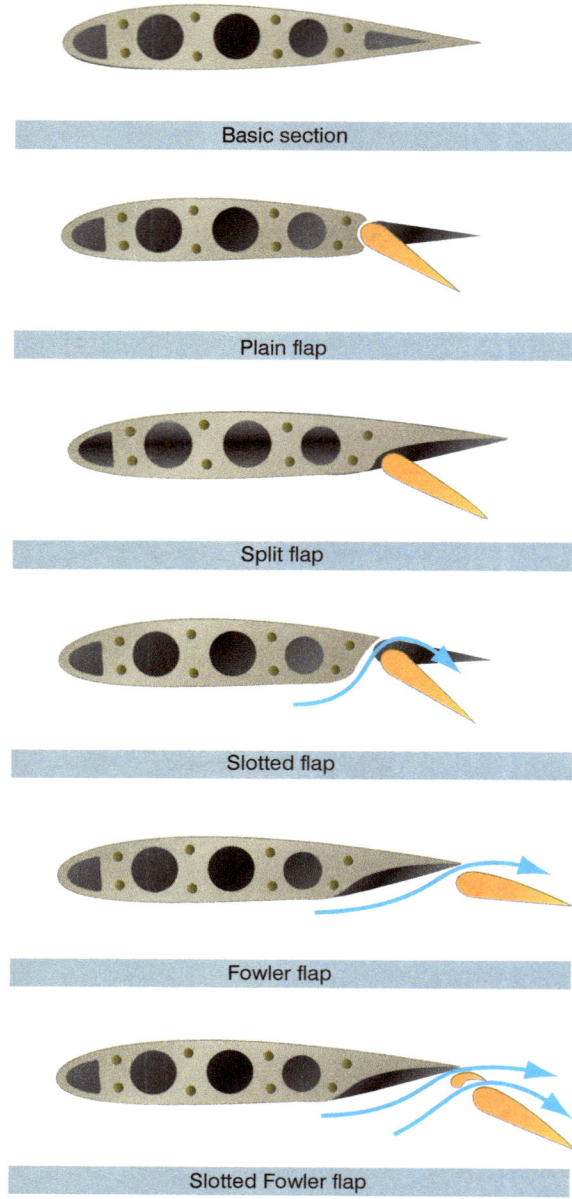

Figure 2-18. The effect of flaps on wing camber and the resulting increase in lift.

Research has shown that the most efficient airfoils for general use at relatively low speeds have the maximum thickness occurring about one-third of the way back from the leading edge of the wing. High-lift wings, and high-lift devices for these types of wings, have been developed that modify the shape of airfoils to produce the desired effect. In general, the amount of lift produced by an airfoil increases with an increase in wing camber.

Camber refers to the curvature of an airfoil. Upper camber refers to the upper surface, lower camber to the lower surface, while mean camber refers to the average of a line that combines of the upper and lower surfaces. Camber is positive when departure from the chord line is outward and negative when it is inward. Thus, high-lift wings have a large positive camber on the upper surface and a slightly negative camber on the lower surface. Flaps added to a wing make it possible to temporarily create more mean camber by increasing both the upper chamber and negative lower camber by extending the movable flap.

PROPELLERS AND ROTORCRAFT

A propeller is simply a revolving wing that provides lift in the horizontal direction. The term for the force produced is thrust when referring to the lift generated by a revolving propeller. Thrust increases as the speed of the propeller is increased and/or if the angle of attack of the propeller blades increases in relationship to the relative airflow. If you orient the "propeller" so that the force produced opposes gravity, it now produces lift and is called a rotor.

The revolving wings, or rotors, of rotorcraft produce lift in the same manner as previously described. But instead of the wind flowing over the wing, the rotor (wing) moves rapidly through the air. It is this movement of the airfoil section through the air, while the vehicle remains stationary, which provides the necessary lift while a rotorcraft is in hovering flight.

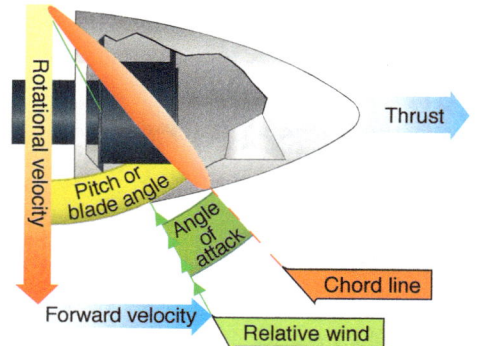

Figure 2-19. A propeller usually produces lift (thrust) in a horizontal direction.

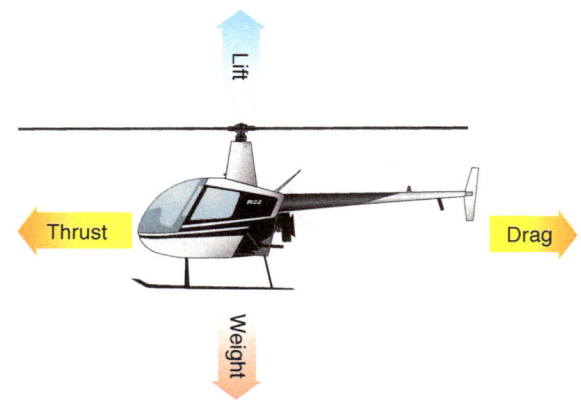

Figure 2-20. The four forces as they apply to a helicopter.

Gravity is the pulling force that tends to draw all bodies within the earth's gravitational field toward the center of the earth. The center of gravity (CG) of an aircraft is defined as the point at which all the weight of the aircraft appears to be concentrated. If the aircraft were able to be supported at its exact CG, it would perfectly balance. The center of gravity is crucial to the operation of an aircraft, as it has a great bearing upon stability.

The desired CG is determined by the general design of the aircraft. The center of the wings lift, (abbreviated as CL) and its relationship to the aircraft's center of gravity, determines an aircraft's stability. The center of lift can shift along the wing depending on many factors, including aircraft speed, weight, and angle of attack. Aircraft designers must estimate how far the center of lift could move for any particular aircraft. They must ensure that the CG always remains in front of the CL. This is essential to provide stable flight. If the center of lift is ever allowed to move ahead of the CG (or conversely if the aircraft is ever loaded such that the CG is aft of the CL), the aircraft will become aerodynamically unstable and virtually impossible to control.

Figure 2-21 shows the resultant down force on the tail resulting from the relationship between CG and CL. Manipulation of this down force, through the elevator control on the horizontal tail, provides flight control for nose up and nose down (pitch).

Loading of the payload, and its effect on the center of gravity of the aircraft, is extremely important for aircraft stability. Too much weight forward and the flight controls (elevator) may not have adequate authority to raise the nose. Too far aft and the aircraft may be unstable in pitch (nose up or down) to the point of being uncontrollable. Poor placement of the CG and CL in a multirotor aircraft may place excessive loads upon motors and flight control systems, or in extreme cases, render those aircraft uncontrollable as well. Care must be taken as the CG can, and will, shift in flight due to burning of fuel, or expending payload, and this shift must be accounted for in the flight planning so as to not exceed center of gravity limitations.

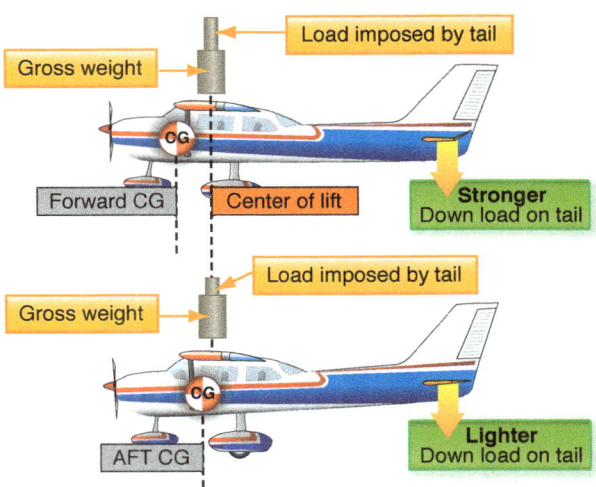

Figure 2-21. Center of gravity is ahead of the center of lift with resulting down force applied to the horizontal stabilizer.

AXES OF MOTION OF AN AIRCRAFT

Whenever an aircraft changes its attitude in flight, it must turn about one or more of three axes.

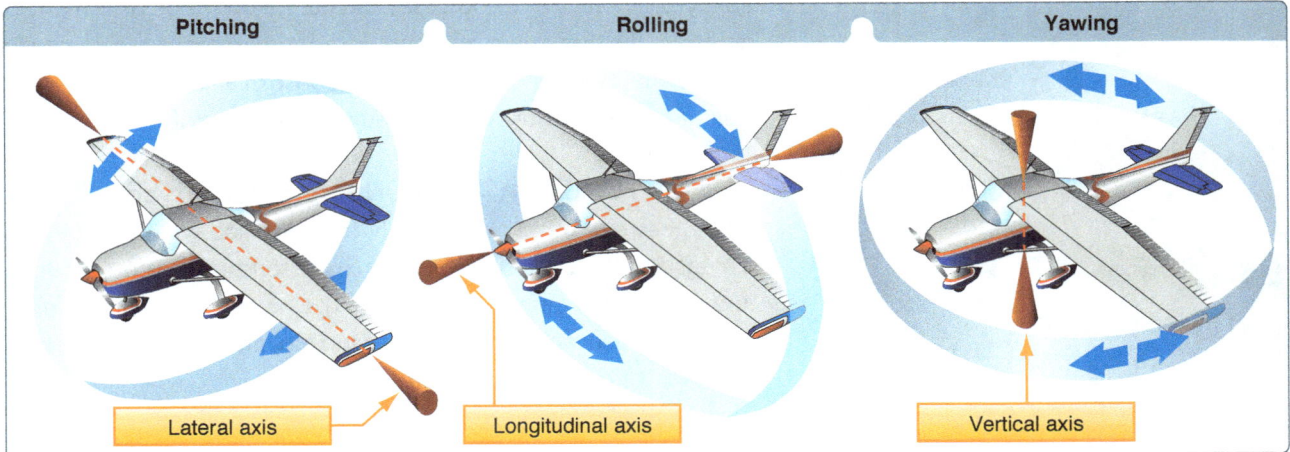

Figure 2-22. The three axes of motion around an aircraft.

Unmanned Aerial Systems: The Definitive Guide

The axes of an aircraft can be considered as imaginary axles around which the aircraft turns like a wheel. The approximate center of the aircraft is where all three axes intersect, with each perpendicular to the other two. The axis that extends lengthwise through the fuselage from the nose to the tail is called the longitudinal axis. Aircraft "roll" around the longitudinal axis. The axis that extends crosswise from wing tip to wing tip is called the lateral, or pitch, axis. The axis that passes through the center or the aircraft, from top to bottom, is called the vertical, or yaw, axis.

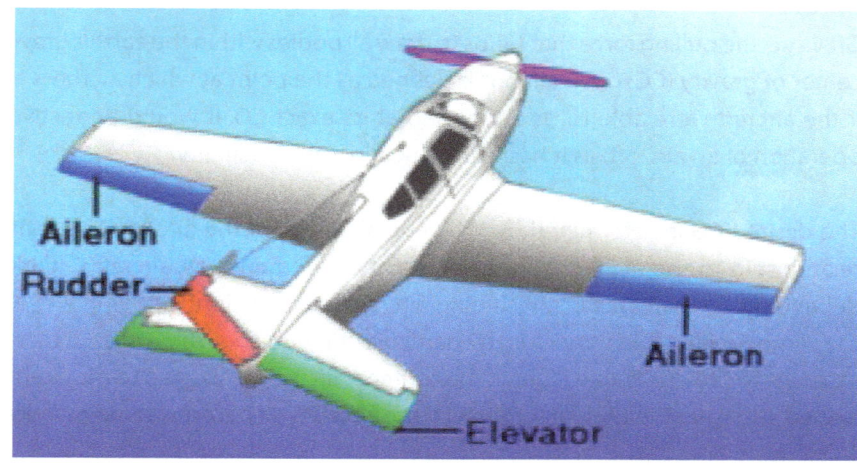

Figure 2-23. Flight controls for conventional fixed-wing aircraft.

The motion of the aircraft around these three axes (roll, pitch, and yaw) is controlled by three control surfaces. Roll is controlled by ailerons, (or elevons in the case of a flying wing), which are usually located at the trailing edge of the wings near the wingtip. Pitch is controlled by the elevators, which are normally located near the rear of the horizontal tail assembly, (or by elevons, again in the case of a flying wing design). Yaw is controlled by the rudder, which is located on the rear of the vertical tail assembly.

AIRCRAFT STABILITY AND CONTROL

Aircraft must have sufficient stability to maintain a constant flight path, yet recover from various upsetting forces such as wind gusts, turbulence, or shifting cargo. Aircraft systems must be designed to provide a proper response to any movement of the controls. This is called flight control and is the act of moving the controls, providing the appropriate aerodynamic force to either keep the aircraft on its current flight path, or changing rotation around one or more axes to redirect the flight path of the aircraft. When an aircraft is said to be controllable, it means that the aircraft responds easily, promptly, and predictably to movement of the controls.

In general, the physical movement of a control surface on an aircraft changes the airflow over the aircraft's surface. This in turn creates a change in the force applied by that control surface, causing the aircraft to rotate around one of its axes of motion. Three important terms concerning the design and operation of an aircraft are aircraft stability, maneuverability, and controllability. Stability is the ability of an aircraft to fly with no control input in a straight-and-level flight path. Maneuverability is the ability of an aircraft to be easily directed along a desired flight path and to withstand any stresses imposed during a change of direction. Controllability is the quality of the response of an aircraft to the pilot or operator's commands while maneuvering the aircraft.

UNIQUE FORCES ACTING ON THE HELICOPTER

The forces described above apply to both fixed-wing and multirotor aircraft. But there are some unique characteristics of rotorcraft stability and control that differ from fixed-wing. One of the primary differences between a helicopter and a fixed-wing aircraft is that a rotorcraft uses the rotor for both thrust and lift.

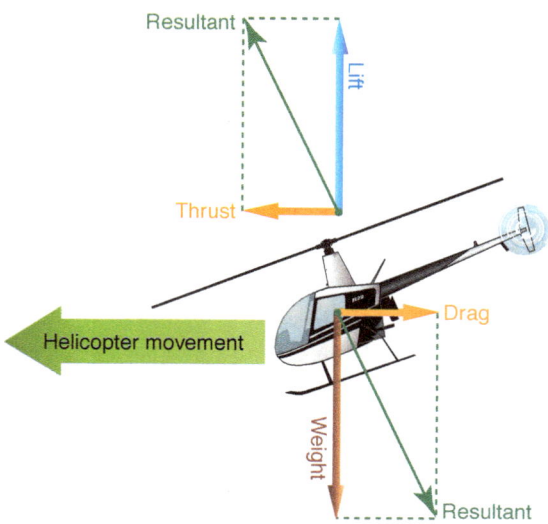

Figure 2-24. Helicopter rotor tilt to achieve forward flight.

A fixed-wing aircraft generally derives most, if not all, of its lift from a fixed airfoil surface (wing) while thrust is provided by some sort of forward facing, rotating airfoil (propeller). The wing on an aircraft can be considered stationary, with wind "flowing" over it. A helicopter, however, derives both lift and thrust from a rotating airfoil called the rotor. The rotor of a helicopter is shaped like a long, thin wing. Instead of wind flowing "over" the rotor, it is the rotor itself moving through the (more or less) stationary air that creates the needed lift. This same rotor must also provide forward (and sometimes sideward) thrust, as well as act as a primary flight control.

In general, the path followed by the rotors delineate a circular path, called the "tip-path plane". This plane of rotation can be viewed as a disk, and from an aerodynamic point of view, the "disk" created by the rotating blades can be changed to adjust the flight of the helicopter. For example, during hovering flight in a no-wind condition, the tip-path plane of a helicopter is horizontal, parallel to the ground. The lift (and thrust) of the rotor blades are directed straight up; while weight and drag act straight down. The sum of the lift must equal the weight in order for the helicopter to hover. If lift equals weight, the helicopter hovers. If lift is less than weight, the helicopter descends. Conversely if lift is greater than weight, the helicopter rises.

To create forward flight, the tip-path plane of the rotors must be slightly tilted forward, thus tilting the total lift-thrust force developed by the rotor blades forward from vertical. This resultant lift-thrust force is actually the sum of two components: lift acting vertically upward and thrust, now acting horizontally in the direction of flight. Now that the helicopter is moving, just like in a fixed-wing, there is weight, the downward acting force to be overcome, as well as drag, the rearward acting or retarding force of inertia and wind resistance. As in a fixed-wing aircraft, in straight-and-level, unaccelerated forward flight, lift equals weight and thrust equals drag. The unique aspect of a rotorcraft is that the lift and thrust are all provided by the rotor.

If during forward flight, lift is made to exceed weight, the helicopter will climb while still traveling forward. If lift is less than weight, the helicopter will descend while still traveling forward. If thrust exceeds drag, the helicopter increases speed; if thrust is less than drag, it decreases in speed.

A unique aspect of rotor based flight is the ability for the aircraft to "slide" in three dimensions. A fixed-wing aircraft, for instance, cannot move sideways. Just like a car, it must be moving forward to also move sideways. It must change its heading to change position left and right. A helicopter however, can "slide" to the left or right without changing heading. For sideward flight to occur, the tip-path plane of the rotors is tilted sideward in the direction that movement is desired, thus tilting the total lift-thrust vector sideward. While moving sideways, the vertical, or lift component, of the rotor is still straight up, but the horizontal, or thrust component, now acts sideward with drag acting in proportional opposition. Similar to forward flight, to "back up" a helicopter, the tip-path plane is tilted rearward, thus tilting lift-thrust vector rearward.

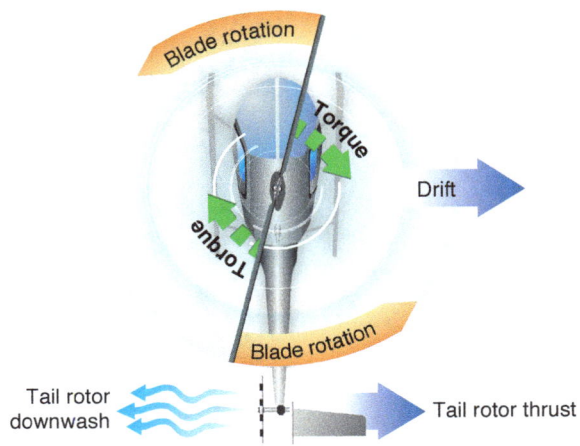

Figure 2-25. The tail rotor is an anti-torque device that also provides yaw control.

Movement around all three axes of a helicopter can be performed simultaneously, while also "sliding" left-right or forward and back. The actual aerodynamics involved are incredibly complicated. Suffice to say that the control mechanisms on a helicopter are very complex and have little in common with those of fixed-wing aircraft.

TORQUE COMPENSATION

Newton's third law of motion states "For every action there is an equal and opposite reaction," and has some very direct implications for rotor based flight. As the rotor of a helicopter turns in one direction, the opposing force created by the rotation causes the fuselage to tend to rotate in the opposite direction. This tendency for the fuselage to rotate (change heading) is

Unmanned Aerial Systems: The Definitive Guide

called torque. Since torque effect on the fuselage is a direct result of engine power supplied to the main rotor, any change in engine power brings about a corresponding change in torque effect. The greater the engine power, the greater the torque effect. The force that compensates for torque and provides for directional control can be produced by various means. The defining factor is dictated by the design of the helicopter, some of which do not have a torque issue as in the case of dual, contra-rotating rotors.

Single rotor helicopters typically have an auxiliary rotor located on the end of the tail boom used to counteract torque. This auxiliary rotor, generally referred to as a tail rotor, is oriented such that it produces thrust in the direction opposite the torque reaction developed by the main rotor. As main rotor speed changes, so must the force produced by the tail rotor. This is usually accomplished by either varying the speed of the tail rotor or changing the angle of the tail rotor blades, thereby changing the (sideways) lift produced by the tail rotor. This is the yaw control of a helicopter.

The tail (or anti-torque) rotor on a helicopter can take the place of a rudder as used on a fixed-wing aircraft. To change the heading of the helicopter, the thrust produced by the tail rotor is either increased or decreased accordingly until the helicopter is headed in the desired direction. Multirotor helicopters change heading differently. In general, the speeds of one or both rotors are adjusted, and the torque produced by the engine is leveraged to turn the helicopter.

UNMANNED MULTIROTOR AERODYNAMICS

There are few parallels within manned aviation to compare to the multirotor systems used in some UAVs. This unique and prolific type of unmanned aircraft propulsion and control system has some unique flight abilities and characteristics. Depending upon the number of lift-producing propellers, or rotors, the multirotor may also be referred to by more specific terms such as; tricopter (3), quadcopter (4), hexacopter (6), or octacopter (8). The generic term "drone" has been used in general to describe unmanned multirotor aircraft. This is a somewhat confusing term however, as the large military aircraft, utilizing fixed-wings, have also been called drones. The proper term to use is multirotor aircraft.

The aerodynamics and controls of a multirotor aircraft share some commonality with helicopters, as well as fixed-wing aircraft, but have unique properties. It is the ability to precisely vary the speed of each motor, thereby varying the propeller's thrust (and resultant torque) that allows the multirotor to be used as a stable, yet controllable, UAV platform. On most small

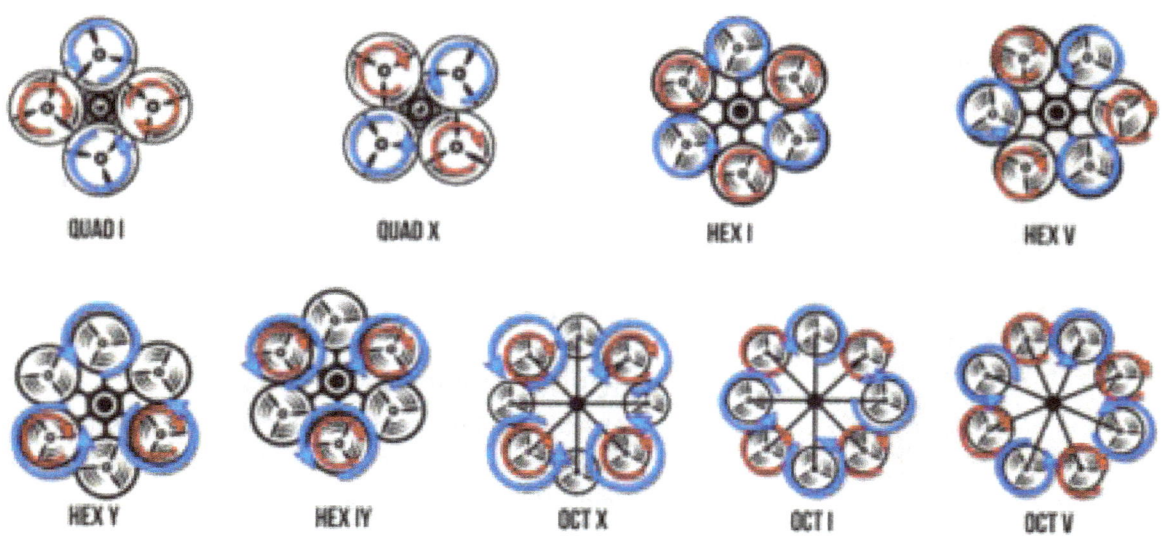

Figure 2-26. Various rotor configurations of the multirotor type UAV.

multirotors, the motor and associated rotor are placed on a structural arm that extends outward from the central hub, or "body," of the aircraft. When a single motor, and associated rotor, is accelerated or decelerated, this increases or decreases the thrust applied to that particular arm. This imbalance of force across the UAV causes the aircraft to pitch forward, roll right or left, or to yaw left and right as needed.

Pitch and roll are easily controlled by changing the speed of the rotors on one side of the aircraft, with a proportional (yet opposite) change applied to the rotor on the other side of the aircraft. For example, to roll a multicopter to the left, the rotor on the right side would increase in speed, thereby increasing lift and raising that side of the aircraft. To pitch the nose of the multirotor up, the front rotor(s) would increase in speed to create more lift. Vertical acceleration (a climb) or a descent, is achieved by either increasing or decreasing all of the motor speeds simultaneously.

Yaw control of multirotors is a little different. It is achieved utilizing the same basic forces that act upon all propellers and rotors. The motors of a multirotor design spin in opposing directions as viewed from above. Each motor counteracts the torque forces of the other motors to achieve stable flight. When two of the opposing motors (rotating in the same direction) are decelerated by the controller, an imbalance occurs that allows the torque effect of the two faster motors to overcome that produced by the slower motors and a yaw rotation occurs. The requirement for stability on a multirotor dictates that each motor be finely controlled to take into account continuous, yet slight, changes in aircraft attitude and direction of flight.

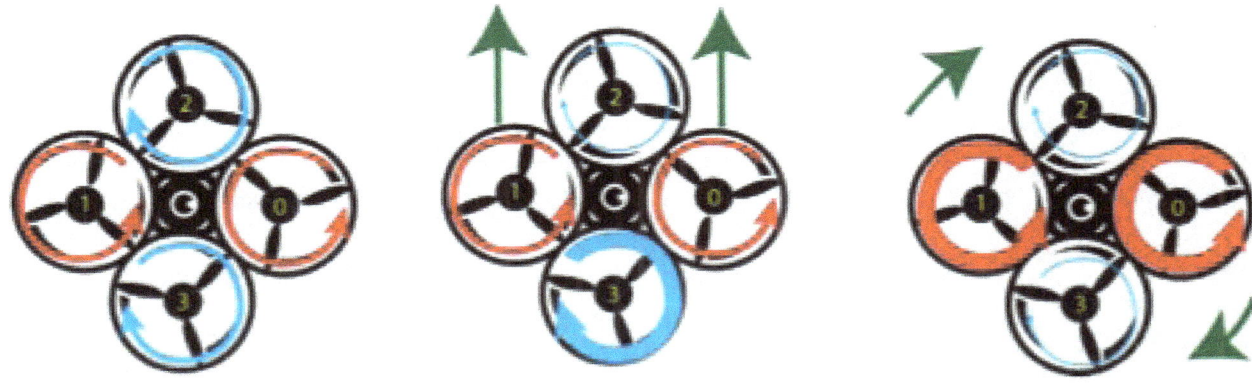

Figure 2-27. Hover, forward flight, and right yaw control of a quadcopter

MULTIROTOR STABILITY

The success of the multirotor type aircraft is a direct result of the ability of electronic control systems developed to stabilize and control the vehicle. Advances in battery and electric motor technology actually preceded the development and flight of the first successful multirotors. However, it was not until the computerized flight controller became affordable, light, and reliable, that the multirotors began to achieve real success. Most fixed-wing and helicopter designs are inherently stable enough to allow flight without computer aided flight control. Not so with the multirotor. Without a digital flight controller, human control of the various motors would be impossible.

FLIGHT CONTROLLER

The flight controller, or flight control board, consists of a set of motion sensors, at least one per axis (roll, pitch, and yaw). This set of gyroscope and accelerometer based sensors measure the motion of the aircraft and send the information to an integrated circuit (IC) computing chip. The speed of the motors is continuously adjusted by the flight control board through electronic speed controls (ESC) that keep the aircraft stable during flight. When a directional command is received from the pilot through the radio receiver, the flight control board accelerates and decelerates the appropriate motors to achieve the desired direction, or directions, of movement.

It is noteworthy that a simple flight control board can only sense movement and direction from a previously known stable condition. It does not know, in absolute terms, where it is actually located on the earth and therefore cannot be geostationary in hover. Wind, or inaccuracies of sensors, will eventually cause the aircraft to drift. If the additional precision of geostationary hovering is desired, a global positioning system (GPS) receiver, and compass are required. Modern autopilot systems that can be installed on higher end UAVs consist of a flight control board, barometer, GPS, and a sensitive compass for geostationary or waypoint seeking flight.

AIRCRAFT LOADS AND STRESS

Unmanned aircraft are exposed to the same fundamental operational stresses as manned aircraft. The intensity of those stresses is not limited by a human pilot, however. This absence of a physically fragile pilot allows tremendous latitude in flight maneuvers and other extreme operations that are only limited by the machine itself.

Aircraft structural members are designed to carry a load or to resist stress. In designing an aircraft, every square inch of wing and fuselage, every rib, spar, and even each attachment fitting must be considered in relation to the physical characteristics of the material of which it is made. Every part of the aircraft must be planned to carry the load to be imposed upon it. The determination of such loads is called stress analysis. Although planning the design is not usually the function of the aircraft operator or technician, it is nevertheless important that they understand, and appreciate, the stresses involved in order to avoid changes in the original design through improper repairs or modifications and to appreciate the flight stress limitations of the aircraft.

The term "stress" is often used interchangeably with the word "strain." While related, they are not the same thing. External loads or forces cause stress. Stress is a material's internal resistance, or counterforce, that opposes deformation. The degree of deformation of a material is strain. When a material is subjected to a load or force that material is deformed, regardless of how strong the material is or how light the load is. There are five major stresses to which all aircraft are subjected:

- Tension
- Compression
- Bending
- Torsion
- Shear

Tension is the stress that resists a force that tends to pull something apart. The engine pulls the aircraft forward, but air resistance tries to hold it back. The result is tension, which stretches the aircraft. The tensile strength of a material is measured in pounds per square inch (psi) and is calculated by dividing the load (in pounds) required to pull the material apart by its cross-sectional area (in square inches).

Compression is the stress that resists a crushing force. The compressive strength of a material is also measured in psi. Compression is the stress that tends to shorten or squeeze aircraft parts. As an example, the top skin of an aircraft wing in flight is in compression, the bottom skin in tension. These loads reverse with the loads imposed during landing as the aircraft weight is removed from the wing and transitioned to the landing gear and fuselage structure.

Torsion is the stress that produces twisting. While moving the aircraft forward, the engine also tends to twist it to one side, but other aircraft components hold it on course. Thus, torsion is created. The torsion strength of a material is its resistance to twisting or torque.

Shear is the stress that resists the force tending to cause one layer of a material to slide over an adjacent layer. Two riveted plates in tension subject the rivets to a shearing force. Usually, the shearing strength of a material is either equal to or less than its tensile or compressive strength. Aircraft parts, especially screws, bolts, and rivets, are often subject to a shearing force.

Bending stress is a combination of compression and tension. The rod shown in figure 2-28 has been shortened (compressed) on the inside of the bend and stretched on the outside of the bend.

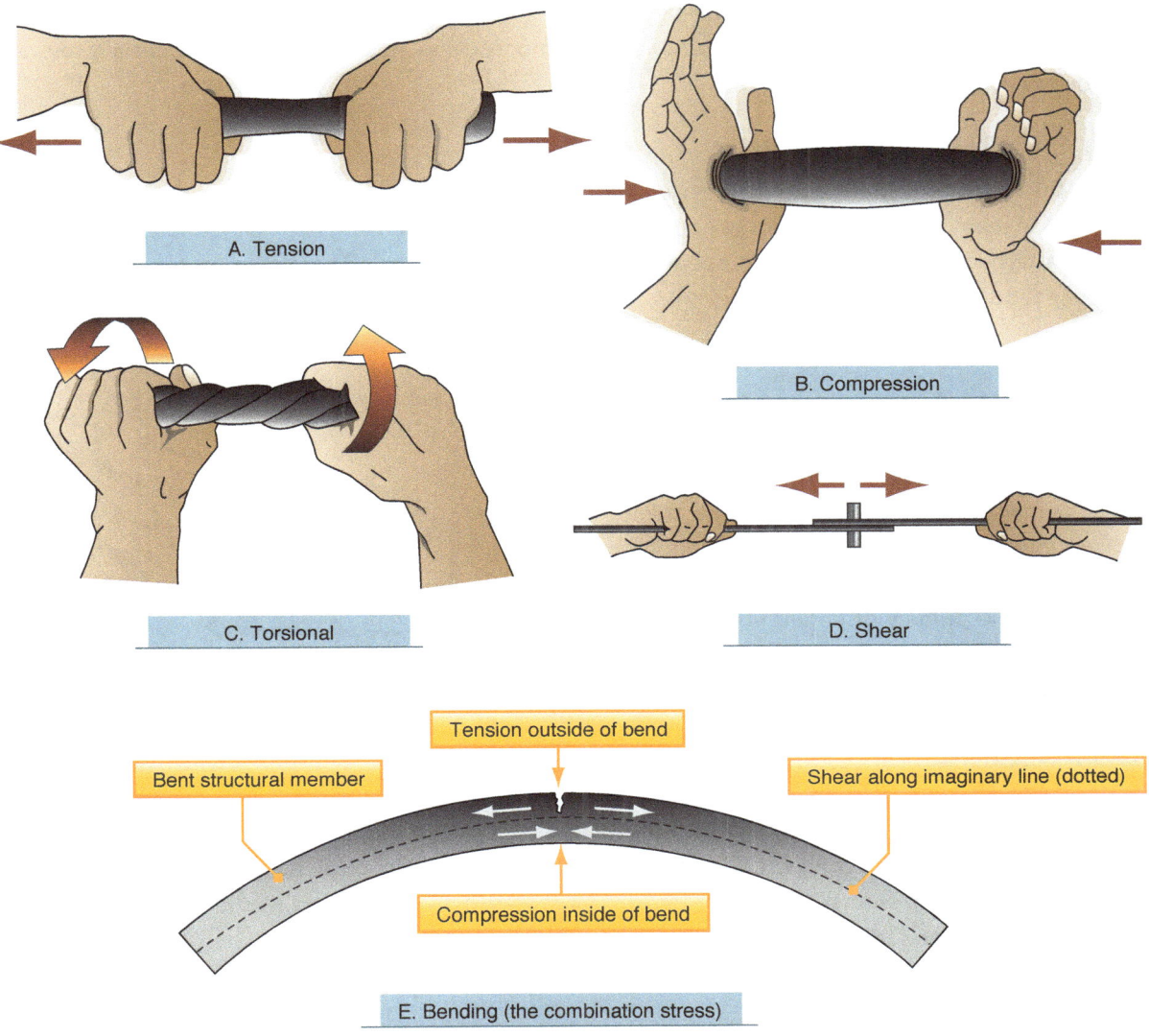

Figure 2-28. Aircraft stresses and their directions of force.

MULTIPLE STRESSES

A single member of any aircraft structure may be subjected to a combination of stresses. In most cases, the structural members are designed to carry end loads rather than side loads. They are designed to be subjected to tension or compression rather than bending. Strength, or resistance to the external loads imposed during operation, may be the principal requirement in certain structures. However, there are numerous other characteristics in addition to designing to control the five major stresses that engineers must consider. For example, cowling, fairings, and similar parts may not be subject to significant loads requiring a high degree of strength. However, these parts must have streamlined shapes to meet aerodynamic requirements, such as reducing drag or directing airflow.

STRESS CONSIDERATIONS IN REPAIR

Inevitably, unmanned aircraft will endure rough landings, ground damage, or other structural damage in operation. Careful consideration of how the structure is designed to endure operational stresses will lead to a repair that restores the strength and aerodynamic properties of the aircraft. Although component replacement is common in commercially available UAVs, there will be occasions when replacement is not the most attractive option and a repair is needed. The repair of manned aircraft load bearing structures of various materials and types is well documented in FAA Advisory Circular AC43-13. This text does not list balsa wood repairs specifically; however, the principles employed in the wood repair chapters are relevant and satisfactory for unmanned aircraft. The repair procedures for composite and metal structures are especially relevant for the latest unmanned systems.

FUSELAGE

The fuselage is the main structure or body of the fixed-wing aircraft. It provides space for cargo, controls, accessories, and other equipment. In many aircraft, the fuselage houses the powerplant. In multiengine aircraft, the engines may be either in the fuselage, attached to the fuselage, or suspended from the wing structure. There are two general types of fuselage construction, truss and monocoque.

TRUSS TYPE

A truss is a rigid framework made up of members, such as beams, struts, and bars which resists deformation by applied loads. The truss-framed fuselage is generally covered with fabric or other suitable material such as mylar. The truss type fuselage frame is usually constructed of tubing or square wooden stock held together in such a manner that all members of the truss can carry both tension and compression loads. The primary distinguishing feature of the truss type construction is that the skin does not carry significant loads and therefore its repair is less critical in nature.

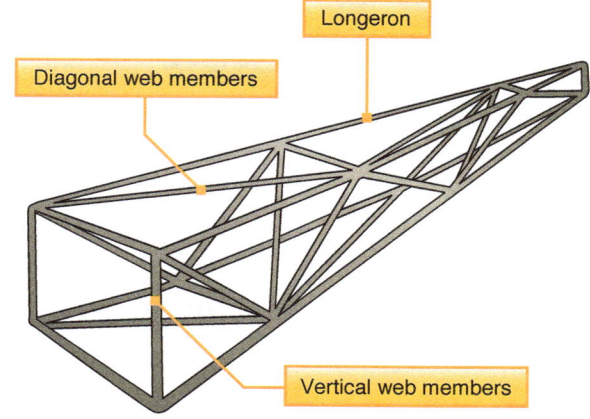

Figure 2-29. The truss type fuselage structure with associated parts.

MONOCOQUE TYPE

The monocoque (single shell) fuselage relies largely on the strength of the skin or covering to carry the primary loads. It is this reliance upon the structural integrity of the skin that makes repairs to the skin surface of this type structure critical to the overall strength and airworthiness of the aircraft. Many composite unmanned aircraft utilized stressed skin or monocoque type construction. The design may be divided into two classes, monocoque and semimonocoque

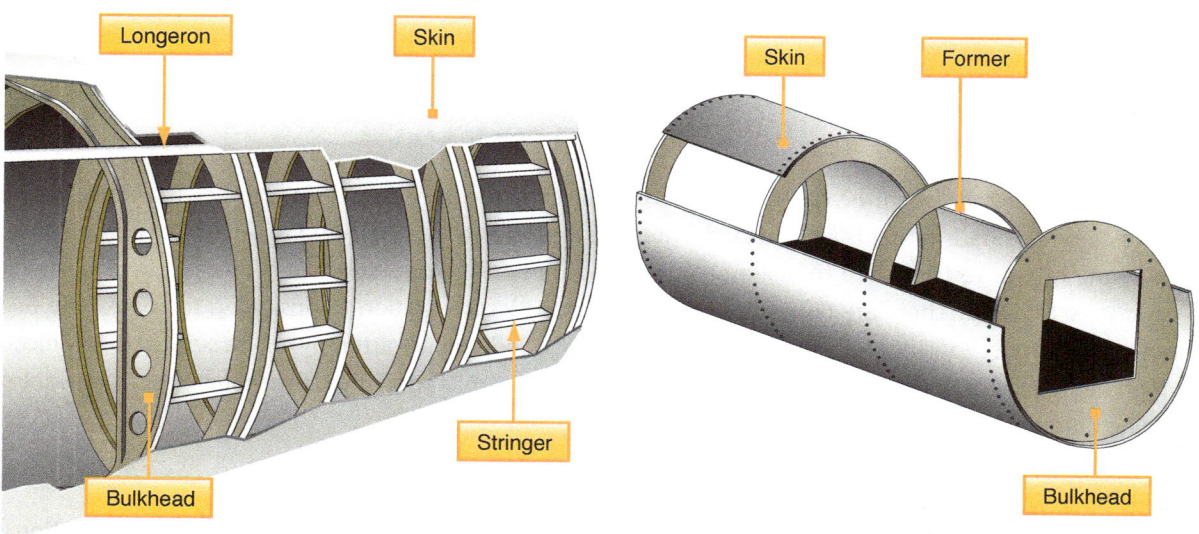

Figure 2-30. Semimonocoque and monocoque fuselage structures.

Most modern aircraft are considered to be of semimonocoque type construction. The true monocoque construction uses formers, frame assemblies, and bulkheads to give shape to the fuselage. The heaviest of these structural members are located at intervals to carry concentrated loads and at points where fittings are used to attach other units such as wings, powerplants, and stabilizers. Since no other bracing members are present, the skin must carry the primary stresses and keep the fuselage rigid. Properly performed skin repairs to this type of structure are essential to preserve their strength.

SEMIMONOCOQUE TYPE

To overcome the strength/weight problem of pure monocoque construction, a modification called semimonocoque construction was developed. It also consists of frame assemblies, bulkheads, and formers as used in the monocoque design, but in addition the skin is reinforced by longitudinal members called longerons. Longerons usually extend across several frame members and help the skin support primary bending loads. Stringers are also used in the semimonocoque fuselage. These longitudinal members are typically more numerous, and lighter in weight, than the longerons. Stringers have some rigidity, but are chiefly used for giving shape and for attachment of the skin. Stringers and longerons together prevent tension and compression from bending the fuselage. Individually, no one of the aforementioned components is strong enough to carry the loads imposed during flight and landing. When combined, however, those components form a strong, rigid framework.

To summarize: in semimonocoque fuselages, the strong, heavy longerons hold the bulkheads and formers. These, in turn, hold the stringers, braces, web members, etc. All are designed to be attached together, and to the skin, to achieve the full strength benefits of semimonocoque design. It is important to recognize that the skin or covering carries part of the load. The fuselage skin thickness can vary with the load carried and the stresses sustained at a particular location. The advantages of the semimonocoque fuselage are many. The bulkheads, frames, stringers, and longerons facilitate the design and construction of a streamlined fuselage that is both rigid and strong. Spreading loads among these structures and the skin means no single piece is failure critical. This means that a semimonocoque fuselage, because of its stressed-skin construction, may withstand considerable damage and still be strong enough to hold together until repairs can be made.

WING SPARS

Spars are the principal structural members of the wing. They correspond to the longerons of the fuselage. They run parallel to the lateral axis of the aircraft, from the fuselage toward the tip of the wing, and are usually attached to the fuselage by wing fittings, plain beams, tubes, or a truss. Spars may be made of metal, wood, or composite materials depending on the design criteria of a specific aircraft. Wooden spars are usually made from spruce, basswood, or composite reinforced balsa. Lamination, the bonding of multiple strips of wood with parallel grain, of solid wood spars is often used to increase strength. Laminated wood can also be found in box shaped spars. As can be seen, most wing spars are basically rectangular in shape with the long dimension of the cross-section oriented up and down in the wing to achieve greatest strength.

WING RIBS

Ribs are the structural crosspieces parallel to the chord line that combine with spars and stringers to make up the framework of the wing. They usually extend from the wing leading edge to the rear spar or the trailing edge of the wing.

Figure 2-31. Spars, ribs, and skin that work together to strengthen the wing structure.

Unmanned Aerial Systems: The Definitive Guide

The ribs give the wing its cambered airfoil shape and transmit the load from the skin and stringers to the spars. Similar, yet smaller, ribs are also used within controls and tail surface structures such as ailerons, elevators, rudders, and stabilizers.

WING SKIN

Often, the skin on a wing is designed to carry part of the flight and ground loads in combination with the spars and ribs. This is known as a stressed-skin design. The lack of extra internal or external bracing requires that the skin share some of the load. Notice the skin is stiffened to aid with this function. The stressed skin wing is very similar to the semimonocoque fuselage type utilizing the skin, ribs, stringers, and longerons in combination to transfer loads. An unmanned aircraft with a foam core wing that has a load bearing covering such as plywood, fiberglass, or balsa is an example of this type of construction.

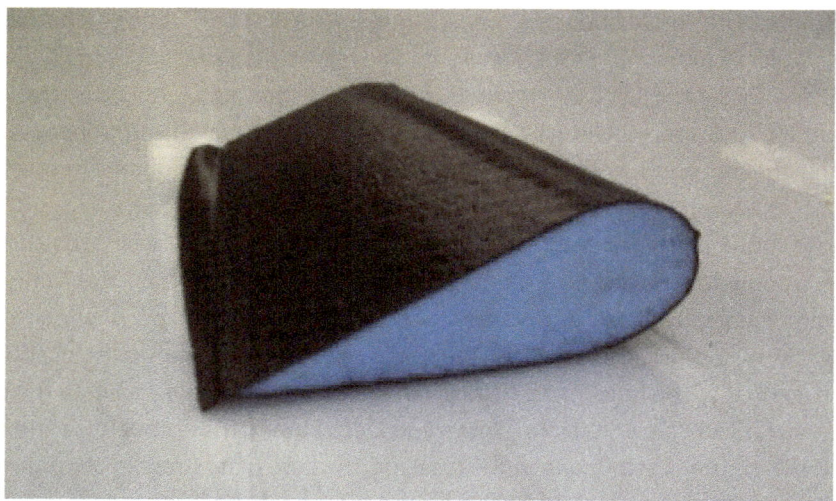

Figure 2-32. Solid skin over a foam core provides increased strength and durability.

CHAPTER 3

AIRCRAFT STRUCTURES, MATERIALS, AND REPAIR

AIRCRAFT STRUCTURAL CONCEPTS

An aircraft is defined as a device used for flight through the air. The FAA has further designated major categories of aircraft: airplane, rotorcraft, glider, and lighter-than-air vehicles. Unmanned aerial systems are not currently a separate category of aircraft, but tend to exist wholly or partly within all of these categories.

This chapter concentrates on the airframes of aircraft; specifically, the fuselage, empennage, nacelles, cowlings and fairings, airfoil surfaces, and landing gear. Also included are various accessories and controls that accompany these structures. The rotors of a helicopter are considered part of the airframe since they are actually rotating wings.

A common type of configuration used in small UAVs is the fixed-wing aircraft. Most small and medium fixed-wing UAVs can be treated much as one would treat a model aircraft. Larger UAVs (55 pounds and heavier) are essentially aircraft and are considered by the FAA to be fully functional airplanes whose structures, maintenance, and repair procedures are governed by applicable aircraft regulations. The maintenance and repair procedures described in this chapter are focused on smaller vehicles (less than 55 pounds), but as they are still considered aircraft by the FAA. Any question about maintaining and/or repairing such aircraft, reference should be made to appropriate FAA aircraft maintenance and repair documents.

The airframe of a fixed-wing aircraft consists of five principal units: the fuselage, wings, empennage, flight control surfaces, and landing gear. Rotorcraft airframes consist of the fuselage, rotor(s) and control systems, tail rotor (on helicopters with a single main rotor), and the landing gear or skids. Multirotor aircraft usually consist of a semi-rigid frame, landing gear, and multiple rotors that provide both propulsion and flight control.

Airframe structural components are constructed from a wide variety of materials. The earliest aircraft were constructed primarily of wood. Steel tubing and the most common material, aluminum, followed. Many newly certified aircraft are built from molded composite materials, such as carbon fiber, fiberglass, and aramid fibers (Kevlar), or even structural foam.

Unmanned Aerial Systems: The Definitive Guide

Chapter 3

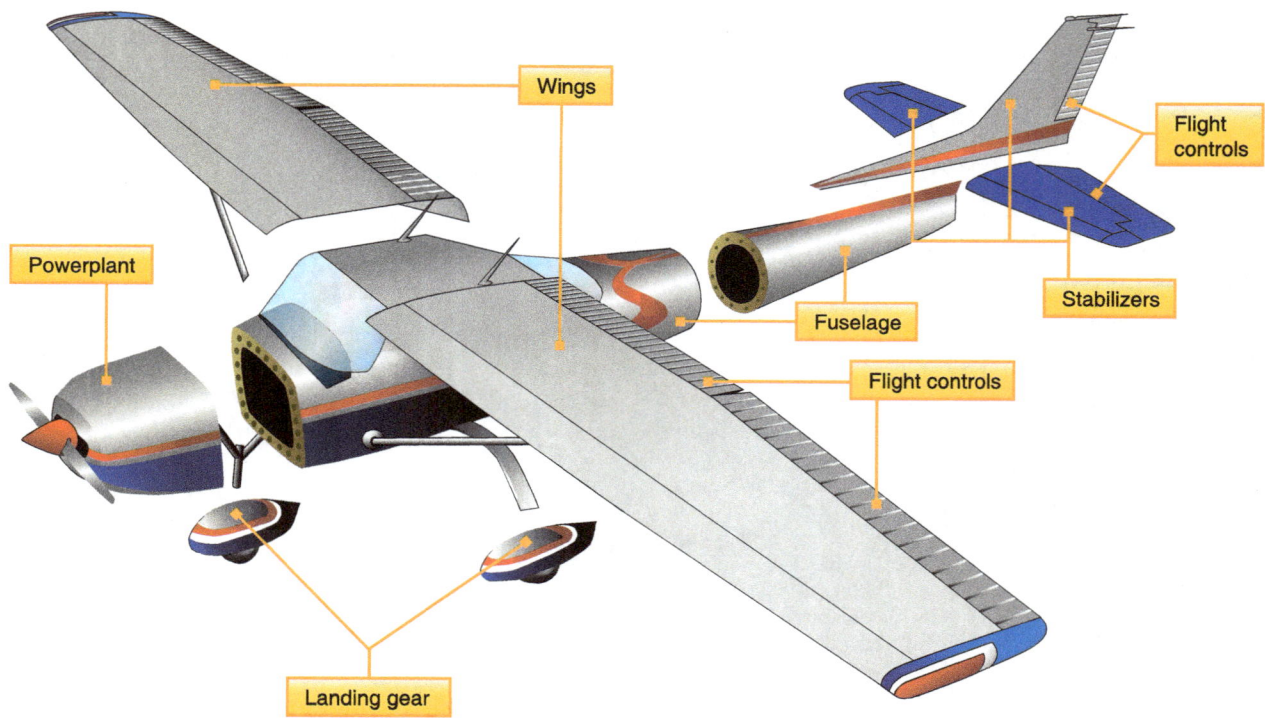

Figure 3-1. Basic aircraft structure and components.

Figure 3-2. Small UAV multirotor with composite structure.

STRESSES IN STRUCTURAL REPAIRS

An aircraft structure must be designed so that it accepts all the stresses imposed upon it by flight and ground loads without any permanent deformation. Any repair made must accept the stresses, carry them across the repair, and then transfer them back into the original structure. Stresses are considered as flowing through the structure, so there must be a continuous path for them, with no abrupt changes along the way. Changes in cross-sectional areas of aircraft structure subject to cycle loading or stresses can result in a stress concentration that may induce fatigue cracking and eventual failure. A scratch or gouge in the surface of a highly stressed piece of metal often causes a stress concentration at the point of damage and could lead to failure of the part.

Forces acting on an aircraft, whether it is on the ground or in flight, introduce pulling, pushing, or twisting forces within the various members of the aircraft structure. While the aircraft is on the ground, the weight of the wings, fuselage, engines, and empennage causes forces to act downward on the wing and stabilizer, along the spars and stringers, and on the bulkheads and formers. These forces are passed from member to member causing bending, twisting, pulling, compression, and shearing forces. As the aircraft takes off, most of the forces in the fuselage continue to act in the same direction. Because of the motion of the aircraft, they increase in intensity. The forces on the wingtips and the wing surfaces, however, reverse direction; instead of being downward forces of weight, they become upward forces of lift. The forces of lift are exerted first against the skin and stringers, then are passed on to the ribs, and finally are transmitted through the spars to be distributed through the fuselage. The wings bend upward slightly at their ends and may flex up and down during flight inducing alternating compression and tension loads as well as torsion.

The five types of stress in an aircraft previously described are tension, compression, shear, bending, and torsion (or twisting). Stresses in an aircraft tend to act in combinations, rather than singly, and this must be considered when repairing a damaged structure. Repair procedures must take into consideration the forces acting upon the original, undamaged structure. The repair will be adequate if it restores the original strength, and aerodynamic characteristics of the structure.

TENSION
Tension is the stress that resists a force that tends to pull things apart. The tensile strength of a material is measured in pounds per square inch (psi) and is calculated by dividing the load (in pounds) required to pull the material apart by its cross-sectional area (in square inches). The strength of a member in tension is determined on the basis of its gross area (or total area), but calculations involving tension must take into consideration the net area of the member. Net area is defined as the gross area minus that removed by drilling holes or by making other changes in the section. Placing rivets or bolts in holes makes no appreciable difference in added strength, as the rivets or bolts will not transfer tensional loads across holes in which they are inserted.

COMPRESSION
Compression is the stress that resists a crushing force, which tends to shorten or squeeze aircraft parts. The compressive strength of a material is also measured in psi. Under a compressive load, an undrilled member is stronger than an identical member with holes drilled through it. However, if a plug of equivalent or stronger material is fitted tightly in a drilled member, it transfers compressive loads across the hole, and the member carries approximately as large a load as if the hole were not there. Thus, for compressive loads, the gross, or total, area may be used in determining the stress in a member if all holes are tightly plugged with equivalent or stronger material.

SHEAR
Shear is the stress that resists the force tending to cause one layer of a material to slide over an adjacent layer. Usually, the shear strength of a material is either equal to or less than its tensile or compressive strength. Shear stress concerns aircraft repairs chiefly from the standpoint of rivet and bolt applications, particularly when attaching sheet metal, because if a rivet used in a shear application gives way, the riveted or bolted parts are pushed sideways. Bearing stress resists the force that the rivet or bolt places on the hole. As a rule, the strength of the fastener should be such that its total shear strength is approximately equal to the total bearing strength of the sheet material.

COMPOUND STRESSES
Torsion is the stress that produces twisting. The torsional strength of a material is its resistance to twisting or torque (twisting stress). The stresses arising from this action are shear stresses caused by the rotation of adjacent planes past each other around a common reference axis at right angles to these planes. Bending is a combination of compression and tension. Both torsion and bending form compound stresses and must be taken into account during any airframe repair.

AEROSPACE MATERIALS AND THEIR PROPERTIES

WOODEN STRUCTURES
Wood was among the first materials used to construct aircraft. Most early aircraft were constructed of wood frames with fabric coverings. Wood is still a common choice of material as it is easy to work with using common hand tools and very strong for its weight. Several forms of wood are commonly used in aircraft:

- Solid wood refers to a component consisting of one piece of wood.
- Laminated wood is an assembly of two or more layers of wood that have been glued together with the grain of all layers or laminations approximately parallel.
- Plywood is an assembled product of wood and glue usually constructed with an odd number of thin plies, or veneers, with the grain of each layer placed 90° with the adjacent ply or plies.
- High-density material includes commercially made products whereby wood and/or wood scraps are fused together to form a wood like material. This is not a structural material but may be found in jigs, supports, and other ground support fixtures.

To insure the strongest possible structure, there are a number of wood defects that should be avoided when constructing or repairing wooden aircraft:
- Compression failure, the breaking of the wood fibers perpendicular to the grain, due to mechanical overload of the wood
- Large knots or pitch pockets
- Cracks of any type
- Wavy or erratic grain
- Mineral streaks
- Decay

ADHESIVES
Adhesives play a critical role in the bonding of aircraft structures. An understanding of the various types, and related terms involved in bonding and adhesives, is helpful to the sUAS operator and technician.
- Close contact adhesive - a non-gap-filling adhesive, which requires some form of pressure (clamps) to insure proper bonding.
- Gap-filling adhesive - suitable for use in joints in which the surfaces to be joined may not be close or in continuous contact and do not require much pressure to bond correctly. Tight fitting joints are still preferable as they provide the best strength and bonding of the materials.
- Glue line - the layer of adhesive joining any two adjacent layers of an assembly.
- Single spread - the application of adhesive to one surface only.
- Double spread - the application of adhesive to both surfaces equally divided between the two surfaces to be joined.
- Open assembly time - the period of time that elapses between the application of the adhesive and the assembly of the components.
- Closed assembly time - the period of time elapsing between the assembly of the joints and the application of pressure.
- Pressing or clamping time - the time during which the components are pressed tightly together under recommended pressure until the adhesive cures.
- Cure time - the manufacturers recommended time interval to enable the adhesive to chemically provide the best adhesion.
- Pot life, working life, or useful life - time elapsed from the mixing of the adhesive components until the mixture must be discarded, because it no longer performs to specifications.
- Epoxy- a two-part synthetic adhesive that is tolerant of minor gaps in the bond line. Available in cure times as short as five minutes for field repairs and rapid bonding, however, longer cure time types have superior strength
- Aliphatic Resin - a carpenter's wood glue that is water resistant when dry
- Cyanoacrylate Adhesive - (super glue) fast setting adhesive that cures by reacting with humidity in the air. May be cured instantly with accelerant for field repairs.

PREPARATION FOR THE APPLICATION OF ADHESIVES
Satisfactory glue joints in aircraft should develop the full strength of the underlying material (wood, fabric, composite, or metal). To produce this result, the conditions involved in gluing must be carefully controlled. These conditions require:
- Performing the gluing operation under the recommended temperature and moisture conditions.
- The surfaces to be joined must be clean, dry, and free from grease, oil, wax, paint, etc.
- Proper adhesive must be selected for the task.
- A uniform film of adhesive must be applied.

The use of proper gluing techniques, including fit, recommended assembly times, and adequate, equal pressure applied to the joint.
- Adequate time, pressure, and temperature to permit the adhesive to cure to its maximum strength.

The manufacturer's directions should be followed for the preparation of any glue or adhesive. To make a satisfactorily bonded joint, it is generally desirable to apply adhesive to both surfaces and join in a thin, even layer. The adhesive can be applied with a brush, glue spreader, applicator bottle, or a grooved rubber roller.

Figure 3-3. Proper gluing technique with minimal squeeze out.

To ensure the maximum strength of the bonded surfaces, apply even force to the joint. Non-uniform gluing pressure commonly results in weak areas and strong areas in the same joint. Pressure may be applied by means of clamps, elastic straps, weight, vacuum bags, or other mechanical devices such as staples or nails. High clamping pressure is neither essential, nor desirable, provided good contact between the surfaces being joined is obtained. Nails and staples are for clamping pressure only and may be removed when the glue cures, or dries, to save weight.

When pressure is applied, a small quantity of glue should be squeezed from the joint. This excess should be removed before it sets. It is important that full pressure be maintained on the joint for the entire cure time of the adhesive as the adhesive does not chemically relink and bond if it is disturbed before fully cured. The full

Figure 3-4. Proper clamping technique.

curing time of the adhesive is dependent on the ambient temperature; therefore, it is important to follow the manufacturer's product instructions carefully for all phases of the gluing operation.

FABRIC COVERINGS

The use of fabric covering on an aircraft offers one primary advantage over other materials: light weight. Finely woven organic fabrics, such as Irish linen and cotton, were the original fabrics used for covering airframes. Their tendency to sag left the aircraft structure exposed to the elements and was detrimental to the lifting surfaces of the wings. To counter this problem, early builders began coating the fabrics with oils and varnishes. Early in aviation, a mixture of cellulose dissolved in nitric acid, called nitrate dope, came into use as an aircraft fabric coating. Nitrate dope protected the fabric, adhered to it well, and tautened it over the airframe. It also gave the fabric a smooth, airtight, and durable finish but was quite flammable. Modern fabric systems use butyrate or vinyl based dope coatings to reduce the overall flammability of the fabric covering.

As the aviation industry developed more powerful engines and more aerodynamic aircraft structures, aluminum became the material of choice. As a covering, aluminum protects the aircraft structure from the elements, is durable, and is not flammable. Although aluminum and composite aircraft now dominate large aircraft construction, fabric and plastic coverings continue to be used in smaller aircraft as they are lightweight and easy to construct and repair.

Large UAS vehicles should be covered with FAA approved, airplane compliant materials. For small and micro UASs, there are a number of model aircraft coverings that have proven suitable. There are three basic types of model aircraft materials: synthetic fabric weaves, plastics, and tissue. Some of these materials are known as iron-on fabrics, or plastics, that have a heat-activated adhesive on one side. Iron-on materials are easy to apply, but over time, the adhesive may eventually release from the structure and the fabric will wrinkle, loosen, or peel off. Other materials heat shrink to fit when heat is carefully applied with an iron or heat gun.

Which material you choose is more a matter of personal preference. Fabrics are more durable, but heavier than plastic films. Plastic films adhere better to the structure but are less puncture resistant and become brittle when cold. Tissue, and the accompanying paint finish required, is the least common covering and seldom used for anything but the lightest airframes.

METALLIC STRUCTURAL MATERIALS

Sheet metal aircraft construction is more common in larger aircraft, but has found its way into smaller aircraft as it is more durable than wood and fabric. Generally, sheet metal made of aluminum alloy can serve as both the structure and outer covering of aircraft, with the parts joined with rivets or other types of fasteners.

Figure 3-5. Plastic film covering for small aircraft showing small wrinkles.

Sheet metal is obtained by rolling metal into flat sheets of various thicknesses ranging from thin (leaf) to plate (pieces thicker than 6 mm or 0.25 inch). The thickness of sheet metal, called gauge, ranges from 8 to 30 with the higher gauge denoting thinner metal. Sheet metal can be cut and bent into a variety of shapes.

Aluminum Alloys Used in Aircraft
Aluminum alloys are the most frequently encountered type of sheet metal in aircraft. In its pure state, aluminum is lightweight, lustrous, and corrosion resistant. The thermal conductivity of aluminum is very high. It is ductile, malleable, and nonmagnetic. When combined with various percentages of other metals (generally copper, manganese, and/or magnesium), aluminum alloys are formed. Aluminum alloys are as lightweight, and stronger, than pure aluminum but they do not possess its corrosion resistance and are usually treated to prevent deterioration.

Clad aluminum is an aluminum alloy of some type with an outer protective coating that improves its corrosion resistance. This coating can be a thin layer of either pure or a different aluminum alloy. To identify grades of aluminum and aluminum alloys, sheet and tubular aluminum stock is usually marked with a standard commercial code marking. The commercial code marking consists of a number that identifies the particular composition of the alloy. An additional letter suffix designates the temper designations and subdivisions of the alloys.
- 1100 aluminum is 99% aluminum and is considered to be "pure" aluminum. 1100 is used where strength is not an important factor, but where light weight and corrosion resistance are desired. 1100 is often used for fuel and oil tanks and cowlings as well as for repairing wingtips and tanks.
- 3003 is slightly stronger than 1100 and is generally used for the same purposes. It contains a small percentage of magnesium and is harder than 1100 aluminum.

- 2014 is used for heavy-duty forgings, plates, and extrusions. It is most commonly used for aircraft fittings, wheels, and major structural components.
- 2024 is generally the "standard" aluminum used for aircraft structures, rivets, hardware, machine screw products, and other miscellaneous structural applications. In addition, this alloy is commonly used for heat-treated parts, airfoil and fuselage skins, extrusions, and fittings.
- 2025 is used extensively for propeller blades.
- 5052 is used where good workability, very good corrosion resistance, high fatigue strength, weld-ability, and moderate static strength are desired. This alloy is found often in fuel, hydraulic, and oil lines.
- 5056 is used for making rivets and cable sheeting and in applications where aluminum comes into contact with magnesium alloys. 5056 is generally resistant to the most common forms of corrosion.
- 6061 is a good general-purpose aluminum used in many different aircraft applications.
- 7075 is one of the highest strength aluminum alloys, but is difficult to work with and form at room temperature.

Various alloys, including 3003, 5052, and 1100 aluminum, are hardened by cold working rather than by heat treatment. Other alloys, including 2017 and 2024, are hardened by heat treatment, cold working, or a combination of the two. Various casting alloys are hardened by heat treatment. In general, one has to be careful when heating aluminum, or when extensive cold working it, as microscopic changes can occur that might lead to premature failure of the metal in use.

STRUCTURAL FASTENERS

Fasteners used to join sheet metal structures come in thousands of shapes and sizes with many of them specialized and specific to certain purposes. Rivets are the most common fastener used in larger aircraft. Rivets are divided into two main groups: solid shank rivets and special purpose blind rivets.

Solid rivets are one of the oldest and most reliable types of fastener. Widely used in aircraft manufacturing, they are relatively low-cost, permanently installed fasteners. In a mass production setting, they are faster to install than nuts and bolts since they adapt well to automatic, high-speed installation tools. Rivets should not be used in tension, as their tensile strengths are quite low relative to their shear strength. Riveted joints are neither airtight, nor watertight, unless special seals or coatings are used. Since rivets are permanently installed, they must be removed by drilling them out. This is a time consuming task, and it also may damage the adjacent structure if it is not done correctly.

Solid rivets are available in several head shapes, but the universal, and the 100° countersunk head, are the most commonly used in aircraft structures. Universal head rivets were developed specifically for the aircraft industry and are protruding head rivets used primarily where the head has no significant effect on the aerodynamics of the aircraft. Countersunk rivets have a flat head with an angular undercut shape that allows the head to fit into a countersunk or dimpled hole. A countersunk rivet is used when aerodynamic drag must be kept to a minimum.

Figure 3-6. Aluminum alloy sheet markings, 2024-T3.

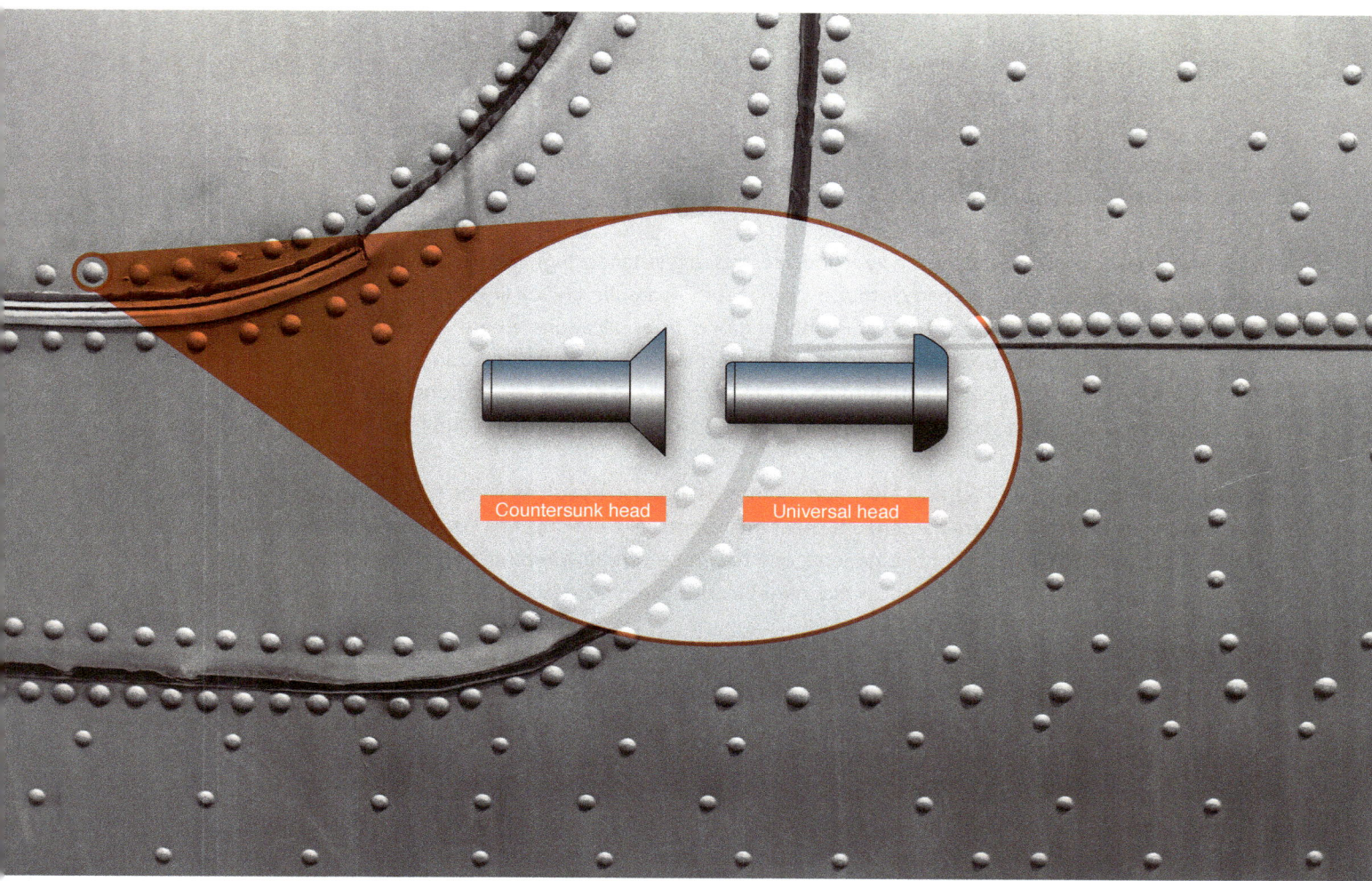

Figure 3-7. Aircraft solid shank rivets.

BLIND RIVETS

During the installation of solid shank rivets, access to both sides of the riveted structure, or part, is required. There are many places on an aircraft where this access is impossible, or where limited space does not permit the use of bulky rivet tools. If it is not possible, or practical, to install solid shank rivets special fasteners have been designed for use. Special purpose fasteners can be used in locations where one side of the rivet cannot be seen or worked. These special fasteners are called blind rivets or blind fasteners. Typically, the locking characteristics of a blind rivet are not as good as those of a driven, solid shank rivet, and they are not used if a driven rivet can possibly be installed. These types of rivets are typically made of aluminum with a steel core, or stem, and can be installed with simple hand tools.

METAL AIRFRAME INSPECTION

When inspecting the metal structure of an aircraft, it is very important to watch for evidence of corrosion both inside, and on outside surfaces. Corrosion is most likely to occur in pockets and corners where moisture may accumulate. While damage to the skin covering caused by impact with an object is plainly evident, a defect, such as distortion or failure of the substructure, may not be apparent until some evidence develops on the surface, such as canted, buckled or wrinkled covering, and loose rivets or working rivets. A working rivet is one that has movement under structural stress, but has not loosened to the extent that movement can be observed. This situation can sometimes be noted by a dark, greasy residue or deterioration of paint and primers around rivet heads. The common term for this is a smoking rivet due to the metallic and corrosion residue trailing back towards the tail of the aircraft as the slipstream carries the debris. External indications of internal damage must be watched for and correctly interpreted. When found, an investigation of the substructure in the vicinity should be made and corrective action taken.

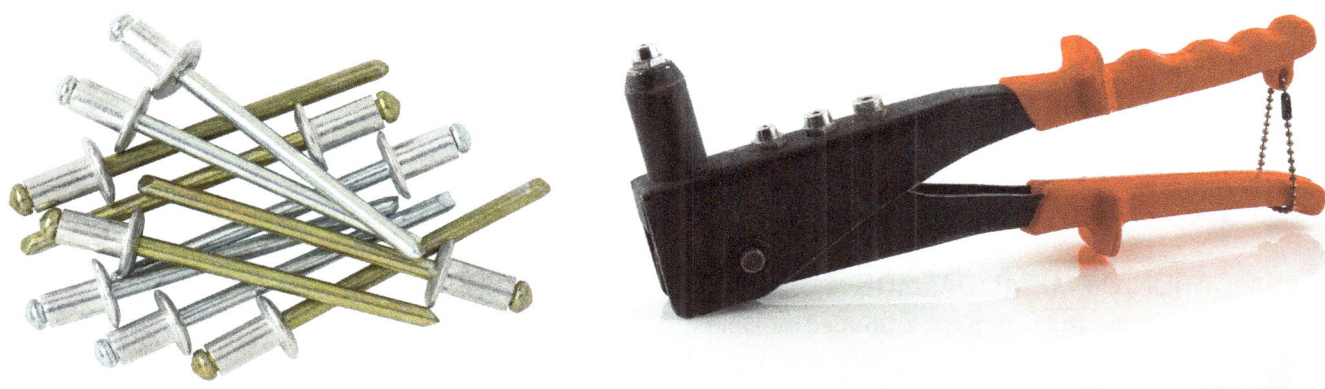

Figure 3-8. Non-structural blind rivets and hand puller installation tool.

Warped wings are usually indicated by the presence of parallel skin wrinkles running diagonally across the wings and extending over a major area. This condition may develop from unusually violent maneuvers, extremely rough air, or extra hard landings. While there may be no actual rupture of any part of the structure, it may have been distorted and weakened. Similar failures may also occur in fuselages. Small cracks in the skin covering may be caused by vibration and are frequently found leading away from rivets. Aluminum alloy surfaces having chipped protective coating, scratches, or worn spots that expose the surface of the metal should be recoated at once, as damaging corrosion may develop rapidly.

Scratches that penetrate the pure aluminum surface layer of clad aluminum permit corrosion to take place in the alloy beneath. A simple visual inspection cannot accurately determine if suspected cracks in major structural members actually exist, nor the full extent of the visible cracks. Special non-destructive inspection techniques are used to find hidden damage.

TYPES OF METALLIC DAMAGE AND DEFECTS

Types of damage and defects that may be observed on aircraft parts are usually defined as follows:
- Brinelling - the occurrence of shallow, spherical depressions in a surface, usually produced by a part having a small radius in contact with the surface under high load.
- Burnishing - the polishing of one surface by sliding contact with a smooth, harder surface. Usually there is no displacement or removal of metal.
- Burr - a small, thin section of metal extending beyond a regular surface, usually located at a corner or on the edge of a hole.
- Corrosion - the loss of metal from the surface by chemical or electrochemical action. The corrosion products are generally removed by mechanical or chemical means.
- Crack - a physical separation of two adjacent portions of metal, evidenced by a fine or thin line across the surface caused by excessive stress at that point. It may extend inward from the surface from a few thousandths of an inch to completely through the section thickness.
- Cut – a loss of metal, usually to an appreciable depth over a relatively long and narrow area, by mechanical means, as would occur with the use of a saw blade, chisel, or sharp-edged stone striking a glancing blow.
- Dent - an indentation in a metal surface produced by an object striking with force. The surface surrounding the indentation is usually slightly upset or distorted.
- Erosion - a loss of metal from the surface by mechanical action of foreign objects, such as grit or fine sand. The eroded area is rough and may be lined in the direction in which the foreign material moved relative to the surface.
- Chattering - a breakdown or deterioration of metal surface by vibratory or chattering action. Although chattering may give the general appearance of metal loss or surface cracking, usually, neither has occurred.
- Galling - a breakdown (or build-up) of metal surfaces due to excessive friction between two parts having relative motion. Particles of the softer metal are torn loose and welded to the harder metal.
- Gouge - a groove in, or breakdown of, a metal surface from contact with foreign material under heavy pressure. Usually it indicates metal loss but may be largely the displacement of material.

Unmanned Aerial Systems: The Definitive Guide

- Inclusion - the presence of foreign or extraneous material wholly within a portion of metal.
- Nick - a local break or notch on an edge. Usually it involves the displacement of metal rather than loss.
- Pitting - a sharp, localized breakdown (small, deep cavity) of metal surface, usually with defined edges.
- Scratch - a slight tear or break in metal surface from light, momentary contact by foreign material.
- Score - a deeper tear or break in metal surface than a scratch. May show discoloration from temperature produced by friction.
- Stain - a change in color, locally causing a noticeably different appearance from the surrounding area.

CLASSIFICATION OF METAL DAMAGE

Damage to an airframe structure may be grouped into four general classes.
- Negligible or minor damage
- Damage repairable by patching
- Damage repairable by insertion
- Complete replacement

In many cases, the availabilities of repair materials, and time, are the most important factors in determining if a part should be repaired or replaced. Negligible or minor damage consists of visually apparent surface damage that does not affect the structural integrity of the component involved. Negligible damage may be left as is or may be corrected by a simple procedure without restricting flight. In most cases, some corrective action must be taken to keep the damage from spreading. Negligible damage areas must be inspected frequently to ensure the damage does not spread. Permissible limits for negligible damage vary for different components of different aircraft and should be carefully researched on an individual basis. Failure to ensure that damages within the specified limit of negligible damage may result in insufficient structural strength of the affected support member for critical flight conditions. Small dents, scratches, cracks, and holes that can be repaired by smoothing, sanding, stop drilling, hammering out, or otherwise repaired without the use of additional materials, fall in this classification.

Damage repairable by patching is any damage exceeding negligible damage limits that can be repaired by installing splice members to bridge the damaged portion of a structural part. The splice members are designed to span the damaged areas and to overlap the existing undamaged surrounding structure. The splice, or patch material used in internal riveted and bolted repairs, is normally the same type of material as the damaged part, but one gauge heavier. In a patch repair, filler plates of the same gauge and type of material as that in the damaged component may be used for bearing purposes, or to return the damaged part to its original contour. Structural fasteners are applied to members, and the surrounding structure, to restore the original load-carrying characteristics of the damaged area. The use of patching depends on the extent of the damage and the accessibility of the component to be repaired.

Damage repairable by insertion is required when the damaged area is too large to be patched or the structure is arranged such that repair members would interfere with structural alignment. In this type of repair, the damaged portion is removed from the structure and replaced by a member identical in material and shape. Splice connections at each end of the insertion member provide for load transfer to the original structure.

Damage necessitating the complete replacement of parts occurs when the location or extent of damage makes repair impractical, when replacement is more economical than repair, or when the damaged part is relatively easy to replace. Castings, forgings, hinges, and small structural members are usually easier to replace than to repair. Some highly stressed members must be replaced because repair would not restore an adequate margin of safety. Most small UAV components, even those as large as complete wings or tail parts, may be easily replaced making repair of major damage impractical.

The following criteria can be used to help decide upon the repair ability of any airframe sheet metal structure:
- Type of damage.
- Type of original material.
- Tools and equipment needed and/or available to make the repair.
- Location of the damage.
- Type of repair required.

In semi or full monocoque construction, the skin of the aircraft carries part or all of the loads. Various specific skin areas are classified as highly critical, semi-critical, or noncritical. Minor damage to the outside skin of the aircraft can be repaired by applying a patch to the inside of the damaged sheet. A filler plug must be installed in the hole made by the removal of the damaged skin area. It plugs the hole and forms a smooth outside surface necessary for aerodynamic smoothness of the aircraft.

The main spar of an aircraft normally refers to the primary spar supporting the wing. Other components of the aircraft may also have members called spars that serve the same function as the spar does in the wing. Because of the load spars carry, it is very important that particular care be taken when repairing this member to ensure the original strength of the structure is not impaired.

WELDING, BRAZING, AND SOLDERING METALS

Rivets and bolts are the most common means of attaching two metal structures to one another. Another method of attaching metal parts is to connect them with melted metal. The three forms of melted metal construction common in aircraft structures are welding, brazing and soldering.

Welding is defined as a process that joins parts by melting both the metal pieces (and some filler metals) until they all flow and mix together, then solidify as a new structure. There are three general types of welding: gas, electric arc, and electric resistance. Each type of welding has several variations and can be used in different situations.

Gas welding is accomplished by heating the ends or edges of metal parts to a molten state with a high temperature flame. Usually another metal is melted into the mix such that when the assembly cools, it is as strong as, or stronger, than the original metal pieces were separately. Electric arc welding is used extensively in large aircraft construction and can be used to join many different types of weldable metals provided that the proper processes and materials are used. Electric resistance welding, usually called either spot or seam welding, is typically used to join thin sheet metal components. When spot welding, two electrodes are held in the jaws of the spot welding machine, and the material to be welded is clamped between them. Pressure is applied to hold the electrodes tightly together and an electrical current is produced that flows through the electrodes and the material. The resistance of the material being welded is so much higher than that of the copper electrodes that enough heat is generated to melt the metal. The pressure on the electrodes forces the molten spots in the two pieces of metal to unite, and this pressure is held after the current stops flowing long enough for the metal to solidify.

Brazing is the joining two pieces of metal using either brass or bronze as the filler metal. Brazing requires less heat than welding and can be used to join metals that may be damaged by high heat. However, because the strength of a brazed joint is not as great as that of a welded joint, brazing is not used for critical structural repairs. When metals are joined by brazing, the base metal parts are not melted. The brazing metal adheres to the base metal by molecular attraction and intergranular penetration; it does not fuse and amalgamate with them.

A method similar to brazing is soldering. Soldering is generally performed only in minor repair jobs and is most often encountered when joining electrical connections. Soldering forms a strong union that has low electrical resistance. Soldering does not require

Figure 3-9. Welding metal parts.

much heat and can be performed using a small propane torch or a portable electrical soldering iron. Solder materials are chiefly alloys of tin and lead although lead-free solder has been developed. The percentages of tin and lead can vary considerably with a corresponding change in their melting points ranging from 293 °F to 592 °F. Half-and-half (50/50) is a common general purpose solder containing equal portions of tin and lead and melts at approximately 360 °F.

Flux is a chemical cleaning agent designed to help reduce the creation of metal oxides during soldering. Metal oxides inhibit the electrical connection and mechanical strength of a solder joint. The two principal types of flux are acid flux, used for metal mending and rosin flux, used in electronics. Rosin flux is used where the corrosiveness of acid flux and vapors released when heated would risk damaging delicate circuitry.

Figure 3-10. Soldering electrical components.

COMPOSITE STRUCTURES

MATERIALS

Composite materials are becoming prevalent in the construction of UAVs. Aircraft parts made from composite materials are usually much lighter in weight than comparable aluminum parts. Other advantages of composite materials are their high strength, relatively low weight, and corrosion resistance. The repair of these materials requires an in-depth knowledge of structures, materials, and tooling however.

Composite materials consist of a combination of different materials combined together to achieve specific structural properties. Unlike the welding of metals, composite materials do not dissolve or merge completely together, but form a new structure with unique properties and strengths. The structural properties of the composite material can be made superior to the individual properties of the materials from which it is constructed. Advanced composite materials are those made of a fibrous material embedded in a resin matrix, generally laminated with fibers oriented in alternating directions to give the material strength and stiffness.

LAMINATES

An isotropic material is one that has uniform strength properties when tested in every direction. Metals are examples of isotropic materials. Anisotropic materials have predominant strength properties oriented in one direction. A fiber material is typically anisotropic and is often used as the primary load-carrying element of some composite materials. Composite components made from fiber reinforced materials can be designed so that the fiber orientation produces optimum mechanical properties, but they can only approach the true isotropic nature of metals, but they are usually much lighter.

Fiber based composites use a matrix material (resin) to support the fibers and bond them together. The matrix transfers any applied loads to the fibers, keeps the fibers in their position and chosen orientation, gives the structure environmental resistance, and determines the maximum service temperature of a composite. A composite structure can be made stronger

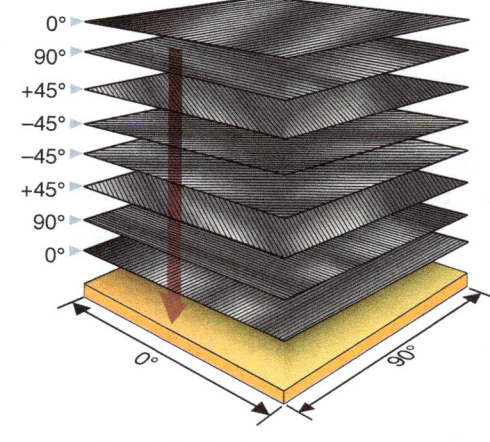

Figure 3-11. Fiber layup orientation.

in many directions by layering plies of material upon one another in varying directions. The structural properties of the component, such as stiffness, dimensional stability, and overall strength, depend on the type, direction, and stacking sequence of the plies. The stacking sequence describes the distribution of ply orientations through the laminate thickness.

TYPES OF COMPOSITE FIBROUS MATERIALS

Fiberglass is one of the oldest, but still widely used, composite products. Fiberglass is composed of individual pieces, woven strands, or matted pads of thin, flexible glass fiber. There are several types of fiberglass used in aviation. Electrical glass, or E-glass, is used in electrical applications as it has a high resistance to current flow. S-glass and S2-glass are fiberglass materials that have a higher strength than E-glass. Fiberglass has advantages over other composite materials in that it is generally inexpensive, has a relatively high chemical and galvanic corrosion resistance, is electrically resistive, and can be worked at room temperature using relatively common household tooling. Fiberglass has a white color and is available as a dry fiber fabric or matrix impregnated (prepreg) material.

CARBON AND/OR GRAPHITE FIBER

Carbon and graphite fibers are based on the hexagonal internal molecular structure (graphene) present in carbon materials. If, at the molecular level, the graphene layers, or planes, are stacked with three-dimensional order, the material is defined as graphite. Graphite fibers are more expensive to manufacture than fiberglass. A simpler form of material that uses only two-dimensional ordering within the layers can be manufactured, and this is known as carbon fiber. Either can be used in aircraft construction and repair and are both generically known as "carbon fiber".

Individual carbon fibers are very stiff and strong: three to ten times stiffer than glass fibers. Carbon fiber can be used for structural aircraft applications due to its high strength and corrosion resistance. Disadvantages include its lower electrical conductivity than aluminum, its high cost, as well as specialized conditions and tools needed to work carbon fiber. Carbon fibers also have a high potential for causing galvanic corrosion when used with metallic fasteners and structures and special protection must be applied when using carbon in these situations. Carbon fiber is typically gray or black in color and is also available as dry fabric or prepreg material.

MATRIX MATERIALS

Resin is a generic term used to designate the polymer used to bind the fibers together into a structural component. There are two general types of polymers: thermoplastic and thermoset. Thermoplastic polymers, which are commonly simply called plastic, are usually shaped into their final form by melting and pressing or injection molding. Thermoplastics will deform or melt when heat is reapplied at a sufficient temperature. Thermoplastics are often used to form components such as aerodynamic fairings and wingtips of small aircraft. Thermoplastics may be heated and reshaped many times. Vacuum forming is a common method of manufacturing thermoplastic components where the plastic is heated until soft and then drawn down over a mold by vacuum to form a rigid shape when cooled.

Figure 3-12. Matrix resins.

Thermosetting plastic, also known as a thermoset, is a petrochemical material that can be made to irreversibly cure. Once shaped, formed, and cured, the material cannot be re-melted or reshaped as thermoplastics can be. Thermosets are somewhat flammable however, and so are seldom used in very high temperature setting such as engines and exhaust systems.

Thermoset plastics can be cured through either a chemical reaction, the application of moderate heat (around 400°F), or through a combination of the two. Thermoset materials are usually liquid or malleable prior to curing and designed to be molded into their final form, or sometimes used as an adhesive. Once cured (hardened), a thermoset resin has assumed its final shape and cannot be reheated and reshaped.

The curing process transforms the resin by cross-linking the molecules permanently, thereby creating a rigid, lightweight structure. Thermoset materials are generally stronger than thermoplastic materials due to this three-dimensional network of bonds and are also better suited to high-temperature applications up to the decomposition temperature. However, they are more brittle. Since their shape is permanent, they tend not to be recyclable.

Thermosetting resins are easily poured or formed into any shape, are compatible with most other materials, and cure readily (by heat or catalyst) into an insoluble solid. Thermosetting resins are also excellent adhesives and bonding agents. Polyester resins are relatively inexpensive, fast processing resins used in some UAV construction and repair. Precautions must be taken however, as polyester resins damage most foam materials and are not suitable for foam core construction unless foam compatibility is determined through testing. One of the disadvantages of using a resin based material is the preparation of the resin and the combining with the fibrous material by "wetting" the fibers. This disadvantage can be minimized through the use of pre-impregnated or prepreg material.

PRE-IMPREGNATED PRODUCTS

Prepreg material consists of a pre-manufactured combination of a matrix and fiber material. It is available in unidirectional form (one direction of reinforcement) and fabric form (several directions of reinforcement). Various tapes, woven fabrics, chopped mat and other materials can be purchased in a prepreg format. Prepreg materials are cured by elevating the temperature of the material after it has been properly shaped or formed.

Prepreg materials must usually be stored in a freezer at a temperature below 0°F to retard the curing process. Many prepreg materials used in aerospace are impregnated with an epoxy resin and are cured at around 300°F. Prepreg materials can be cured in an autoclave, or by using an oven, heat blanket or other portable heat source. Prepregs are typically purchased and stored in a sealed plastic bag to avoid moisture contamination. Prepregs have a definite shelf life due to the unavoidable slow curing of the matrix materials, even when cold. Their expiration date from time of manufacture determines their viable period for use in aerospace applications.

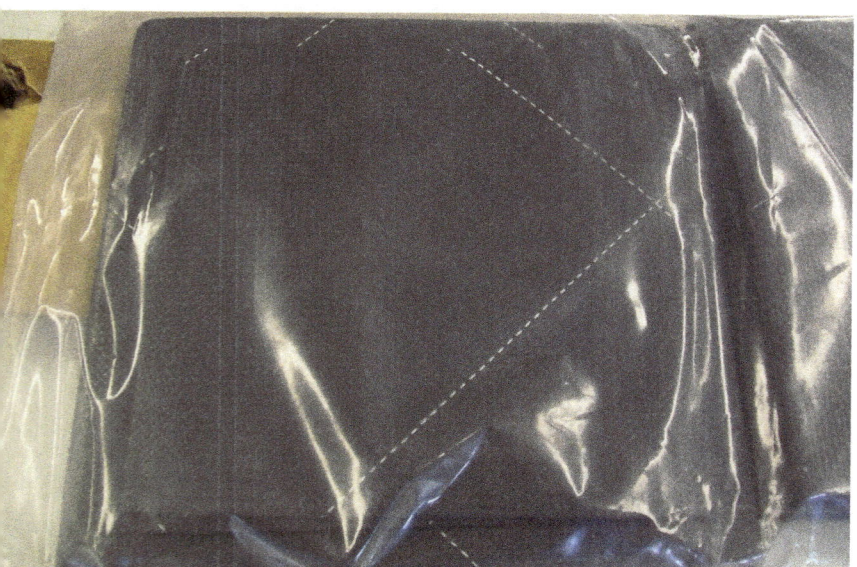

Figure 3-13. Prepreg materials.

WET LAYUP PROCESS

Dry fiber materials, such as carbon and fiberglass, are used for many aircraft repair procedures. The dry fabric is manually impregnated (wetted) with a resin during the repair work. This process is called wet layup. The main advantage of using a wet layup process is that the fiber and resin component parts can be stored separately for a long time at room temperature. Another advantage is that wet layups can usually be cured at room temperature. Although, an elevated temperature can be used to speed up the curing process and increase the strength. Disadvantages of wet lay-ups are that the process is messy and the resultant material is likely less uniform in strength and weight than one created using prepreg materials.

SANDWICH STRUCTURES

A sandwich structural component is usually a panel that consists of two relatively thin sheets bonded to, and separated by, a relatively thick, lightweight core. The core supports the face sheets against buckling and resists shear loads. The core provides shear strength and compression stiffness. Composite sandwich construction is most often fabricated using autoclave cure, press cure, or vacuum bag cure and is difficult to construct in the field. Sandwich construction has high bending stiffness at minimal weight in comparison to aluminum and composite laminate construction. One of the most common sandwich construction materials is honeycomb.

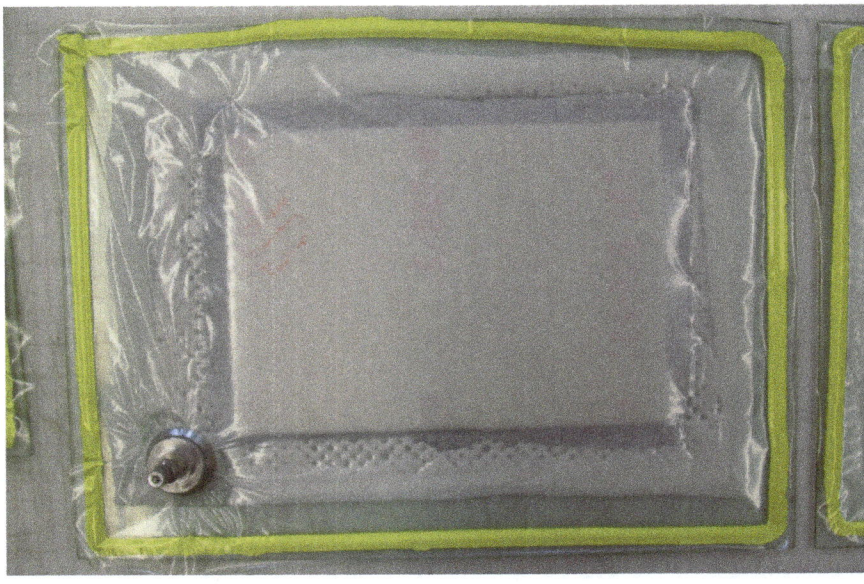

Figure 3-14. Wet layup.

Most honeycombs are anisotropic. Increasing the core thickness greatly increases the stiffness of the honeycomb construction, while the weight increase is minimal. Due to the high stiffness of a honeycomb type construction, it may not be necessary to use external stiffeners, such as stringers and frames.

Most honeycomb structures used in aircraft construction have aluminum, fiberglass or carbon fiber face sheets. The internal honeycomb is composed of a lightweight material such as paper, cardboard or metallic foil. Carbon fiber face sheets cannot be used with aluminum honeycomb core material, because it causes the aluminum to corrode. Some of the materials found in common sandwich construction include:
- Kraft paper - A relatively low strength paper based component with good insulating properties. It is widely available and is relatively low in cost.
- Thermoplastics - provide good insulating properties as well as good energy absorption and/or redirection. It is both moisture and chemical resistant, is fairly environmentally compatible, and can be produced at a relatively low cost.
- Aluminum - has a very good strength-to-weight ratio, good heat transfer properties, and electromagnetic shielding properties, is machinable, and can be produced at a relatively low cost.
- Steel - has good heat transfer properties, electromagnetic shielding properties, and is heat resistant but is heavier than most components.
- Aramid paper - A type of paper that is flame resistant. It has good insulating properties as well.
- Fiberglass - harder to form than paper but is strong, has good insulating properties, and is fairly low cost.
- Carbon Fiber - excellent strength to weight ratio and other physical properties, but hard to construct and very expensive.
- Ceramics - is very heat resistant, has good insulating properties, but is also very expensive.

FOAM CORE STRUCTURES

Foam core structures can be used to give strength and shape to all sorts of aircraft parts including wing tips, flight controls, fuselage sections, wings, and wing ribs. Foams are typically heavier than honeycomb and not as strong but can be much easier to shape, field manufacturer and repair. In some situations, foam can be used as the entire load bearing structure for very small aircraft. A variety of foams can be used as core material including:

Figure 3-15. Various honeycomb structures.

- Polystyrene (better known as Styrofoam) - has a tightly closed cell structure and no voids between cells; high compressive strength and good resistance to water penetration. It can be easily can be cut with a hot wire to make different shapes.
- Phenolic foam - has very good fire-resistant properties and is relatively very low density, but also low strength properties.
- Polyurethane - can be used for producing the fuselage, wing tips, and other curved parts of small aircraft. It is relatively inexpensive, fuel resistant, and compatible with most adhesives. Polyurethane cannot be cut with a hot a hot wire to form shapes, but it is easily contoured with sharp bladed tools and sanding equipment.
- Polypropylene - can be shaped with a hot wire and is compatible with most adhesives and epoxy resins but cannot be used with polyester resins. It easily dissolves when put in contact with many chemicals, fuels, adhesives and solvents.
- Polyvinyl chloride (PVC) - is a closed cell, medium- to high-density foam with high compression strength, durability, and excellent fire resistance. It can be formed and bent using heat and is compatible with polyester, vinyl ester, and epoxy resins.
- Polymethacrylimide (Rohacell) - is closed-cell foam used for lightweight sandwich construction. It has excellent mechanical properties, high stability under heat and has good solvent resistance. It is more expensive than the other types of foams, but has greater mechanical properties.
- Balsa Wood - is a natural wood product with elongated closed cells that somewhat mimic foam. Balsa wood is available in a variety of grades and shapes. Its density is less than one-half the density of conventional wood products. Balsa does however have a higher density than foam cores. Balsa is fairly cheap and can be shaped using common hand tools and processes.

COMPOSITE STRUCTURAL DAMAGE

Damage to composite structures, whether they be fuselage, wing, tail, or other components, can occur within the composite material itself, or as part of the assembly. This can include damage in the matrix and fibers, or broken elements of the structural component. Fiber breakage can be critical because structures are typically designed to have the fiber carry most of the load. Fiber failure is typically limited to an area near the near the point of impact that

Figure 3-16. Aircraft foam wing tip and elevon structure.

caused the damage. Damaged fiber normally requires the removal and repair of that portion of the component or more likely a complete component replacement.

Matrix imperfections, or damage, can slightly reduce some of the material strength properties but are seldom critical to the structure, unless the matrix degradation is widespread. An accumulation of a significant number of matrix cracks can cause the degradation of the matrix. For laminates designed to transmit loads with their fibers only, a very slight reduction of strength occurs when the matrix is damaged. A significant number of matrix cracks, or micro-cracks, can significantly reduce the effectiveness of the fiber-resin interface however. Matrix imperfections may develop into delaminations, which are a more critical type of damage.

Delamination and debonds can form between the layers in the laminate. Delaminations form from matrix cracks or from low-energy impact. Debonds can also form from production nonadhesion along the bondline between two elements and initiate delamination in adjacent laminate layers. Under certain conditions, delaminations or debonds can grow when subjected to repeated loading and can cause catastrophic failure when the laminate is loaded in compression. The criticality of delaminations or debonds depend on the size of the delaminated areas, the number of delaminations at a given location and the structural load placed on the component at the specific location. Ultraviolet (UV) light can also affect the strength of composite materials. Composite structures need to be protected by a top coating to prevent the effects of UV light.

INSPECTION OF COMPOSITE MATERIALS

A visual inspection is the primary inspection method used to verify the surface integrity of composite structures. Most types of damage will make some permanent change to the composite surface, making the damage visible. Once damage is detected, the affected area needs to be inspected closer using flashlights, magnifying glasses, mirrors, or borescopes. These tools are used to magnify defects that otherwise might not be seen easily and to allow visual inspection of areas that are not readily accessible.

Physical impact damage, wrinkles, discoloration due to overheating, foreign matter imperfections, blisters, and debonding are some of the discrepancies that can be detected with a visual inspection. Visual inspection cannot find internal flaws in the composite, such as delaminations, debonds, and matrix crazing. More sophisticated techniques are needed to detect these types of defects.

NONDESTRUCTIVE INSPECTION, COMPOSITES

Various forms of nondestructive inspection (NDI) can be used to determine the internal integrity of composite structures. Audible sonic testing (coin tapping) makes use of frequencies in the audible range (10 Hz to 20 Hz) to determine if there

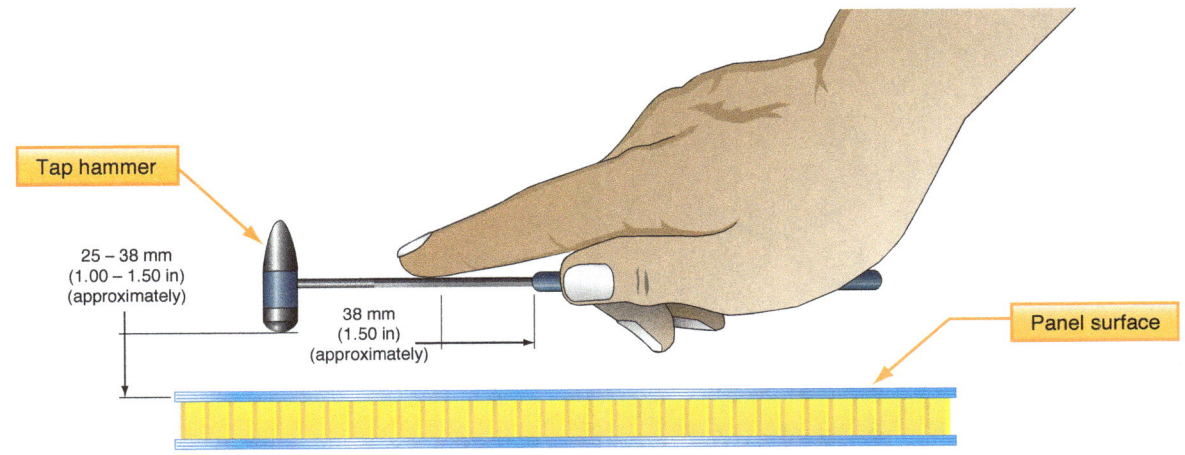

Figure 3-17. Tap testing composite materials.

are internal delaminations or imperfections in a composite part. Tap testing is the most common technique used for the detection of delamination and/or debond. The method is accomplished by carefully tapping the inspection area with a solid round disk or lightweight hammer-like device and listening to the response of the structure to the hammer. A clear, sharp, ringing sound is indicative of a well-bonded solid structure, while a dull or thud-like sound indicates a discrepant area.

Tap testing is effective on thin skin to stiffener bond lines, honeycomb sandwich, with thin face sheets, or even near the surface of thick laminates. One of the problems with this method is that internal elements of the structure, such as wing ribs or longerons, might produce pitch changes that are interpreted as defects, when in fact they are present by design.

Ultrasonic inspection has proven to be a very useful tool for the detection of internal delaminations, voids, or inconsistencies in composite components not otherwise discernable using visual or tap methodology. Ultrasonic inspection uses sound wave energy with a frequency above the audible range to detect delaminations or other discontinuities. A high-frequency sound wave is introduced into the part and is directed by the inspector. The sound is monitored and displayed as it travels through the part.

Ultrasonic sound waves have properties similar to light waves. When an ultrasonic wave strikes an interrupting object, the wave or energy is either absorbed or reflected back to the surface. The disrupted or diminished sonic energy is then picked up by a receiving transducer and converted into a display on an oscilloscope or a chart recorder. The display allows the operator to evaluate the discrepant indications comparatively with those areas known to be good. Ultrasonic inspection requires specialized equipment and a well-trained operator.

COMPOSITE REPAIR TECHNIQUES

Both prepreg and dry fabrics can be cut with hand tools, such as scissors, pizza cutters, and knives. Carbon fiber material is difficult to cut and wears tool surfaces quickly. A squeegee and a brush are used to impregnate dry fibers with resin for wet layup. Markers, rulers, and circle templates are used to make a repair layout. Air-driven power tools, such as drill motors, routers, and grinders, are used to shape and cut composite materials. Electric motors are not recommended, as carbon is a conductive material that can cause an electrical short circuit. If electric tools are used, they need to be of the totally enclosed type.

Figure 3-18. Composite structure repair process.

A caul plate made from aluminum is often used to support the part during the cure cycle. A mold release agent, or parting film, is applied to the caul plate so that the part does not attach to the caul plate. A thin caul plate is also used on top of the repair when a heat bonder is used.

Repairs of composite aircraft components are often facilitated with a technique known as vacuum bagging. A plastic bag is sealed around the repair area. Air is then removed from the bag, which allows repair plies to be drawn together with no air trapped in between. Atmospheric pressure bears on the repair and a strong, secure bond is created. Several processing materials are used for vacuum bagging a part. These materials do not become part of the repair and are discarded after the repair process. Vacuum bags are especially useful for applying pressure to bottom wing surfaces when the aircraft is too large to invert during the repair process.

Release agents, also called mold release agents, are used so that the part comes off the tool or caul plate easily after curing. A bleeder ply is usually installed to create a path for the air and volatiles to escape from the repair. Excess resin is collected in the bleeder. Bleeder material could be made of a layer of fiberglass or a nonwoven polyester. Vacuum bag sealing tape, also called sticky tape, is used to seal the vacuum bag to the part or tool.

Solid release films are used so that the prepreg or wet layup plies do not stick to the working surface or caul plate. Solid release film is also used to prevent the resins from bleeding through and damaging the heat blanket or caul plate if they are used. The vacuum bag material provides a tough layer between the repair and the atmosphere. The vacuum bag material is available in different temperature ratings, so make sure that the material used for the repair can handle the cure temperature. Most vacuum bag materials are one-time use, but material made from flexible silicon rubber is reusable.

Composite materials can be cured in ovens using various pressure application methods. The oven uses heated air circulated at high speed to cure the matrix materials. Typical oven cure temperatures are 250°F to 350°F. Ovens have a temperature sensor to feed temperature data back to the oven controller.

Simpler but less precise heating methods include electrical resistance heat blankets, infrared heat lamps, and hot air devices. All heating devices must be controlled by some means so that the correct amount of heat can be applied. This is particularly important for repairs using prepreg material and adhesives, as controlled heating and cooling rates are usually prescribed.

A heat bonder is a portable device that automatically controls heating based on temperature feedback from the repair area. Heat bonders also have a vacuum pump that supplies and monitors the vacuum in the vacuum bag. The heat bonder controls the cure cycle with thermocouples that are placed near the repair. Modern heat bonders can run many different types of cure programs and cure cycle data can be printed out or uploaded to a computer.

A heat blanket is a flexible heater. It is made of two layers of silicon rubber with a metal resistance heater between the two layers of silicon. Heat blankets are a common method of applying heat for repairs on the aircraft. Heat blankets may be controlled manually; however, they are usually used in conjunction with a heat bonder. Heat is transferred from the blanket via conduction. Consequently, the heat blanket must conform to and be in contact with the part, which is usually accomplished using vacuum bag pressure.

Infrared heat lamps can also be used for elevated temperature curing of composites if a vacuum bag is not utilized. However, they are generally not effective for producing curing temperatures above 150°F, or for areas larger than two square feet. It is also difficult to control the heat applied with a lamp, and lamps tend to generate high-surface temperatures quickly. If controlled by thermostats, heat lamps can be useful in applying curing heat to large or irregular surfaces.

PREPREG COMPOSITES

Prepreg is a fabric or tape that is impregnated with a resin during the manufacturing process. The resin system is ready to be cut and cured. Prepreg material must be stored in a freezer below 0°F to prevent premature curing of the resin. The material is typically placed on a roll and a backing material is placed on one side of the material so that the prepreg does not stick together. The prepreg material is sticky at room temperature and adheres to other plies easily during the stack-up process. You must remove the prepreg from the freezer and let the material thaw, which might take 8 hours for a full roll. Prepreg material is temperature sensitive. Excessively high temperatures cause the material to begin curing, and excessively low temperatures make the material difficult to handle. Prepare the prepreg repair plies in a controlled temperature environment and bring them to the repair area immediately before using them.

Figure 3-19. Wood truss type aircraft structural repair.

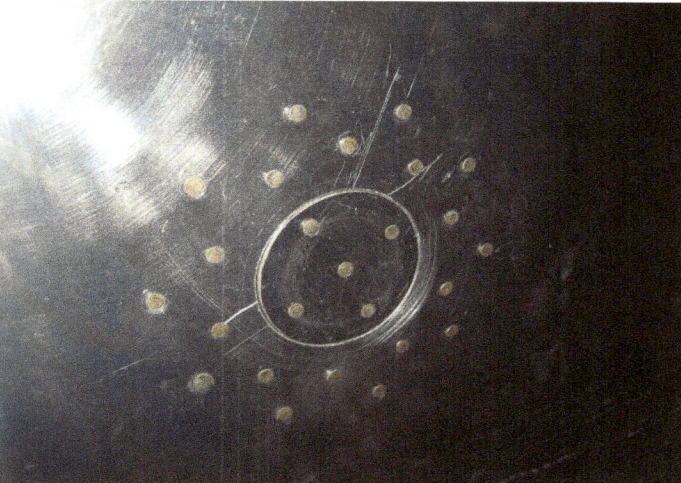

Figure 3-20. Monocoque aircraft construction skin repair, flush patch.

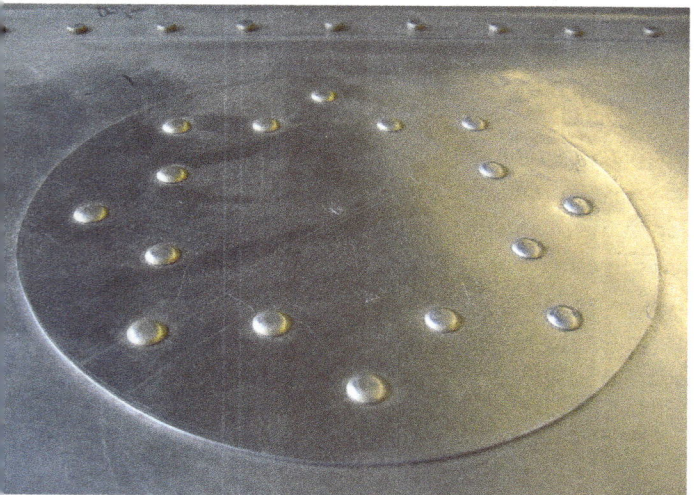

Figure 3-21. Semi-monocoque aircraft structural repair, surface patch.

Composite materials can be used to structurally repair, restore, or enhance aluminum, steel, and titanium components. Bonded composite doublers have the ability to slow or stop fatigue crack growth, replace lost structural area due to corrosion grind-outs, and structurally enhance areas with small and negative margins. This technology has often been referred to as a combination of metal bonding and conventional on-aircraft composite bonded repair. Boron prepreg tape with an epoxy resin is most often used for this application.

AIRCRAFT STRUCTURES, DAMAGE AND REPAIR

FUSELAGE

As mentioned previously, there are two general types of aircraft construction: truss and monocoque. A truss is a rigid framework made up of members, such as beams, struts, and other solid members. A truss fuselage frame is usually constructed of wood or metal connected together in such a manner that the truss carries the loads imposed on the fuselage. Any repair to a truss frame must replicate the load carrying capability of the original structure. A truss frame and is generally covered with some lightweight material. This material generally does not carry much of the load imposed on the frame and is, therefore, less demanding to repair.

A monocoque (or single shell) structure relies largely on the strength of the skin, or covering, to carry the imposed loads. A true monocoque construction would be similar to the body of a plastic model airplane; just an external shell that carries the entire load. Some very small aircraft can be true monocoque in their construction but it is difficult to build a large aircraft in a truly monocoque manner that is both lightweight, yet strong enough to be airworthy.

Larger aircraft are primarily semi-monocoque in design. This design consists of frame assemblies, bulkheads, and formers reinforced by longitudinal members called longerons or stringers. Longerons usually extend across several frame members and help the skin support primary bending loads. Stringers are more numerous, and lighter in weight, than the longerons and are there to provide shape to the structure. Any skin damage to a monocoque, or semimonocoque airframe, requires that the original strength of the aircraft skin be maintained across the repair.

A more modern form of light aircraft construction uses high-density foam in place of many of the above mentioned fuselage components. In one form of construction, similar to semi-monocoque, the foam is cut into the shape of the structure, and then covered with structural wood, fiberglass or carbon fiber. The foam provides the overall shape, but the stresses and loads imposed on the aircraft are almost entirely born by the structural skin. In very small aircraft that will not undergo much stress, the foam itself can be designed to both create the overall shape as well as handle the stresses and strains placed on the aircraft. This type of construction is not well suited to an airframe required to carry any significant load, but can be used for what are essentially lightweight models or prototypes.

The type of foam typically used in small aircraft construction is expanded polyolefin or EPO foam. This type of foam is highly tolerant of impacts and distortion. If compressed, bent, or twisted, it tends to return to its original shape. In general, foam should be considered to be load bearing, and any substantial cracks, divots, or missing pieces of foam need to be replaced and reinforced in a manner that its original strength is maintained.

Figure 3-22. Nonstructural foam hatch repair by filling and shaping.

WINGS

Wing components are usually manufactured from wood, foam, or metal. Aircraft with wood wing spars may have wood or metal ribs while larger aircraft with metal spars have metal ribs. The wings of many small unmanned aircraft are one piece and may not include spanwise reinforcements such as spars, depending upon the weight of the aircraft. On larger aircraft, each wing (left and right) is constructed as a separate component. These wing sections may be joined by a tubular or rectangular spar or alternatively, the inboard end of the wing includes fittings that attach the wing to the fuselage. The area around this attach point is often covered with a fairing to achieve smooth airflow. This fairing may be as simple as vinyl tape on the smallest UAVs.

The wing of an aircraft can be attached to the fuselage at the top, mid-fuselage, or at the bottom. They may extend perpendicular to the horizontal plane of the fuselage or can angle up or down slightly. This angle is known as wing dihedral.

Figure 3-23. Tubular spars within a removable wing panel to carry flight and landing loads.

The wing design for any given aircraft depends on a number of factors, such as size, weight to be carried, use of the aircraft, desired speed in flight and while landing, as well as any other specific performance requirement. The wings are designated left and right, corresponding to the left and right sides of the aircraft as viewed from the rear of the aircraft.

Most often wings are fully cantilevered in their design and construction. Wings described as fully cantilevered means that they are built so that external bracing is not necessary. Instead, the wings are supported by internal structural members and the skin of the aircraft. Non-cantilevered wings use external struts, or cables, to assist in supporting the wing and carrying the aerodynamic and landing loads. Wings can be constructed from aluminum, fabric covered wood, foam covered with fiberglass or carbon fiber, or entirely from high-density foam. The internal structures of most wings made of metal, or wood and fabric, are made up of spars and stringers running span wise (wingtip to wingtip) and ribs and formers running chord wise (leading edge to trailing edge). The spars are the principle structural members of a wing. They support the total load born by the wing skin, which includes the weight of the fuselage, landing gear, payload and propulsion system. The significant repair of any wing structure, whether internally or externally braced, must be considered carefully.

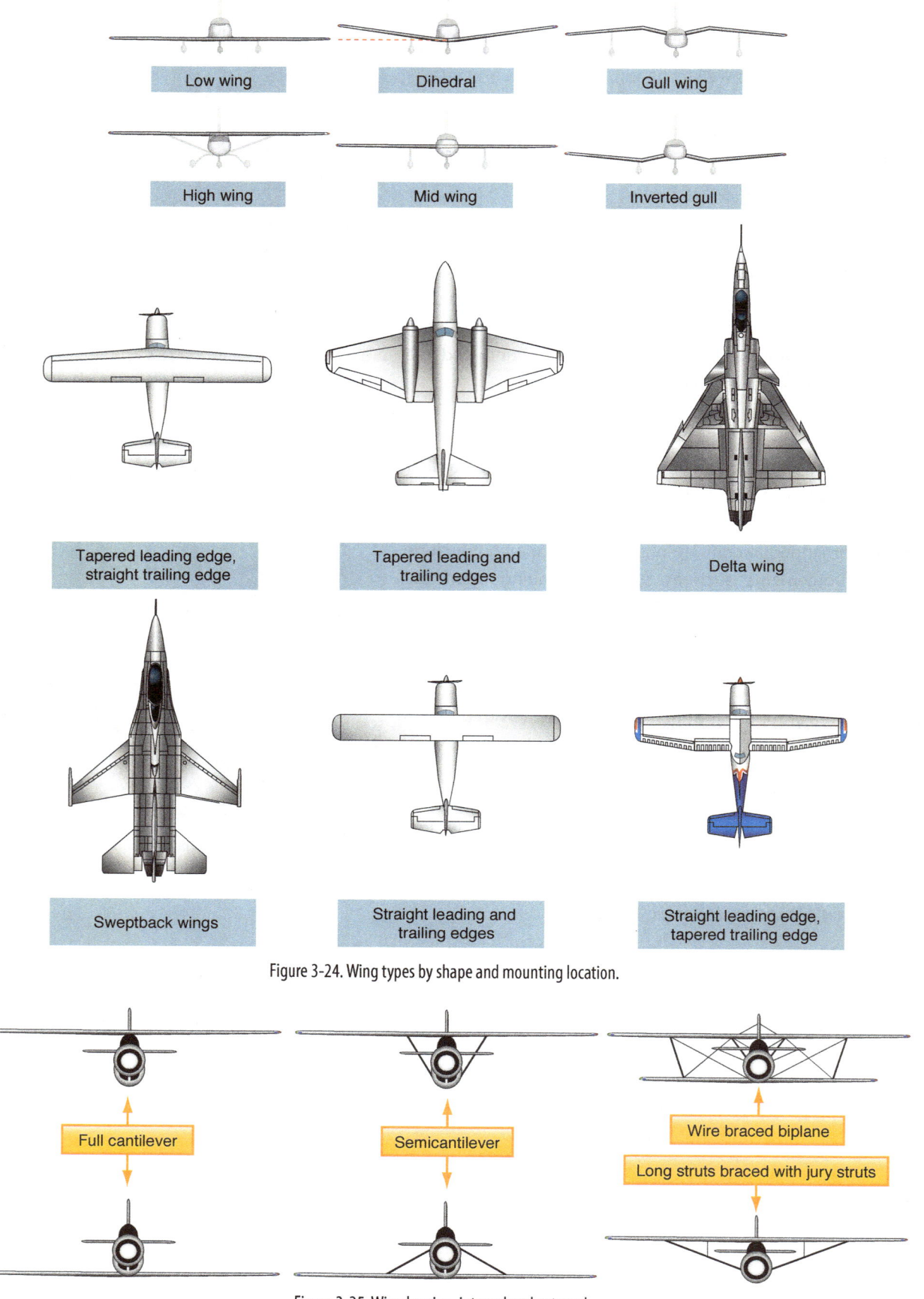

Figure 3-24. Wing types by shape and mounting location.

Figure 3-25. Wing bracing, internal and external.

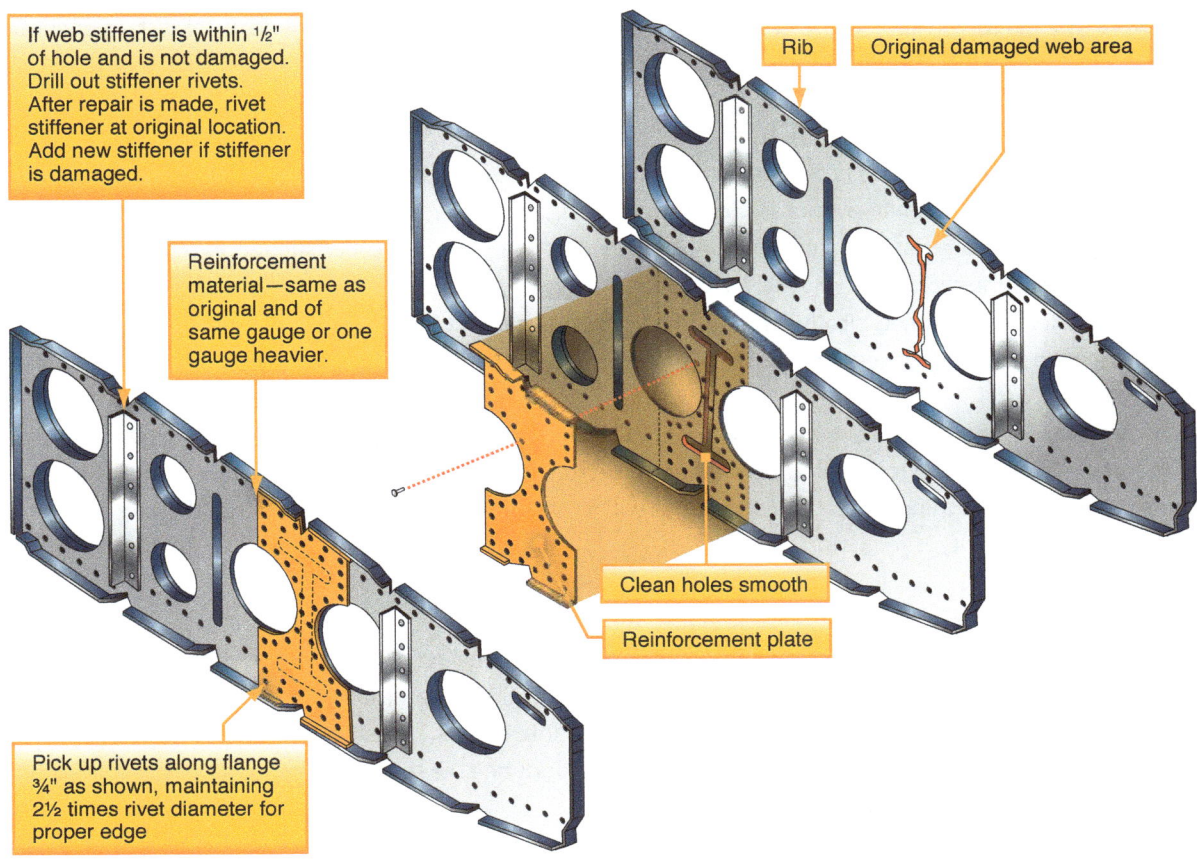

Figure 3-26. Internal wing structural rib repair example.

EMPENNAGE

The empennage of an aircraft is also known as the tail. Most empennage designs consist of a tail cone, fixed aerodynamic surfaces or stabilizers, and movable aerodynamic surfaces. The tail cone serves to close and streamline the aft end of most fuselages.

The other components of the empennage include fixed surfaces that stabilize the aircraft and movable surfaces that direct an aircraft during flight. The fixed surfaces are usually the horizontal stabilizer and vertical stabilizer. The movable surfaces include a rudder, located at the aft edge of the vertical stabilizer, and an elevator, located at the aft edge the horizontal stabilizer. The internal structure of the empennage is similar to that used in wing construction so the repairs will be similar, although lighter and smaller.

FLIGHT CONTROL SURFACES

The directional control of a fixed-wing aircraft takes place around the lateral, longitudinal, and vertical axes by means of flight control surfaces. The primary flight control surfaces on a fixed-wing aircraft include the ailerons, elevator, and the rudder. The ailerons are attached to the trailing edge of both wings and when moved, roll the aircraft. The elevator is attached to the trailing edge of the horizontal stabilizer and causes the aircraft to change its pitch angle for climb and descent. The rudder is attached to the trailing edge of the vertical stabilizer and rotates the aircraft side to side for

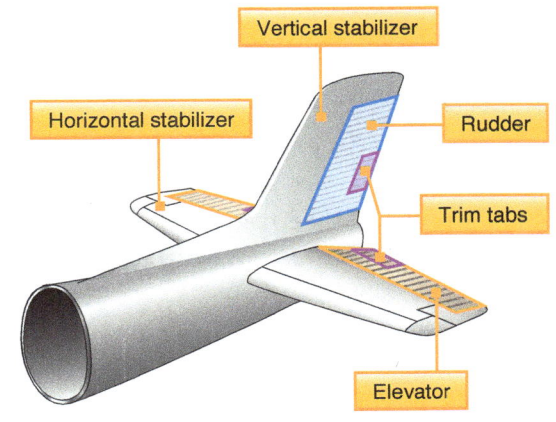

Figure 3-27. Aircraft tail surfaces.

Unmanned Aerial Systems: The Definitive Guide

directional control in yaw. Flight controls are actuated in a variety of ways that include a mechanical system of control cables and pulleys, pushrods, electric actuators (servos), or a combination of systems can be employed.

DUAL PURPOSE FLIGHT CONTROL SURFACES

The ailerons, elevators, and rudder are considered conventional control surfaces. However, some aircraft are designed with control surfaces that may serve dual purposes. For example, delta wing aircraft typically employ elevons to perform the combined functions of the ailerons and the elevator. A ruddervator can be used on an aircraft with a "V" tail configuration to combine the action of the rudder and elevator. Dual-purpose control systems can help eliminate weight and structure by combining control elements. They typically employ a more complicated actuating system involving mixing of the control inputs to achieve the desired combination of control movements.

Repairs to controls must preserve the balance of the control or flutter may result. Flutter is the uncontrolled rapid oscillation of a control surface in flight. This oscillation can lead to structural damage or loss of the entire control surface from the aircraft. Controls on UAVs weighing fewer than 55 pounds will most commonly be replaced, rather than repaired, to preserve balance and structural integrity.

FABRIC

If a damaged section of fabric must be repaired, there are a number of considerations that must be taken into account. If the damaged area is large, and might take an inordinate amount (weight) of repair material, this could imbalance the vehicle, impairing its flight characteristics. It might be simpler, safer, and more efficient to remove all the material and recover rather than attempt to repair a heavily damaged section of fabric. You might be able to affect a temporary field-repair simply using tape or a bonding agent, but a permanent repair is preferable.

If a repair is to be conducted, you must first remove the topcoat of paint across the entire area to be repaired. You will then need to remove the damaged section of fabric. It is preferable to remove the fabric back to a structural member of some sort to support the new fabric patch.

After removing the damaged fabric, a replacement must be fashioned and put into place. If a total fabric replacement is being conducted, the original fabric can be used as a pattern. If a patch is to be installed, the patch must be made larger so as to provide significant overlap. You must consider the airflow over the patch when designing the repair. It might be preferable to make a patch larger than what seems necessary to insure that the airflow over the patch does not tend to lift and separate it from the main structure.

Once the old fabric has been cut away, the patch can be installed and attached to the airframe with special fabric adhesive. After the adhesive has cured, you might need to "smooth" the edges of the repair by liberally applying additional layers of fabric sealer, called "dope". When the adhesive has cured fully, the repair can be repainted.

LANDING GEAR

The landing gear support the aircraft during landing and while it is resting on the ground. Simple aircraft that fly at low speeds generally have fixed gear that does not retract during flight. Faster, more complex aircraft have retractable landing gear. Lightweight fairings and wheel pants can be used to reduce air friction and drag on fixed gear aircraft. Landing gear must be designed to be strong enough to withstand the forces of landing when the aircraft is fully loaded, while also remaining as light in weight as possible.

To aid with the potentially high impact of landing, most landing gear have a means of either absorbing shock, or accepting shock and distributing it, so that the structure is not damaged. Not all aircraft landing gear are configured with wheels. Rotorcraft, for example, have such high maneuverability and low landing speeds that a set of fixed skids is common and quite functional.

Some small UASs eliminate the landing gear altogether and simply land on the bottom of the fuselage itself. This design works well for UAVs that do not takeoff and/or land on hard surface runways.

There are two basic configurations of airplane landing gear: conventional gear (or tail wheel) and tricycle gear. Tail wheel landing gear dominated early aviation and therefore have become known as conventional gear. In addition to the two main wheels, which are positioned under most of the weight of the aircraft, a conventional gear aircraft also has a smaller wheel located at the aft end of the fuselage. Often this tail wheel is steerable by spring attachments to the rudder. This eliminates a separate control system with associated weight and complexity.

Figure 3-28. Conventional landing gear with steerable tailwheel.

Conventional gear designs can cause the aircraft to "ground loop" when landing. A ground loop occurs when the tail of the aircraft swings around and comes forward of the nose of the aircraft. This happens due to the two main wheels being forward of the aircraft's center of gravity. The tail wheel is aft. If the aircraft swerves at all upon landing, and the tail wheel swings out wider than the main gear, this pulls the center of gravity out to the side and forward, causing the aircraft to pivot around the main wheels. Tailwheel configurations are not especially desirable on small UAVs due to this handling difficulty.

The tricycle landing gear configuration is the most prevalent configuration used in modern aviation. In addition to the main wheels, a nose wheel is installed at the front of the fuselage. This keeps the center of gravity forward of the main wheels, but behind the nose gear. This virtually eliminates ground loops since the center of gravity follows the nose wheel and always remains between the main wheels. The nose wheel is normally steerable, which simplifies ground handling and maneuvering. Repairs to landing gear are usually in the form of component replacement in large and small aircraft. The loads imposed on the gear, and their flexibility requirements, make repair impractical in all but very minor damage.

Figure 3-29. Tricycle landing gear with main wheel fairings.

HELICOPTER STRUCTURE

The structure of a helicopter is designed to complement its unique flight characteristics. The airframe of a helicopter can be constructed of wood, metal or composite materials. Since a helicopter can take off and/or land vertically, they are often not equipped with wheels. Very often a helicopter's landing gear is composed of a simple set of metal skids. As with fixed-wing aircraft, helicopter fuselages and tail booms are often truss-type or semi-monocoque structures of stress-skin design with similar repairs being employed.

Figure 3-30. Helicopter with landing gear skids and ground handling dolly.

CHAPTER 4

ELECTRICITY, ELECTRICAL, COMMUNICATIONS AND NAVIGATION SYSTEMS

BASIC ELECTRICITY

Electricity is the flow of electrons through a material known as a conductor. These electrons can be harnessed to perform some sort of electrical work as they pass through various devices. This flow of electrons is known as a current flow. Current (electrons) flows from a source, through the conductor (usually a wire) to one or more devices, then back to the source. This circular flow path is called an electrical circuit.

CURRENT

The amount of electrons flowing through any circuit is called current. Current is a measurement of the total amount of electron flow. Current is measured in terms of amperes or "amps". The more electrons that flow through a circuit, the more "amps". The electrical abbreviation for amps when used in formulas or on drawings is the capital letter "I".

When discussing current, there are two schools of thought concerning the directional flow of electricity. Conventional current theory assumes that electrons flow from positive (+) to negative (−). The other theory, called electron flow theory, assumes that electrons flow from negative to positive. Both conventional flow and electron flow theories are used in industry. In aviation, as well as this text, it is assumed that electrons flow from negative to positive. From a practical standpoint, it makes little difference which way you assume the current is flowing, so long as your chosen method is used consistently.

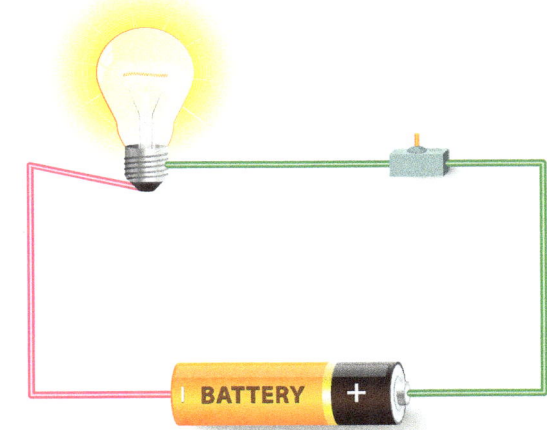

Figure 4-1. Electrical Circuit.

Unmanned Aerial Systems: The Definitive Guide

VOLTAGE

Unlike current, which is easy to visualize as a flow, voltage is a variable measured between two points. Voltage can be considered as the electromotive force (emf), or electrical pressure, that moves the electrons in a circuit. The symbol for emf or voltage is the capital letter "E" or is sometimes represented by the letter "V".

As an example, across the terminals of a battery in an automobile circuit, voltage is measured as a difference of 12 volts. In other words, there is an electromotive force of 12 volts available to push the electrons (current) through the circuit. There cannot be current flow through a circuit unless there is voltage created by a battery, generator, power cell or some other power generating or storing source.

RESISTANCE

The fundamental properties of current and voltage are related to a third property known as resistance. In any closed electrical circuit, when voltage is applied, a current will result. For any given voltage (pressure) the resistance of the conductor determines the amount of current that flows. In general, the greater the circuit resistance, the less the current. If the resistance is reduced, then the current increases. This voltage increase is linear in nature and can be calculated using Ohm's law. Ohm's law generally states that as current flows through the circuit the various devices performing some sort of work decrease the pressure (voltage) of the current as it flows through each device. This loss of voltage due to work being performed by a device is called a "voltage drop".

CONDUCTORS AND INSULATORS

Although current can be forced to flow through most any material, the word "conductor" usually refers to materials that offer low resistance to current flow, and the word "insulator" describes materials that offer high resistance to current. There is no distinct dividing line between conductors and insulators; under the proper conditions, all types of material conduct some current. Materials offering a resistance to current flow midway between the best conductors and the poorest conductors (insulators) are sometimes referred to as "semiconductors," and find their greatest application in the field of transistors and integrated circuits.

The best conductors are primarily metals such as silver, copper, gold, and aluminum, but some nonmetals, such as carbon and water, can be conductors as well. The resistance of a conductor is dependent on the type of conductor material. Copper is usually considered the best available conductor, since a copper wire of a particular diameter offers a lower resistance to current flow than an aluminum wire of the same diameter.

Figure 4-2. Electrical conductors (copper wires) surrounded by (plastic) insulation.

However, aluminum is much lighter than copper, and for this reason, as well as cost considerations, aluminum is often the conductor of choice when weight is a factor. Materials such as rubber, glass, ceramics, and plastic are poor conductors and are usually used as insulators. The current flow in some of these materials is so low that it is usually considered zero.

The resistance of a metallic conductor is directly proportional to its length. The longer the length of a given wire, the greater the resistance. The resistance of a conductor is also inversely proportional to its cross-sectional area. If a thicker wire is used, (the cross-sectional area is increased), the resistance to current flow is reduced. Another factor influencing the resistance of a conductor is temperature. Although some substances, such as carbon, show a decrease in resistance as the surrounding temperature increases, most materials used as conductors increase their resistance as temperature increases. The unit used to measure resistance is called an ohm. The symbol for the ohm is the Greek letter omega (Ω). In mathematical formulas, the capital letter "R" refers to resistance. The resistance of a conductor, and the voltage applied to it, determine the number of amperes of current flowing through the conductor.

Ohm's law states that E (voltage) =I (current) times R (resistance). So according to this law, 1 ohm of resistance in a circuit will limit the current flow to 1 ampere when a voltage of 1 volt is applied. As long as you can measure, or know, two of the three variables listed above (E, I or R), you can use Ohm's law to calculate the missing variable. Some versions of Ohm's law refer to voltage as "V". Ohm's law can be used to calculate the current flow in any circuit.

POWER
The ability of electricity to accomplish something useful is known as power. Power is a rate of energy usage. It is a combination of the pressure (volts) and flow (amps). Power is expressed in terms of watts, which can be calculated by multiplying volts times amps. For example, a light bulb plugged into a 12 volt circuit, with 5 amps flowing through it would cause a 60 watt power draw on the circuit. Watts is a measure of how much electron flow is needed to power any particular device.

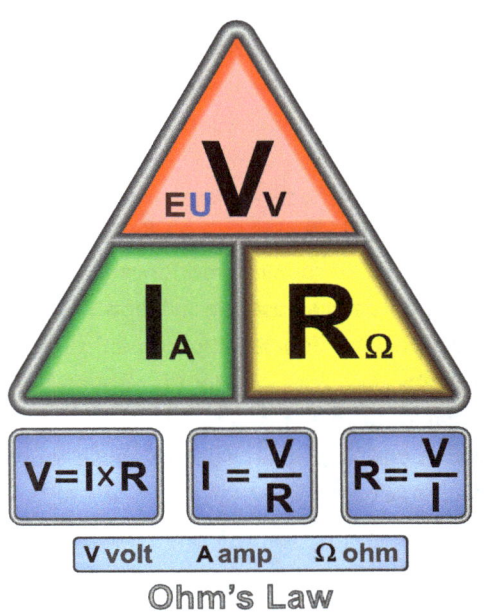
Figure 4-3. Ohms law calculations.

Electrical power used over a span of time is a measure of energy consumption rate. A common unit of energy consumption is the term watt-hour. A watt-hour specification is a way to describe how much total electrical energy is available from any electrical storage device such as a battery. If, for an example, a battery is rated at 100 watt-hours, it can discharge 100 watts for one hour. At that point it will go dead as it has run out of electrons. Or alternatively, it could discharge one watt for 100 hours.

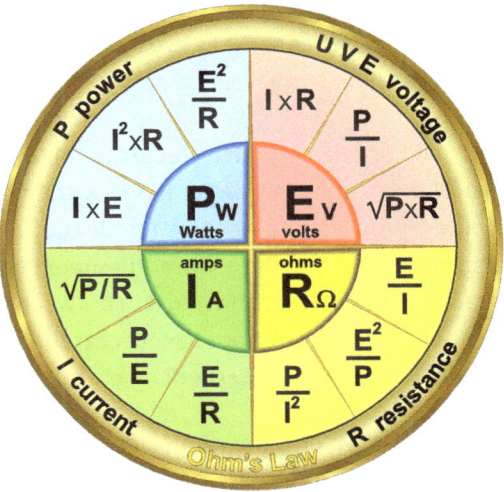
Figure 4-4. Power calculations.

Most small batteries are not capable of storing that much energy. In many cases, small batteries can only store a couple of 1/100ths or 1/1000ths of an amp. The term milliampere is used to measure the capacity of small batteries. A milliampere (mA) or milliamp is 1000th of an amp. A milliamp-hour (mAh) is equivalent to 1/1000th of an amp per hour. If you are using a storage device with limited capacity to supply your circuit with electricity, you will want to reduce the current draw (amps) to as little as possible so as to extend the life of the power source.

ELECTRICAL ENERGY PRODUCTION
Electrical energy can be produced by a number of methods. The five most commonly used in aviation are pressure, chemical, thermal, solar and mechanical.

PRESSURE
Pressure generation of electricity is known as piezoelectric generation. Electricity generated by this method is dependent upon the application of mechanical pressure on a dielectric or nonconducting crystal. The most common piezoelectric materials used today are crystalline quartz or specially formulated ceramics, as well as some other exotic materials. The application of force on the piezoelectric material produces an electric polarization proportional to the force applied. This polarization establishes a voltage across the crystal. If a circuit is connected to the crystal, a flow of current will occur. The exact opposite

effect can be observed if a voltage is applied to the faces of the crystal. This causes the crystal to mechanically change shape in proportion to the applied voltage.

Both of these effects are known as the piezoelectric effect. Piezo materials are used extensively in transducers used to convert mechanical motion into an electrical signal. Common devices used in aviation include microphones and other vibration-sensing elements. The opposite effect, whereby mechanical output is derived from an electrical signal input to a crystal is widely used in headphones as well as small speakers such as those found on portable electronic devices.

CHEMICAL

Chemical energy can also be used to create electricity. The most common form of this is the battery. Fuel cells are another up and coming form of chemically generated electricity. Batteries come in two forms; liquid (or wet) and dry cell (sealed) batteries.

Wet cell batteries produce electricity through the use of two different metals submerged in a chemical solution, typically an acid. The positive terminal of the battery is attached to one of the metals, the negative terminal is attached to the other. The reaction between the acid and the metals causes electrons to collect around the negative battery terminal, thereby producing a potential voltage.

If the electrochemical reaction that releases energy is reversible, the battery type is known as a secondary cell. The battery found in your car is typically a secondary-cell battery. The electrolyte is sulfuric acid (battery acid). As the battery continues to provide electrons, the acid is chemically changed and depleted of free electrons. When current is applied back into the battery, the acid is "recharged" and the battery will be able to supply power again. Depleting the battery of its charge, then recharging it is called a "battery cycle". Every time a battery is cycled it loses a little of its total holding capacity. Eventually, after enough cycles, the battery will be unable to store any charge and will need to be replaced.

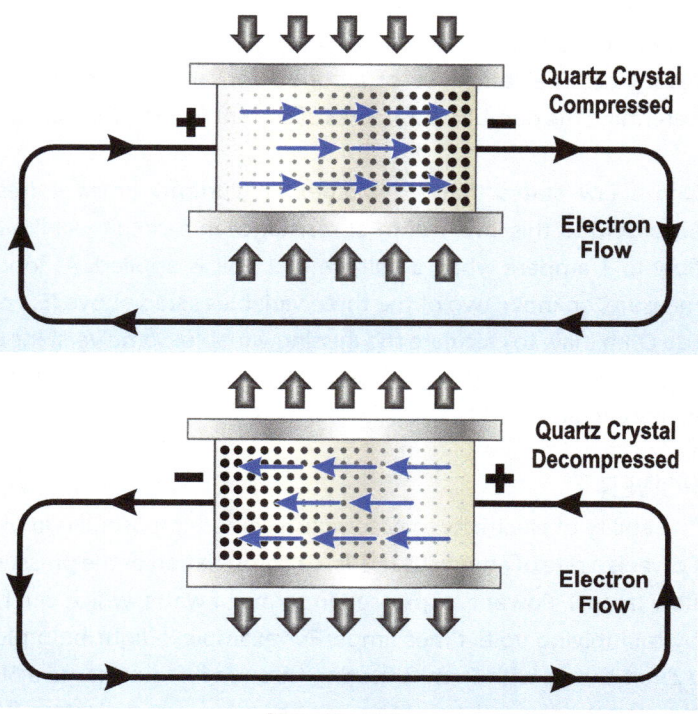

Figure 4-5. Piezoelectricity.

Figure 4-6. Wet cell battery.

The term battery life cycle is defined as the number of complete charge/discharge cycles a battery can perform before its normal charging capacity falls below 80% of its rated capacity. Battery life can vary anywhere from 500 to 1,300 cycles. Various factors can cause deterioration of a battery and shorten its service life. Over-charging, too rapid a discharge, or leaving a battery in a low, or discharged condition for a long period of time will reduce the batteries capacity to recharge.

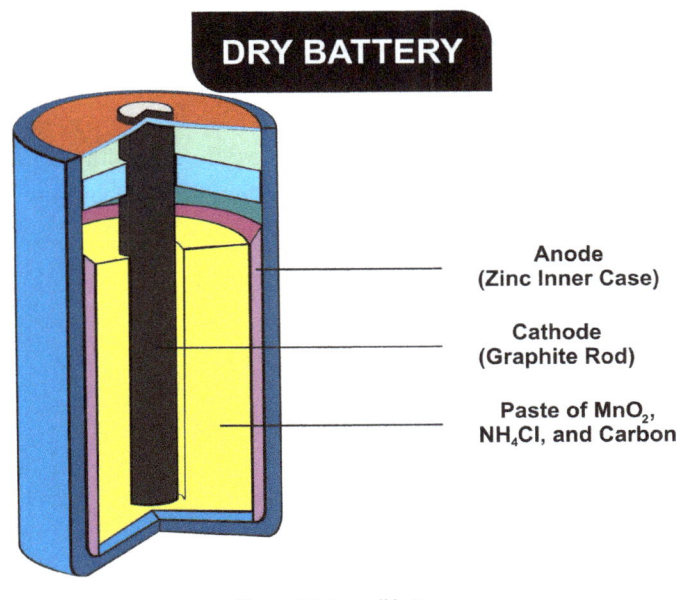

Figure 4-7. Dry cell battery.

Some wet-cell batteries require venting to discharge the pressure created when the battery is recharged. These type of batteries might need to occasionally be refilled with water (distilled) to maintain their capacity. Caution needs to be exercised when servicing these batteries as the acid contained within is very corrosive. Care must also be taken when utilizing these batteries to insure that the acids don't spill out of the battery during normal operations. If spilled, battery acid will corrode or destroy almost any surface it comes into contact with. Some wet cell batteries are sealed. They do not need refilling, and are unlikely to spill, but are still considered wet cell batteries.

The dry cell is the most common type of small battery and is similar in its characteristics to that of an electrolytic cell. This type of a battery is basically designed with a metal electrode or graphite rod acting as the positive terminal, immersed in an electrolytic paste primarily alkaline based—the opposite of acid base wet cells. This assembly is encased in a metal container, usually made of zinc, which itself acts as the negative terminal. The battery then operates similar to a wet cell.

When the battery is discharging an electrochemical reaction takes place, resulting in one of the metals being consumed. Because of this consumption, the charging process is not reversible as it is in a wet cell battery. Attempting to reverse the chemical reaction in a dry cell of this type is dangerous and can lead to a battery explosion. There are specially designed dry cells that can be recharged however, but they are all prominently labelled as being rechargeable. Dry cell batteries are commonly used to power items such as flashlights, radio transmitters, or other small consumer electronics. The most common dry cells used today are alkaline, silver-oxide and lithium batteries.

FUEL CELLS

A fuel cell is similar in many ways to a wet cell battery. It operates by converting the chemical energy available in fuel into electricity. Hydrogen, alcohol or other hydrocarbons can be used as the fuel. Fuel cells are different from secondary batteries in that they consume the fuel and cannot be recharged by simply reversing the current flow. When the fuel in a fuel cell is depleted, it needs to be replaced. Fuel cells can produce electricity continuously for as long as fuel is available to convert. There are byproducts to this consumption process, but in many cases it is simply water, or water vapor, that can be vented overboard. Fuel cells do create heat as well that also needs to be vented or controlled in some manner.

Fuel cells are classified by the type of electrolyte (fuel) they use. Fuel cells come in a variety of sizes but generally produce relatively small amounts of electricity. To create a workable system, fuel cells are usually joined together in series to increase the voltage and current to an acceptable level.

Figure 4-8. Hydrogen fuel cell.

Unmanned Aerial Systems: The Definitive Guide

THERMAL ELECTRICITY GENERATION

Electricity can be created simply from having two differing metals touch one another. As the temperature at the junction of the two materials is increased, a current can be produced. In aviation, this property is commonly used in thermocouples. Thermocouples are pairs of dissimilar metal wires joined at one end, which generate a voltage between the two wires proportional to the temperature at the junction. Different metal combinations can be used to create different voltages. This property is used for temperature measurement instruments such as cylinder head and exhaust gas temperature gauges.

SOLAR ENERGY

A solar cell or a photovoltaic cell is a device that converts light energy into electricity. These cells contains chemical elements that, when exposed to light energy, release electrons. Photons in sunlight are taken in by the solar panel or cell, where they are then absorbed by semiconducting materials, such as silicon. The photons impacting the cell materials cause electrons in the cell to break loose from their atoms, allowing them to flow through the material to produce electricity.

Figure 4-9. Solar panel.

MECHANICAL GENERATORS

If you rotate a coil of wire through a magnetic field, current is generated. If you rotate a large enough coil fast enough, a usable current can be created. A device to accomplish this is known as a generator. Generators essentially convert mechanical energy to electrical energy. The mechanical energy might be from a hydro or steam turbine or, in the case of an aircraft or automobile, a direct connection to the internal combustion engine powering the vehicle. In general, the faster you spin the generator, the higher the current potential (amps) of the generator. Most generators develop DC current, but can be designed to create AC. A device of this type is most commonly called an alternator.

DIRECT AND ALTERNATING CURRENT

If the current flow in a circuit is generally in one direction, it is commonly referred to as a direct current or DC circuit. Most battery powered, as well as computer controlled systems, are direct current circuits. It was discovered long ago that if the current in a circuit could be made to go back and forth very quickly, the components in the circuit could be made much smaller. This led to the advent of alternating current or AC circuits. Many of the principles, characteristics, and effects of AC are similar to those of direct current. In general, AC circuitry is used in household and commercial airline systems; DC is used in smaller, mobile applications like aircraft and automobiles.

Figure 4-10. Mechanically driven generator.

Alternating current has largely replaced direct current in commercial power systems for a number of reasons. It can be transmitted over long distances more readily and more economically than direct current, since AC voltages can be increased or decreased by means of transformers. Because more and more units are being operated electrically in airplanes, the power requirements are such that a number of advantages can be realized by using AC. Space and weight can be saved, since AC devices, especially motors, are smaller and simpler than DC devices.

CIRCUIT PROTECTION DEVICES

Perhaps the most serious trouble in a circuit is a "direct short". This term describes a situation in which some point in the circuit, where full system voltage is present, comes into direct contact with the return side of the circuit (sometime referred to as "ground"). This "short circuit" establishes a path for current flow that contains no resistance other than that present in the wires carrying the current, and these wires have very little resistance.

Since most wires used in aircraft electrical circuits are fairly small compared to those found in household or commercial circuits, their current carrying capacity is quite limited. Any current flow in excess of normal, such as would occur in the case of a direct short, could cause a rapid generation of heat. If the excessive current flow caused by the short is left unchecked, the heat in the wire will continue to increase, possibly causing a portion of the wire to melt or catch fire. At the very least, the wire could burn through, opening the circuit, rendering it unusable.

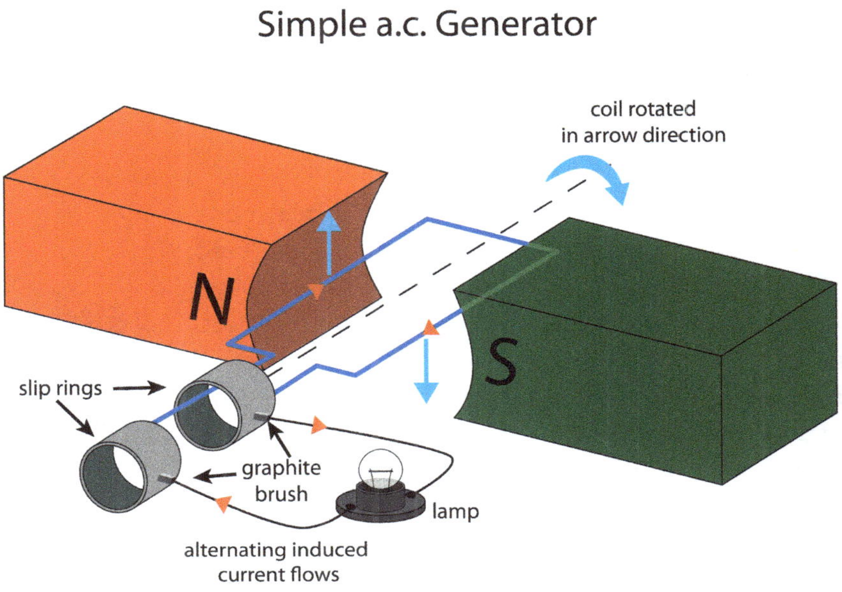

To protect aircraft electrical systems from damage and failure caused by excessive current, several kinds of protective devices are installed in electrical systems. Fuses, circuit breakers, and other thermal protectors are used for this purpose. Circuit protective devices, as the name implies, all have a common purpose—to protect the units and the wires in the circuit. Some are designed primarily to protect the wiring and to open the circuit in such a way as to stop the current flow when the current becomes greater than the wires can safely carry. Other devices are designed to protect a unit in the circuit by stopping the current flow to it when the unit becomes excessively warm. They all work a little differently, but in general they act as an automatic switch, stopping current flow in a circuit before any serious wiring damage can occur.

Figure 4-11. Simple alternating current generator.

Figure 4-12. Inline fuse and circuit breaker.

Unmanned Aerial Systems: The Definitive Guide

SWITCHES

Switches control the current flow in most aircraft electrical circuits. A switch is used to start, stop, or change the direction of the current flow in a circuit. The number of poles, throws, and positions they have designate the type of switch as well as its function.

The term pole refers to the number of circuits that can be completed through the switch at any one time. Throw indicates the number of circuits, or paths for current, that are possible to complete through each pole of the switch. Positions indicates the number of places at which the switch will come to rest opening or closing one or more circuits. A wall switch in your house is an example of a single-pole, single-throw (SPST) switch. There are many types of simple switches. The most common include knife, toggle and push button switches.

SWITCH TYPES

Knife switches consist of a flat metal blade, hinged at one end, with an insulating handle for operation, and a fixed contact. When the switch is closed, current flows through the hinged pivot and blade and through the fixed contact. The knife and contacts are typically formed of copper, steel, or brass, depending on the application. Knife switches are not usually used in operational circuitry, but can be used as cut-off switches to completely disconnect a circuit from its power source in an emergency.

Figure 4-13. Toggle switch with safety cover.

Toggle switches are similar in function but are normally completely enclosed and manually actuated by a mechanical lever, handle, or rocking mechanism. Toggle switches are available in many different styles and sizes, and are used in numerous applications. Many are designed to provide the simultaneous actuation of multiple sets of electrical contacts, or the control of large amounts of electric current or main voltages. A classic example of an enclosed toggle switch is the wall mounted light switch found in many homes.

Mercury switches are commonly used in household applications but are sometime found in electronic level detectors. Mercury is an electrically conductive, liquid metal. A mercury switch consists of a drop of mercury contained inside a glass bulb with two or more contacts. The contacts pass through the glass, and are connected by the mercury when the bulb is tilted to make the mercury roll on to them. The "silent" wall switch in your house is probably a mercury switch.

Pushbutton switches are similar to toggle switches but have one stationary contact and one movable contact. The movable contact is attached to the pushbutton. The pushbutton is either an insulator itself or is insulated from the contact. This switch is spring loaded and can be designed either for momentary contact (like a doorbell), or designed such that each push of the button "toggles" the switch condition (like an on/off button on an appliance). Micro switches are usually pushbutton switches that open or close a circuit with a very small movement of the tripping device, usually 1/16 of an inch or less. These are primarily used as limit switches to provide automatic control of landing gears, actuator motors, and the like.

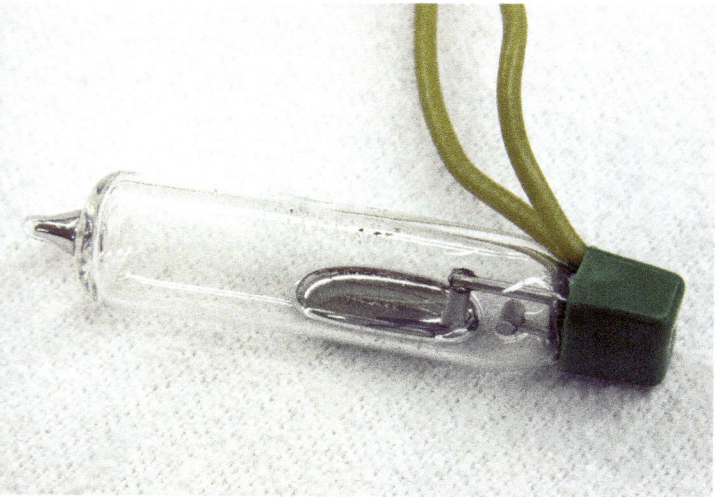

Figure 4-14. Glass tube mercury switch.

MOTORS

The reverse of a generator is a motor. Motors essentially convert electrical energy into mechanical energy. For the most part, the more voltage or current supplied to a motor, the higher the power or speed of the motor. A motor in which speed can be controlled is called a variable speed motor. Some motors are designed such that by reversing the direction of current flow, the direction of a motor's rotation is reversed as well.

CIRCUITS

The series circuit is the most basic electrical circuit. A simple series circuit can have nothing more than a voltage source, a conductor, and a resistor or some other powered device such as a motor or light. This type of circuit is classified as a series circuit as the components are connected end-to-end, so that the same current flows through each component equally. There is only one path for the current to take and everything is in series with one another. In a series circuit, current and voltage travel through each component. If there is a break in the circuit, either via a switch or a component failure, current will cease to flow in the entire circuit.

Figure 4-15. Pushbutton switch.

Figure 4-16. Electric motor.

A circuit in which two or more electrical resistances or loads are connected across the same voltage source is called a parallel circuit. The primary difference between the series circuit and the parallel circuit is that more than one path is provided for the current in the parallel circuit. Each of these parallel paths is called a branch. In a parallel circuit, current and voltage split proportionally to the resistance (load) encountered in each branch. If there is a break in the circuit (past the branch point), current will cease to flow in that branch but will still be available to the other branches.

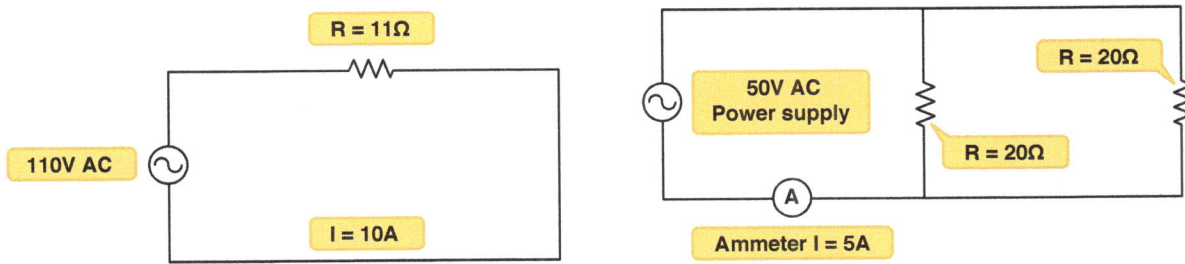

Figure 4-17. Series and parallel circuits.

SEMICONDUCTORS

Pure silicon is normally a good insulator, but that characteristic can be modified by adding a small amount of various materials, such as germanium. Arsenic and phosphorus are also sometimes used. If two different silicon based materials are placed in contact with one another, a component called a diode is created. Diodes can be designed to control whether current will flow across the junction, in what direction it can flow, and what will be emitted by the diode itself. Diodes are a good way to make certain circuits "one-way" or to control the current flow electronically instead of using a manual switch.

Unmanned Aerial Systems: The Definitive Guide

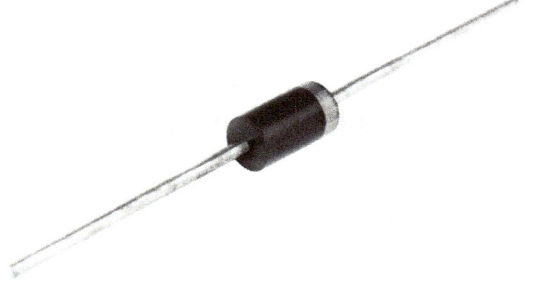
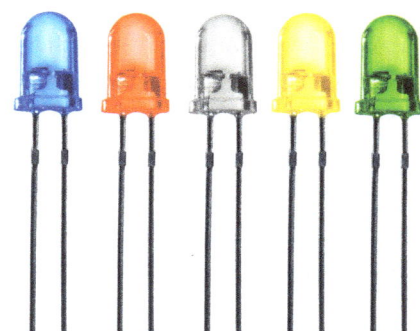

Figure 4-18. Switching and light-emitting diodes (LED).

The unique characteristics of semiconductor material have allowed for the development of many specialized types of diodes. Most electrical components put out heat as a byproduct of their operation. A light-emitting diode (LED) dissipates excess energy as light. By using different elements in the chemical composition of the diode, an LED can be designed to radiate different colors, such as red, green, yellow, blue and even infrared. The advantages of LEDs over incandescent lamps are longer life, lower voltage, faster on and off operations, and less dissipated heat.

Liquid crystal displays (LCD) are similar to diodes but require less power to operate than an LED. A specially designed liquid crystal is encapsulated between two glass plates. When voltage is not applied to the LCD, the display is clear. But when voltage is applied, it results in a change of color that can be used to build different kinds of displays. LCDs are commonly used for mobile phone, tablet, and laptop computer displays. Many large LCD displays are backlighted for increased contrast and easier viewing.

Figure 4-19. LCD used as a display on an electrical multimeter.

LOGIC CIRCUITS

Diodes and transistors (which are basically controllable on-off diodes) can be connected together into something known as a logic circuit. Logic circuits operate in a binary mode where voltage can create one of two logic conditions. This can be either 1 or 0, or could be considered as on-off or true-false. Circuits can be designed and programmed to perform binary logic operations that can provide useful information or control circuits and equipment. In most modern logic circuits, thousands, if not millions, of diode-like functions have been placed on one small chip called a microprocessor.

A microprocessor is a device that can be programmed to perform arithmetic and logical operations and other functions in a preordered sequence. The microprocessor is usually used as the central processing unit (CPU) in today's computer systems and can be connected to other components, such as memory chips as well as input-output and sensor or control circuits. Some microprocessors can be purchased preprogrammed to perform certain operations, others can be programmed in the lab, while those used in computers can be reprogrammed infinitely. Microprocessors normally operate using a DC voltage of about 5 volts and can generate significant heat as they perform millions of micro switching operations every second as part of their programming.

Figure 4-20. Integrated microprocessor chip.

INSTRUMENT SYSTEMS

INSTRUMENT COMPONENTS
Aircraft instrument systems are used to indicate the position or condition of aircraft subsystems or the aircraft itself. There are two components to any instrument or instrumentation system. The function of the first is to sense the condition while the other is to display the information. In direct sensing, both of these functions take place in a single unit. Remote-sensing instruments have a sensor unit that captures the information which is then sent to a separate display unit. The connection between the sensor and the display can be accomplished in many ways including electricity, liquid (pressure), or pneumatic (pressure or vacuum). Newer instrument systems utilize data buses to transfer electronic information digitally.

INSTRUMENT CLASSIFICATIONS
There are three basic kinds of instruments used in aircraft: flight attitude and performance, propulsion, and position indicating and navigation instruments.

- **Flight instruments** sense and display the aircraft's flight attitude. These includes basic flight instruments, such as the altimeter and airspeed indicator, as well as the attitude indicator, turn coordinator, and vertical speed indicator.

- **Propulsion instruments** display the important operating parameters of the aircraft's propulsion system. These include speed, quantity, pressure, and temperature indications. The most common engine instruments are the fuel/oil quantity and pressure gauges, engine speed tachometers, and various system temperature gauges.

- **Navigation instruments** sense and display information used by the aircraft controller or the aircraft itself to determine position as well as provide guidance along a planned course. This includes compasses, as well as position determination sensors that measure navigation information provided by external transmitters.

INSTRUMENT OPERATING PRINCIPLES
Aircraft instruments are classified according to the principles upon which they operate. Some use mechanical methods to measure pressure and temperature. Others utilize magnetism and electricity. Newer instrument systems utilize solid state sensors and computers to process and display information.

Pressure-sensing instruments can be either direct reading or remote sensing. Pressure measurement involves some sort of mechanism that can sense either absolute or changes in pressure of either a liquid or air. The type of pressure needed to be measured often makes one sensing mechanism more suited for use in a particular instance. The three fundamental pressure-sensing mechanisms used in aircraft instrument systems are the Bourdon tube, diaphragm or bellows, or solid-state sensing devices.

A Bourdon tube is illustrated in Figure 4-21. The open end of this coiled tube is fixed in place and the other end is sealed and free to move. When a fluid or gas flows into the open end of the tube, the unfixed portion of the coiled tube straightens. The higher the pressure, the more the tube straightens. When the pressure is reduced, the tube recoils. A pointer or sensor is attached to the moving end of the tube. By calibrating this motion, a face or dial of the instrument can be created.

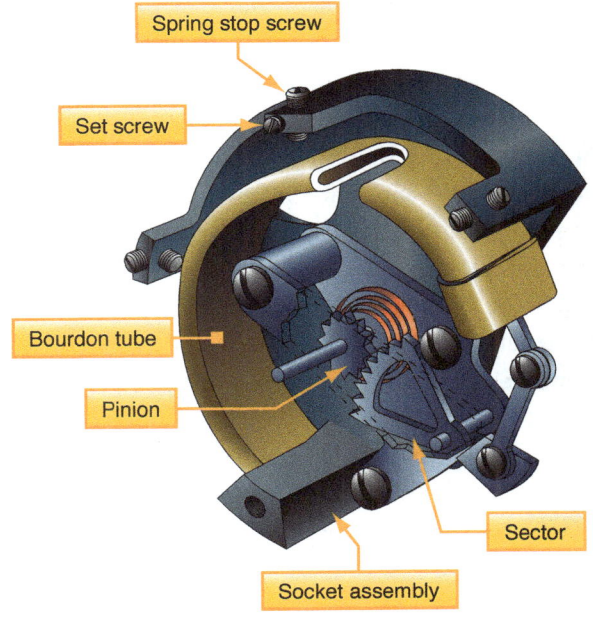

Figure 4-21. Bourdon tube instrument.

The Bourdon tube is the mechanism used in many pressure gauges found on larger aircraft. When high pressures need to be measured, the tube is designed to be stiff. Gauges used to indicate lower pressures use a more flexible tube that uncoils and coils more readily. Most Bourdon tubes are made from brass, bronze, or copper.

Pressure of a heated liquid or gas increases as temperature increases, Bourdon tubes can use this characteristic to measure temperature as well. This is accomplished by essentially calibrating the instrument differently and relabeling the face of the gauge with a temperature scale. Since the sensing and display of pressure information using a Bourdon tube mechanism usually occurs in a single instrument housing, they are most often direct reading gauges. But a Bourdon tube sensing device can also be used remotely if properly designed.

A diaphragm and bellows are two other similar sensing mechanisms employed in aircraft instruments for pressure measurement. A diaphragm is a hollow, thin-walled metal disk, usually corrugated. When pressure is introduced through an opening on one side of the disk, the entire disk expands. By placing linkages in contact with the other side of the disk, the movement of the pressurized diaphragm can be transferred to a pointer that registers against a scale on the instrument face. If sealed to the outside atmosphere, diaphragms and bellows are called aneroids.

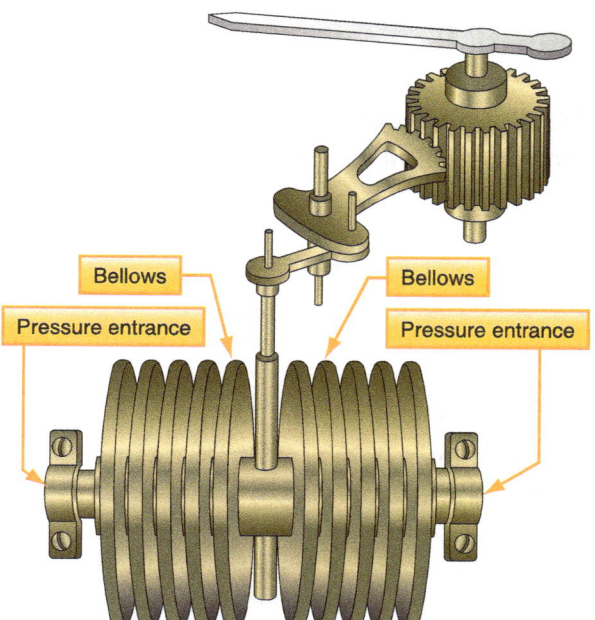

Figure 4-22. Bellows unit.

When a number of diaphragm chambers are connected together, the device is called a bellows. This accordion-like assembly of diaphragms can be very useful when measuring the difference in pressure between two gases, called differential pressure. Just as with a single diaphragm, it is the movement of the side walls of the bellows assembly that correlates with changes in pressure and to which a pointer linkage is attached.

Aneroid pressure sensing devices are often located inside a single instrument housing that contains the pointer and instrument dial. Remote sensing systems also make use of a diaphragm or bellows. The pressure sensitive aneroid can be located remotely on the engine or airframe as a transducer that converts pressure into an

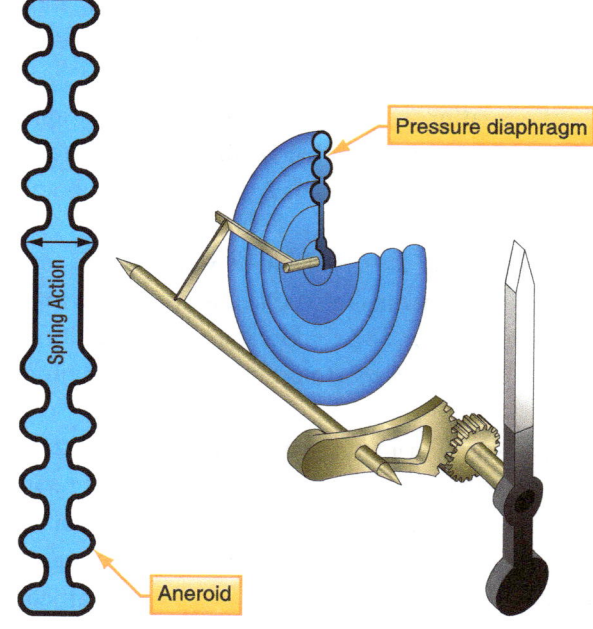

Figure 4-23. Aneroid sensing mechanism.

electrical signal. This transducer transmits the signal to a gauge or to a computer for processing and subsequent display. This computer is often known as the air data computer, or simply ADC.

Solid-state micro technology pressure sensors are increasingly being used in aircraft to determine critical pressures needed for operation. Many of these sensors provide a digital output that can be easily processed by electronic computers. Solid-state sensors used in most aviation applications typically utilize either varying electrical output, or resistance changes, when pressure changes are sensed. Piezoelectric, piezo resistor, and semiconductor chip sensors are the most commonly used in UASs.

In the typical sensor, tiny wires are embedded in the crystal or pressure-sensitive semiconductor. When pressure deflects the crystal, a small amount of electricity is created or, in the case of a semiconductor chip and some crystals, the resistance changes. Since the current and resistance change in proportion to the amount of deflection, outputs can be calibrated and used to display pressure values. Nearly all of the pressure information needed for engine, airframe, and flight instruments can be captured and/or calculated through the use of solid-state pressure sensors in combination with temperature sensors. Solid-state pressure-sensing systems are usually remote sensing systems.

TYPES OF PRESSURE

A pressure indication is really a comparison of two forces. Pressure is commonly measure in pounds per square inch, or psi. Absolute pressure is a measurement comparing the measured force to that created in a total vacuum. Many aircraft instruments, such as the altimeter, the rate-of-climb indicator, and the manifold pressure gauge make use of absolute pressure. Absolute pressure is the difference between the pressure being measured and an absolute vacuum.

In aviation, there is a commonly used pressure known as standard pressure. Standard pressure refers to an established or standard value that has been created for atmospheric pressure. This standard pressure value is 29.92 inches of mercury, 1,013.2

Figure 4-24. Tire pressure gauge (gauge pressure).

hectopascal (hPa), or 14.7 psi. All of these values are averages since the atmosphere is continuously fluctuating. They are used by engineers when designing instrument systems and are sometimes used by technicians and pilots.

Another type of pressure measurement used in aviation is gauge pressure. Gauge pressure is the difference between the pressure to be measured and the ambient atmospheric pressure. For example, if a pressure gauge were inserted into a deflated balloon, it would indicate an absolute pressure of 14.7 psi but a gauge pressure of 0 psi. Gauge pressure is easily measured and is obtained by ignoring the effect of the atmosphere exerting its pressure on everything.

In another example, take a tire located at sea level, filled with air and checked with a gauge to read 32 psi, (gauge pressure). The approximately 15 psi of atmospheric air pressing on the outside of the tire is ignored. If an absolute pressure gauge were attached to the tire, it would read about 47 psi; the 32psi pressure in the tire plus the roughly 15 psi already existing in the atmosphere at sea level. But at about 5,000 feet above sea level (the approximate elevation of Denver, Colorado), the air pressure in the atmosphere is only about 12 psi. If the tire was inflated to 32 psi (gauge) at that altitude, the absolute pressure in the tire would be only 44 psi (32 psi gauge plus 12 psi atmospheric).

Gauge pressure measurements are simple and widely useful. They eliminate the need to measure varying atmospheric pressure to indicate or monitor a particular pressure situation. When generally discussing pressure, unless otherwise indicated or specifically mentioned, gauge pressure should be assumed, unless the pressure measurement is of a type known to require absolute pressure.

In many instances in aviation, it is desirable to compare the pressures of two different elements to arrive at useful information for operating the aircraft. When two pressures are compared, the measurement is known as differential pressure and the gauge is a differential pressure gauge. An aircraft's airspeed indicator is a differential pressure gauge. It compares ram air to ambient air pressure to determine how fast the aircraft is moving. An engine pressure ratio (EPR) gauge is also a differential pressure gauge. It compares the pressure at the inlet of the engine with that at the outlet to indicate the power developed by the engine.

PRESSURE MEASURING INSTRUMENTS

One of the most important instruments used to determine the health of an engine is the engine oil pressure gauge. In reciprocating and turbine engines, oil is used to both lubricate and cool bearing surfaces where parts are rotating or sliding past each other at high speeds. A loss of pressurized oil to these areas would rapidly cause excessive friction and over temperature conditions, potentially leading to catastrophic engine failure.

In reciprocating engines, the manifold pressure gauge indicates the pressure of the air in the engine's induction manifold. This is an indication of power being developed by the engine. The higher the pressure of the fuel air mixture going into the engine, the more power it can produce. For normally aspirated engines, this means that an indication near atmospheric pressure is the maximum. Turbocharged or supercharged engines pressurize the air being mixed with the fuel, so full power indications are above atmospheric pressure. Most manifold pressure gauges are calibrated in inches of mercury, although digital displays may have the option to

Figure 4-25. Engine performance gauges.

display in a different scale. Manifold pressure is measured in absolute pressure. Therefore the pressure indicated on the gauge when the aircraft is not operating should be about 29.92 inches of mercury (or 14.7 psi), the ambient air pressure at sea level. Since air pressure changes at a rate of about one inch of mercury per 1000 ft. change in altitude, the elevation of the airport/aircraft must be taken into account when interpreting manifold pressure.

Turbine engines have their own pressure indication system used to indicate the total power being developed by the engine. This measurement is called engine pressure ratio (EPR). EPR compares the pressure of the engines exhaust to the pressure of the ram air at the inlet of the engine. After adjusting for temperature, altitude, and other factors, an EPR gauge presents an indication of the thrust being developed by the engine. Since the EPR gauge compares two pressures, it is a differential pressure gauge.

An internal combustion driven aircraft usually needs to pump fuel from the holding tank to the engine inlet and/or controls. Fuel is typically pumped out of fuel tanks located on various parts of the aircraft. A malfunctioning fuel pump, or a tank that has been emptied, is a condition that requires immediate attention. While direct-sensing fuel pressure gauges using Bourdon tubes, diaphragms, and bellows sensing arrangements exist, it is particularly undesirable to run a fuel line any great distance to an instrument display or sensor, due to the potential for fire should a leak develop. The preferred arrangement in aircraft is to place a sealed sensing mechanism in the fuel tank itself and send a send a signal to a remotely located indicator.

PRESSURE SWITCHES

Sometimes a system is designed to simply monitor whether the pressure developed by a certain operating system is too high or too low, so that an action can take place should one of these conditions occur. This can be accomplished through the use of a pressure switch.

A pressure switch is a device usually made to open or close an electric circuit when a certain pressure is reached. Pressure switches can be designed such that the electric circuit is normally open and closes when a certain pressure is sensed, or the circuit can be normally closed and then opened when the activation pressure is reached. Pressure switches contain a diaphragm to which the pressure being sensed is applied on one side. The opposite side of the diaphragm is connected to a mechanical switching mechanism for an electric circuit.

Small fluctuations or a buildup of pressure moves the diaphragm, but not enough to throw the switch. Only when pressure meets or exceeds a preset level designed into the switch does the diaphragm move and the mechanical device activates to close the switch and complete the circuit. Each switch is rated to close (or open) at a specific pressure, which cannot normally be modified.

A low oil pressure indication switch is a common example of how pressure switches are employed. It is installed in an engine so pressurized oil can be applied to the switch's diaphragm. Upon starting the engine, oil pressure increases and the pressure against the diaphragm is sufficient to hold the contacts in the switch open. As such, current does not flow through the circuit and no indication of low oil pressure is given. Should

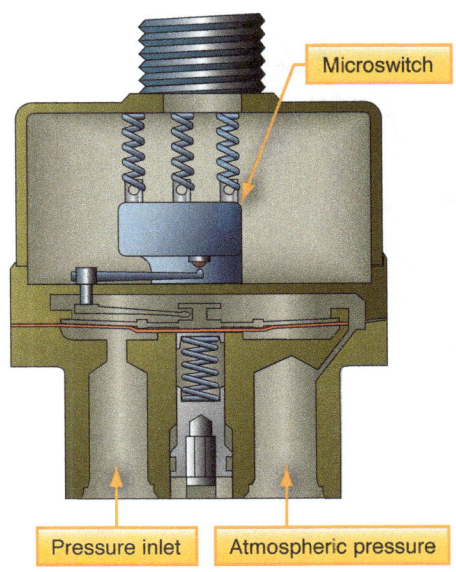

Figure 4-26. Pressure sensor and switch.

a loss of oil pressure occur, the pressure against the diaphragm becomes insufficient to hold the switched contacts open. When the contacts close, they close the circuit to the low oil pressure indicator to warn of the situation. Pressure warning systems are usually designed such that a system failure, such as a clogged or leaking line leading to the instrument, also causes the switch to close and the warning indicator to activate.

PITOT-STATIC SYSTEMS

Some of the most important flight instruments derive their indications from measuring air pressure around or impacting the aircraft. Gathering and distributing these various air pressures is the function of the pitot-static system. On simple aircraft, this may consist of a pitot head with impact and static air pressure ports and tubing connecting these air pressure pickup points to the instruments, or transducers, which require air for their indications. The altimeter, airspeed indicator, and vertical speed indicator are the three most common pitot-static instruments.

In a typical pitot-static system, the head, or pitot tube, collects ram air and static pressure for use by the flight instruments. The aft section of the pitot tube is often equipped with small holes on the top and bottom surfaces that are designed to collect air pressure that is at atmospheric pressure in a static, or still, condition. The ram air entering the pitot tube is directed to the airspeed indicator. The static pressure is connected to the airspeed indicator, altimeter and the vertical speed indicator.

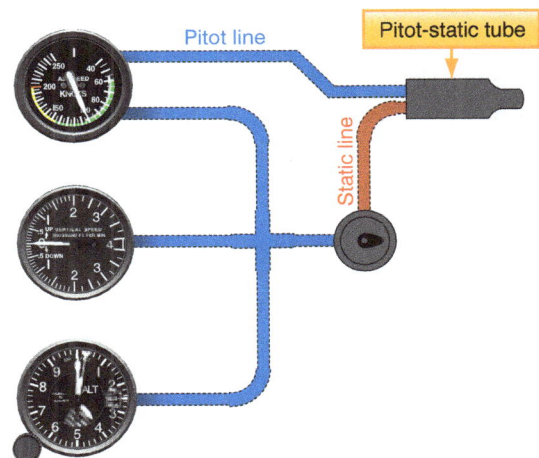

Figure 4-27. Basic pitot-static system.

The pitot-static tube is mounted on the outside of the aircraft at a point where the air is least likely to be turbulent. It is pointed in a forward direction parallel to the aircraft's line of flight. The location may vary. Some are installed in the nose of the aircraft, while others may be located on a wing. A few may even be found near the tail of the aircraft. Various designs exist but the function remains the same: to capture impact (dynamic) air pressure and static air pressure, and direct them to the instruments or autopilot as needed.

Unmanned Aerial Systems: The Definitive Guide

Figure 4-28. PITOT-SYAMC tube.

ALTIMETERS AND ALTITUDE

An altimeter is used to indicate the height of the aircraft above a predetermined level, such as sea level or the terrain beneath the aircraft. The most common way to measure this distance is rooted in discoveries made by scientists centuries ago: as altitude increases, air pressure decreases. The amount that it decreases is measurable and consistent for any given altitude change. Therefore, by measuring air pressure, altitude can be determined. Altimeters that measure the aircraft's altitude by measuring the pressure of the atmospheric air, are known as pressure altimeters.

Figure 4-29. Airspeed indicator and altimeter.

An altimeter is designed to measure the ambient air pressure at any given location and altitude. In aircraft, it is connected to the static vent. The relationship between the measured pressure and the altitude is indicated on the instrument, which is usually calibrated in feet, but could be in meters as well. Altimeters are direct-reading instruments that measure absolute pressure but indicate that pressure as altitude.

An aneroid or aneroid bellows is the core of the pressure altimeter's inner workings. Attached to this sealed diaphragm are the linkages and gears that connect it to the indicating pointer. Static air pressure enters the airtight instrument case and surrounds the aneroid. At sea level, the altimeter indicates zero. As the aircraft climbs, ambient air pressure decreases, the aneroid expands and displays the increasing altitude on the altimeter. As the aircraft descends, the air pressure around the aneroid increases and the pointer moves in the opposite direction.

The face, or dial, of an analog altimeter is read similarly to a clock. As the longest pointer moves around the dial, it registers altitude in hundreds of feet. One complete revolution of this pointer equals 1,000 feet of altitude. The second longest pointer moves more slowly indicating altitude in thousands of feet. Once around the dial for this pointer is equal to 10,000 feet. Some altimeters are equipped with a third pointer that registers altitude in 10,000 foot increments. Digital altimeters are also available, with the altitude indicated in a numeric digital fashion; very often using an LED display.

Figure 4-30. Altimeter.

Accurate measurement of altitude is important for numerous reasons. For example, avoidance of tall obstacles and rising terrain relies on precise altitude indication, as does flying at a prescribed altitude. Measuring altitude with a pressure measuring device is fraught with additional complications however. Steps must be taken to correct the altitude indication, compensating for factors that can cause an inaccurate display. One major factor that affects pressure altitude measurement is the naturally occurring pressure variations throughout the atmosphere.

Different air masses routinely move over the earth's surface, each with inherent pressure characteristics. To maintain altimeter accuracy despite this naturally occurring change in atmospheric pressure, a means for compensating for this variation has been devised. An adjustable pressure scale visible on the face of an analog altimeter, known as a barometric or Kollsman window, can be adjusted to correct for these natural variations in the ambient atmospheric pressure. By entering the current known air pressure, (also known as the altimeter setting), in the window, the altimeter can be made to indicate the actual altitude above sea level. This altitude is known as indicated altitude.

UAV aircraft have the same requirements as manned aircraft regarding accurate altitude indications. Communication with air traffic control (ATC) and terrain avoidance are prime examples. Another need for accurate altitude information is the regulatory requirement to be at, or below, certain altitudes. Geo-fencing, the establishment of vertical and horizontal limits of flight for the UAV, is a function reliant upon accurate altitude measurement. Most autonomous systems use a combination of an onboard barometer and GPS information to determine altitude accurately.

Indicated altitude is not the same as actual altitude above the ground. When adjusting the altimeter using the Kollsman window, the resultant indication is the altitude above the average, (or mean) sea level. This altitude, (abbreviated as msl), is the most common altitude used in aviation as it insures that all aircraft are measuring altitude from a common datum (sea level). To determine an aircraft's actual altitude above the ground or obstructions, the altitude of the ground (also referenced in feet above sea level) must be subtracted from the altimeter reading. For example, if an aircraft's altimeter indicated 2,300 ft. msl but the ground below was actually located 1,400 ft. above sea level, the aircraft would only be 900 ft. above ground level (agl).

Altimeters can be adjusted to read altitude above ground level. This is accomplished by adjusting the pressure compensation such that the altimeter indicates an altitude of zero feet while on the ground prior to takeoff. From that point on (assuming no changes in atmospheric conditions), the altimeter will indicate feet above the departure airport. This is useful when operating in close proximity to the ground or obstructions or when landing and departing from the same location, but care must be taken not to use or report this altitude when communicating with other aircraft or air traffic control, as they are expecting altitude measured above sea level.

SPEED AND DISTANCE MEASUREMENTS

In normal situations outside of aviation, a "mile" is normally considered to be a "statute mile" (sm). A statue mile is 5,280 feet. When we commonly refer to speed, we are really referring to statue miles per hour (smph) or simply miles per hour (mph). In metric measuring countries, the standard for measuring speed is kilometers per hour (or kph).

In aviation, the standard measurement for distance is the nautical mile. The technical definition of a nautical mile is one minute of arc measured along any meridian. By international agreement it has been set at exactly 1,852 meters, which is about 6,076 feet. Nautical miles are the international standard for both marine and aviation navigation. An aircraft (or a boat) that travels one nautical mile per hour (nmph) is said to be traveling at one knot. The history behind the term knot is complicated but a knot is approximately 1.151 mph.

Nautical miles and knots are the most common distance and speed measurements used in aviation. Statute miles are used in meteorological measurements. Meters and meters per sec (m/s) are also common distance and speed measurements that may be encountered. One knot equals approximately 0.514 meters per second and also equals approximately 1.852 kilometers per hour. A conversion table is presented below.

APPROXIMATE CONVERSIONS BETWEEN UNITS OF SPEED

	m/s	km/h	mph	knot	ft/s
1 m/s=	1.0	3.6	2.24	1.94	3.28
1 km/h=	0.28	1.0	0.62	0.54	0.91
1 mph=	0.45	1.61	1.0	0.87	1.47
1 ft/s=	0.30	1.10	0.68	0.59	1.0

AIRSPEED INDICATORS

The airspeed indicator is a primary flight instrument that is a differential pressure gauge. Ram air pressure from the aircraft's pitot tube is directed into a diaphragm in the airspeed instrument case. Static air pressure from the aircraft static source is directed into the case surrounding the diaphragm. As the speed of the aircraft varies, the ram air pressure varies, expanding or contracting the diaphragm. Linkages attached to the diaphragm causes a pointer to move over the instrument face, which is calibrated in knots (kts) or miles per hour (mph).

The relationship between the ram air pressure and static air pressure produces an indication known as indicated airspeed (IAS). As the total air pressure declines as an aircraft climbs, the ram air pressure will decrease, even if the aircraft remains at the same speed. By comparing ram air pressure to static pressure (which also decreases proportionally with altitude), the change in air pressure with altitude can be compensated for.

As with the altimeter, there are other factors that must be considered in measuring airspeed throughout all phases of flight. These can cause inaccurate readings or indications that are not always useful. In analog airspeed indicators, the factors are often compensated for with ingenious mechanisms inside the case and on the instrument dial face. Digital flight instruments can have calculations performed in the air data computer (ADC) so that accurate information is always displayed.

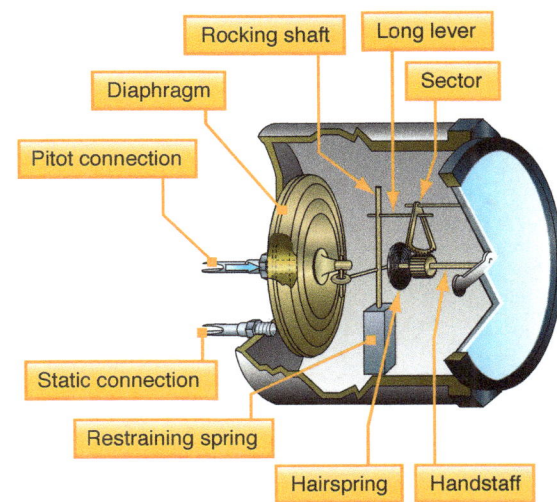

Figure 4-31. Airspeed Indicator.

Calibrated airspeed (CAS) takes into account errors due to position error of the pitot static pickups. It is impossible to locate the pitot tube such that ram air is always heading directly into the tube. Calibrated airspeed corrects for this as well as the nonlinear nature of the pitot static pressure differential when displayed on a linear scale. Analog airspeed indicators must be manually re-corrected and may come with a correction chart that allows cross-referencing of indicated airspeed to calibrated airspeed for various flight conditions. These differences are typically very small and often are ignored. Digital instruments have these corrections performed in the ADC.

Indicated airspeed does not take into account temperature and air pressure differences from standard that naturally exist in the atmosphere. These factors can greatly affect airspeed indications and calculations. What is known as true airspeed or TAS, would be the same as calibrated airspeed if the flight occurred when standard day conditions exist. But when atmospheric temperature or pressure varies from standard, the relationship between the ram air pressure and static pressure is altered and must be compensated for if one wants to know the actual airspeed of the aircraft through the air (TAS). Calibrated to true airspeed conversions must be calculated using graphs and tables, or can be performed automatically by a computer.

The advantage of digital flight instrument systems is that all of these calculations can be accomplished by an air data computer. Ram air from the pitot tube and static air from the static vent is directed to the sensing portion of the ADC as are external temperature information as well. This information can be manipulated and calculations performed so a true airspeed value can be digitally calculated.

None of the previous mentioned airspeeds actually describe the speed of the aircraft over the ground. This speed, known as ground speed (GS) must take into account the wind speed and direction. Without an external input of these parameters, the pitot-static system cannot calculate ground speed. In most cases, ground speed is derived from the aircrafts navigation system.

MECHANICAL MOTION INDICATORS
There are many instruments on an aircraft that indicate the mechanical motion of a component of the aircraft. The tachometer, or tach, is one such instrument. A tachometer indicates the speed of any rotating device such as the crankshaft of an engine, a propeller or helicopter rotor speed, or even the speed of an electric motor. It can be a direct or remote-indicating instrument, the dial of which is calibrated to indicate revolutions per minutes (rpm). On reciprocating engines, a tach is typically used to monitor engine power and to ensure the engine is operated within certified limits. Gas turbine engines also utilize

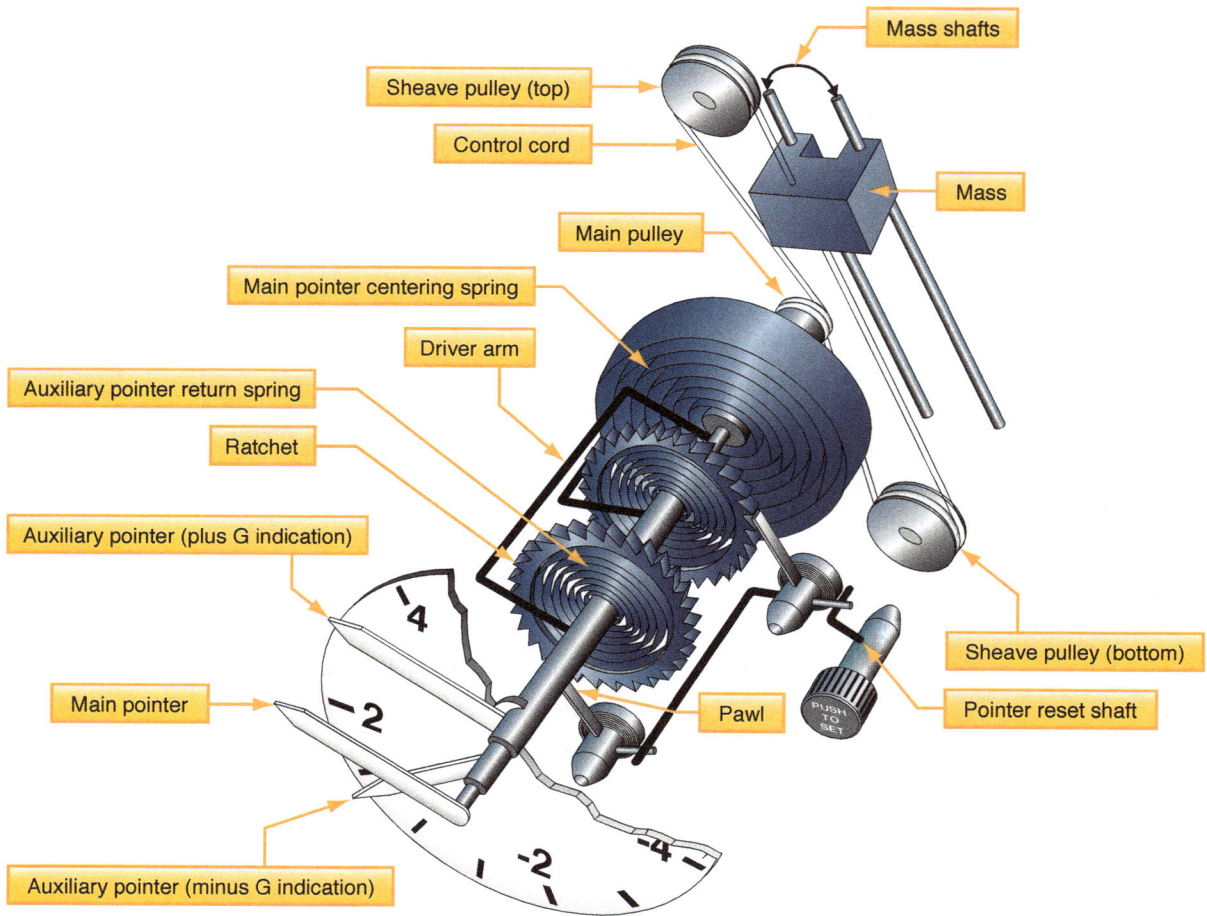

Figure 4-32. Mechanical accelerometer.

tachometers. They monitor the speed of the compressor sections of the engine. Turbine engine tachometers are calibrated in percentage of rpm with 100 percent corresponding to optimum turbine speed. This allows similar operating procedures despite the varied actual engine rpm of different engines.

ACCELEROMETERS

An accelerometer is an instrument that measures acceleration. It is used to monitor the forces acting upon an airframe. Accelerometers are also used in some navigation systems. Single and multi-axis accelerometers are available. Accelerometers can also be designed into computer microchip assemblies. Some navigation systems make use of multi-axis accelerometers to continuously calculate the location of the aircraft in a three dimensional plane.

In some systems, solid-state sensors are employed, such as piezoelectric crystalline devices. In these instruments, when an accelerating force is applied, the amount of resistance, current flow, or capacitance changes in direct relationship to the size of the force and can be measured. Laser accelerometers can also be used to determine precise changes in speed and direction. In general a laser unit will measure minute changes in the phase and frequency of a transmitted laser signal to determine the aircraft change in movement.

STALL WARNING AND ANGLE OF ATTACK INDICATORS

An aircraft's angle of attack (AOA) is the angle formed between the wing chord centerline and the relative wind. At or above a certain angle, turbulent airflow over the wing surfaces is insufficient to create enough lift to keep the aircraft flying, and a stall occurs. An instrument that monitors the AOA allows such a condition to be avoided.

A simple form of an AOA warning device is a switch that enables a tone or light to be produced as the critical angle of attack is approached. These systems are composed of an electric switch that opens and closes a circuit to a warning horn or light. The switch is located near the point of air stagnation on the wing leading edge. A small lightly sprung tab activates the switch. At normal angles of attack, the tab is held down by air that diverges at the point of stagnation and flows under the wing. This holds the switch open. As the angle of attack increases, the point of stagnation moves down. The divergent air that flows up and over the wing then pushes the tab upward to close the switch and complete the circuit to the horn or light.

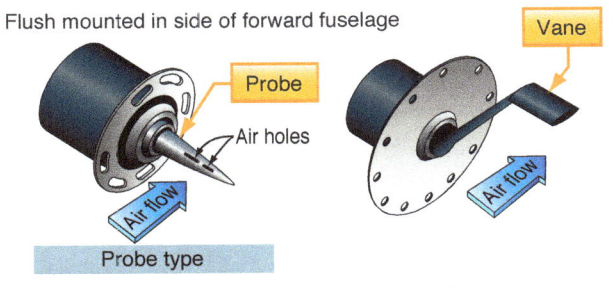

This system provides an approximation of the true angle of attack, and is useful in avoiding stall situations. A true AOA sensing and indicating system can be installed that measures the true angle of the wind flowing over the aircraft. This system is usually comprised of a small moving metal vane installed on the side of the fuselage that can accurately determine the direction of airflow over the wing. It is usually designed to furnish angle of attack information to both a display device as well as input into other systems like the air data computer. In small autonomous UAVs that lack AOA indicators, test flights to determine stall speed are accomplished and then the autopilot is set to maintain the aircraft speed above this critical point.

Figure 4-33. Angle of attack indicating system.

TEMPERATURE MEASURING INSTRUMENTS

The temperature of a number of different items must be known for aircraft to be operated safely and properly. These include engine oil, carburetor mixture, inlet air, outside air, engine cylinder head, and exhaust gas temperature. External sensor packages may also be installed that measure non-airframe related temperatures. Many different types of thermometers have been used to collect and present temperature information. These include both non-electric and electric temperature indicators.

NON-ELECTRIC TEMPERATURE INDICATORS

The physical characteristics of most materials change when exposed to changes in temperature. The changes are consistent, such as the expansion or contraction of solids, liquids, and gases. The coefficient of expansion of

Figure 4-34. Engine temperature indicator.

different materials varies and is unique to each material. Most everyone is familiar with the liquid mercury thermometer. As the temperature of the mercury increases, it expands up a narrow passage that has a graduated scale upon it to read the temperature associated with that expansion.

The temperature sensing element of a bimetallic thermometer is made of two dissimilar metals strips bonded together. Each metal expands and contracts at a different rate when temperature changes. One end of the bimetallic strip is fixed, the other end is coiled. A pointer is attached to the coiled end which is set in the instrument housing. When the bimetallic strip is heated, the two metals expand. Since their expansion rates differ and they are attached to one another, the effect is that the coiled end tries to uncoil as one metal expands faster than the other. This moves the pointer across the dial face of the instrument. When the temperature drops, the metals contract at different rates, which tends to tighten the coil and move the

Unmanned Aerial Systems: The Definitive Guide

pointer in the opposite direction. This type of measuring instrument can either be direct reading, or the thermometer can be equipped with a remote sensor that transmits the movement to an indicating device.

ELECTRICAL TEMPERATURE MEASURING INDICATORS

The use of electricity to measure temperature is very common in aviation. Many different measuring and indication systems can be found on aircraft. Certain temperature ranges are more suitably measured by one or another type of system. The principle parts of any electrical thermometer are the temperature-sensitive element (or bulb), the indicating instrument, and the connecting wires. As the temperature changes, the resistance of the temperature sensitive element changes, thereby changing the current flow in the circuit which can be directly measured. Electrical resistance thermometers are widely used in aviation to measure carburetor air, oil, and free air temperatures.

DIRECTION INDICATING INSTRUMENTS

Many instruments exist to aid in the navigation of an aircraft. An indication of direction is critical to navigation. The magnetic compass is a direction finding instrument. It is a simple instrument that makes use of the earth's magnetic field. Using this principle, the magnetic compass was created, and has been used, for centuries.

Figure 4-35. Aircraft compass or heading indicator.

Within an aircraft compass, permanent magnets are attached to a float mounted on a pivot free to rotate. The magnets rotate to align with the earth's magnetic field. A numerical compass card, usually graduated in 5° increments, is constructed around the perimeter of the float. It serves as the instrument dial. The entire assembly is enclosed in a sealed case filled with a liquid similar to kerosene. This somewhat dampens vibration and oscillation of the moving float assembly and decreases friction. On the front of the case, a glass face allows the numbers on the rotating float to be referenced against a vertical lubber line. The magnetic heading of the aircraft is determined by observing the number aligned with the lubber line.

Magnetic indicating systems always reference the magnetic north pole, which is not located at the same place as the true north pole. The angular difference between these two poles is known as variation. Across the U.S. the difference between magnetic and true north (variation) is usually less than 15 degrees, but in some areas of the world it can be over 50 degrees. If precision is needed while flying, the variation between these two poles must be taken into account.

SOLID STATE MAGNETOMETERS

Solid state magnetometers are used onboard many modern aircraft. They have no moving parts and are extremely accurate. Tiny layered structures react to magnetism on a molecular level. These devices sense the direction to the earth's magnetic poles, and are free from the oscillation that plagues a standard magnetic compass. They feature integrated processing algorithms and easy integration with digital systems. The information they derive can be routed to an electrically driven heading indicator, or sent to the aircraft navigational system directly. Magnetometers are very sensitive to magnetic interference and should be located away from such fields, or shielded to prevent large errors in direction determination.

ATTITUDE INDICATORS

The attitude indicator, or artificial horizon, is one of the most essential flight instruments for an aircraft. It provides pitch and roll information. A mechanical attitude indicator operates using a gyroscope rotating in a horizontal plane. It mimics the actual horizon through the principle of rigidity in space. As the aircraft pitches and rolls in relation to the actual horizon, the gyro gimbals allow the aircraft and instrument housing to pitch and roll around the gyro rotor that remains parallel to the ground.

In an aircraft, a horizontal representation of the airplane in miniature is fixed to the instrument housing. A painted hemisphere simulating the horizon, sky, and the ground is attached to the gyro. The sky and ground meet at what is called the horizon bar. The relationship between the horizon bar and the miniature airplane are the same as those of the aircraft and the actual horizon. Graduated scales reference the degrees of pitch and roll.

Attitude indicator gyroscopes can be either vacuum-driven or electrically driven. In a vacuum-driven system, air is sucked through a filter and then through the attitude indicator in a manner that spins the gyro rotor inside. An erecting mechanism is built into the instrument to assist in keeping the gyro rotor rotating in the intended plane. After air engages the scalloped

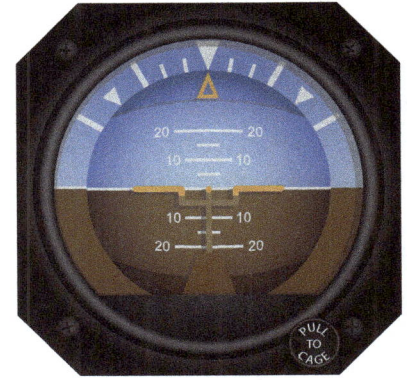

Figure 4-36. Aircraft attitude indicator.

drive on the rotor, it flows from the instrument to the vacuum pump through ports and is exhausted overboard. Electrically driven attitude indicators are very similar to vacuum driven indicators. The main difference is in the drive mechanism. Inside an electrically driven gyro, a small electric motor is connected to the gyro rotor. Other than the gyro driving system, both vacuum-driven and electric gyros operate similarly.

It is possible to simulate an attitude sensing and indicator system using accelerometers. Assuming that the system is preset when the aircraft is "level" accelerometers can be used to determine if the nose dips, rises or if the aircraft banks. Accelerometer based attitude indicating systems are not true attitude systems as they essentially mathematically calculate what the aircrafts attitude should be, without actually measuring it. The heads up display or HUD, of modern UAS ground station displays are of this type.

COMMUNICATION AND NAVIGATION SYSTEMS

ANALOG AND DIGITAL SIGNALS

Electronic devices can convert instrument data, audio sounds, as well as visual images, into electrical signals. These signals can then be transmitted to receivers that convert the signal back into its original format. Electronic circuits are designed to perform this function in two very different ways. Analog circuity processes the input by continuously varying some parameter such as voltage, current, amplitude, frequency, or phase in proportion to the input level. For example, an analog microphone alters a continuous current flowing through it when sound is applied. The alteration in the signal type, or strength, transmits the input characteristics to a receiver that can reconvert it back to its original format.

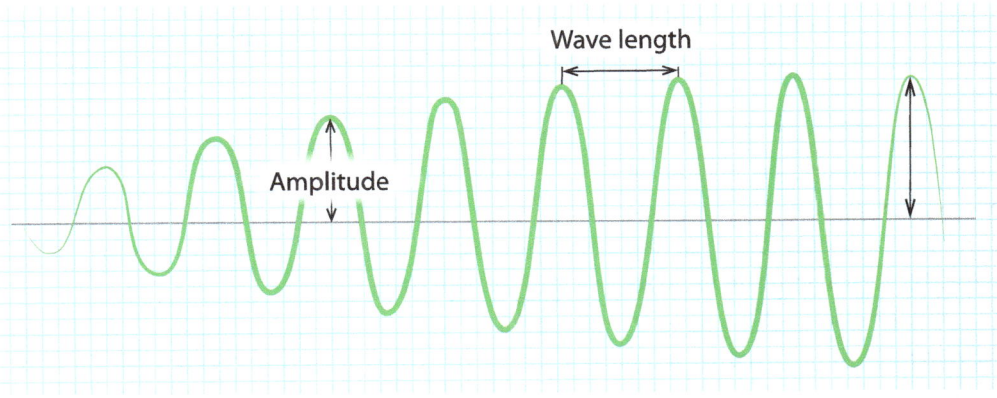

Figure 4-37. Radio signal with amplitude changes.

A digital electronic system operates quite differently, however. For example, a digital transducer takes short, discrete samples of the input and transmits these as pulses to the receiver. This signal is interpreted as either a series of ones or zeros, and those numbers are then used by the receiver to "rebuild" the original. The faster the sampling rate, the more information can be transmitted, and the more accurate the recreation of the original event.

A significant advantage of digital transmission over analog is the control of noise. Noise is any alteration of the signal not present in the original but introduced by the transmission system itself. For example, an analog microphone uses a noise sensitive transducer to modify a voltage that varies in proportion to the volume and tone of the input sound. But other factors such as electrostatic activity and circuitry imperfections can, and will, continuously modify the microphone voltage as well. It may be only a small addition to the signal, but it wasn't in the original. When the signal gets reproduced by a speaker, unoriginal sound will be introduced into the system. This unintended modifier is called noise or interference.

During the processing of digitized data however, there is little or no signal degradation due to noise. The information captured by a digital system is converted into a string of binary code. These ones and zeros are electronically created as a sequence of voltage or no voltage and carried through many processing stages. Since the voltage needed to represent a "one" is considerably higher than any noise that might be created by the system, unintended noise is represented by a fairly low voltage (a zero) and is canceled out of the system.

RADIO COMMUNICATION

Much of aviation communication and navigation is accomplished through the use of radio. A radio wave is an electromagnetic transmission invisible to the human eye that can be encoded with information, and has the ability to penetrate many solid or semi-solid structures. The atmosphere is naturally filled with many type of electromagnetic waves such as gamma and x-rays, ultraviolet, infrared, and visible light rays, as well all manner of radio waves. Each occurs at a specific frequency and has a corresponding wavelength. The relationship between frequency and wavelength is inversely proportional. A high frequency wave has a short wave length and a low frequency wave has a long wave length. Figure 4-38 illustrates the radio spectrum that includes the range of common aviation radio frequencies and their applications. The Federal Communications Commission (FCC) controls the assignment of frequency usage for radio communications.

Radio waves are essentially alternating currents of a fixed frequency. Radios feed electrons into a length of conductor that is resonant at that frequency. Electrical resonance for every circuit occurs at a specific frequency based on the length of the conductor used as an antenna. A properly tuned resonance circuit can actually generate higher voltages and currents than what are fed into them. This characteristic is the basis for radio communications.

The wavelength of a radio transmission is the actual distance from one wave peak to another as viewed on an oscilloscope. If the receiving antenna is designed correctly, it can capture (resonate) the transmission and direct the signal into the radio receiver for amplification. For the best reception, the antenna should be one wavelength long. That is impractical in many ways, however, as some wavelengths used in aviation can be several feet long. This might also require antennas to have multiple conductors: one tuned to each and every frequency that might be used.

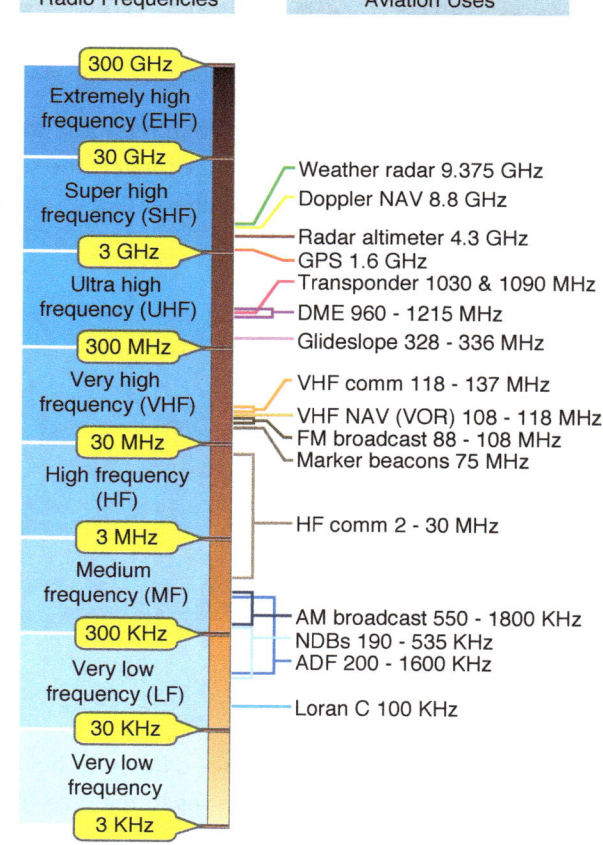

Figure 4-38. Radio frequency spectrum used in aviation.

This problem is solved by using antennas tuned to the middle of the desired frequency range, proportional in length to one wavelength. In other words, the antenna might not be designed to be one full wavelength long, but instead might be ½, ¼, or some other common multiple. Although an antenna of this type is not quite as efficient as a full wavelength antenna, it can still be made to work on an aircraft.

RADIO WAVE CREATION AND TRANSMISSION

If an alternating current is applied to a radio antenna, it will travel the length of the antenna, collapse, then travel the length of the antenna in the opposite direction. The number of times it does this every second is known as the radio wave frequency or radio frequency. These radio waves are continuously produced so long as the AC signal is applied to the antenna. If the current is modified in some manner, information (such as audio or video) can be encoded into the signal.

Figure 4-39. Various aviation radio antennas.

Radio waves propagate out into space at the frequency of the supplied signal. Radio waves are directional and travel at the speed of light: 186,000 miles per second. The distance they travel, however, depends on the frequency and the amplification of the signal sent to the antenna. Radio waves of different frequencies have unique characteristics as they propagate through the atmosphere. Very low frequency (VLF), low frequency (LF), and medium frequency (MF) waves have relatively long wavelengths and utilize correspondingly long antennas. Radio waves produced at these frequencies are known as ground waves or surface waves. This is because they follow the curvature of the earth as they travel from the broadcast antenna to the receiving antenna. Ground waves are particularly useful for long distance transmissions.

Higher frequency radio waves travel in a straight line and do not curve to follow the earth's surface. This limits transmissions to receiving antennas within line-of-sight of the broadcast antenna. Some high frequency (HF) radio waves bounce off of the ionosphere layer of the atmosphere. This refraction extends the range of HF signals beyond line-of-sight. As a result, transoceanic aircraft often use HF radios for voice communication. These kinds of radio waves are known as sky waves.

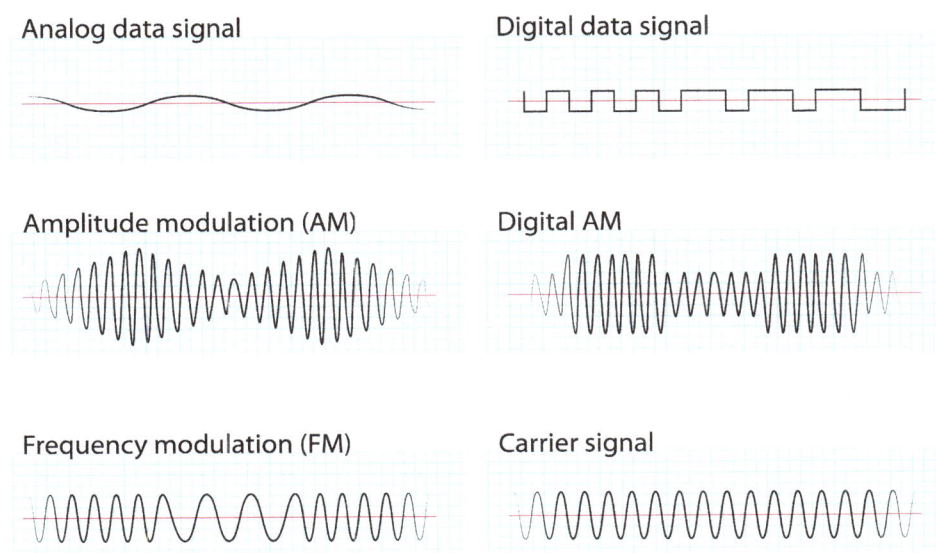

Figure 4-40. Radio wave amplitude, frequency, and modulation.

Unmanned Aerial Systems: The Definitive Guide

At the very high, ultra-high and super high frequency (VHF/UHF/SHF) end of the spectrum, waves are only capable of line-of-sight transmission and do not refract off of the ionosphere. Many aviation communication and navigation systems, as well as internet communications and control devices, operate within this frequency range.

The production and broadcast of radio waves in itself does not convey any significant information, however. The basic radio wave discussed previously is known as a carrier wave. To transmit and receive useful information, this wave must be altered or modulated by an information signal. The information signal contains the unique voice or data information to be conveyed. The modulated carrier wave carries the information from the transmitting radio to the receiving radio via their respective antennas.

In general, only a limited amount of information can be transmitted via each individual wave. Low frequency radio waves cannot carry as much information (modulation) as can be carried by radio waves transmitted at higher frequencies. That is why medium frequency AM radio does not tend to sound as good as very high frequency FM radio stations. The FM station can carry more information within its signal, increasing the fidelity of the transmission.

Two common methods of modulating carrier waves are amplitude modulation (AM) and frequency modulation (FM). A radio wave can be altered to carry useful information by modulating the amplitude (or the strength/height) of the wave. For example, when transmitting voice via AM, the analog signal from a microphone would be amplified and then superimposed over the carrier wave signal. As the microphone provides changing input, the transmitted signal would be amplified proportionally.

When this modulated carrier wave strikes the receiving antenna, a voltage is generated in reverse of what was applied to the transmitter antenna. The signal is weak and must be amplified before it can be demodulated. Demodulation is the process of removing the original information from the carrier wave. Electronic circuits designed into the receiver essentially remove the carrier wave, leaving something similar to the original input signal. This signal can then be amplified to drive speakers or other output devices.

Amplitude modulation provides limited fidelity. Atmospheric noises, or static, alter the amplitude of a carrier wave making it difficult to separate the intended amplitude modulation and that which is caused by static. High data transfer rates, such as those needed by computers or high fidelity music, are poor candidates for amplitude modulation radio. AM is simpler to create and decipher however, which is why it has gained widespread usage. AM is primarily used for voice transmission today, as there is really not that much encoded information needed to recreate a speaking voice. AM is still used in aircraft communication radio systems. Amplitude modulated VHF communication radios are the primary communication radios used in aviation. They operate in the frequency range from 118.000 MHz to 136.975 MHz. VHF radios are used for communications between aircraft and air traffic control (ATC), as well as air-to-air communication between aircraft.

Frequency modulation (FM) is superior to AM for carrying and deciphering information on radio waves. A carrier wave modulated by FM maintains a constant amplitude. However, the information signal alters the frequency of the carrier wave in proportion to the strength of the signal. Thus, the signal is represented as slight variations to the normally consistent timing of the oscillations of the carrier wave. Since the transmitter oscillator output fluctuates during modulation to represent the information signal, the bandwidth needed for FM is greater than that needed for AM radio. This restricts the use of FM in that each signal uses more of the assigned spectrum (bandwidth) than a similar AM transmission.

Noise and static can be removed much easier from FM signals, however. FM has a steady current flow and requires less power to produce since modulating a constant frequency takes less power than modulating the amplitude of a signal. Demodulation of an FM signal is similar to that of an AM receiver.

RADIO ANTENNAS

Antennas are simply conductors with lengths proportional to the wavelength of the frequency to be transmitted or received. All antennas are made of conductors but the exact shape and material from which an antenna is made can alter its transmitting and/or receiving characteristics. When a signal is applied to an antenna, it has a certain frequency. There is a corresponding wavelength for that frequency. An antenna half the length of a received signals wavelength is most resonant meaning that it is able to maximize voltage and current creation. This creates the strongest signal to be radiated by the transmitting antenna. It also facilitates capture of the wave and maximum induced voltage if it is also used as the receiving antenna.

Many radios, especially voice communication radios, use the same antenna for transmitting and receiving. Multichannel radios could use a different length antenna for each frequency, however this is impractical. Acceptable performance can exist from a single antenna half the wavelength of a median frequency. Many radios use a tuning circuit to adjust the effective length of the antenna to match the wavelength of the desired frequency. The physical antenna length is a compromise when using a multichannel communication or navigation device that must be electronically tuned for the best performance.

Figure 4-41. Simple whip antenna.

A formula can be used to find the ideal length of a half wavelength antenna required for a particular frequency. VHF radio frequencies used by aircraft communication radios are 118.00 - 136.975 MHz. The corresponding half wavelengths of these frequencies are 40 to 50 inches. Pure half wavelength VHF antennas are relatively long. Antennas one-quarter of the wavelength or smaller are often used instead. This is possible on metal aircraft because when mounted on, and connected to, a metal fuselage, a ground plane is formed and the fuselage acts as the missing one-quarter length of the half wavelength antenna. Non-metallic aircraft cannot use the airframe as part of the antenna and thereby incur significant signal loss when using shorter antennas.

The strength of the radio signal varies depending on the type of antenna and the angular proximity to it. All antennas, even those that are omnidirectional, radiate a stronger signal in some directions compared others. This is known as antenna field directivity. Receiving antennas with the same polarization as the transmitting antenna generate the strongest signal. A vertically polarized antenna is mounted up and down. It radiates waves out in all directions. To receive the strongest signal from these waves, the receiving antenna should also be positioned vertically. Many vertical and horizontal antennas on aircraft are mounted at a slight angle off plane. This allows the antenna to receive a weak signal, rather than no signal at all, when the polarization of the receiving antenna is not identical to the transmitting antenna.

COMMONLY USED UNMANNED AIRCRAFT ANTENNAS

Unmanned aircraft utilize various antenna types for transmission and reception of radio telemetry, video, and manual flight control, among other applications. The payload carried by the aircraft may also have radio transmission and reception capability utilizing specific antenna and frequencies. These antennas have unique properties for each type of radio frequency or equipment type. Some antennas are particularly sensitive to physical orientation. Antenna must be positioned properly, or a significant degradation of performance may occur. Increasing the power of the transmitter is not usually the best solution for poor antenna design and placement. The increased power may interfere with, or entirely block, other necessary radio signals. It is best to optimize antenna performance first, and then seek to increase the power of the signal later if needed.

There are 4 types of antenna in common use in UAVs: the skew-planar wheel, cloverleaf, dipole, and patch antennas.

Unmanned Aerial Systems: The Definitive Guide

SKEW-PLANAR WHEEL ANTENNA

The skew-planar wheel type antenna is a form of circular cloverleaf with four lobes offset 90 degrees from one another. This antenna is best suited for video reception, particularly first person view or FPV; however, it may be used as a transmitting antenna as well. This antenna is omnidirectional meaning that it performs equally well in any directional orientation

CLOVERLEAF ANTENNA

The cloverleaf is a term for a circular, omnidirectional antenna that has three lobes resembling the leaves of the common clover plant. This antenna is primarily used for video transmission and reception and is an improvement over one piece, linear-dipole type antennas. The circular orientation of the cloverleaf antenna provides for more reliable video reception, especially in the case of long range FPV applications. The primary disadvantage of any circular antenna is that their construction is neither compact, nor particularly aerodynamic.

DIPOLE ANTENNA

The dipole antenna (sometimes called the rubber ducky) is the standard factory antenna received with most telemetry and video systems. The dipole is a linear antenna requiring that both the transmitter and receiver be aligned either vertically or horizontally for best signal reception. Aircraft in flight move continuously however, thereby disrupting this alignment and causing degraded performance when using this type of antenna.

PATCH ANTENNA

The patch antenna is a highly directional antenna developed for long range use. Good performance is available from this type but it must be oriented with the flat "face" of the antenna towards the aircraft. This is acceptable for flights at a distance but can become a problem as the aircraft comes closer, possibly circling behind the operator and ground station. Mechanical antenna trackers can be used to solve this problem with the ground receiver antenna automatically rotating to the optimum position for best reception.

ANTENNA WIRING

Transmitters and receivers must be connected to their antennas via conductive wire. These transmission lines are coaxial cable, also known as coax. Coax consists of a center wire conductor surrounded by a semi rigid insulator. Surrounding the wire and insulator material is a conductive, braided cover that runs the length of the cable. Finally, a waterproof

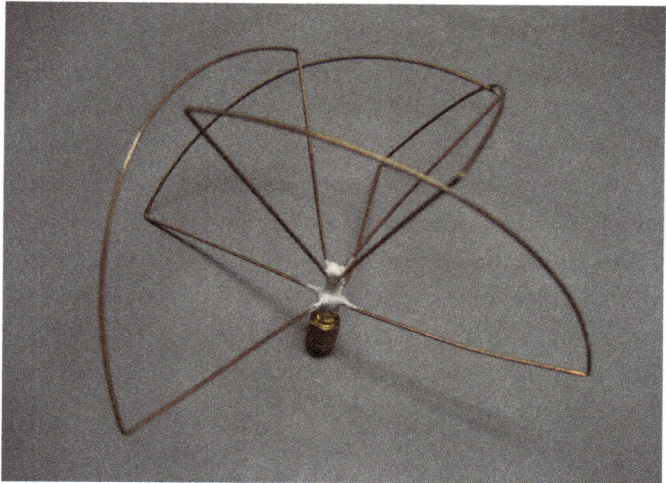

Figure 4-42. The skew-planar wheel antenna.

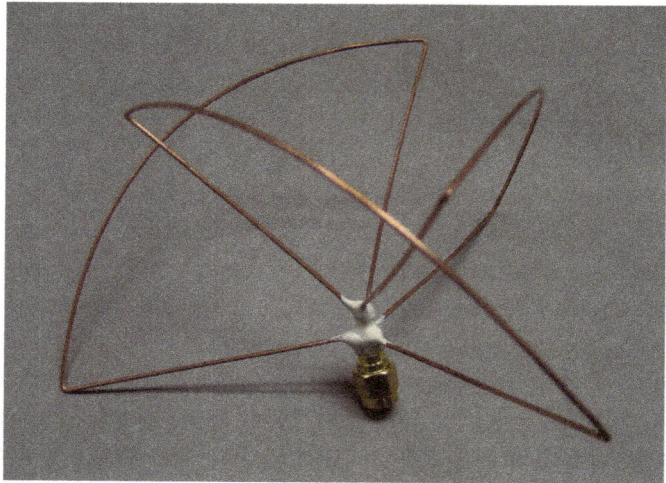

Figure 4-43. The cloverleaf antenna.

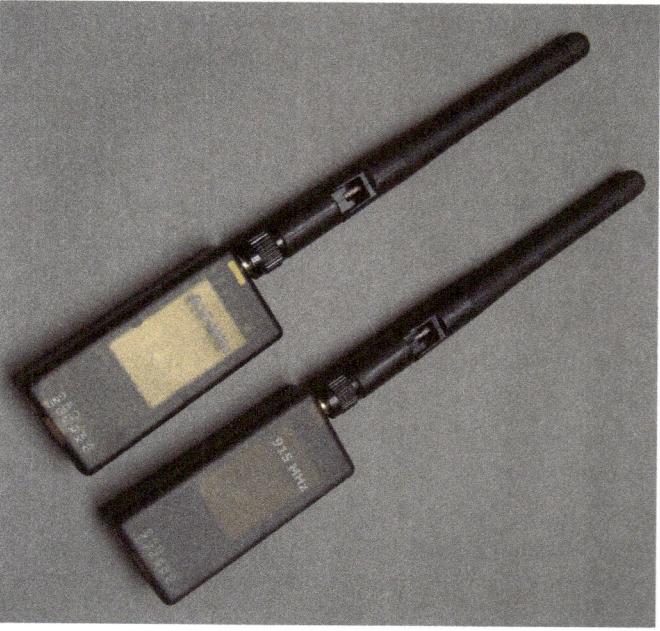

Figure 4-44. The common dipole linear antenna.

covering is set around the braided shield to protect the entire assembly from the elements. The braided cover in the coax shields the inner conductor from any external fields that could induce noise into the circuit. It also prevents the fields generated by the internal conductor from radiating a signal prior to reaching the antenna.

For optimum performance, the resistance (more properly called impedance) of the transmission line should be equal to the impedance of the antenna. In aviation applications, this is often approximately 50 ohms. Special connectors are used for coaxial cable to insure proper and tight connects and to minimize signal leakage or loss.

Figure 4-45. Two patch antennas, video and telemetry, with tracking stand.

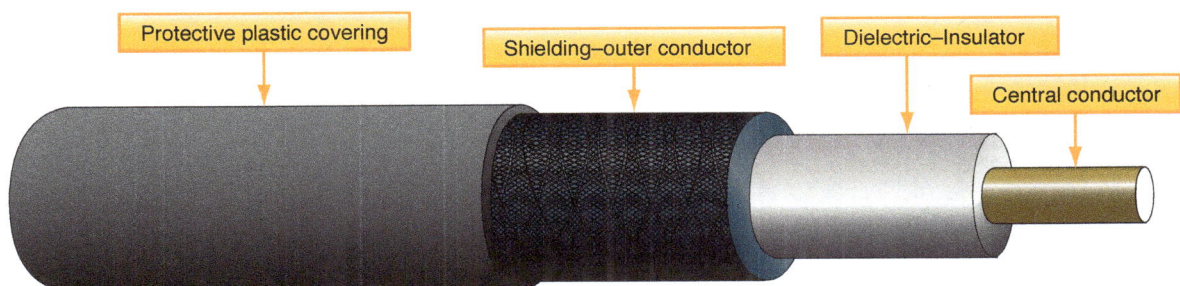

Figure 4-46. Coaxial cable assembly.

TRANSCEIVERS

A transceiver is a communication radio that transmits and receives. The same frequency is used for both. When transmitting, the receiver does not function. The push to talk (PTT) switch blocks the receiving circuitry and allows the transmitter to be active. In a transceiver, some of the circuitry is shared by the transmitting and receiving functions of the device, as is the antenna. This saves space as well as the number of components used. Aviation transceivers are half duplex type systems that permit communication in both directions using a single frequency, but only one user can speak at a time. This differs from full duplex systems (such as mobile phones) that permit multiple user to both speak and listen simultaneously.

INTERNET WI-FI

A wireless network uses radio waves to connect mobile devices to the internet. It is a digital system using just two frequencies. The devices usually have to be "paired" to the system using an ID and password. There are also security protocols that can be installed to insure that only approved users can access the network.

The device that physically connects to the internet is called a router. The router is a radio transmitter and receiver that connects with each approved mobile device and allows that device to communicate with the internet. The radios used for Wi-Fi are like other radio systems but operate digitally, sending signals

Figure 4-47. Icom Hand held aviation band transmitter and receiver.

Unmanned Aerial Systems: The Definitive Guide

comprised of a string of ones and zeros. Wi-Fi routers operate on one or both of two frequencies: 2.4 GHz or 5.0 GHz. This frequency is considerably higher than most radios permitting the signal to carry more data.

There are a number of standards that permit the router to connect to mobile devices. The IEEE 802.11 standard is the most common. This standard was developed in 1997 and has since been updated many times. Most IEEE compatible devices state which standard they use by appending a letter to the standard. For example, the first version of internet routers used the 802.11a specification. The

Figure 4-48. Wireless Wi-Fi routers.

modification produced the 802.11b standard, and so on. Each standard generally improved the data carrying capacity of the system and was more or less backward compatible. This means that an 802.11g router could talk to an 802.11b compliant device, but that the reverse wouldn't necessarily be true.

Wi-Fi devices operate with fairly short antennas, measured in inches. The devices are also limited in power to reduce interference with nearby units. This affects the range of a Wi-Fi router. A general rule of thumb is that a router can pair up with a device about a hundred feet away if both are located indoors. The range can extend up to 300 feet if used outdoors and no obstructions or interference are present.

Radio signal interference from other devices can negatively impact Wi-Fi operation and range. The 2.4 GHz frequency is used by a number of other consumer devices that can interfere with long distance Wi-Fi communications. Wi-Fi range extenders can be added to a system to overcome some of these difficulties.

MOBILE PHONE TECHNOLOGY

Mobile phones operate as small radio transmitters and receivers similar to those used in aviation. The frequency of operation is not adjustable however. Each phone (and commercial network) has its own set of frequencies and mode of operation. A phone designed to operate on one system (or in one country) may not work on another operators system.

There are generally two mobile phone operating standards and protocols: CDMA and GSM. CDMA stands for code division multiple access and is primarily used in the United States. GSM (global system for mobile communications) is a worldwide standard used in the U.S. and most of the rest of the world.

Figure 4-49. Mobile phone tower.

Each system operates differently and are incompatible with one another. A CDMA based phone cannot connect to a GSM network for instance. A phone designed for use in the US will use different frequencies than those used in Europe as well. Any mobile phone installation therefore needs to be carefully paired with the provider to be used and the effective coverage area must be determined.

Mobile phones are fairly low powered with a range of only a couple of miles. This restricts usage on the ground to areas with direct line of site access to a mobile phone tower. Airborne transmitters are another matter however. As an aircraft climbs to a higher altitude, it can be "seen" by more cell phone towers. This can cause an interference problem which is why the use of mobile phones in manned aircraft is restricted. This does make it easier for an aircraft to receive mobile phone transmissions however. As the aircraft climbs, more phones come "into view" and can be potentially communicated with.

Mobile phone technology and frequencies are not well suited to high data transfers, but can be used in some situations. As mobile phone technology has improved, the data transfer rates have increased as well, but they are nowhere near, nor are they likely to compare to that which Wi-Fi can provide.

BLUETOOTH

Bluetooth is a communications protocol primarily designed for low-power consumption, with a short range of usually 100 meters or less. Bluetooth is a wireless technology operating in the UHF radio band from 2.4 to 2.485 GHz. Bluetooth devices must be "paired" to communicate with one another. Bluetooth is not considered a highly secure communications systems but is designed to permit two device located in close proximity to one another to maintain a communications lockup. The data transfer rates for Bluetooth are similar to those of Wi-Fi.

AVIATION NAVIGATION SYSTEMS

VOR

One of the first modern electronic navigation systems used in manned aviation was the VHF Omnidirectional Range, or VOR. VORs operate on an assigned frequency between 108.00 and 117.90 MHz. The VOR receiver on board the aircraft measures the phase difference between two signals transmitted by the VOR to determine the direction of the aircraft in relation to the transmitter. VORs operate "line of sight", which can severely reduce their range. An observer on the ground might only be able to pick up a VOR station 3-5 miles away. But at an altitude of 1,000 ft. or more above the ground, the VOR should have a range in excess of 50 miles.

To use a VOR, the receiver must be turned to the proper frequency. The receiver then indicates in which direction the aircraft is in relation to the ground station. This direction is stated as a "radial". For example, if you were east of a VOR, you would be on the 90° radial. Someone due south of the VOR would be on the 180° radial, west is the 270° radial and north is the 360° radial.

TACTICAL AIR NAVIGATION (TACAN)

The VOR system has deficiencies that make it unusable for certain military operations. The Department of Defense has developed an alternative navigation system known as tactical air navigation (TACAN). TACAN operates in the UHF band and provides distance as well as bearing information.

Figure 4-50. VORTAC ground station.

Unmanned Aerial Systems: The Definitive Guide

The FAA and the Department of Defense have worked together to develop a multi-mode VOR and TACAN based navigation system designed such that civilian aircraft use TACAN to provide distance information while still using VOR for azimuth information. This combined navigation aid is known as VORTAC and has become the world wide navigation standard. It is however being rapidly supplanted by the more accurate global navigation satellite system.

GLOBAL NAVIGATION SATELLITE SYSTEM

The Global Navigation Satellite System (GNSS) is the accepted term for navigation systems that provide global navigation via space-based satellite systems. GNSS transmitters are typically located on low earth orbit satellites permitting users with fairly small, inexpensive receivers to determine their location in three dimensions (latitude, longitude, and altitude). As long as the transmitters are within the sight line of a number of satellites, the receivers can determine their location within a few meters or even feet.

The Global Positioning System (GPS), is the United States GNSS system and is operated by the Air Force. The Russian GLONASS navigation system is also operational. The European Union is developing a system called Galileo, as are China (Compass), Japan, and India. Due to its accuracy and worldwide availability, GNSS has been designated by ICAO as the future aviation navigation system.

GLOBAL POSITIONING SYSTEM

GPS is a space-based positioning, velocity, and time system composed of a minimum of twenty-four satellites in six orbital planes. The satellites operate in circular orbits arranged so that at any one time users worldwide are able to view a minimum of five satellites (see Figure 4-51). GPS operations are based on the concept of ranging and triangulation from a group of satellites in space that act as precise reference points.

A GPS receiver determines location by comparing the travel time of radio signals from multiple satellites. Each satellite transmits a specific code, called a course/acquisition (CA) code that contains information on the satellite's position, an extremely precise GPS system time, clock error, and the accuracy of the transmitted data. The GPS receiver on the aircraft matches each satellite's CA code with an identical code contained in the receiver's database. By comparing the reception time from each satellite, the receiver can calculate its position relative to each satellite. The aircraft GPS receiver then mathematically determines its position by triangulation.

Figure 4-51. GPS satellite constellation.

Using stored information, the GPS receiver can also compute navigational information such as distance and bearing to a point, ground speed, estimated time enroute, estimated time of arrival, and winds aloft. It does this by using the aircraft's known latitude/longitude, measuring relative movement, and referencing these to a database built into the receiver.

GNSS AUGMENTATION

GNSS signals provide accuracy for enroute and two-dimensional navigation, but they do not provide acceptable vertical or lateral guidance for automated landings or other precision operations. The standard GNSS signal needs to be augmented to provide this capability. This can be accomplished by using a Satellite Based Augmentation System (SBAS), Ground Based Augmentation System (GBAS), or Aircraft Based Augmentation System (ABAS).

SATELLITE BASED AUGMENTATION SYSTEMS

SBASs comprise a network of ground reference stations that collect satellite signals and send them to one or more ground processing centers. The centers compare the overall signal inaccuracy from each station and compute a differential correction. This correction is sent to one or more geostationary satellites that transmit the augmentation message information back to users on the ground.

There are multiple SBASs being developed and/or in operation. Most operate regionally, over each countries airspace. One currently operational SBAS is the U.S. operated wide area augmentation system (WAAS).

WAAS uses a network of precisely located ground reference stations that monitor transmitted GPS satellite signals. These stations are located throughout the United States (primarily co-located with ARTCCs) as well as in Canada and Mexico. The ground reference stations collect and process error information and send it to the WAAS master station. The master station more or less "averages" the error and develops a correction message that is then sent to users via geostationary satellites located above the United States. Using WAAS, GPS signal accuracy is improved from about plus or minus 20 meters to approximately 2 meters both horizontally and vertically.

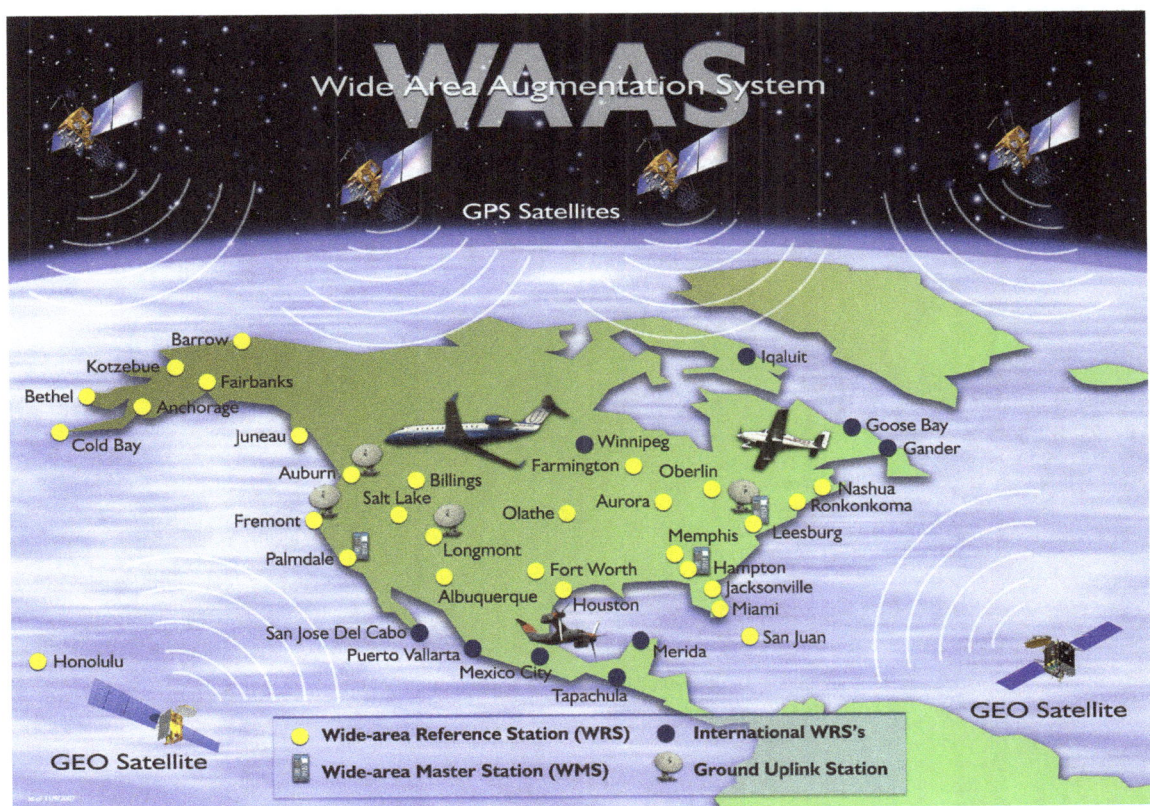

Figure 4-52. Wide Area Augmentation System, a satellite based GPS augmentation system.

GROUND-BASED AUGMENTATION SYSTEM

Aircraft using GBAS receive augmentation information directly from a local ground-based transmitter. GBAS is similar to SBAS with the exception that the system error is measured, corrected, and transmitted in only one local geographic area (about 30 nm radius), thereby making the augmentation differential calculation very accurate. The augmentation message is sent only to aircraft in the local area, usually by some form of domestic radio communication.

Local, privately owned GBAS systems can be purchased to augment GPS accuracy within a very limited area. Surveyors, builders and others sometimes employ these systems to improve the accuracy of GPS systems used in the field.

ADS-B

The successful proliferation of global navigation satellite systems (GNSS), such as GPS, has led to the development of an air traffic control tool known as automatic dependent surveillance broadcast (ADS-B). ADS-B combines the positioning information available from a GPS receiver with on-board flight status information such as location, altitude, and velocity. It then broadcasts this information to other ADS-B equipped aircraft and ground stations using a discrete UHF frequency. Airborne receivers use the information to plot the location and movement of the transmitting aircraft on the electronic flight deck display of manned aircraft. Inexpensive ground stations can be constructed to display information on local ADS-B equipped aircraft, including potentially unmanned aircraft, as well as to share information with other ground stations that are part of the network.

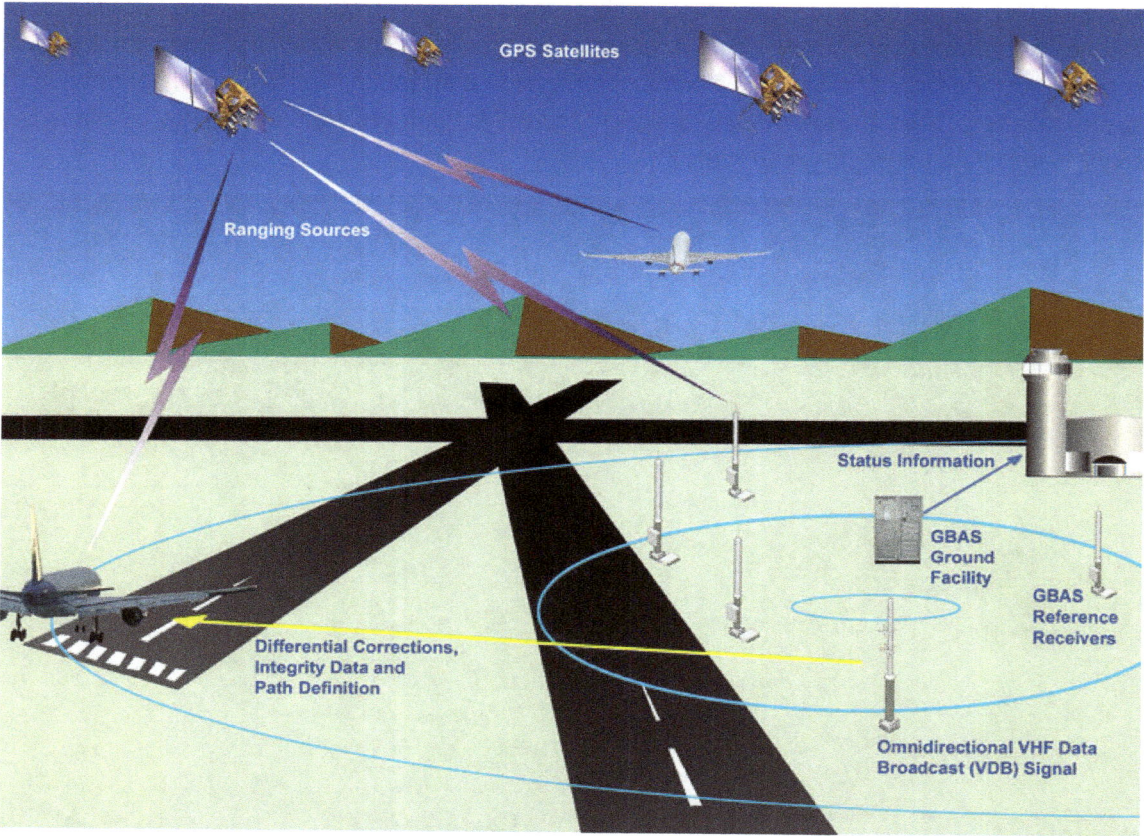

Figure 4-53. GBAS-ground based GPS augmentation system.

CHAPTER 5

POWERPLANT THEORY AND OPERATION

Powerplant systems used in unmanned aircraft can be one of many different types commonly used in aerospace applications. There are designs utilizing turbines, reciprocating piston engines, as well as electric motor drive. The UAS designer's choice of propulsion is often defined by the proposed mission of the aircraft. Each propulsion system has advantages and disadvantage in areas such as thrust to weight ratio, endurance, vibration, noise, and reliability. Each powerplant is unique in its need for cooling, lubrication, fuel metering, inspection, and maintenance. An entire text could be written on the attributes of each type of propulsion system, but in this book we will explore the more common types of propulsion in widespread use with the acknowledgment that there are variations of each type with their own unique operational characteristics.

INTERNAL COMBUSTION-RECIPROCATING ENGINES

An internal combustion engine is a device for releasing stored energy from a fuel into heat, then converting this heat energy into mechanical energy. The relationships between pressure, volume, and temperature of gases are important to understanding the basic principles of engine operation. In general, fuel (usually in liquid form) is vaporized and mixed with air, forced or drawn into a cylinder, compressed by a piston, and then ignited by an electric spark. The resultant heat energy from the burning fuel air mixture is converted into mechanical energy and then into work. Figure 5-1 illustrates the various engine components necessary to accomplish this conversion.

RECIPROCATING ENGINE OPERATION

The operating cycle of an internal combustion reciprocating engine includes a series of events that include induction, compression, ignition and burning, followed by expansion and exhausting of the fuel air (F/A) mixture. The liquid fuel is mixed with the required amount of air prior to reaching the intake valve of the engine cylinder itself. A valve in the top, or head, of the cylinder opens to permit the fuel air mixture to enter the cylinder. This valve then closes, and the piston moves up to compress the trapped fuel air mixture. The compressed mixture is then ignited, and the resultant gases, due to combustion, expand very rapidly. This expansion forces the piston to move away from the cylinder head.

Unmanned Aerial Systems: The Definitive Guide

This downward motion of the piston acting on the crankshaft through the connecting rod is converted into a circular, or rotary, motion by the crankshaft. When the piston reaches the bottom of the cylinder a different valve opens allowing the burned gases to escape, with the momentum of the crankshaft forcing the piston back up in the cylinder where it is ready for the next event in the cycle. At that point the cycle repeats itself.

The valve in the cylinder head that opens to let in a fresh charge of the fuel air mixture is called the intake valve. The valve permits the escape of the burnt gases is called the exhaust valve. These valves are opened and closed at the proper times by the valve-operating mechanism of the engine. This mechanism can be either mechanically or electronically controlled.

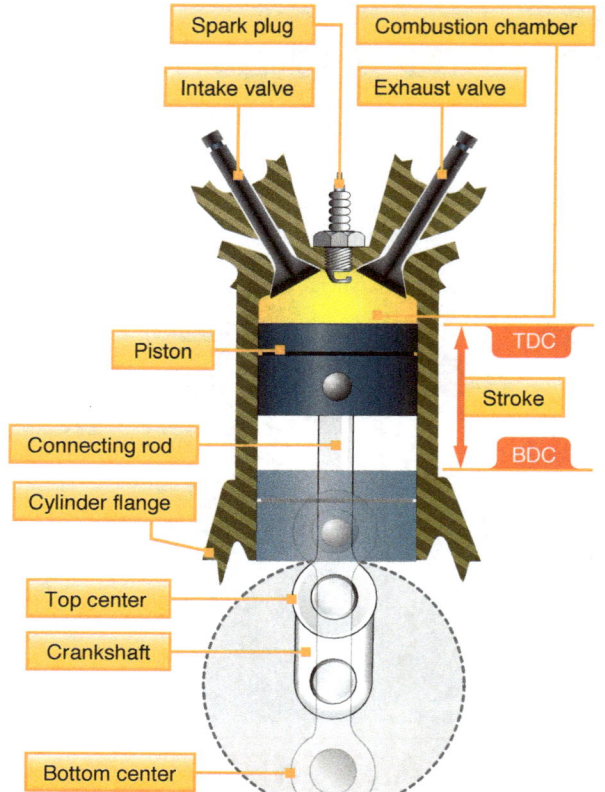

Figure 5-1. Reciprocating engine cylinder components.

INTERNAL COMBUSTION ENGINE TERMINOLOGY

- Cycle - the number of strokes a piston is required to accomplish to complete a single thermodynamic cycle in the engine. This is typically two or four.
- Cylinder bore - the inside diameter of a specific cylinder.
- Top dead center (TDC) - the position where the piston is the farthest from the crankshaft, or at the "top" of the cylinder with the connecting rod parallel with the cylinder wall.
- Bottom dead center (BDC) - the position where the piston is closest to the crankshaft, or at the "bottom" of the cylinder with the connecting rod parallel with the cylinder wall.
- Stroke - the distance the piston moves from one end of the cylinder to the other, specifically from top dead center to bottom dead center, or vice versa.
- Valve timing - the precise location, or measurement, that defines when a valve either opens or closes. Valve timing is usually defined as the point when the crankshaft is a certain number of rotational degrees prior to, or after, either TDC or BDC.
- Ignition timing - the precise measurement that defines when the fuel air mixture is ignited and is usually expressed in degrees of crankshaft rotation before TDC.
- Spark plug - an electrical device that produces a short, high voltage spark intended to ignite the fuel air mixture in the cylinder.
- Piston displacement - the volume the piston moves through during a single, complete revolution of the crankshaft from BDC to TDC.
- Engine displacement - the total displacement of all the cylinders.

There are several different operating cycles used in internal combustion engines. The most common found in aeronautical use include four-stroke, two-stroke, and diesel type cycles.

FOUR-STROKE OR FOUR-CYCLE ENGINE

The vast majority of manned aircraft reciprocating engines operate using the four-stroke cycle, sometimes called the Otto cycle after its originator, the German physicist Nikolaus August Otto. The four cycle engine has many advantages for use in aircraft. In this type of engine, four strokes of the piston are required to complete the required series of events or operating cycle of each cylinder. Two complete revolutions of the crankshaft (720 degrees) are required for the four strokes; thus, each cylinder in an engine of this type fires once in every two revolutions of the crankshaft.

The timing of the ignition, and the valve events, vary considerably from engine to engine. Many factors influence the timing of a specific engine, and it is very important that the engine manufacturer's timing recommendations be followed. The timing of the valve and ignition events is always specified in degrees of crankshaft travel. A certain amount of crankshaft travel is required to open a valve fully; therefore, any timing specified in engine documentation or discussion represents the start of the opening of the valve rather than the full-open position.

INTAKE STROKE

During the intake stroke, the piston is pulled downward in the cylinder by the rotation of the crankshaft. This reduces the pressure in the cylinder and causes fresh air under atmospheric pressure to flow through the carburetor, which meters and adds the proper amount of fuel. The fuel air mixture is then directed through pipes to the intake valves, then into the cylinders. The quantity (or weight) of the fuel air mixture introduced to the engine is controlled by the carburetor or other metering device. In general, the amount of fuel air allowed to enter the cylinder depends upon the amount of throttle opening. The more the throttle is open, the more fuel air can enter the engine; therefore more power, or speed, will likely be produced. Restricting the amount of fuel air entering the engine proportionally reduces the power produced.

The intake valve controls entry of the fuel air mixture into the cylinder and is opened prior to the piston reaching TDC on the exhaust stroke. This early opening permits a greater quantity of the fuel air mixture to enter the cylinder. The timing of the valve opening before the piston reaches TDC is limited by several factors, such as the possibility that hot gases remaining in the cylinder from the previous cycle may flash back into the intake pipe and the induction system. In most high-power aircraft engines, both the intake and the exhaust valves may be open simultaneously for a short time when the piston approaches TDC at the start of the intake stroke.

VALVE TIMING

When the intake valve opens before TDC on the exhaust stroke it is called valve lead. Likewise the closing of the exhaust valve after the piston has passed TDC and has started the intake stroke is called valve lag. The time that both valves are open is called valve overlap. Valve overlap is designed to aid in cooling the cylinder internally by circulating the cool incoming fuel air mixture. Valve overlap also increases the amount of the fuel air mixture induced into the cylinder, and aids in scavenging the byproducts of combustion from the cylinder.

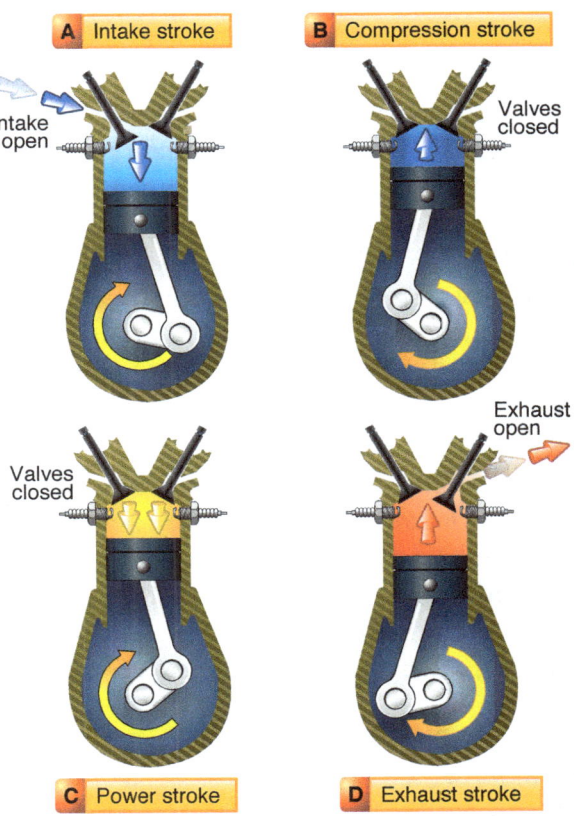

Figure 5-2. The four strokes of an internal combustion engine.

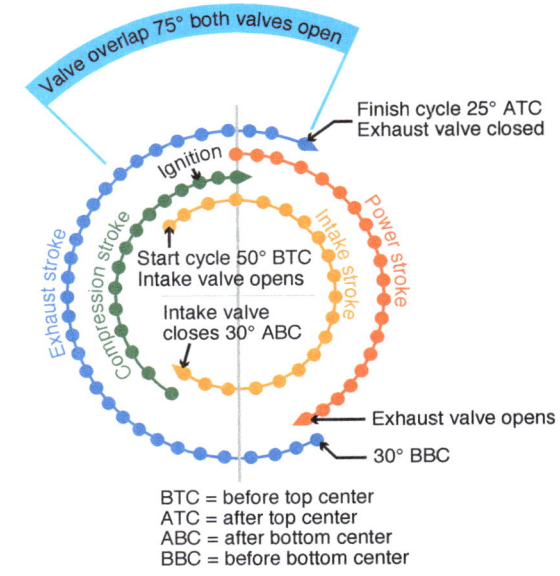

Figure 5-3. Valve timing expressed in degrees of crankshaft rotation.

The intake valve is timed to close when the crankshaft is about 50° to 75° beyond BDC on the compression stroke. This allows the momentum of the incoming gases to fill the cylinder with the fuel air mixture more completely. Because of the comparatively large volume of the cylinder available when the piston is near BDC, the slight upward travel of the piston during this time does not have a great effect on the incoming flow of gases. If allowed to stay open too long, however, late timing can force the fuel air mixture back through the intake valve and defeat the purpose of the late closing of the intake valve.

COMPRESSION STROKE AND IGNITION

After the intake valve is closed, the continued upward travel of the piston compresses the fuel air mixture. As the piston approached TDC, the fuel air mixture is ignited by an electric spark from the spark plug. To ensure complete combustion of the fuel air mixture, the ignition timing will normally be set to approximately 20° to 35° before TDC. Many factors affect the specific ignition timing of a particular engine and the manufacturer has expended considerable time in research and testing to determine the best settings.

Most engines incorporate devices for adjusting the ignition timing, and it is important that the system be timed according to the engine manufacturer's recommendations. Some systems are designed to vary the timing according to the speed of, and the power produced, by the engine. The ignition timing can be either mechanically or electronically controlled. In most small UAS aircraft equipped with reciprocating engines, electronic ignition control varies the timing which provides both easy starting of the engine as well as peak horsepower production.

POWER STROKE

As the piston moves through the TDC position at the end of the compression stroke and starts down on the power stroke, it is pushed downward by the rapid expansion of the burning gases within the cylinder head. This force can be greater than 15 tons (30,000 psi) at maximum power output of the engine. The temperature of the burning gases in the cylinder may be between 3,000° and 4,000 °F. As the piston is forced downward during the power stroke by the pressure of the burning gases, the movement of the connecting rod is converted to rotary motion by the crankshaft. This motion is then usually transmitted by a shaft to the propeller.

EXHAUST VALVE

As the burning gases expand, the temperature quickly drops to within safe limits and the gases are released to flow out through the exhaust port. The timing of the exhaust valve opening is determined by, among other considerations, the desirability of using as much of the expansive force as possible and of scavenging the cylinder of the burnt fuel air mixture as completely and rapidly as possible. The exhaust valve may be opened considerably before the piston reaches BDC on the power stroke (on some engines at 50° and 75° before BDC) while there is still some pressure in the cylinder. This timing is such that the internal pressure remaining in the cylinder can be used to force the gases out of the exhaust port as soon as possible. This process helps remove excess heat from the cylinder and avoids overheating the cylinder and the piston. Thorough scavenging of the cylinder is very important, as any exhaust products remaining in the cylinder may dilute the incoming fuel air charge at the start of the next cycle, reducing the overall power output of the engine.

EXHAUST STROKE

As the piston travels through BDC at the completion of the power stroke and starts upward on the exhaust stroke, it begins to push the burned exhaust gases out the exhaust port. As the last of the burnt fuel air mixture leaves the cylinder, the speed of the gases leaving the cylinder creates a low pressure in the cylinder which speeds the flow of the fresh fuel air charge into the cylinder as the intake valve opens. The intake valve is timed to open at anywhere from 8° to 55° before TDC on the exhaust stroke to take advantage of this low pressure. The four cycles of the engine then repeat themselves. If the engine has more than one cylinder (and most do), the cycles are staggered so that the power stroke occurs at different times, spreading the load (and the resultant vibration) equally among cylinders. The fact that only one cylinder at a time is usually producing power induces significant vibration possibilities into the engine however.

TWO-STROKE ENGINES

The two-stroke engine has re-emerged in popularity primarily finding use in ultra-light, light sport (LSA), and many experimental aircraft, as well as unmanned applications. As the name implies, two-stroke engines require only one upstroke and one down stroke of the piston to complete the required series of events in the cylinder. Thus, the engine completes the operating cycle in one revolution of the crankshaft (360 degrees).

The intake and exhaust functions are accomplished during the same stroke. Two cycle engines eliminate the need for intake and exhaust valves by using piston ports to control the inlet and exhaust of air. Instead of a valve opening and closing, the inlet (and exhaust) ports are situated on the side of the cylinder, and the physical movement of the piston passing the port opens and closes the opening.

Figure 5-4. Twin cylinder, opposed, two stroke engine.

Most small two-stroke engines cannot be lubricated by oil contained in the crankcase, since this area of the engine ends up being used to control the fuel air mixture entering the cylinder. In many smaller engines, lubricating oil must be premixed with the fuel. As the fuel air mixture (containing oil) passes through the crankcase, it lubricates many of the moving parts of the engine such as the crankshaft and piston. Special two-stroke oils are available specifically designed to mix with gasoline and burn without leaving unburnt oil or ash in the cylinder.

The two stroke system of operation is simple and eliminates many moving parts. They do tend to run hotter and faster than comparable four cycle engines however. Two cycle engines can be either air or water cooled and generally require a gear or belt reduction system between the engine and propeller to optimize engine and propeller rpm efficiencies respectively. The engine normally operates at a higher rpm for efficient operation, but the propeller is more efficient at lower operating speeds and needs some form speed reduction system installed.

Two-stroke engines provide a higher power-to-weight ratio, usually in a narrow range of rotational speeds called the "power band". Compared to four-stroke engines, they have a greatly reduced number of moving parts, are more compact and significantly lighter.

DIESEL CYCLE ENGINES

A diesel cycle depends on high compression pressures to provide the ignition of the fuel air charge in the cylinder. No spark, or ignition system, is utilized in a compression ignition engine such as a diesel. Just as in gasoline powered engines, air (without any fuel) is drawn in the cylinder and compressed by the piston. But at its maximum pressure the fuel is sprayed (injected) into the cylinder. At this point, the high pressure and temperature in the cylinder causes the fuel to self-ignite, thus increasing the internal pressure of the cylinder. This drives the piston down, eventually turning the crankshaft.

DIESEL ENGINE FUEL

Diesel engines typically operate at significantly higher pressures than similar gasoline fueled engines. If gasoline were used in a diesel engine, it would ignite too early in the cycle and would be unable to provide significant power. Diesel fuel is similar to kerosene and can tolerate higher pressures without self-igniting. The aviation equivalent of diesel fuel is called Jet-A.

There are many types of diesel cycle engines in use including two-stroke and four-stroke diesels. Various water and air cooled piston engines have been developed for aircraft use that can operate on Jet-A fuel using the diesel cycle. In addition, it is possible to use specially conditioned diesel fuel in modified spark ignition engines for unmanned propulsion. The 5 horsepower, Lycoming EL-005 powerplant is an example of this type of engine.

ENGINE POWER AND EFFICIENCY CALCULATIONS

All aircraft engines are rated according to their ability to do work and produce power. An understanding of the terms, work, and power, and how they are calculated, are necessary to properly match an engine to the required UAS application.

WORK

Work is defined as force multiplied by distance. Work is accomplished (and measured) as the magnitude of a force acting on a body multiplied by the distance through which the force acts.

$$\text{Work (W)} = \text{Force (F)} \times \text{Distance (D)}$$

Work can be expressed in different ways and measurements. One of the most commonly used standards is called foot-pounds (ft-lbs). As an example, if a one-pound mass were raised vertically one foot, it would be said that one ft-lb of work had been performed. The greater the mass of the object and/or the greater the distance moved, the greater the work (in ft-lbs) performed.

HORSEPOWER

A common unit of mechanical power is expressed as horsepower (hp). Late in the 18th century, James Watt, the inventor of the steam engine, calculated that an English workhorse could work for a reasonable length of time at the rate of 550 ft-lbs per second, or 33,000 ft-lbs per minute. From his observations came the unit of horsepower, which has become the standard unit of mechanical power in the English system of measurement.

Work is the product of force and distance, and power is work per unit of time. Consequently, if a 33,000 lb. weight is lifted a vertical distance of 1 foot in 1 minute, the power expended is 33,000 ft-lbs per minute or exactly 1 horsepower. To calculate the horsepower rating of an engine, you must divide the power developed in ft-lbs per minute by 33,000, or the power in ft-lbs per second by 550.

Work is performed not only when a force is applied for lifting; force may be applied in any direction. If a 100-lb weight is dragged along the ground, a force is still being applied, even though the direction of the resulting motion is approximately horizontal. The amount of this force would depend upon the roughness (friction) of the ground. If the weight were attached to a spring scale graduated in pounds, then dragged by pulling on the scale handle, the amount of force required could be measured. Assume, for example, that the force required to move a 100 pound object horizontally is 90 pounds, and the object is moved 660 feet in 2 minutes. The amount of work performed in the 2 minutes would total 59,400 ft-lbs, or 29,700 ft-lbs per minute. Since 1 hp equals 33,000 ft-lb per minute, the horsepower expended in this example would be 29,700 ft-lbs divided by 33,000 ft-lbs, or 0.9 hp.

In electrical terms 746 watts (voltage x amperage) equals approximately 1 horsepower. This calculation is useful when evaluating electrically propelled unmanned aircraft as compared to conventional piston engine aircraft horsepower ratings.

PISTON DISPLACEMENT

If other factors remain equal, the greater the piston displacement in an internal combustion engine, the greater the horsepower the engine is capable of developing. When a piston moves from BDC to TDC, it displaces a specific volume. The volume displaced by the piston is known as piston displacement and is expressed in cubic inches (CI) for most American-made engines and cubic centimeters (cc) for others. The piston displacement of one cylinder may be obtained by multiplying the area of the cross-section of the cylinder by the total distance the piston moves in the cylinder in one stroke. For multi-cylinder engines, this product is multiplied by the number of cylinders to get the total piston displacement of the engine. Since the volume (V) of a geometric cylinder equals the area (A) of the base multiplied by the height (h), it is expressed mathematically as: $V = A \times h$. The area of the base is the area of the cross-section of the cylinder.

AREA OF A CIRCLE

To find the area of a circle, it is necessary to use the number pi (π). This number represents the ratio of the circumference to the diameter of any circle. Pi cannot be stated exactly as it is a never-ending decimal number. Expressed to four decimal places, 3.1416 can be considered equivalent to π and is accurate enough for most computations. The area of a circle, as in a rectangle or triangle, is expressed in square units. One-half the diameter of a circle is known as the radius. The area of any circle can be found by multiplying π times the square of the radius (r). The formula is: $A = \pi r^2$.

COMPRESSION RATIO

All internal combustion engines must compress and burn the fuel air mixture to extract a reasonable amount of work from each power stroke. The fuel air charge in the cylinder can be compared to a coil spring in that the more it is compressed; the more work it is potentially capable of performing. The compression ratio of an engine is a comparison of the volume of space in a cylinder when the piston is at the bottom of the stroke to the volume of space when the piston is at the top of the stroke. This comparison is expressed as a ratio, hence the term compression ratio.

For example, if there are 140 cubic inches of space in the cylinder when the piston is at the bottom dead center and 20 cubic inches of space when the piston is at top dead center, the compression ratio would be 140 to 20. If this ratio is expressed in fraction form, it would be 140/20 or 7 to 1, usually represented as 7:1. This is a common, but relatively low compression ratio allowing fuels to be used of lower octane, however, the horsepower output could be improved with higher compressions.

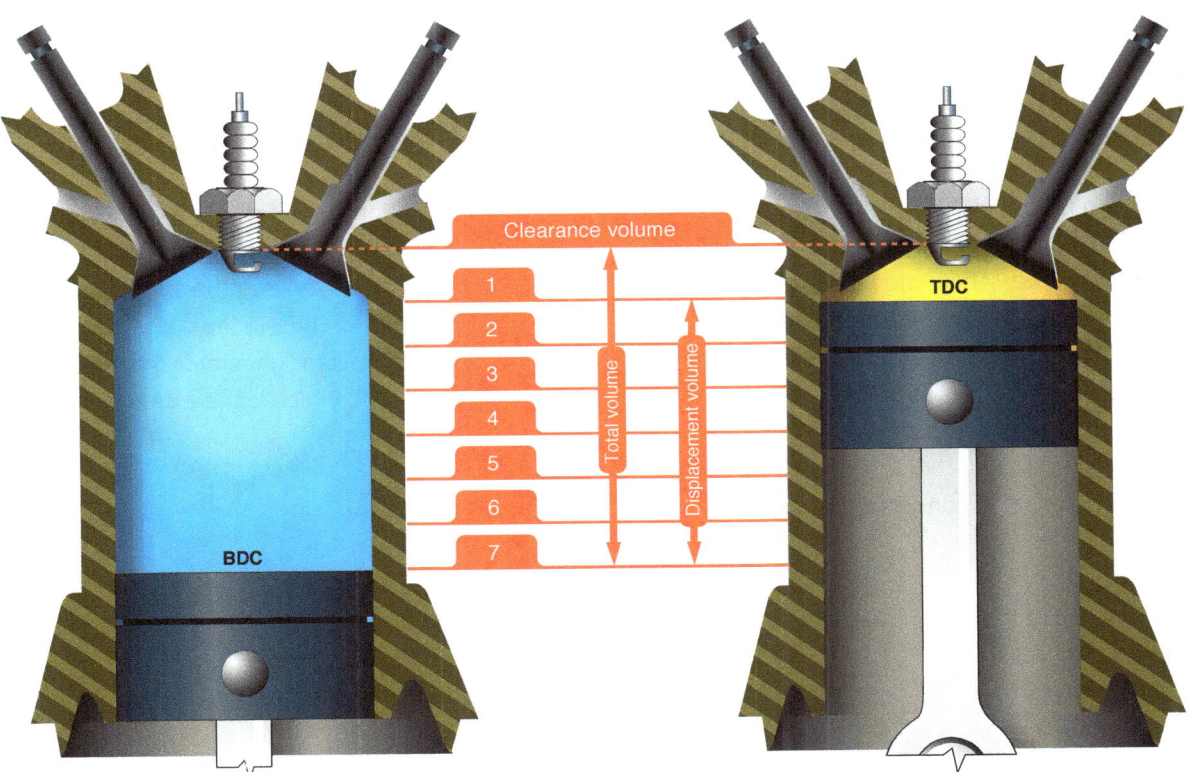

Figure 5-5. Compression ratio of engines.

Compression ratio is one of many factors that affect the maximum horsepower developed by an engine. In general, the higher the compression ratio of an engine, the more power can be extracted from a given amount of fuel. High compression ratios however require stronger (and heavier) engines and tend to produce excessive heat and accompanying accelerated wear. Depending on the type and grade of fuel used, if the compression ratio becomes is too high, pre-ignition or detonation can occur in the cylinder which can subsequently damage the engine. Compression ratio, ignition timing, fuel qualities, as well as engine design, all contribute to the efficiency and performance of various piston engine powerplants.

GAS TURBINE ENGINE CHARACTERISTICS

Gas turbine engines installed in unmanned aircraft range from small model aircraft based units to powerplants utilized by the largest of the world's unmanned aircraft. The advantages of gas turbine engines include light weight in relation to the thrust developed, good fuel economy, low vibration, and the ability to operate efficiently at high altitude. Civilian UAVs have been thus far limited in the types of operations that would make use of the gas turbine's inherent strengths. As regulations allowing higher altitudes and speeds are introduced, the gas turbine propulsion system will see increased implementation in UASs.

Figure 5-6. Gas turbine powered UAV.

GAS TURBINE TYPES AND OPERATION

In a reciprocating engine, the intake, compression, combustion, and exhaust cycles all take place in the combustion chamber. Consequently, each must have exclusive occupancy of the combustion chamber during its respective part of the engine's cycle. A feature of the gas turbine is that separate sections of the engine are devoted to each cycle, and all functions are performed simultaneously without interruption. This is one reason turbine engine vibration is less than that found in a reciprocating engine. Without the continuous stopping and reaccelerating of the engines internal parts, vibration is reduced. This reduction in vibration leads to longer service life and reduced stress on the engine.

A gas turbine engine is typically composed of a rotating compressor, a combustion chamber, and a turbine coupled to the compressor with a rotating shaft. In a gas turbine engine, air flows through the compressor section designed to increases its pressure. As the compressed air moves towards the combustion chamber, fuel is sprayed into the air and ignited. The high temperature/pressure air then expands out of the rear of the engine turning a turbine wheel in the process. The turbine shaft is connected to, and drives the compressor as well as any other devices such as an electric generator that are coupled to the shaft. The energy not used to drive various components of the engine create thrust, which is the essential force that drives the engine forward.

A typical gas turbine engine consists of the following components:
- Air inlet
- Compressor
- Fuel injector and combustion chamber
- Turbine and drive shaft
- Exhaust section
- Accessory section
- The systems necessary for starting, lubrication, fuel supply, and auxiliary purposes, such as anti-icing, cooling, and pressurization.

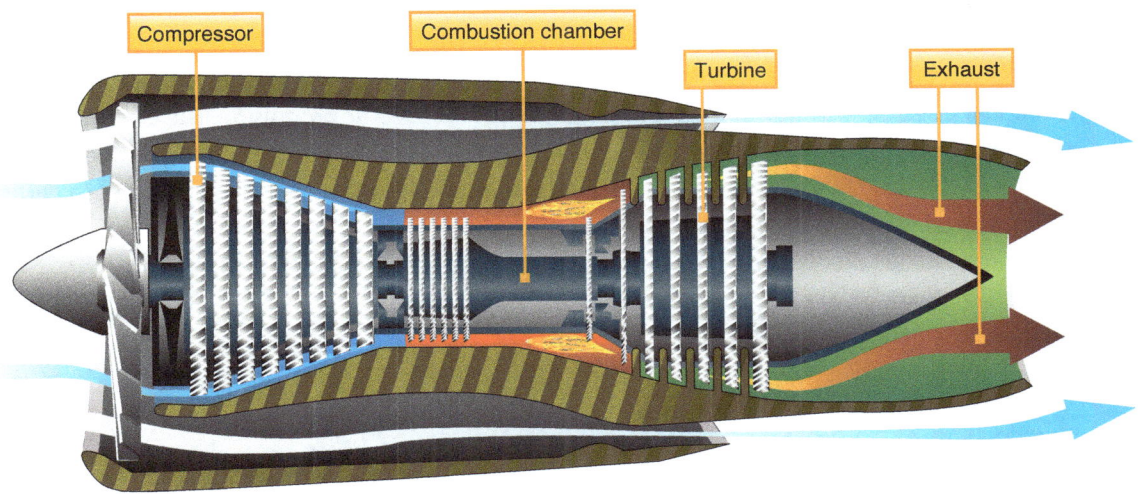

Figure 5-7. The main components of a gas turbine engine.

Four types of gas turbine engines can be used to propel and power aircraft. These are turbofan, turboprop, turboshaft, and turbojet engines. The difference between these four types of aircraft turbine powerplants is primarily the type of compressor, or compressors, for which the engine is designed. The "turbojet" or simply "jet" was once used to describe any gas turbine engine used in aircraft. As gas turbine technology evolved, other jet engine types were developed to take the place of the turbojet engine.

The pure turbojet engine is rarely used today as it has inherent problems with noise and fuel consumption. Most modern "jet" aircraft now use a turbofan engine. The turbofan engine is designed to turn a large fan, or set of fans, at the front of the engine in addition to the compressor. These large fans produce about 80 percent of the total thrust of the engine. A turbofan engine is quieter and has better fuel consumption, than a turbojet.

Figure 5-8. A turbofan engine characterized by the large fan blades at the front of the engine.

A turboshaft engine is a gas turbine engine designed to transfer rotational horsepower through a shaft connected to a transmission. The transmission lets the gas turbine engine run at its peak and most efficient speed while reducing the speed, and increasing the torque available at the output shaft. Turboshaft engines have found use in unmanned rotorcraft that have the need to lift heavy loads, reduce vibration, and provide lengthy flight duration. Turboshaft engines can come in many different styles, shapes, and horsepower ranges. A turboprop engine is similar to a turboshaft engine, as it is designed to turn a standard aircraft propeller. A turboprop engine is usually connected to the propeller via a transmission and a drive shaft.

Gas turbine engines can operate on a variety of fuels. They typically utilize a form of kerosene similar to diesel fuel. In aviation, this fuel is designated as Jet-A fuel. Gas turbines can also operate on aviation or automobile gasoline as well as other flammable liquids.

ELECTRIC MOTOR PROPULSION CHARACTERISTICS

The majority of small UAVs, whether rotary or fixed wing, utilize electric motor propulsion. As battery technology advances, larger and larger unmanned aircraft, as well as manned aircraft, will utilize electric propulsion. The electric motor offers many advantages over other engine types as they have low vibration, zero emissions, precise speed control, long life, and near silent operation. Much as the size of the gas tank dictates flight duration in fueled aircraft, the duration of a particular electric motor system is determined by the battery capacity onboard the aircraft and the electrical load placed upon that battery by the motor/propeller combination. The electric motor speed, as well as other features, are controlled by an electronic speed control or ESC.

TYPES OF ELECTRIC MOTORS

There are many variations of electric motors used in unmanned aircraft. Each has unique properties that lend themselves to various mission profiles. In the past, brushed, direct current (DC) motors, with or without a propeller reduction gearbox, were the only choice available. As electronic speed controls became capable of switching power to the windings of the motor, instead of using brushes riding on a commutator to control rpm and rotation, the brushless motor became the preferred type of motor in UAVs. The elimination of the brushes was a major improvement in many ways. Brushless motors are typically 85-90% efficient whereas brushed DC motors are more like 75-80% efficient. An additional problem with brushed motors is that brushes spark as they pass over commutators and they create inductive circuits that cause magnetic and radio frequency interference (EMI, RFI), heat, loss of efficiency, friction, and required frequent replacement. The electrical interference caused by the brushes is of particular concern to unmanned operators as the sensitive electronics onboard has to be shielded from this interference, or minimized at the motor source, with attenuating capacitors. Brushed motors can be identified by the visible brush housing at the rear of the motor and two input wires from the ESC. Brushless motors will typically have three wires and lack the brush housing and brushes.

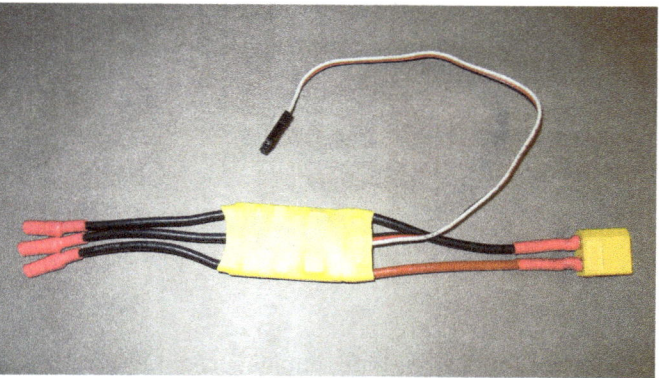

Figure 5-9. A simple brushless electronic speed control (ESC).

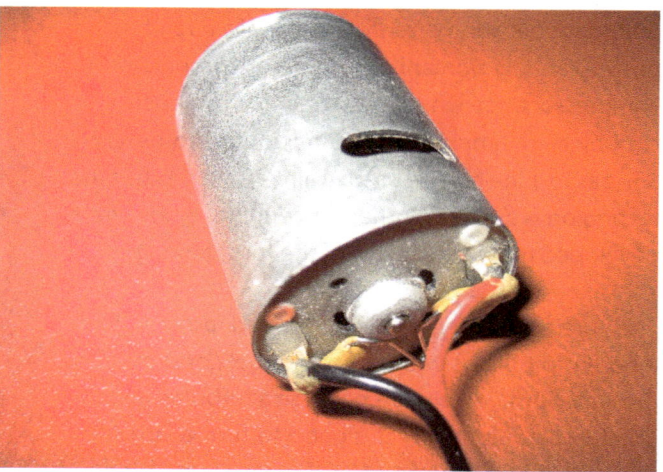

Figure 5-10. Brushed DC motor.

ELECTRONIC SPEED CONTROL (ESC)

The modern ESC is used primarily to control the speed of an electric motor. ESCs are sized and selected based upon their ability to flow current to the motor without overheating or damage. Other features include soft start, braking, battery eliminator circuits (BEC), and selectable power-versus-duration modes of operation. ESCs are programmable by the user to enable or disable features to tailor their operation to specific unmanned aircraft. As an example, the brake feature can be used to stop the output shaft rapidly, (and to keep

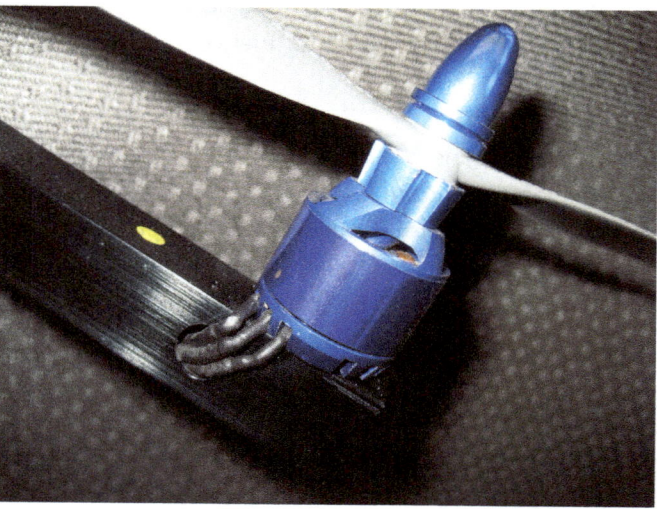

Figure 5-11. Brushless DC motor with distinctive three-wire connection.

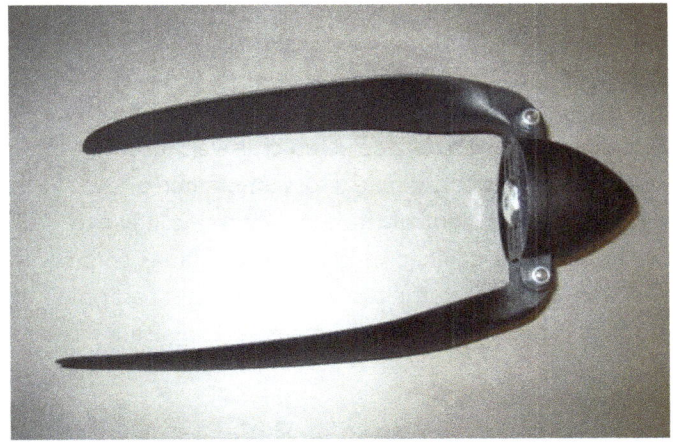

Figure 5-12. Folding propeller for use with brake function of ESC.

Figure 5-13. Programming card for accessing and modifying ESC functions.

it stopped), until the operator again accelerates the motor. UAVs configured to use a folding propeller, which reduce aerodynamic drag during gliding portions of flight, are one common use of the brake function.

The power, versus duration, function allows the operator to control the amount of current available to the motor thereby optimizing either flight time or maximum power, as the needs of the aircraft or mission require. The battery eliminator circuit is used to power radio receivers and autopilots from the main motor battery without need for a dedicated flight control battery, thereby saving valuable weight. The various features and options available from a particular ESC are usually programmed with a programming card. This card greatly simplifies accessing the various features of the ESC.

INRUNNER VERSUS OUTRUNNER MOTORS

Specific aircraft thrust requirements, whether it be high or low speed, often dictate the choice of inrunner versus outrunner electric motors. Inrunner motors have fixed coils mounted to the outer casing with magnets mounted to the motor shaft. The shaft spins inside the casing, hence the term "inrunner". The inrunner motor is especially suited to high rpm ducted fan type propulsion.

Outrunner motors have permanent magnets mounted on the large diameter outer casing. The outer casing is spun around the fixed coils in the center of the motor casing, hence the term "outrunner". It is the increased distance from the central windings (coils) of the motor to the magnets that increases the torque potential of outrunner types. Outrunner motors are designed for higher torque to turn large propellers. Their ability to increase torque at lower rpm has essentially eliminated the gearbox requirement for larger propellers.

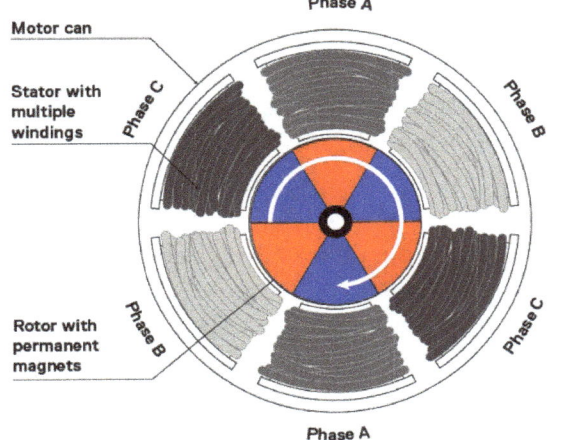
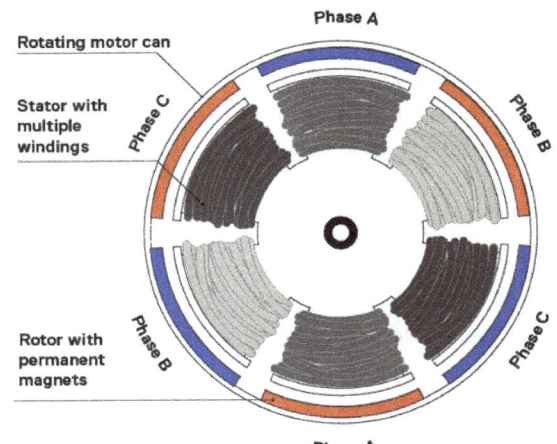

Figure 5-14. Inrunner vs. outrunner type motors.

Unmanned Aerial Systems: The Definitive Guide

ELECTRIC MOTOR POWER RATINGS AND SELECTION

Electric motor propelled unmanned aircraft must be powered adequately to carry the airframe and payload aloft. Some reserve of power above the minimum is needed to accelerate away from a hand launch, climb satisfactorily after a catapult launch, maintain control in the case of multirotors, or provide rapid climb potential to a selected cruise altitude. For most propulsion purposes, the total weight of the aircraft and payload will need to be considered. Most unmanned aircraft have very high performance in speed, duration, and climb when not carrying the weight of the data gathering payload. This must be considered when test flights are performed without payloads. A faux payload of inexpensive lead is commonly used to simulate the weight of high value payloads when an unmanned aircraft is in the test flight and flight test phase of development. Only after the aircraft has proven itself to meet the mission requirements will expensive or delicate payload systems be carried aloft in place of the lead.

The addition of the payload has a significant effect upon the power required in many cases. The ultimate load that a particular design is capable of carrying can be approximated through calculations, however, actual flight tests are needed to determine a satisfactory balance between weight and desired stability and control. The payload carried by a particular unmanned aircraft may vary considerably from mission to mission and it is the responsibility of the operator to be aware of, and adjust for, lighter or heavier loading within the performance capabilities of the aircraft. Information regarding loading and balance limits will be found in the particular unmanned aircraft specifications. Just as manned aircraft have Type Certificate Data Sheets (TCDS), Pilots Operating Handbooks (POH), and performance charts, the unmanned aircraft should have these documents available for reference as well.

WATT-MOTOR COMPARISON

A watt is a unit of electrical power derived from multiplying voltage by amperage. Experience with many unmanned aircraft designs has produced a range of watt levels that correspond to aircraft wing loadings, weights, and desired performance. An estimate of 50-100 watts needed per pound of aircraft weight has proven to be reasonable for small UAV designs. 50 watts per pound provides adequate power for large wing area models with a light wing loading, while 150 watts per pound is better suited to heavier or higher performance type aircraft. This wattage estimate has also been correlated to the various nitro methane fueled, glow (assisted compression ignition) powered engines commonly available in the past. For example, a .40 cubic inch sized glow engine powered aircraft would require an approximately 752 watt electric power system for the equivalent performance of the fueled engine.

It is useful to remember when estimating and converting that 746 watts is equal to one horsepower. It is overly simplistic to select a particular watt rated motor and depend upon it to perform satisfactorily in an unmanned aircraft. A host of factors contribute to the overall aircraft performance including wing area, total vehicle weight, propeller size and efficiency, battery capacity, and quality of the various components, to name a few. There are online calculators that can be utilized to take the various factors of specific aircraft into consideration and recommend an adequate electric power system. It should be noted that these calculators are useful but may be based upon inaccurate assumptions and estimates. The ultimate validation of an unmanned electric power system is still the careful and accurate flight test performance measurements. This is best accomplished through autopilot data logging capability with careful post-flight analysis.

KV OR KV MOTOR RATING

The term KV is used in small aircraft design and refers to the speed constant of a motor. KV is defined as the number of revolutions per minute a motor will turn when one volt is applied if no load is attached to the motor. It could generally be considered similar to a revolutions per volt measurement. For example, a 3000kV brushless motor will turn at 30,000 rpm if 10 volts is applied to its terminals. KV is the unloaded rpm of an electric motor shaft at a specific selected voltage. This number, by itself, is not especially useful for determining performance. A propeller or rotor is normally attached to the shaft which will place a load on the motor affecting the speed. The KV rating of a motor is related to the power output from a motor, or more usefully, the torque level of a motor.

```
KV .............................................................................. 1400
Configuration ........................................................ 12N14P
Stator Diameter .................................................... 18mm
Stator Length ......................................................... 6mm
Shaft Diameter ....................................................... 2mm
Motor Dimensions (Dia x Len) ................... Φ23x18.5mm
Weight (g) ................................................................ 18g
Idle Current @ 10v (A) ........................................... 0.2A
No. of Cells (Lipo) ................................................... 2-3S
Max Continuous Current (A) 180S ......................... 12A
Max Continuous Power (W) 180S ........................... 96W
Max Efficiency Current ............................. (2-7A)>85%
Internal Resistance ............................................ 325mΩ
```

Figure 5-15. Sample electric motor specifications.

Figure 5-16. Clockwise rotation, low KV motor.

The KV of a motor is determined by the number of winds on the motor armature (or turns) and the strength of the magnets. KV permits a better understanding of the torque that can be expected from any particular motor. It is a good way to compare motor performance. In general, a low KV motor has more winds of thinner wire, it will carry more volts at fewer amps, produce higher torque, and can turn a bigger propeller. A high KV motor has less winds of thicker wire and will carry more amps, at fewer volts, and spin a smaller propeller at higher rpm. Both larger/ low speed and smaller/high speed, propellers have their place when selecting electric power systems.

POWERPLANT INSPECTION AND MAINTENANCE

Of all the propulsion systems used in unmanned aircraft, the liquid fueled powerplant has the highest requirement for inspection, maintenance, and repair. Vibration, heat expansion and contraction, moving parts with associated wear, lubricating oil breakdown, and internal contamination all take their toll on the service life of powerplants. In the case of brushless electric motors with sealed bearings, they have limited maintenance requirements, however their performance should still be measured periodically. This is primarily accomplished by measuring maximum rpm with a known good battery and ESC. The motor, propeller, battery, wiring, connections, and ESC work as a system and failures in any one component will affect the others. This is especially critical in multirotor aircraft that rely upon the satisfactory performance of each motor for lift and control.

FUELED ENGINE MAINTENANCE

Piston and gas turbine type engines, by design, convert fuel and air to heat. This heating and cooling, with subsequent stress on the materials that comprise the engine, can cause wear, cracking, corrosion, erosion, and fatigue. Vibration also takes its toll on engine parts. It is beneficial to perform routine inspections and service on these engines if reliable operation is desired. Selection of the proper lubricating oil, combined with scheduled oil changes, with filter inspections for contaminates, is important.

Two stroke engines are especially prone to sparkplug fouling as the lubricating oil is often mixed with the fuel and burnt in the combustion chamber. This feature requires frequent sparkplug service or replacement. A thorough checklist that may be used for insuring the integrity of an engine inspection program may be found in FAA's recommended powerplant inspection checklist 14 CFR Part 43, Appendix D. This checklist is also useful for inspecting the airframe and propellers of aircraft and can serve as a foundation for an unmanned aircraft inspection program.

CHAPTER 6

FLIGHT CONTROL

CONTROL SYSTEMS

The control systems for unmanned aircraft can be classified as either manual, assisted manual, or autonomous. Each requires specific equipment onboard the aircraft to perform the guidance, stability, and control functions. Each type of control may be used during different phases of a flight. For example, an aircraft may be taken off from the ground by manual control, stabilized in climb by an autopilot (assisted manual), commanded to fly to a series of waypoints (autonomous), finally descending back to earth for landing using manual control.

First person view (FPV) control is considered to be a form of assisted manual flight. In this method of control, the operator uses an onboard camera and radio link to send live video to a viewing screen or goggles on the ground. The aircraft is controlled manually via this live video feed which can include an overlaid heads up display (HUD) for critical aircraft attitude and systems information. Payload function control, such as camera triggering, are not directly flight control related and as such will be discussed in a later chapter.

MANUAL FLIGHT CONTROL

Traditionally, radio controlled model aircraft only had the ability to respond directly to operator commands. Much like manned aircraft operations, model aircraft operators relied upon the inherent stability of the aircraft with the operator having the ability to control the aircrafts flight path as desired. The flight control system typically consisted of a manual flight control transmitter on the ground, with a receiver, battery, and servo motors located on the aircraft.

The servos are electric motors connected to a gear system that moves the control surfaces through pushrods in proportion to the operator's selected control stick movement. A small movement

Figure 6-1. Manual flight control with FPV link.

Unmanned Aerial Systems: The Definitive Guide

of the transmitter control stick by the operator would produce a small movement of the aircraft control surface, while a large movement of the stick produced a large control surface deflection. This is called proportional control and was a major milestone in the development of successful recreational radio control models.

The radio control link between the ground transmitter and the airborne receiver was a frequency modulated radio signal in the 72 MHz band. Other frequencies were used but were much less popular. Every system had a receiver onboard the aircraft matching the frequency used by the transmitter. This method of command and control required that only one aircraft at a time be operated using one of the available frequencies. If multiple operators attempted to use the same frequency, the airborne receiver could not distinguish the correct signal. Two or more transmitters operating on the same frequency would lead to radio interference that could cause a loss of control and possibly a loss of the aircraft. This interference problem was alleviated with the introduction of spread spectrum technology radio systems that are in use today.

Spread spectrum radio control technology operates in the 2.4 GHz frequency band and eliminates most forms of common interference. A spread spectrum system assigns a unique identification code to every radio transmitter. The receiver on board the aircraft is programmed to identify and lock onto the signal from the paired transmitter ignoring others. This is known as binding.

The transmitter and receiver are now bound together as a unique and matched set. Once locked together, the transmitted signal can be spread over a wide frequency band. The receiver can distinguish the signal from the paired transmitter and can ignore other systems. This entire process is accomplished quickly so that even if signal information is lost or corrupted momentarily, the aircraft does not respond to a faulty signal or a transmission from another controller. This type of encryption has its origins in military systems, permitting many operators and aircraft to fly simultaneously with no perceptible radio interference.

ASSISTED MANUAL CONTROL

Manual flight control was used for many years before modern autopilots were developed. There have been many evolutionary steps in technology along the way. The piezo gyroscope, or gyro, was one such device that helped make assisted manual flight possible. A gyroscope is a very stable device that is able to sense any movement of an aircraft. A basic gyro senses movement around one dimension, (roll, pitch or yaw), while more modern gyros can sense all three.

On UAVs, gyros are typically installed between the radio receiver onboard the aircraft and the servo that controls movement around one or more axes of flight (elevator for pitch, ailerons for roll, or rudder for yaw). The gyro can sense any deviations from level flight and can be used to level the aircraft. When a turn, climb, or descent was commanded by the operator, the stabilization provided by the gyro was overridden and a signal would be sent to the servo to move

Figure 6-2. Typical manual flight controller with smart phone video feed.

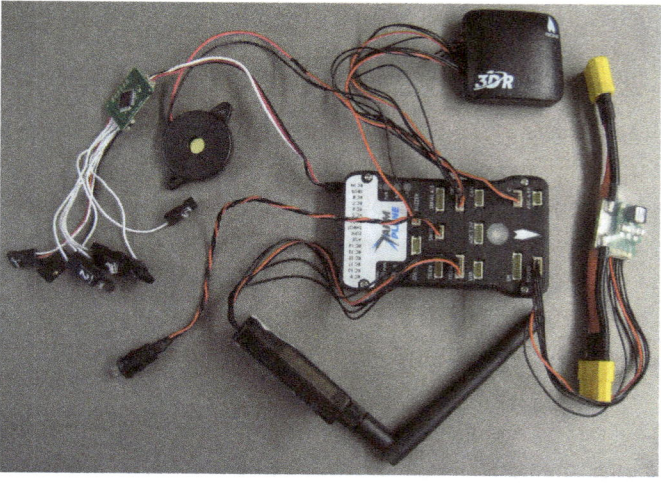

Figure 6-3. Flight stabilization autopilot and manual flight receiver.

the control surface. When the flight control transmitter sticks were released (centered) by the operator, a properly adjusted gyro would automatically move the aircraft's control surfaces, through the servos, to maintain level flight.

Early unmanned aircraft, initially used for aerial photography of agricultural fields, took advantage of the piezo gyro to position the aircraft, and therefore the camera lens, as perpendicular to the ground as possible so as not to skew the resultant images. As the aircrafts altitude and distance from the operator increased, it became increasingly difficult to visually and manually level the aircraft for accurate imaging. Use of the piezo gyro solved this important challenge to early precision agriculture UAV operations.

AUTONOMOUS FLIGHT CONTROL

The ability to operate autonomously, along a preprogrammed flight path, is the hallmark of the modern unmanned aircraft. The ability to easily and automatically control an aircraft's precise speed, location, and direction has opened up an enormous number of possibilities for applied research, surveillance, cinematography, and a host of other aerial applications.

Early autopilot systems with their associated wiring and battery power demands were large, heavy, expensive, and unreliable. Variations in atmospheric conditions, such as temperature changes and barometric pressure changes, required frequent recalibration of the autopilot sensors. Simply moving the aircraft from a warm environment to a cold runway, without compensating for the temperature changes, could render the system highly inaccurate and unreliable.

Today's autopilots have dramatically improved in all areas including compensating for changes in the environment, cost, size, reliability, accuracy, and system weight. Modern autopilots function with inputs from a variety of sources including the barometer/altimeter, GPS, magnetometers (compass), optional manual flight receiver, and airspeed sensors. Inertial measurement units (IMU), which are actually a combination of gyroscopes and accelerometers, can sense motion in any one of the axes of the aircraft. The autopilot can then adjust the flight path of the aircraft accordingly. This method of measuring directional acceleration can be further enhanced and corrected with data received from GPS satellites, as well as other sensors. The inputs from the various sensors are routed to a central processor that uses a mathematical algorithm to correct and adjust the aircraft's position. These same sensors and inputs permit the autopilot to direct the aircraft to fly to a selected GPS location or waypoint as programmed by the operator.

Figure 6-4. UAV electronic controls installed.

Figure 6-5. Vehicle mounted autopilot.

FLIGHT MODES

There are other functions, or modes, of autopilot operation that are available to the operator including, but not limited to:

Autonomous mode - Autonomous flight (AUTO) is the navigation of an aircraft to and from a predetermined set of waypoints, navigated in series. This is a popular mode for mapping or agricultural imaging flights. In autonomous flight, the aircraft potentially flies entirely on its own without operator input from takeoff to landing. Autonomous flight relies upon an autopilot, GPS receiver, and a calibrated, sensitive, and accurate magnetometer or compass. Autonomous flight can be interrupted at any time by the operator if a collision hazard exists with a manned aircraft, or other malfunction occurs, by manually selecting another mode with the transmitter. It is important that the operator and/or observer visually monitor the aircraft at all times when in autonomous flight. Only a few seconds may be available to avoid collisions or loss of the aircraft.

Figure 6-6. Mode selector switches.

Return to Launch - Return to launch (RTL) mode is selected if the operator wishes the aircraft to automatically return to the point where the flight initiated. The RTL location may be the point that the motors were armed for operation, in the case of a multirotor aircraft, or the point that the GPS signals became satisfactory for flight (3D lock) in the case of a fixed wing aircraft. It is important to know how each system is designed to RTL. For example, arming a multirotor aircraft while still in a vehicle or while in a working area means that the autopilot will attempt to return to that point if the RTL mode is selected. That location may be too close to observers, bystanders, or equipment, creating a potential safety problem. RTL is only usable if the autopilot is still receiving accurate GPS and compass information that can provide a solid location fix for the aircraft, and can be maintained during the flight back to launch. If the navigational sensors are compromised, RTL will not function reliably and another flight mode must be selected that does not rely on the faulty sensors in order to avoid a fly away or crash.

Stability mode - The stability (STB) mode relies on internal IMU stability information and can be useful when the aircraft is being controlled in line of sight but has lost the ability to navigate back to the operator due to loss of GPS or compass functionality. At the limits of an operator's vision, aircraft orientation and directional control can be difficult. If a control problem is encountered, switching to STB will stabilize the aircraft. If operating a multirotor aircraft, pushing forward on the control stick and observing the direction of travel of the aircraft may help the operator regain orientation. If a fixed wing aircraft, initiating a turn will raise a wing and possibly reveal the direction of travel. Once the operators can accurately observe the orientation and direction of travel of the aircraft, control can then be established. Regardless of the method used, it is good practice to remain close enough to regain control of the aircraft if the autopilot autonomous function must be abandoned for any reason during the flight.

Loiter mode - Loiter (LTR) mode is the ability to hold an aircraft at a fixed point in the air both horizontally and vertically. This mode requires accurate compass, barometer/altimeter, and GPS inputs and is considered a geostationary mode. Wind drift and turbulence will be compensated for automatically as the aircraft holds a fixed position over the earth. This mode is especially useful for cinematography or surveillance activities as the position of the aircraft can be fixed while a gimbaled camera is focused and adjusted for desired images. The workload of the operator is reduced in this mode as they do not have to concentrate on flying the aircraft and can instead concentrate on camera control.

Depending on the sophistication of the installed autopilot system and software, there can be other modes that can be selected. A limitation of having multiple selectable modes is the ability of the operator to remember which switch controls which modes. Labeling the transmitter may help, but often with only a few seconds to avoid a crash. The operator may have to change modes quickly and precisely by memory.

TELEMETRY

Autopilot systems can also provide a means of two-way communications with the aircraft, in the form of a radio telemetry link. This linkup commonly uses either 433 or 915 MHz, and permits a computer, usually a laptop on the ground, to display many of the aircraft's operating parameters. The parameters displayed can be customized but will typically include items such as aircraft speed, altitude, aircraft attitude (artificial horizon), as well as selected operating mode, number of GPS satellites in view, percent battery charge remaining, and so on.

The information received by the laptop through this telemetry link is generated by the autopilot and provides real time flight monitoring as well as post flight review of data logs. System malfunctions during a flight such as a bad compass signal may be displayed, alerting the operator or observer to a problem in real time.

Telemetry is a two-way link and the aircraft autopilot can be controlled during flight using this link. Modes may be changed, cameras controlled, and other flight functions selected from the ground. Some operators choose to solely fly using the telemetry radio link and have eliminated the manual flight transmitter from their systems. Their ground based computer then becomes the sole means of controlling the aircraft. This is only feasible with purely autonomous functions of the autopilot as no manual control system is available. When operating in this manner, the manual flight control transmitter might be considered as a secondary, or even redundant, control device. If the radio telemetry link is lost however, the manual controller can provide options for the operator that might otherwise be unavailable.

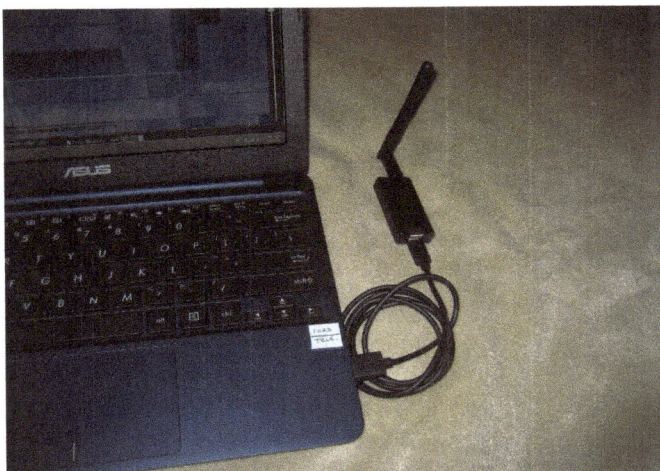

Figure 6-7. Radio telemetry for transmission and reception of UAV data.

Figure 6-8. Heads Up Display (HUD).

DATA LOGGING

As previously mentioned, data logging is an important capability provided by the autopilot. The data gathered in flight can be stored onboard the autopilot. Typically, over 100 different flight parameters can be recorded at a rate of multiple times per second. Aircraft location, altitude, speed, sensor status, servo position, current, and voltage are but a few of the possible data points. This information can be downloaded after a flight and is extremely valuable in evaluating the aircraft overall system health and performance. As an engineering and research tool the data logging function of the autopilot is unparalleled.

An example of the usefulness of the data logs is the measurement of the effect of motor current upon compass error. As the aircraft flies and the electric current varies with the speed of the motor, the magnetic field surrounding the motor power wires will vary. This magnetic field, referred to as electromagnetic interference (EMI), can cause compass errors to be introduced making it difficult for the autopilot to navigate reliably. Analyzing the motor current and compass error data after the flight might detect a correlation between the two. If, for example, a problem was discovered, shielding around the wires or other adjustments might need to be made to protect the compass.

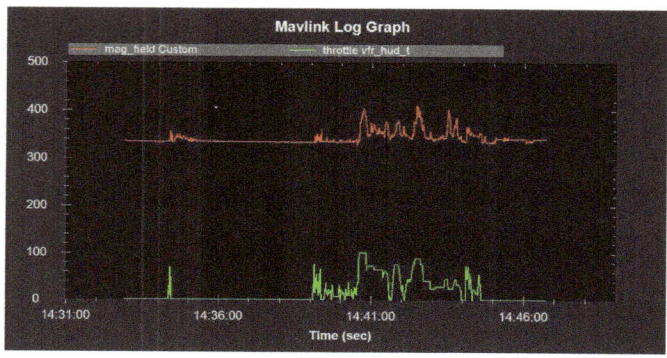

Figure 6-9. Motor and compass interference showing engine speed and interference.

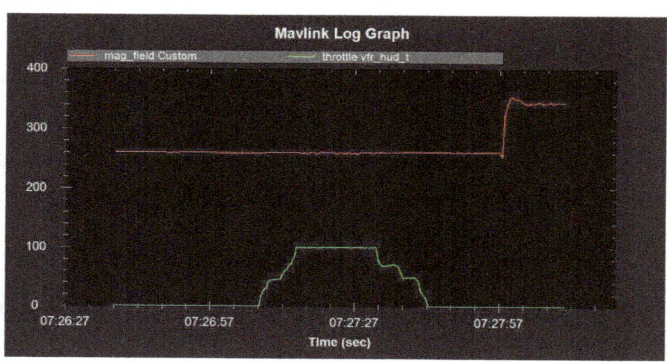

Figure 6-10. Motor and compass interference showing engine speed and interference after shielding.

The graphs in Figures 6-9 and 6-10 were generated utilizing data log information and clearly show the before and after effects of shielding the motor power wires to minimize compass interference.

FAILSAFE SYSTEMS

Failsafe systems are actions the aircraft, or operator, may take in the event of a failure or loss of control signal. The failsafe is preselected by the operator prior to flight, and may be changed as the flight profiles change. For instance, if the loss of the telemetry radio signal occurs for a set number of seconds, in one failsafe mode, the aircraft might automatically circle in place, return to launch, or immediately land. The successful demonstration of failsafe actions is a required part of FAA granting an approved operating area, or certificate of authorization (COA), and provides a margin of safety in the event of unforeseen failures. Failsafe systems are not always electronic in nature and may include parachute deployment, engine shutdown, or other actions designed to satisfy safety requirements

FIRMWARE

Autopilots for UAVs are somewhat generic in nature and can be used in a variety of vehicles. The firmware is the coding installed into the memory of the autopilot that adapts the autopilot to various types of aircraft. For example, a fixed wing aircraft has different flight control and stability requirements than a multirotor. The same basic autopilot might be used for each, but different firmware would have to be installed. Even then, firmware is a generic set of performance parameters which may need to be adjusted to suit different operations or specific aircraft. Some autopilot firmware is "open source", which means the code is freely accessible and can be modified by users. Open source software is a means by which improved, or highly customized, control algorithms may be created and distributed for use by users.

Figure 6-11. Parachute deployment for failsafe.

Figure 6-12. Programming an autopilot.

AUTOPILOT TUNING

Autopilot authority for any particular aircraft is adjusted by changing PID values. A proportional-integral-derivative controller (PID controller) is a control loop feedback mechanism (controller) widely used in robotic control systems as well as in UAS autopilot systems. Changing a PID value lets the operator modify and/or customize the performance of their aircraft. It allows the operator to increase or decrease the control and stability response of the aircraft. This is useful for adjusting the autopilot authority to provide better flight maneuverability or more docile, stable, training type flights.

PID values are interpreted in terms of time. P is the present error, I is the accumulation of past errors, and D is a prediction of future errors, based on the current rate of change. By increasing and decreasing the three parameters in the PID controller algorithm, the operator can provide custom performance values to adjust a flight system to suit their needs.

The PID values of the most basic flight controllers are adjusted up and down as needed to tune aircraft control responses to operator preferences. Very high relative PID values provide highly responsive stability control but may be too sensitive causing the aircraft to oscillate in flight. Relatively low values may cause the aircraft to wander and have limited stability. Flight tests and observation of behavior will guide the operator in selecting the correct PID values for each aircraft and operator.

AUTOPILOT INSTALLATION

The modern autopilot is a very sensitive instrument. It can be affected by the surrounding electromagnetic (EMI) environment, excessive vibration, as well as the temperature and airflow environment in which it operates. Many autopilot problems can be avoided by careful attention to the autopilot installation and location.

Vibration can affect the inertial measurement unit's accuracy and therefore the autopilot's ability to control flight. The autopilot should be carefully isolated from airframe vibration by the use of vibration deadening materials. Foam ear plugs, Moongel acoustic dampener pads, neoprene foam, and rubber or silicone isolators are all commonly used to reduce the transfer of vibration from the airframe to autopilot. It should be noted that the mounting must be firm enough

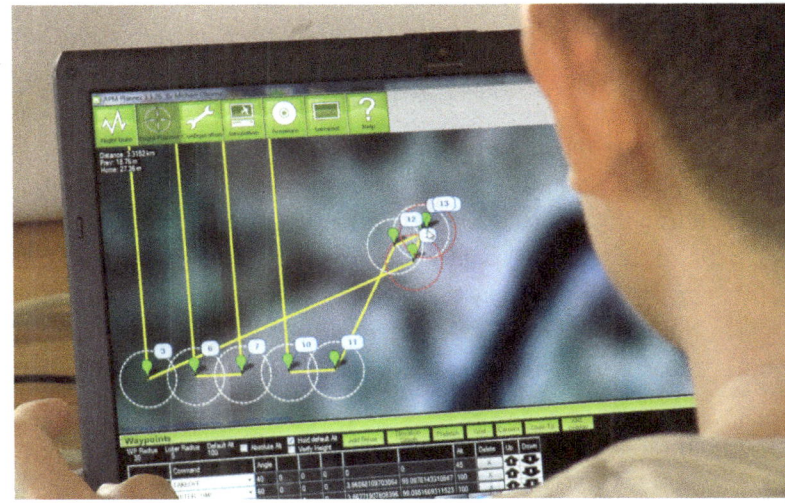

Figure 6-13. Autopilot performance tuning.

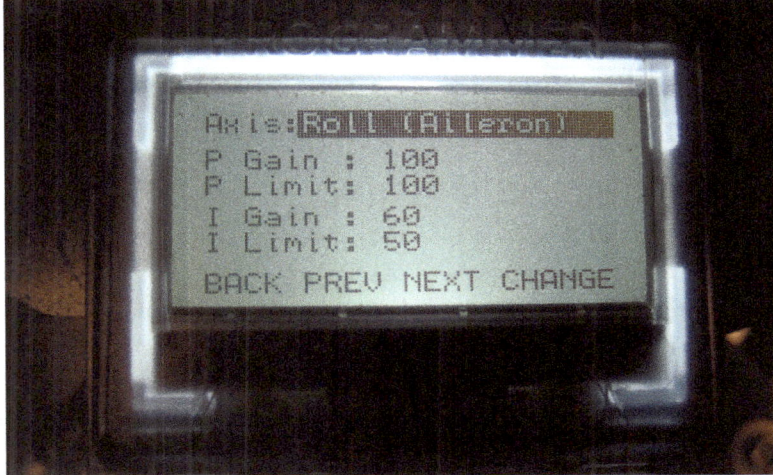

Figure 6-14. Autopilot adjustment (PI) gains and limits.

Figure 6-15. Autopilot mounted on foam with EMI shield located underneath.

for the autopilot to receive feedback from aircraft movement, but not so firm as to transfer unnecessary vibration. Some experimentation may be required with various products to achieve the best balance of absorption and rigidity.

The isolation of the autopilot (in particular its magnetometer or compass) from unwanted magnetism may be accomplished by shielding either the electro-magnetism producing parts and/or the autopilot itself. This is commonly accomplished through the use of self-adhesive metallic tape. This tape can be used to either contain magnetic fields, or to isolate and protect sensitive components from outside magnetic fields. This tape can be made of aluminum, copper, or custom material designed specifically to shield EMI. Proper shielding can be difficult to obtain and a thorough understanding and testing of the autopilot may be necessary after installation. There are apps for smart phones and tablets that can be used to detect and measure magnetic fields (as well as vibration) and are indispensable to tracking down EMI interference.

Another way to isolate the compass and/or autopilot is by moving it physically away from the offending components. In general, EMI is reduced by the square of the distance between components. So it is good practice to place possible offenders as far away as physically possible. In many UAVs, the compass and GPS are mounted on the top of the aircraft or on a short, nonmetallic post extending above the aircraft. The most troublesome interference producing components are the electric motors and their associated power wiring.

When installing autopilots and GPS units it should be noted that if an external GPS has an arrow indicator shown on the exterior case, the orientation of the arrow is to the front of the aircraft and this indicates that the component is a combination GPS/compass unit. A GPS only, external receiver will not have an arrow and may be oriented in any direction.

AUTONOMOUS TESTING

After the autopilot, telemetry, and the associated receivers and wiring have been are installed, the aircraft is ready for initial testing. For safety reasons, the aircraft propeller, or rotors of a multirotor aircraft, should be removed for all ground tests. The first test is to verify that the flight control movements operate correctly in manual mode. In the United States, mode 2 is the preferred manual transmitter control arrangement. This configuration places the throttle and rudder on the left control stick and the ailerons and elevator on the right. Pushing forward (up) on the throttle (left) stick should result in an rpm of the drive motor(s) or engine. Likewise, pushing forward the right stick should lower the nose of the aircraft, which should cause the elevator control surface to move down. This should cause the rear most rotor in a multirotor to rotate faster. Pulling the stick back should create the opposite control reaction. If these actions do not produce the expected results, the servo directions may be reversed easily by changing the programming of the transmitter or the direction of the throttle control.

Verifying the controls operate correctly is the first step towards a safe test flight. The next step is to verify that the autopilot moves the flight controls in the desired direction. To test the autopilot, the aircraft's radio and control system should be powered up with autonomous mode with stability control enabled on the autopilot.

To test an autopilot installed on a fixed wing aircraft, begin by physically lowering the nose of the aircraft and see if the autopilot attempts to keep the aircraft "level". When the nose of the aircraft is lowered, the elevator should move

Figure 6-16. Mode 2 manual flight transmitter.

smoothly to the up position as if the autopilot is trying to raise the nose of the aircraft. If the nose is physically raised, the autopilot should adjust the flight controls to lower the nose of the aircraft. Likewise, if the aircraft is physically rolled to the left, the left aileron should lower while the right aileron rises in an attempt to return the aircraft level flight. The opposite should occur when the aircraft is banked to the right.

A multirotor aircraft may be similarly tested by observing which motors accelerate as the aircraft is pitched forward and back, left and right. This test is accomplished with the propellers removed for safety. When all of the controls move in the desired direction in both manual and autonomous modes, it is time to test fly the aircraft.

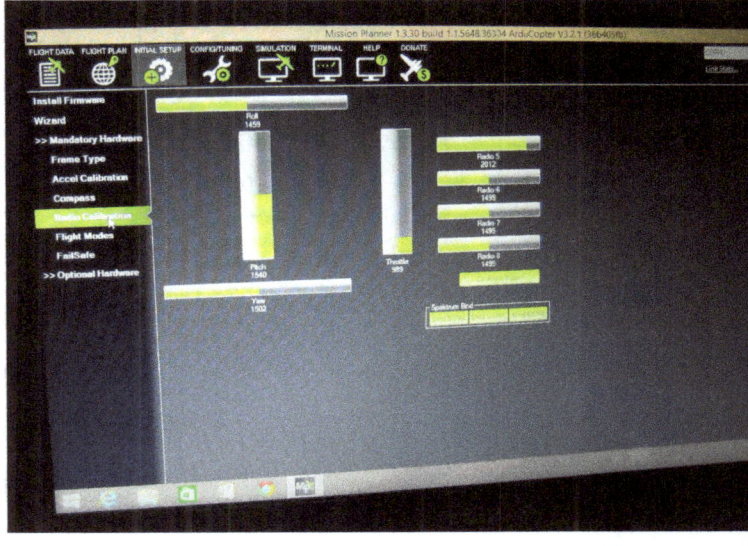

Figure 6-17. Calibrating manual flight controller for autopilot.

TEST FLIGHT AND FLIGHT TEST

An unmanned aircraft test flight is used to determine whether the aircraft is functioning and performing as expected. Reducing the risk factors of a test flight are very important. Test flights should be performed in unpopulated areas, during optimal weather conditions, and with calm or very light winds. An experienced operator should be at the controls. The initial test flight may reveal serious weaknesses in the aircraft or systems that will need to be addressed before continuing to the flight test phase.

Flight test, on the other hand, is a series of flights conducted to determine the performance, duration, and operating characteristics of a specific aircraft. Tuning of autopilot PID values, adjustment of control deflections, and the development of the unique operating techniques and precautions for the specific aircraft are accomplished. During flight test, changes should be made one at a time and the effects of those changes recorded, preferably in writing. Flight test is a logical, methodical process to gather data and flight experience with the aircraft.

The data logging capability of the autopilot is crucial to the accuracy of the flight test phase and significant performance numbers should be recorded for future reference. Typically, it is useful to know such things as takeoff distance and speed, climb speed and rate, cruise speed, and approach to landing speed, with landing rollout distances, to name a few. This data can be used not only to evaluate aircraft performance in the future but can also be used to evaluate the effects of any airframe and/or engine modifications or the addition of extra payload at a future time. This information can also be used to generate the aircraft's operating handbook, develop performance charts, specifications, and determine operating limits. In particular, the flight duration and overall stability of a multirotor type aircraft can be seriously degraded as payload is increased. It is in the flight test phase that these characteristics are discovered and operating limitations can be established.

FIRST PERSON VIEW (FPV)

Ground receivers can be used to capture the radio signal from the UAV and process it for viewing on a monitor or goggles. The video can easily be recorded in high resolution

Figure 6-18. FPV goggles.

on a memory card, and saved for later viewing as well. FPV flight takes practice and can be difficult for an operator to maintain situational awareness, particularly while learning how to fly a specific aircraft. The FAA line of sight requirements may be satisfied by employing the use of a dedicated observer. They can assist with aircraft position, distance determination, as well as assist in maintaining clearance from manned aircraft and objects as well.

Any aircraft flown solely by FPV must have certain equipment onboard. A video camera, radio transmitter, and usually a dedicated battery pack are required. The aircraft mounted video transmitter is limited in power by Federal Communications Commission (FCC) regulations. The available frequencies for FPV are 900 MHz, 1.2 & 1.3GHz, 2.3 & 2.4 GHz, and 5.8GHz. Of these choices, 5.8GHz has the least interference problems and best all-around performance. The primary limitation of the 5.8 GHz band is that anything positioned between the transmitter and receiver will potentially block reception. This limitation should not be a problem if the observer insures that line of sight contact with the aircraft is maintained at all times.

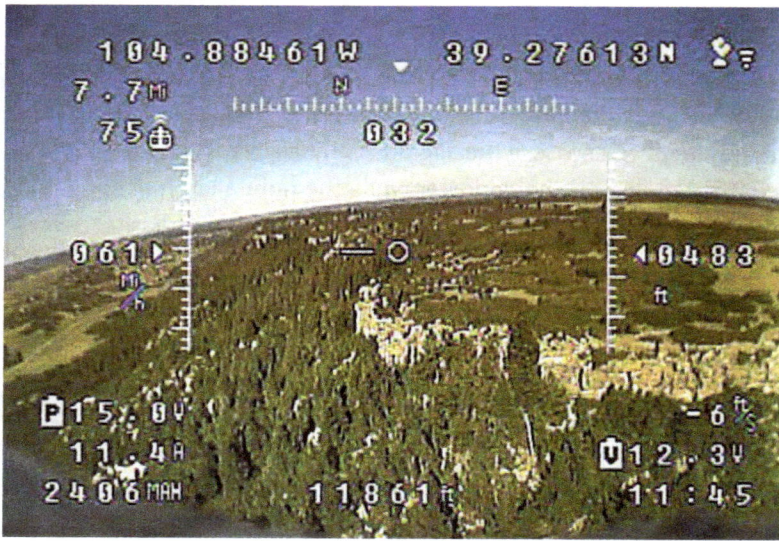

Figure 6-19. FPV monitor screen with on screen display (OSD).

Most modern manual flight control transmitters operate on 2.4 GHz so that frequency is only available for video transmission if you are operating an older transmitter on the 72 MHz band. The power of the onboard transmitter is not as important as the antennas used to transmit and receive. In fact, an extremely powerful onboard video transmitter can potentially interfere with the flight-2 control and telemetry radios of the UAS. The radio frequency interference (RFI) created by and/or affecting your aircraft can be measured with a portable frequency scanner if interference seems to be a problem. Proper physical location of sensitive components as well as proper shielding often can mitigate RFI challenges.

Figure 6-20. Radio frequency interference analyzer.

116   Unmanned Aerial Systems: The Definitive Guide

CHAPTER 7

SENSORS AND PAYLOADS

The unmanned aircraft is designed as a working aircraft. The sensors, cameras, or other payload carried by the aircraft are the primary purpose for which it is designed, tested, and flown. The aircraft should complement the proposed payload in such a way as to enhance the ability of the payload to gather the desired data. The payloads monetary value can often exceed the value of the entire aircraft with the aircraft designed around the payload requirements.

UASs can carry many different types of payload, with new applications being imagined daily. This requires the airframes to be designed and built with future system needs in mind. Some of the more common civilian types of payloads currently carried include cameras, air or water sampling equipment, sound recording microphones, and other forms of imaging equipment such as thermal and hyper-spectral imagers. Future payloads will likely include other types of sensors, commercial deliveries, and high altitude electronic equipment such as mobile phone transmitters, aerial sensors (pointed down at the ground as well as up into space), as well as other yet to be imagined payloads.

PAYLOAD INSTALLATION

The first concern of the designer and operator when considering the payload to be carried is normally its weight. Additional issues include the vibration environment as well as any EMI or RFI emissions the payload, or aircraft systems, may be subject to. There might also be environmental concerns such as temperature, pressure, and humidity that need to be taken into consideration as well.

The total weight of the payload will ultimately help determine the size and capability of the aircraft needed. Once an aircraft has been selected that can safely carry the weight of the payload and its associated support equipment, the vibration sensitivity of the payload needs to be addressed. Many cameras will not produce usable image data in a

Figure 7-1. Hyperspectral camera used for agricultural imaging.

Unmanned Aerial Systems: The Definitive Guide

high vibration environment and may even be damaged. The most troublesome installations are often found when a vibration sensitive payload is combined with a reciprocating piston engine. Many larger single cylinder engines, common in the model aviation community, have vibration levels measuring over 7g's in one or more axes. In many cases, this extreme vibration will need to be controlled through careful isolation of the payload from the engine and/or airframe. Vibration dampening of the engine itself, through isolating mounts, has shown to be ineffective in practice however. Electric motor propulsion is a much preferred option if at all feasible.

EMI and RFI emissions must also be monitored closely. A payload utilizing the same frequency, or one close to that used by the autopilot or controls, can interfere with proper flight control functions. Likewise, the ignition system of a piston engine can create radio frequency interference that can cause malfunctions in sensitive payload electronics. Knowledge and testing of the electronic emissions of both the aircraft and payload, their sensitivity, and their interactions with one another is of utmost importance if the mission of the aircraft is to be successful.

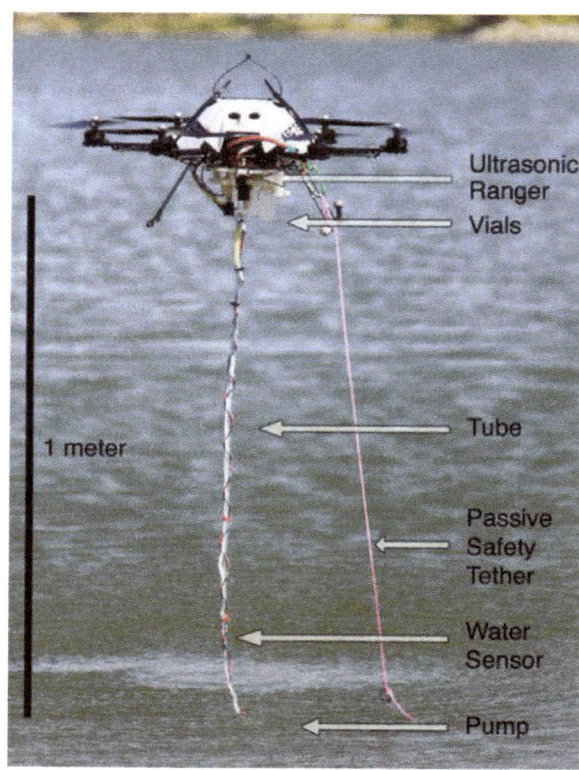

Figure 7-2. Multicopter drawing water sample.

Another consideration when designing or selecting a UAV is that the payload likely needs to be easily removable for downloading data, adjustments, charging batteries, or maintenance. This may have to be accomplished in the field with little support and/or equipment. Ease of removal is as important as the tolerance for mishandling the payload. The system should be designed such that payloads can be easily attached and/or removed with a minimal chance of damaging the airframe in any way.

PAYLOAD INTEGRATION

The term used to describe the process of marrying a particular payload to a particular unmanned aircraft is "integration". Factors related to the safe and efficient integration of the payload within the aircraft must be considered during the design and operation of the aircraft. Integration begins with the proposed physical mounting of the payload and continues until final stages of flight testing are complete with improvements and adjustments throughout the process. Vibration, EMI, and RFI can present real challenges to payload integration. As with the flight test of the UAV, integration should be approached methodically with an appropriate data gathering and documenting system set up to insure that issues can be addressed as they arise.

PAYLOAD MOUNTING SYSTEMS

Cameras are one of the most common UAS payloads. A camera gimbal installed on the aircraft allows rotation of a camera in one or more directions independent of the aircraft flight direction or orientation. The gimbal is commonly installed below the aircraft providing an unobstructed view of the surrounding area without

Figure 7-3. Camera mounted in vibration dampening gel on removable retainer plate.

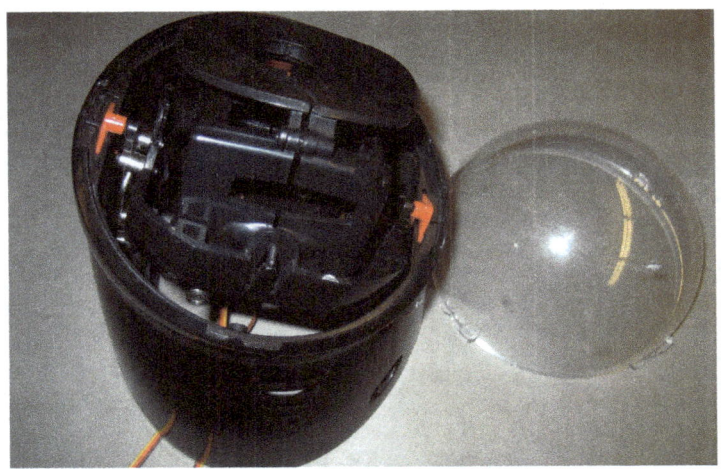

Figure 7-4. Gimbal camera nose pod with clear plastic cover.

airframe components blocking the images. Common use of the gimbaled camera was pioneered in recreational, cinematography, and surveillance operations. Precision agriculture, as well as similar applications, primarily use straight down imaging and therefore have little need for swiveling or rotating of the camera. A gimbal is needed when the senor must be focused on a specific spot or location while the aircraft moves. Even a "hovering" aircraft moves ever so slightly and might need a gimbaled payload. The gimbal and sensor package can be mounted out in the open or may be enclosed in a pod, or enclosure, to protect sensitive optics and mechanisms from the outside environment.

The camera gimbal movement must be controlled in some fashion. It can be controlled by either an automatic system or manually by the operator. The servo type gimbal control is the oldest, most inexpensive, and the most basic control mechanism. A servo motor moves the camera mounting system, either by direct operator control from a radio control transmitter, or through a stabilized control board. The autopilot may also be used as the camera control system, eliminating the need for an independent control board. Multiple servos can be installed, each assigned to rotate, tilt, or level the camera. A separate radio channel is required for motion around each axis. Simple tilt only systems are the most basic but are useful on multirotor aircraft as the multirotor itself can provide the rotation (yaw) desired.

Figure 7-5. Camera mounted to gimbal.

The brushless electric motor gimbal is an improvement over the servo type as it offers rapid, precise control of the camera position. Each desired action of the camera will have an associated electric motor controlled through an electronic control. Another advantage of the motor type gimbal is the ability to rotate through 360 degrees, unlike a servo type which has limited output travel. Brushless motors have a higher current draw than a comparable servo requiring a larger power source however, thereby adding weight to the aircraft. This type of gimbal also requires the addition of a dedicated electronic speed control to power each of the motors.

GYRO STABILIZATION

With the addition of software and camera controllers, both the servo and motor type gimbals can be gyro stabilized. Much like an autopilot for the camera, this feature steadies the video image and allows point monitoring of a specific location regardless of aircraft movement. The operator still retains the ability to direct the camera as desired, but once pointed, the gyros stabilize the camera and mount adjusting for aircraft movement. Gyro stabilization has many benefits for video production as it removes the sense of motion that may be distracting to the viewer. Precision agriculture and surveillance applications may also benefit from a stabilized camera able to point directly earthward regardless of aircraft attitude.

AIR SAMPLING PAYLOADS

Most air sampling systems onboard unmanned aircraft require access to clean, undisturbed air to obtain the most accurate results. When utilizing multirotor aircraft, a remote intake for the air sample may be necessary to avoid the turbulent air

Figure 7-6. Brushless, stabilized gimbal.

below the aircraft. Another concern with larger fixed wing and helicopter systems is the exhaust emissions of the powerplant contaminating the sample. This issue is normally addressed by placing the sample probe in the front of the aircraft and the engine in the rear.

ACOUSTIC PAYLOADS

Sound reception as well as recording from airborne microphones is another form of UAS payload application. This payload type is not deployed just for surveillance type applications; they are also used to study natural events. For example, scientists using UAVS are studying the ultrasonic sounds used by bats while hunting food and mental mapping their surroundings for navigational purposes. When using any type of sound based sensor, acoustic interference from the propulsion or lifting parts of the aircraft might occur as some frequencies interfere with the payload sensors. This interference might occur at frequencies that the human ear cannot hear but nevertheless must be addressed through potential modifications to the microphone, aircraft, or operating techniques.

UNCONVENTIONAL PAYLOADS

There are a number of proposed uses for UASs that involve innovative payloads and systems. They are far too numerous to discuss in this chapter, and there are many concepts that have yet to be identified. Some of the more commonly suggested payloads include:

- Ultrasonic imaging and rangefinders
- Non-visible light cameras such as UV, infrared, and various thermal imagers
- Radar and laser scanning systems
- Radio and/or internet transceivers to provide wide area or localized emergency gap coverage
- Air quality sensors including smog, CO_2, and other systems
- Weather sensors including temperature, pressure, and humidity devices

Whatever the use, the UAV must be designed to safely carry these payloads and have the ability to operate them correctly while in flight. One of the most important payload considerations in UAS operations is weight and balance.

WEIGHT AND BALANCE
One of the most important factors in UAS operation is proper weight and balance of the aircraft. Weight and balance includes both the total weight of the aircraft and its payload, as well as the effect of weight on its overall balance. Too much weight can reduce the performance of the aircraft and may cause a structural failure. Improper balance of the weight affects the maneuverability and stability of the aircraft and may even make it potentially unflyable.

AIRCRAFT WEIGHT
Weight is a major factor in the design, construction, and operation of all UAVs. Excessive weight reduces the efficiency of an aircraft and its load carrying capacity. When an aircraft is designed, it is usually made as light as the required structural strength will allow, with the wings or rotors designed to support the maximum allowable weight. When the weight of an aircraft is increased, the wings or rotors must produce additional lift to support the load. The total load is not only the static weight of the aircraft, but also dynamic loads imposed by flight maneuvers. For example, the wings of an aircraft weighing 50 pounds in total must support 50 pounds in level flight. But when the airplane is turned smoothly and sharply at a bank angle of 60°, the dynamic load requires the wings to support twice this weight, or 100 pounds. Quick, uncoordinated maneuvers or flight into turbulence can impose substantially higher dynamic loads on the structure such that structural failure could occur.

These dynamic forces are measured in "Gs". One G is equal to the normal force of gravity. Two Gs equals twice the force of gravity, exposing the aircraft structure and its components to a force equal to twice its weight. Three Gs is three times the weight, and so on. Manned aircraft are typically designed such that the structure can sustain a load factor (G) of 3.8 times its weight. With no fragile pilot onboard, small UAVs can easily be subjected to forces of 4 to 5 Gs or more. At five Gs, every pound of weight added to an aircraft requires that the structure be strong enough to support an additional five pounds. For this reason, a maximum weight for every aircraft should be established and rigidly adhered to as the structural components of the aircraft will likely be subjected to substantial forces while in flight.

EFFECTS OF WEIGHT
A lightly loaded aircraft will usually perform better than expected and will not be subject to any over stress condition. An overloaded aircraft will experience many problems however including:
- A higher takeoff speed, resulting in a longer takeoff run.
- The rate and angle of climb will be reduced.
- The service ceiling of the aircraft will be reduced.
- The cruising speed will be reduced.
- The cruising range or flight time will be shortened.
- Aircraft maneuverability will be decreased.
- A longer landing roll will be required as the landing speed will be higher.
- Excessive loads may be imposed on the structure, especially the landing gear.

The structural weight of an empty aircraft is more or less static. The operator cannot remove required components of the aircraft to make it lighter. The only variables generally modified by the operator are the weight of the fuel and the payload. Batteries and other non-combustible power sources are still considered as "fuel" for the purpose of weight and balance. In general, decreasing (or increasing) the weight of fuel carried permits a one to one increase (or reduction) in the payload that can be carried. Aircraft using combustible fuels actually lose weight during flight, and this weight reduction must be taken into account when calculating a vehicle's balance and stability. Electrically powered aircraft do not see a significant weight change as the batteries deplete however.

The easiest way to determine the weight of an aircraft is to either place it on a scale (or scales if large enough) or to measure the weight using a sling arrangement, holding the aircraft from above. In either case, the scales should be checked for accuracy prior to calculating the weight of the aircraft. The aircraft should be weighed empty (minus fuel and payload) as well as fully fueled and then with the payload installed. This information should be recorded to assist in further calculating the balance and stability of the aircraft.

A template such as that shown in Table 7-1 can be used to document the aircraft weight and balance information.

- The empty weight of the aircraft is defined as its weight with everything installed except the fuel and the payload.
- Fuel weight can be calculated by weighing the aircraft without fuel, then with fuel. The difference is the weight of the fuel.
- Payload should be weighed prior to installation on the aircraft.
- Total weight can either be directly measured by weighing the aircraft in its takeoff configuration or calculated as the empty weight plus fuel and payload.
- Landing weight can be calculated as the total weight minus the fuel used during flight.

WEIGHT AND BALANCE TEMPLATE

Empty Weight	Fuel Weight	Payload Weight	Total Weight (Takeoff)	Fuel Used During Flight	Landing Weight

Table 7-1. Weight and Balance table example.

WEIGHT LIMITATIONS

Aircraft designers should set a maximum weight for an aircraft, basing this calculation on the lift the wings or rotors can provide under the operational conditions for which the aircraft is designed. The structural strength of the aircraft will also limit the maximum weight the aircraft can safely carry. As significant G loads are likely be encountered in flight, the total weight of the aircraft at takeoff should never exceed the predetermined maximum aircraft weight limit.

CENTER OF GRAVITY

The center of gravity (CG) of an aircraft is that point around which the aircraft rotates when moving through one of the three axes of motion (roll, pitch and yaw). Another way to think about it is that the center of gravity is that point at which the total weight of the aircraft is assumed to be concentrated. The center of gravity is that point over which the aircraft would balance if it could be suspended in some way from that point.

The center of gravity can be calculated in three dimensions: longitudinally, laterally and vertically. In general, based upon the configuration of most aircraft, the vertical CG is seldom calculated, but it must be considered for some stability and loading problems. These will be discussed later in this chapter. Since most aircraft "look the same" on both the left and right sides, lateral stability is usually less of a problem for fixed wing aircraft, but is important for rotorcraft. Longitudinal stability is important for all aircraft and must be calculated before each flight.

The ideal location of the (longitudinal) center of gravity on a fixed with aircraft is slightly ahead of the center of lift provided by the wings. In this configuration, the aircraft tends to pitch down, with the down force provided by the horizontal stabilizer in the tail keeping the airplane level. To remain stable, the CG must always remain forward of the center of lift (CL). If the CG approaches the CL, or even gets behind it, the aircraft will uncontrollably pitch up, stall and crash. If the CG moves too far forward of the CL however, the tail will be unable to provide sufficient down force, and the aircraft will enter an unrecoverable dive. Therefore both forward and rearward limits to the center of gravity must be established and adhered to.

The CG limits of production aircraft have been very carefully determined by the designers and confirmed during test flying of the aircraft. Some model aircraft have limits published as well, but many do not, and any aircraft self-designed and built will need to have their own limits established. In general, for fixed wing aircraft that have straight wings, the CG should be located somewhere between 20% and 35% of the mean aerodynamic chord (MAC) of the wing. To provide maximum stability, it should probably be closer to 25%-30% of the MAC. The mean aerodynamic chord of a wing can be determined by measuring the "width" of the wing. Since many UAVs use a straight, non-swept wing, this measurement is pretty straightforward.

For example, as shown in Table 7-2 if a wing were 12 inches wide (30 cm), percentage MAC positions could be easily calculated and could be marked on the wing. This set of calculations can easily be made for any MAC and wing configuration.

CENTER OF GRAVITY CALCULATION

There are two ways to determine the CG of small UASs: mathematically and using a balance stand. The mathematical method is more precise (and is the only method allowable for use on large UAVs) and needs to be fully understood. The center of gravity of any aircraft is calculated as follows:

1. The aircraft must be weighed using accurate, sensitive, and preferably calibrated scales. At least three scales must be used or a single scale with spacer blocks to keep the aircraft level as the single scale is moved from wheel to wheel. A fixed wing aircraft is normally weighed by placing the scales under the landing gear. Aircraft without landing gear can still be weighed using this method by placing stands where the gear would be located. The weight of the stand needs to be removed from any calculation however.
2. The distance of each scale (longitudinally) from a common reference point (called a datum) must be established. This distance is known as the "arm". A common datum point is the forward most part of the aircraft.
3. Multiply each scale weight by its arm, which results in a "moment".
4. Add the scale weights together to get a total weight of the aircraft.
5. Add all calculated moments together to get a total moment for the aircraft
6. Divide the total moment by the total weight. The result is the center of gravity measured in distance from the datum.

MAC CALCULATIONS

Distance from the Leading Edge In:

%MAC	Centimeters	Inches
20%	6.0	2.4
25%	7.5	3.0
30%	9.0	3.6
35%	10.5	4.2

Table 7-2. MAC calculations table.

CALCULATING AN AIRCRAFT'S CG

For example, if a fully loaded aircraft were placed on three scales, and the following weights were determined, the weight and balance calculation would look something like.

Forward scale (#1) =17
Left scale (#2) = 24
Right scale (#3) = 26

If the aircraft in question had a 12 inch wide wing, and the leading edge was at datum location XX, This aircraft would have a CG located at 35% of the MAC.

SAMPLE CENTER OF GRAVITY TABLE

Scale	Weight	Arm	Moment
#1			
#2			
#3			
Total			
Total Moment/Total Weight = (This is Center of Gravity)			0.00

Table 7-3. Sample Center of Gravity calculation table.

You should probably perform this calculation first with the aircraft fully loaded (payload) but with no fuel. This would simulate the most extreme landing situation. You would then add fuel and calculate the fully loaded CG. This would simulate the most extreme takeoff situation. So long as both CGs remain within limits, you have assured initial stability of the aircraft.

STABILITY AND BALANCE

Balance control refers to the location of the CG of an aircraft. CG location is important to aircraft stability, which determines safety in flight. CG must be located and remain within specific limits during the entire flight. If the CG is not within the CG limits previously described, you will need to either move payload or adjust the location of movable aircraft components until correct balance is achieved. As a last resort, some form of ballast or dead weight could be added to the aircraft. Care must be taken when adding ballast as this not only adds weight to the aircraft, it may also add stress to the aircraft in a location that was not so designed. Lead is a common material used for ballast as it is compact, yet very heavy. It is imperative that ballast be mounted securely so that it cannot become dislodged in flight or the aircraft might become uncontrollable and crash as a result.

CENTER OF GRAVITY TABLE

Scale	Weight	Arm	Moment
#1	17	12	204
#2	24	23	552
#3	26	23	598
Total	67	-	1357
Total Moment/Total Weight = (This is Center of Gravity)			20.21

Table 7-4. Center of Gravity calculation table.

You must check the weight and balance over the entire flight profile to ensure stability. In general, that means fully loaded with fuel, and also with minimum or no fuel. If you are going to add (or drop) payload in flight, those conditions also have to be considered. These can either be calculated or actually weighed to ensure that the aircraft CG remains within limits.

ROTORCRAFT STABILITY

Rotorcraft weight and balance is a little more complicated. On a single rotor aircraft, the center of lift is assumed to occur at the point of the rotor shaft. With multi rotor aircraft, the geometric center of all the rotors is considered to be the center of lift.

In general, the center of gravity of any rotorcraft should be as close to the center of lift, both laterally and longitudinally. When calculating the lateral CG of a rotorcraft, the rotor axle is often used as the datum, as this simplifies the calculations. Arms to the left of the rotor centerpoint are considered to be negative, while arms to the right are positive. If the rotorcraft has a nose wheel, the weight from it can be disregarded when calculating lateral stability, assuming the nose gear is centered along the airframe. If the helicopter is skid equipped, the weight measured at each skid can be used for the calculation.

		LONGITUDINAL			LATERAL	
Scale	Weight	Arm	Moment	Arm	Moment	
#1	11	5	55	0	0	
#2	44	14	616	+5	220	
#3	46	14	644	-5	-230	
Total	101		1354		-10	
Total Moment/Total Weight = Center of Gravity		Longitudinal CG = 13.01			Lateral CG = 0.10	

Table 7-5. Sample Helicopter Weight and Balance Table.

The goal of weight distribution on a helicopter is to insure that the CG is as close to the CL in both lateral and longitudinal directions as possible. If it is not, the helicopter will tend to "tilt" in the heavy direction, necessitating a constant compensation from the rotor. This not only diverts needed power and weight carrying capability from the aircraft, but also limits the amount of control authority present on that side if the aircraft were to encounter turbulence when its level flight is disturbed.

Multirotor aircraft can be considered similar to helicopters. The center of lift is most likely located very near the exact center of the aircraft. As multirotor aircraft do not usually have conventional landing gear, some sort of stand may need to be constructed that will hold the multirotor on the scales.

MECHANICAL BALANCING

An easy (but less accurate) method of balancing a small UAS is to balance the aircraft either on two fingers or a specially built balance stand. For a fixed wing aircraft, you place the tips of a finger (or the balance stand) under each wing, a couple of inches out from the fuselage sides. Then lift the plane up and let it hang freely.

A correctly balanced vehicle will either be level or have the nose pointing slightly downwards. If the aircraft does not balance in a level position, move your fingers (or the aircraft position on the stand) in unison, either fore or aft until the aircraft remains balanced. Once accomplished, mark or note your finger positions; you have just established where along the MAC the CG is located.

SPECIAL STABILITY ISSUES

The stability conditions discussed so far are called "static stability". They are stability measurements calculated without considering the movement of the aircraft or payload while in flight. Dynamic stability is a measurement of stability during flight. Positive dynamic stability is generally assumed to exist whenever an aircraft's attitude is changed (by either turbulence or intentional control movements) and the aircraft tends to return back to its original attitude. Negative dynamic stability is a condition whereby when an aircraft's attitude is changed, the movement around the axis of control increases and becomes more pronounced with each oscillation. An aircraft with negative dynamic stability is virtually uncontrollable by any manual flight means and may require a computer controlled flight system to avoid crashing.

Entire textbooks have been written about dynamic aerodynamic stability. The primary cause of longitudinal instability in an aircraft occurs if the CG is allowed be either very close to, or beyond the limitations of the aircraft. Another cause of dynamic instability, primarily found in UAVs is the improper positioning of payload in the vertical axis. In general, any weight placed below the aircrafts actual CG location will make the aircraft more dynamically stable; but weights placed above the CG will tend to create instability. In other words, it's best to keep heavy payload below the rotors or wings, not above them. It is common practice to place payload and cargo bays very near, or directly below, the center of gravity of a UAV.

CHAPTER 8

AIRSPACE OPERATIONS

The Federal Aviation Administration has the authority and the responsibility to provide for safe aircraft operations within the airspace of the United States. Details concerning the FAAs operational authority over UASs are covered in chapter 11 This chapter primarily covers airspace operations of both manned aircraft and UAVs.

AIRSPACE

To provide aircraft operators with flexibility while still insuring appropriate levels of safety, the airspace above the United States has been categorized into different classes with specific requirements and different rules for operating in each. Differing airspace classifications and rules permit the FAA to provide varying levels of security and control. In general, airspace classification is designed to provide maximum separation and active control in areas of dense or high-speed flight operations. The requirements for operating in each airspace area differ based on the type of aircraft operation commonly found within each.

IFR, or instrument flight rules, specify the procedures used by aircraft when the air traffic control (ATC) system provides separation from other aircraft. IFR aircraft are required to file flight plans and receive operating clearances, while maintaining contact with and adhering to ATC instructions. Airline, military, most corporate, and many general aviation flights are conducted under IFR. VFR, or visual flight rules, specify the rules by which aircraft can operate without using ATC.

UAS operators and VFR pilots provide their own separation from IFR and other VFR aircraft using the "see and avoid" principle. VFR is primarily used by smaller and slower aircraft and is limited to areas without a lot of air traffic and only during periods of good weather. Small UASs primarily operate under VFR rules and procedures. Larger UASs or any UAS operation being conducted when it is difficult for the operator to provide separation would need to be operated under IFR. As of now, there are no current or proposed procedures or regulations for operating a UAV under IFR rules. Those operations that have been permitted required special exceptions from the FAA.

Unmanned Aerial Systems: The Definitive Guide

AIRSPACE CLASSIFICATIONS

To delineate how both IFR and VFR operations are to be conducted, the airspace above the U.S. has been classified into one of four general categories with overall operating policies for each.

- Positive controlled airspace (PCA) - ATC separates all aircraft, whether IFR or VFR.
- Controlled airspace - ATC separates IFR aircraft but VFR pilots provide their own separation.
- Uncontrolled airspace - pilots provide their own separation, regardless of whether they are IFR or VFR.
- Special use airspace (SUAS) - airspace within which there are special operating restrictions and rules.

AIRSPACE CLASSES AND NAVIGATIONAL CHARTS

To differentiate the services offered in controlled and uncontrolled airspace, the FAA has developed seven standardized airspace categories, defined as: Class A, B, C, D, E, F and G. Classes A through E are designated as controlled airspace. Class F is an international airspace designator not currently used in the U.S. Class G is uncontrolled airspace. In general, Class A airspace is the most restrictive airspace. Class G airspace is the least restrictive with few ATC services provided. Class B, C, D, and E airspace spans the range of services. Special use airspace has been defined by the FAA to restrict certain special operations as well.

In general, UAS operations under instrument flight rules (IFR) are not permitted. Some special military drone operations are conducted in IFR, but for all intents and purposes, civilian UAS flights must operate in VFR conditions at all times.

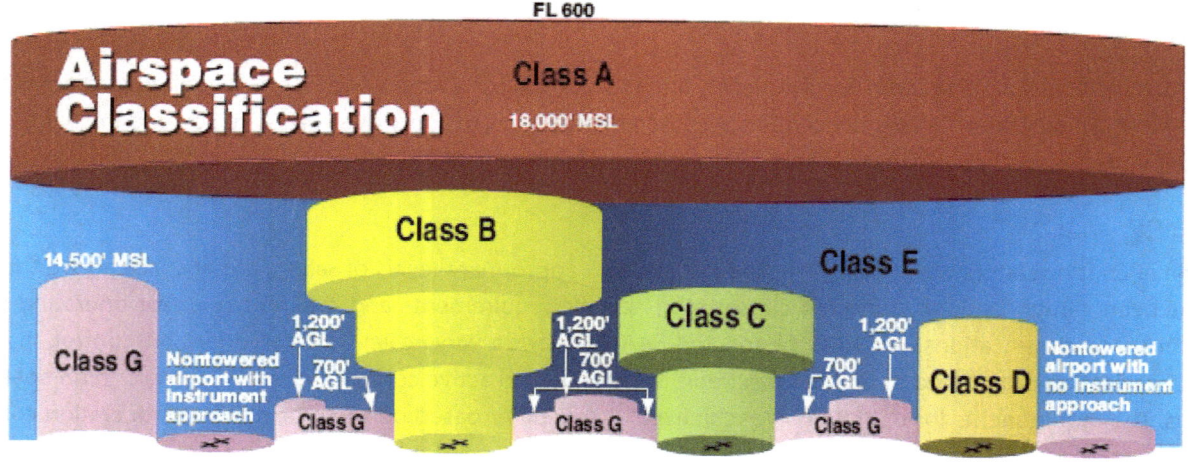

Figure 8-1. Airspace classes in the U.S.

IFR FLIGHT IN CONTROLLED AIRSPACE (CLASS A, B, C, D, AND E)

Within controlled airspace, air traffic controllers are always required to separate IFR aircraft and are sometimes required to separate VFR aircraft. IFR aircraft must file a flight plan and receive a clearance to operate in controlled airspace. Since VFR aircraft can operate in areas of controlled airspace as well, (sometime without contacting ATC), it remains the responsibility of operators to see and avoid IFR aircraft, regardless of the services being provided by the air traffic controller.

UAS AND VFR FLIGHT IN CONTROLLED AIRSPACE (CLASS A, B, C, D, AND E)

VFR and UAS flight is not permitted in Class A airspace. In class B, C, D, and E, UAS and VFR flight may be permitted so long as certain requirements are met. Operation in any one of these classes of airspace requires that the pilot or operator see and avoid all other aircraft, whether IFR or VFR, regardless of whether an ATC facility is involved.

IFR FLIGHT IN UNCONTROLLED AIRSPACE (CLASS G)

Within uncontrolled airspace, air traffic controllers are not able to, nor permitted, to provide any aircraft separation services. If an IFR aircraft wishes to operate in controlled airspace, it is the pilot's responsibility to separate their vehicle from all obstructions and/or other aircraft. Once the aircraft enters controlled airspace, ATC separation services will be provided to IFR aircraft. A flight plan is not required to operate IFR in uncontrolled airspace, but a flight plan and clearance would be required if the aircraft were to transition to or pass through any area of controlled airspace.

UAS AND VFR FLIGHT IN UNCONTROLLED AIRSPACE (CLASS G)

Just as with IFR flight within uncontrolled airspace, air traffic controllers are not able, nor permitted, to provide any aircraft separation services to any aircraft in class G airspace. If an operator wishes to operate in uncontrolled airspace, they may do so, as long as the weather permits the pilot or operator to separate their vehicle from all obstructions and/or nearby aircraft. A flight plan is not required to operate in uncontrolled airspace.

AERONAUTICAL CHARTING

Maps used by pilots in the early 1920s were common road maps available at automobile service stations. These maps were unsuitable for aerial navigation since they lacked the necessary landmark information needed to accurately navigate from one airport to the next. The U.S. government began to print air navigation charts around that time, and these charts are now known as sectional charts.

SECTIONAL CHARTS

Sectional charts are aeronautical charts scaled 1:500,000 or about 8 statute miles to the inch. Sectional charts are still used today and depict the relevant information needed by pilots to navigate accurately and safely. This information includes cities, highways, railroads, airport locations, terrain features, and distinctive objects. Sectional charts also depict navigation aids, federal airways, and air traffic control facilities.

Some pilots carry world aeronautical charts (WACs) instead of sectionals during IFR flights. (See figure 8-3).WACs are similar to sectionals but are scaled 1:1,000,000 or about 16 miles to the inch. They present less-detailed information to the pilot but cover a larger area than a sectional chart.

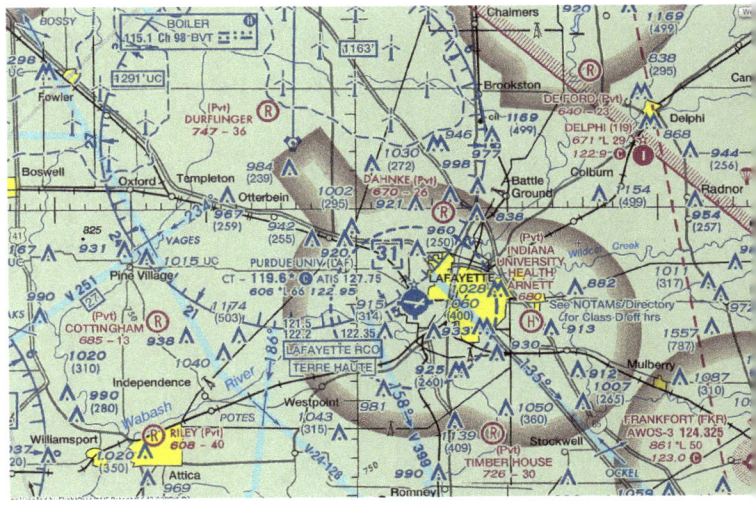

Figure 8-2. Sectional chart excerpt.

INSTRUMENT CHARTS

Pilots navigating using IFR charts and procedures Pilots flying using instrument flight rules (IFR) have more demanding navigational needs. Depending on their cruising altitude, operators use either low altitude (below 18,000 ft.) or high altitude (18,000 ft. and above) enroute charts to navigate from airport to airport. These charts are similar to sectionals and WACs but omit most terrain and other ground based information used by VFR operators. IFR charts provide electronic navigational information as well as radio frequencies and cruising altitude information. An excellent guide to understanding both VFR and IFR charts can be downloaded from the FAA publications website. The document is entitled "Aeronautical Chart Users Guide".

AIR TRAFFIC CONTROL FACILITIES

Air traffic control, usually abbreviated as ATC, exists not only to provide for the safety of aircraft as they travel from airport to airport, but also to effectively and efficiently manage all the resources needed to operate the complex system of navigation aids (navaids), communications, and traffic management systems, as well as air traffic control facilities. This combination of facilities is commonly known in the U.S. as the national airspace system or NAS.

Unmanned Aerial Systems: The Definitive Guide

Chapter 8

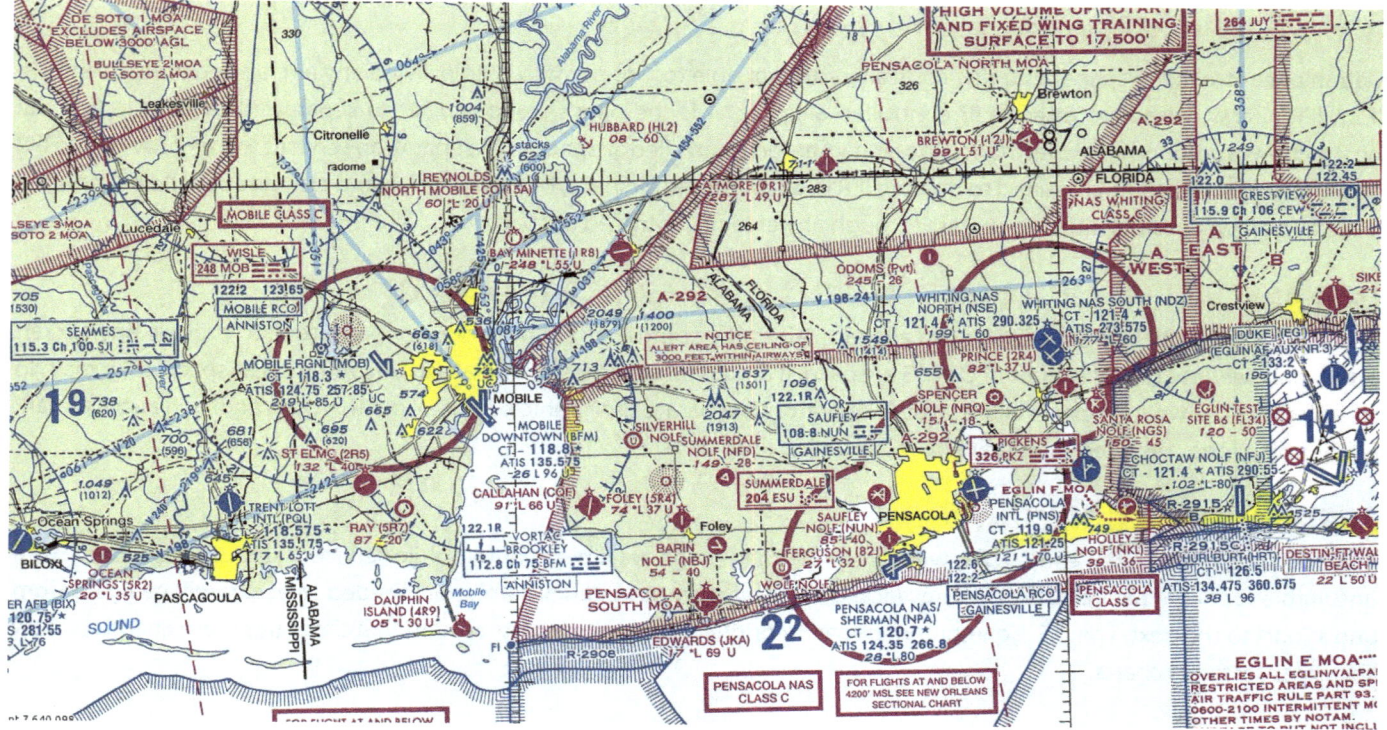

Figure 8-3. World aeronautical chart (WAC) excerpt.

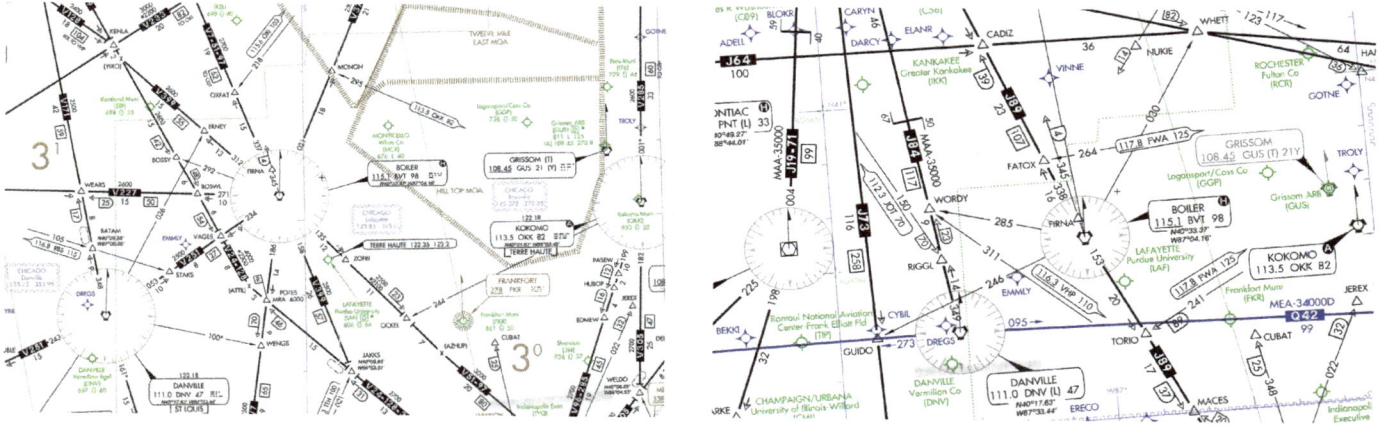

Figure 8-4. Low altitudes IFR chart.

Figure 8-5. High altitude IFR chart.

CONTROL TOWERS

Air traffic controllers working in the glass enclosed control tower cabs manage traffic within a radius of a few miles of the airport using both visual and electronic means. They instruct pilots and operators during taxiing, takeoff, and landing, and they grant clearances for aircraft to fly. Tower controllers ensure minimum separation distances between landing and departing aircraft, transfer control to radar controllers when aircraft leave their airspace, and receive control of aircraft for flights coming into their airspace.

TERMINAL RADAR APPROACH CONTROL (TRACON)

Air traffic controllers working in TRACONs typically manage traffic, using radar, within a 40-mile radius of the primary airport up to 10,000-15,000 feet above the airport. They separate departing and arriving flights, and grant clearances for aircraft to fly through the TRACON's airspace. These controllers ensure that aircraft maintain minimum separation while within their airspace, transfer control of aircraft to tower or enroute center controllers when the aircraft leave their airspace, and receive control of aircraft for flights coming into their airspace.

TRACON airspace is usually divided into discrete sectors that can provide services to eithersingle or multiple airports. Consolidated or large TRACONs in major metropolitan areas provide service to several primary airports. Their airspace is divided into areas of specialization, each of which contains groups of sectors.

A consolidated TRACON is a standalone air traffic control facility that provides radar control service to aircraft arriving or departing the primary airport and adjacent airports as well as to aircraft transiting the facility's airspace. Consolidated TRACONs are not specifically related to any one control tower or airport, and may not even by located at or near an airport.

COMBINED RADAR APPROACH CONTROL AND TOWER WITH RADAR

A Combined Radar Approach Control and Tower with Radar is an air traffic control facility that provides radar control services to aircraft arriving or departing the primary airport and adjacent airports and to aircraft transiting the facility's airspace, but it also has a tower to control traffic landing and departing at the primary airport. This facility would be operationally divided into two functional areas: radar approach control and tower. These two functional areas might be located within the same facility or in close proximity to one another. Controllers assigned to this facility would be certified and commonly work in both areas.

ENROUTE AIR TRAFFIC CONTROL

Air Route Traffic Control Centers (ARTCC) separate aircraft (primarily IFR) flying outside of or above TRACON airspace. They also provide approach control services to small airports where no TRACON service is provided. Each center's airspace is divided into smaller, more manageable blocks of airspace called areas and sectors.

FLIGHT SERVICE STATIONS

Flight Service Stations (FSSs) primarily provide preflight, in-flight, and enroute communications and weather services to private and corporate aircraft. FSSs also coordinate search and rescue operations and provide operational support to air shows, conventions, and other aviation events.

Flight Services Stations were previously owned and operated by the FAA. Due to the inherent limitations of radio communications in the early twentieth century, FSS stations were initially placed along major air routes spaced every 30 to 50 miles. As air travel grew, this eventually resulted in hundreds of stations across the country.

In 1985, the FAA embarked on a consolidation program to establish a limited number of "super" or Automated Flight Service Stations (AFSS). The FAA consolidated the FSS network and reduced the number of facilities to about 100 during this time period. In 2005, the FAA awarded a private contract for the operation and staffing of AFSSs in the continental United States, Puerto Rico, and Hawaii to the Lockheed-Martin (LM) Corporation. Flight service stations in Alaska are still operated by the FAA. LM assumed responsibility for providing flight services at these stations beginning in October 2005. The FAA still provides oversight, but LM has the operational authority to deliver all FSS services. These services are provided to operators through a system of FSS hubs located in Virginia, Arizona, and Texas. All flight service specialists complete FAA-approved air traffic control training and are certified by the National Weather Service (NWS) as pilot weather briefers.

ATC SERVICES IN DIFFERENT AIRSPACE CLASSES

The separation and services provided by ATC to aircraft differ based upon the airspace within which they are operating as well as the type of operation being conducted (IFR or VFR). Class A airspace generally exists at and above 18,000 ft. The federal aviation regulations require that every aircraft operating within Class A airspace operate under instrument flight rules and receive a clearance from ATC. VFR and UAS flight is not permitted in Class A airspace. Class A airspace is not specifically designated on navigational charts.

Chapter 8

Figure 8-6. Class B airspace as depicted on a VFR navigation chart.

Class B airspace exists around the nation's busiest airports from the earth's surface up to an altitude of about 10,000 ft. Class B airspace "rings" the primary airport and may have a number of areas that do not extend down to the ground. Under the UAS rules proposed by the 2015 NPRM, UASs can operate in Class B airspace if they have received permission from the ATC facility (normally the TRACON) that has responsibility for that airspace.

Class C airspace surrounds medium-activity airports. Class C airspace extends from the Earth's surface, up to about 4,000 feet above ground level. There is normally at least one shelf of airspace that does not extend to the earth's surface. Under the UAS rules proposed by the 2015 NPRM, UAS operators will need permission to operate in Class C airspace. This permission can be obtained from the controlling TRACON.

Class D airspace exists from the earth's surface up to 2,500 feet above the airport elevation. Class D airspace surrounds airports that have an operating control tower. Both IFR and VFR pilots are required to establish two-way radio communication with the air traffic control tower prior to entering the Class D airspace. Under the rules proposed by the 2015 NPRM, UAS operators need to obtain permission to operate in Class D airspace.

Class D airspace is depicted on sectional charts by blue dashed lines. Since a control tower within class D airspace most likely does not have radar, they are unable to separate aircraft from each other, but can advise pilots of possible traffic. If a control tower operates less than 24 hours per day, when the tower is closed, the airspace reverts to Class E.

Generally, if the airspace is not Class A, B, C, or D, and not very close to the ground (700 ft. or 1,200 ft. AGL), it will be designated as Class E airspace. In general, across the continental U.S., Class E airspace begins 1,200 ft. above the ground and extends upward until reaching the base of Class A airspace (18,000 ft.).

In some areas of the country, to accommodate airport instrument approaches, the base of Class E airspace is designated as 700' above the ground. This area is so designated on sectional charts with magenta shading. There are some areas of the country where Class E airspace extends to the ground. Those areas are designated on sectional charts with dashed magenta lines. Under the UAS rules proposed by the 2015 NPRM, individuals wishing to operate UASs in Class E airspace must obtain permission from the controlling agency. The controlling agency may be difficult to determine, as it could be a nearby TRACON or possibly the ARTCC. The digital Airport/Facility Directory published online by the FAA will normally list a facility associated with each airport. Although it may not in fact be the controlling facility, they should be able to provide appropriate contact information.

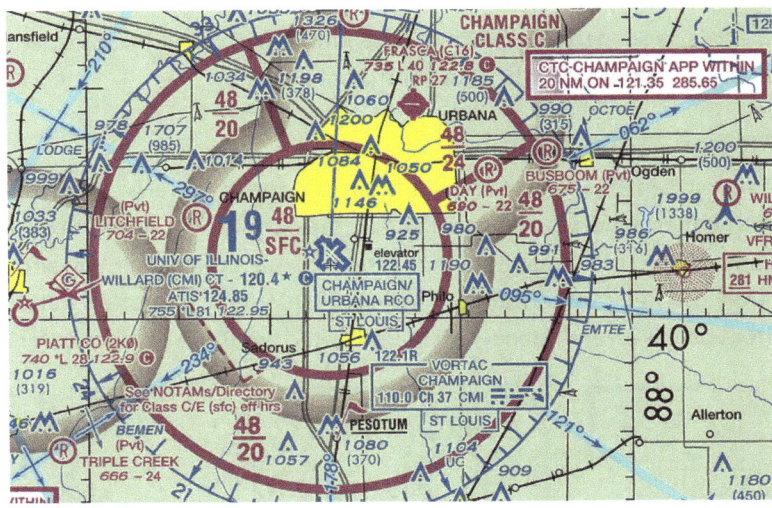

Figure 8-7. Class C airspace as depicted on a VFR navigation chart.

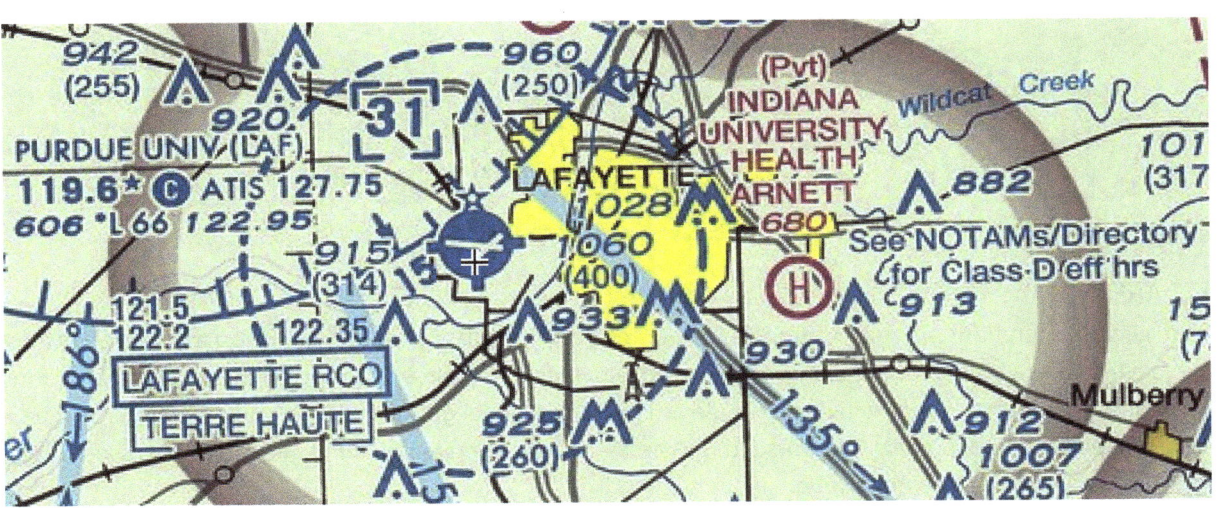

Figure 8-8. Class D airspace as depicted on a VFR navigation chart.

CLASS F AND G AIRSPACE

Class F airspace is not used in the United States. It is used internationally in areas of limited ATC capability. Class G airspace is used in the U.S. however and is defined as airspace within which ATC services are not provided to any aircraft. In general, if airspace is not Class A, B, C, D or E, it is Class G. Most of the Class G airspace in this country is located away from major airports and below 1,200 feet AGL. Under the proposed UAS rules, most UAS operations will be conducted in Class G airspace.

SPECIAL USE AIRSPACE

In numerous areas scattered around the United States, it is in the national interest to either restrict or completely prohibit the flight of civilian aircraft. The U.S. government, through the Federal Aviation Regulations, has designated these areas as special use airspace. Special use airspace is designed to either confine unique aircraft operations or to entirely prohibit flight within the specified area. Unless otherwise noted, all of the following examples of special use airspace are published on VFR and IFR navigation charts and are designated in appropriate aeronautical publications. Operations in, or infringement of, special use airspace can have some serious implications for UAS operators. The most current depiction of special use airspace can be obtained from the FAA at http://sua.faa.gov/.

PROHIBITED AREAS

A prohibited area is airspace where aircraft operations are absolutely prohibited by law. These areas are directly concerned with either national security or public safety. Among the prohibited areas are the White House, the Capitol Building, and Camp David. The regulations expressly prohibit either IFR or VFR aircraft from entering such areas without specific (and very rarely granted) authorization. Air traffic controllers are not permitted to authorize civilian aircraft operations within these areas unless an emergency exists. Prohibited areas are numbered for reference prefixed with the letter "P".

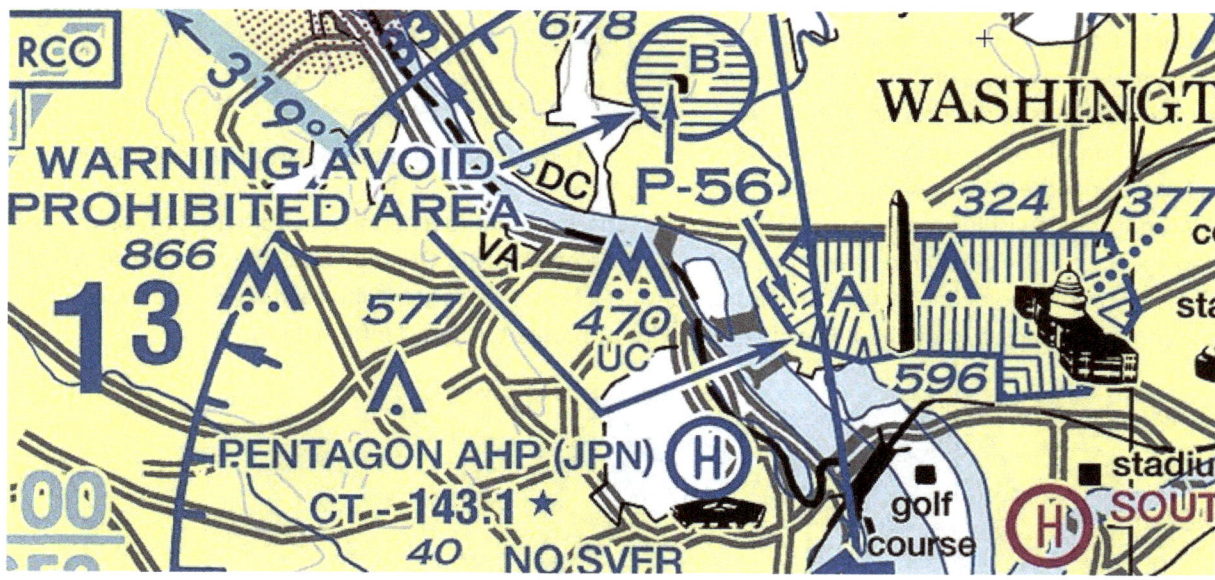

Figure 8-9. Prohibited areas over Washington, D.C.

RESTRICTED AREAS

Locations where aircraft operations are not prohibited at all times but are subject to some restriction are labeled restricted areas. They are located where both airborne and ground-based activities are routinely conducted that may be hazardous to either the aircraft or its occupants. These activities include artillery firing, aerial gunnery, and high-energy laser and missile testing. Some restricted areas are in effect 24 hours a day, whereas others operate part-time. Restricted areas are available for civilian flight whenever they are not active. Restricted areas are numbered for reference prefixed with the letter "R" and are normally controlled by the appropriate air route traffic control center.

TEMPORARY FLIGHT RESTRICTIONS

The FAA may impose temporary flight restrictions (TFRs) around any incident or accident that has the potential for attracting a sufficient number of aircraft to create a hazard to either other aircraft in the air or people on the ground. Temporary flight restrictions may be imposed around earthquake, flood, fire, or aircraft crash sites. TFRs essentially operate like temporary, ad-hoc restricted areas.

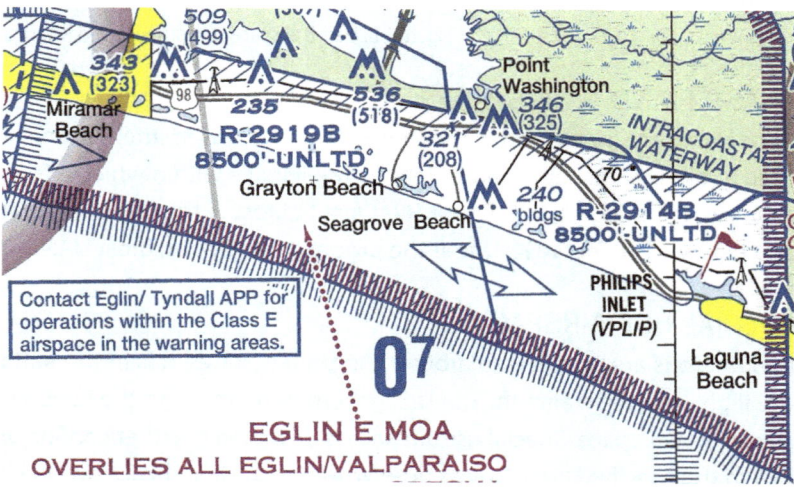

Figure 8-10. Restricted area in northwest Florida.

When a temporary flight restriction is imposed, the FAA notifies UAS operators by issuing a notice to airmen (NOTAM). These notices are distributed nationwide to FAA air traffic control towers, air route traffic control centers, and flight service stations, who then relay the information to UAS operators. In addition, NOTAMs are transmitted to the airlines, military services, and many independent UAS operators-briefing companies who make the information available to their subscribers. An up to date list of TFRs can be obtained at http://tfr.faa.gov/. The dimensions of the TFR, the effective dates and time, and the reason for the imposition of the TFR are provided, as is the identity of the controlling agency. By their very nature, TFRs are dynamic; therefore the UAS operator should check the status of TFRs prior to every flight.

SPECIAL FLIGHT RULES AREAS

There have been special flight rules areas (SFRAs) around the United States for many years and are primarily found in either areas with congested/complex airspace (Anchorage) or areas with large numbers of VFR flights (Grand Canyon and Los Angeles). Following the attacks of September 2001, the airspace around Washington underwent a number of changes designed to restrict flight operations. After a number of VFR accidents in and around New York City, special flight rules were set up there as well. All of these areas of special flight rules are codified in part 93 (special air traffic rules) of the Federal Aviation Regulations and affect the following areas:

Anchorage	AK
Ketchikan	AK
Grand Canyon	AZ
Luke AFB	AZ
Los Angeles	CA
Washington	D.C.
Valparaiso	FL (Eglin AFB)
New York	NY
Niagara Falls	NY
Lorain County	OH (Cleveland area)

Table 8-1. Special flight rules areas.

In order to fly within any of these SFRAs, UAS operators must conform to the routes, procedures and altitudes specified in FAR 93 or may be subject to penalty by the FAA. Air traffic procedures for these areas may be modified from the standard to incorporate these requirements. Although most of these do not currently affect UAS operators, the existence of and the reasons for the creation of each of these areas should be taken into account before flying within the vicinity of FAR part 93 airspace.

DC FLIGHT RESTRICTED ZONE AND SPECIAL FLIGHT RULES AREA

The FAA established the Washington, D.C. Flight Restricted Zone and Special Flight Rules Area in 2003 to restrict air traffic around the nation's capital. There are very specific rules and penalties for violating the rules pursuant to flying within this airspace. At present, most of the restrictions concern piloted aircraft, but could be expanded in the future. UAS operators who do not adhere to the proper procedures could be detained and interviewed by law enforcement personnel. The DC FRZ extends outward roughly 30 nm in radius from Washington, D.C. and extends vertically from the ground up to, but not including, FL 180.

WARNING AREA

A warning area is airspace located over international waters where operations that may be hazardous to nonparticipating aircraft are routinely conducted. The activities conducted in a warning area are usually similar to those performed in a restricted area. Since warning areas are located in international airspace, neither the United States nor any other government has the right to restrict the flight of aircraft through these areas. Both IFR and VFR aircraft may operate in warning areas, but they do so at their own risk.

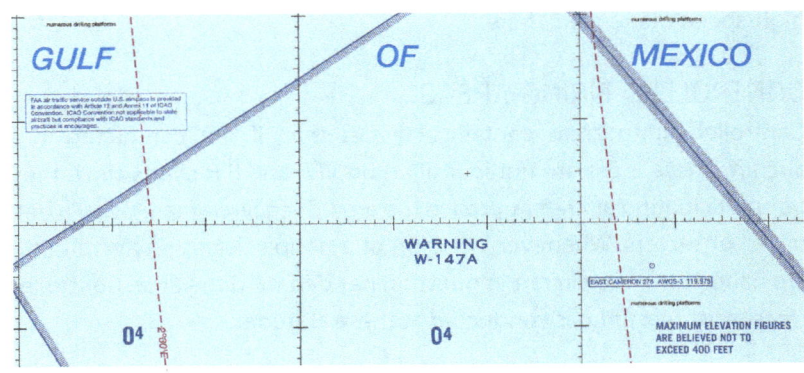

Figure 8-11. Warning area located in the Gulf of Mexico.

Unmanned Aerial Systems: The Definitive Guide

MILITARY OPERATIONS AREA

A military operations area (MOA) is designated airspace where military flight training activities routinely take place that might prove hazardous to civilian aircraft. Some of the flight training being conducted by military aircraft requires acrobatic maneuvers to be practiced on or near a federal airway. Although acrobatic flight along a federal airway is forbidden by federal regulation, the Department of Defense has been exempted if the maneuvers are conducted within an MOA.

MILITARY TRAINING ROUTES

Military UAS operators are required to practice low-level, high-speed, combat-training flights. The maneuvers performed during these training flights make the "see and avoid" concept of traffic separation difficult without increased vigilance on the part of both military and civilian operators. To assist civilian operators to avoid military aircraft, the FAA and the Department of Defense have mutually agreed to participate in the military training route (MTR) program. Through this program, designated MTR routes have been designated by both the FAA and the DOD and are depicted on VFR navigation charts as "VR" routes.

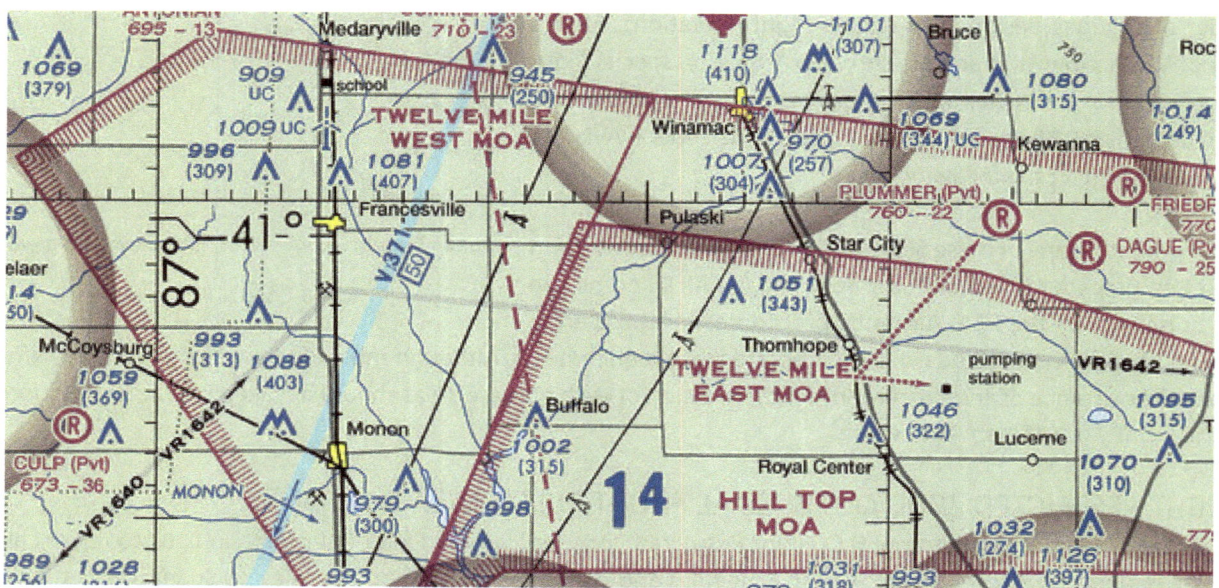

Figure 8-12. MOAs and military training routes.

ALERT AREAS

Alert areas are airspace that may contain a large number of high-performance military training aircraft conducting routine training exercises. Although there are no legal restrictions to civilian aircraft flying through an alert area, both IFR and VFR operators transiting the area should be aware of the large numbers of military aircraft that may be practicing nonacrobatic high-speed maneuvers there.

CONTROLLED FIRING AREAS

Controlled firing areas contain activities that, if not conducted in a controlled environment, could be hazardous to aircraft. These areas are not identified on VFR and IFR charts since the controlling agency suspends its activities whenever nonparticipating aircraft approach the area. Such aircraft are usually detected by the use of spotter aircraft, radar, or ground-based observers. Whenever intrusion of a nonparticipating aircraft into a controlled firing area is detected, the test firings are halted until the aircraft in question has departed the area. Controlled firing areas predominantly affect low flying aircraft since most test firing is conducted at these altitudes.

NATIONAL SECURITY AREAS

National security areas (NSAs) consist of airspace established at locations where increased security and safety of ground facilities are required. VFR operators are requested to voluntarily avoid flying through NSAs whenever possible.

COMMUNICATIONS SYSTEMS

RADIO PHRASEOLOGY

The operation of the air traffic control system ultimately depends on reliable and accurate communication between UAS operators and air traffic controllers. Virtually every instruction, procedure, or clearance used to separate or assist aircraft relies on written or verbal communication. Any miscommunication between participants in the air traffic control system might contribute to or even be the direct cause of an aircraft accident with a subsequent loss of life. Radio is the primary means of ATC communication although various forms of digital (text and graphic) transmission of information is slowly becoming available.

To ensure that miscommunication is kept to a minimum, it is imperative that standard phraseology and procedures be used when communicating with pilots, operators, or controllers. The FAA and ICAO have agreed on a relatively common set of communication practices, but there are some difference between the standards defined by each agency. For the purpose of this text, FAA practices and procedures will be utilized.

STANDARD PRONUNCIATION

Certain letters and numbers may sound similar to one another when spoken over low-fidelity radio or telephone equipment. In addition, accents and dialects may make it difficult to discern and identify the exact content of a message. To alleviate this problem, a standard for pronunciation of letters and numbers has been approved by ICAO and adopted by the FAA.

NUMBERS

Numbers can be stated in two different ways: group form or individually. In general, unless specified otherwise, each number should be enunciated individually unless group form pronunciation is stipulated. For example the number 10 would be pronounced individually as "one zero", but in group form would be "ten". The number 1246 would be pronounced individually as "one two four six", but in group form as "twelve forty six". The following table indicates how letters and numbers should be commonly pronounced.

ALTITUDES

Unless otherwise specified, every altitude used in the ATC system is measured above mean sea level (MSL). The only routine exception are cloud ceilings, which are measured above ground level (AGL). Use of an AGL altitude requires the pilot or operator to explicitly indicate that the altitude being stated is above ground level. Altitudes should be separated into thousands and hundreds, with the thousands are always pronounced separate from the hundreds. Each digit of the thousands number should be enunciated individually, whereas the hundreds should be pronounced in group form. For example, the altitude 3,900 ft. would be pronounced "three thousand niner hundred". An altitude of 12,500 ft. would be pronounced as "one two thousand fife hundred". 17,000 ft. would be pronounced "one seven thousand".

CHARACTER	NUMBER	PRONUNCIATION
0	Zero	Zee-ro
1	One	Wun
2	Two	Too
3	Three	Tree
4	Four	Fow-er
5	Five	Fife
6	Six	Six
7	Seven	Sev-en
8	Eight	Ait
9	Nine	Nin-er

Table 8-2(A). Standard pronunciation of numbers table.

CHARACTER	WORD	PRONUNCIATION
A	Alpha	Al-fah
B	Bravo	Brah-voh
C	Charlie	Char-lee
D	Delta	Del-ta
E	Echo	Eck-oh
F	Foxtrot	Foks-trot
G	Golf	Golf
H	Hotel	Hoh-tell
I	India	In-dee-ah
J	Juliett	Jewlee-ett
K	Kilo	Key-loh
L	Lima	Lee-mah
M	Michael	Michael
N	November	Nov-em-ber
O	Oscar	Oss-cah
P	Papa	Pah-pah
Q	Quebec	Key-beck
R	Romeo	Row-me-oh
S	Sierra	See-air-ah
T	Tango	Tang-go
U	Uniform	You-nee-form
V	Victor	Vik-tah
W	Whiskey	Wiss-key
X	X-ray	Ecks-ray
Y	Yankee	Yang-key
Z	Zulu	Zoo-loo

Table 8-2(B). Standard pronunciation of letters table.

FLIGHT LEVELS

At or above 18,000 ft. MSL, all altitudes are called flight levels (FL). When communicating, flight levels should be preceded by the words "flight level," and each number should be enunciated individually. For example, 18,000 ft. MSL would be considered as FL180 and would be pronounced "flight level one eight zero". FL390 would be pronounced as "flight level three niner zero.

TIME

A common system of time measurement is essential to the safe operation of the ATC system. The FAA and ICAO have agreed that local time is not to be used within ATC. Instead, every ATC facility around the world must use the same time standard, known as coordinated universal time (UTC). UTC is the same as local time in Greenwich, England, which is located on the 0° line of longitude, known as the prime meridian. UTC was previously known as Greenwich Mean Time (GMT).

TIME ZONE	DIFFERENCE
Eastern standard time (EST)	5 hours
Eastern daylight time (EDT)	4 hours
Central standard time (CST)	6 hours
Central daylight time (CDT)	5 hours
Mountain standard time (MST)	7 hours
Mountain daylight time (MDT)	6 hours
Pacific standard time (PST)	8 hours
Pacific daylight time (PDT)	7 hours
Alaskan standard time (AST)	9 hours
Alaskan daylight time (ADT)	8 hours

Table 8-3. Standard time zones.

The use of UTC around the world eliminates the question of which time zone a facility or aircraft is located in. In addition, the use of UTC eliminates the need for "a.m." and "p.m." by using a 24-hour clock system. UTC is always issued as a four-digit number, and the word "o'clock" is never pronounced. For example, 6:20 a.m. becomes 0620, and 6:20 p.m. becomes 1820. Local time is converted to UTC by adding the number of hours indicated in the following chart (Table 8-3):

To convert from local time to UTC, convert the local time to a 24-hour clock, and then add the required time difference. To convert from UTC to local time, subtract the difference and convert from a 24-hour to a 12-hour format.

For example:
4:35 a.m. (EST) is 0435 (EST), which is 0935 (UTC)
9:13 p.m. (PDT) is 2113 (PDT), which is 0413 (UTC) the next day
1125 (UTC) is 0425 (MST), which is 4:25 a.m. (MST)

To prevent any confusion when issuing time, pilots and operators should suffix any UTC time with the word "zulu" and any local time with the word "local."

ALTIMETER SETTINGS

The proper barometric pressure must be used to insure that an altimeter indicates the correct altitude above mean sea level. Altimeter settings are enunciated by pronouncing every digit without the decimal point preceded by the word "altimeter":

ALTIMETER SETTING	PRONUNCIATION
29.92	Altimeter two niner niner two
30.16	Altimeter tree zero one six

Table 8-4. Altimeter setting pronunciations.

WIND DIRECTION AND VELOCITY

Wind direction at airports is always determined in reference to magnetic north and indicates the direction that the wind is blowing from. The direction is always rounded off to the nearest 10°. Thus, a wind blowing from north to south is a 360° wind; a wind from the east is a 90° wind. The international standard for measuring wind velocity requires that wind speeds be measured in knots; 1 knot equals approximately 1.15 miles per hour. Wind direction and velocity information is always preceded by the word "wind," with each digit of the wind direction enunciated individually. The wind direction is then followed by the word "at" and the wind velocity in knots, with each digit enunciated individually. If the wind direction is constantly changing, the word "variable" is suffixed to the average wind direction. If the wind velocity is constantly changing, the word "gusts" and the peak speed are suffixed to the wind speed. Here are some examples:

WIND DIRECTION	WIND SPEED	PRONUNCIATION
From the north	15 knots	Wind three six zero at one five
From the east	10 knots with occasional gusts to 25 knots	Wind zero niner zero at one zero gusts two five

Table 8-5. Wind direction pronunciations.

HEADINGS

Aircraft headings are also measured in reference to magnetic north. If the heading contains fewer than three digits, it should be preceded by a sufficient number of zeros to make a three-digit number. Aircraft headings should always be preceded by the word "heading," with each of the three digits enunciated individually. Unless absolutely necessary, headings are normally issued in even ten degree increments. Table 8-6.

HEADING	PRONUNCIATION
090°	Heading zero niner zero
125°	Heading one two fife
250°	Heading two fife zero

Table 8-6. Example heading pronunciations.

RADIO FREQUENCIES

When pronouncing issuing radio frequencies, each digit is enunciated individually. Current VHF communications radios use 25 kHz spacing between assigned frequencies. For instance, the next usable frequency above 119.600 is 119.625, followed by 119.650, 119.675, and 119.700. The first number after the decimal is always pronounced, whether or not it is a zero. But if the second number after the decimal is a zero, it is not pronounced. The third number after the decimal is never pronounced, since it is always either a zero or a five and can be assumed. VHF and UHF communication and navigation frequencies always use the decimal point. The decimal is pronounced as "point".

FREQUENCY	PRONUNCIATION
119.600 MHz	One one niner point six
343.000 MHz	Three four three point zero
123.050 MHz	One two three point zero five
131.725 MHz	One three one point seven two five

Table 8-7. Frequency pronunciations.

AIRCRAFT SPEEDS

Aircraft speeds, like wind speeds, are always measured in knots. Airspeeds are always expressed with each digit enunciated individually and suffixed with the word "knots," as in the speed Table 8-8.

Unmanned Aerial Systems: The Definitive Guide

AIR TRAFFIC CONTROL FACILITIES

ATC facilities are identified by name, using the name of the city where the facility is located followed by the type of facility or the operating position being communicated with. If a particular city has two or more airports, the airport name is used instead of the city name. Approach controls and centers are always named after the largest nearby city.

AIRWAYS, ROUTES, AND NAVIGATION AID DESCRIPTIONS

Airways are always described with the route identification pronounced in group form. The route number is prefixed with "victor" if it is a low-altitude airway, "jay" if it is a high altitude airway, and "tango" or "Q" if it a GPS based route.

AIRCRAFT IDENTIFICATION

Aircraft are identified using procedures that help eliminate confusion and misdirected instructions. The assigned aircraft identification call signs used by UAS operators and controllers vary depending on the type of operation in which the aircraft is involved. If the aircraft is a scheduled airline flight, the FAA has authorized the use of a distinctive airline name that should be used when communicating with that aircraft. In addition to this name, every airline flight has been issued a flight number by the airline itself. The approved aircraft identification consists of the airline name, followed by the flight number pronounced in group form (such as "United twenty-six eleven").

SPEED	PRONUNCIATION
250	Two fife zero knots
95	Niner fife knots

Table 8-8. Speed table.

FACILITY TYPE	PRONUNCIATION
Local control	Tower
Ground control	Ground
Clearance delivery	Clearance
Air route traffic control center	Center
Flight service station	Radio
Approach control	Approach
Departure control	Departure

Table 8-9. Air traffic control facilities.

ROUTE	PRONUNCIATION
V251	Victor two fifty-one
J97	Jay ninety-seven
T368	Tango tree sixty-eight
Q12	Cue twelve

Table 8-10. Route table.

Most authorized airline names are easily recognizable, although a few are somewhat unusual. These approved airline names have been selected to ensure that no two sound similar. Every airline has also been issued a three-letter designator to be used in written communications concerning the aircraft. A list of air carrier names and their three-letter identifiers can be found in the Contractions Handbook published by the FAA. Some larger corporate flight operations as well as flight schools have been issued identifiers as well.

General aviation, as well as UAS aircraft, call signs consist of the type of aircraft plus a unique serial number assigned by the FAA. The call sign may contain up to five numbers or letters. When the call sign is pronounced, each character is enunciated individually. Every U.S. aircraft's serial number is preceded by the letter N, signifying that it is registered in the United States. During routine communications, this letter is usually not pronounced but can be used if the pilot or operator wishes. Aircraft registered in other countries have aircraft identification numbers or letters preceded with a letter other than N.

Military aircraft are assigned a variety of call signs that may include five numbers, one word followed by numbers, or two letters followed by numbers. Each word is pronounced in full with the letters and numbers enunciated individually. The aircraft's call sign is always prefixed with the name of the military service, as in the following examples (Table 8-11):

CALL SIGN	MILITARY SERVICE	PRONUNCIATION
C693	Coast Guard	Coast Guard six niner tree
R23956	Army	Army two three niner fife six
VV1963	Navy	Navy one niner six tree
VM4257	Marine	Marine four two fife seven
A14932	Air Force	Air Force one four niner tree two

Table 8-11. Airspace classes in the U.S.

Figure 8-13. VORTAC ground station.

NAVIGATION SYSTEMS

Pilots using IFR procedures utilize a number of navigation aids that UAS operators need to be familiar with. UASs with advanced navigation systems may even utilize some of these systems. In any case, the UAS operator should at least become familiar with the technology so as to be able to understand the navigation of piloted aircraft. Some of these systems are designed to be used strictly for enroute navigation, others are designed to guide aircraft to the runway for landing. Some navigation aids can be used for both purposes.

VHF OMNIDIRECTIONAL RANGE (VOR)

One of the first modern electronic navigation systems was the VOR. The VOR was selected as the international civil navigation standard in 1949 by the International Civil Aviation Organization and is still used world-wide. VORs are assigned a frequency between 108.10 and 117.90 MHz. The VOR receiver on board the aircraft measures the phase difference between two signals transmitted by the VOR to determine the direction of the aircraft in relation to the transmitter.

When the aircraft is directly east of the VOR, it is said to be on the 90° radial of the VOR. An aircraft directly south of the VOR will on the 180° radial, west is the 270 degree radial and north is the 360 degree radial. There are potentially 360 different courses (radials) that the UAS operators can select to fly.

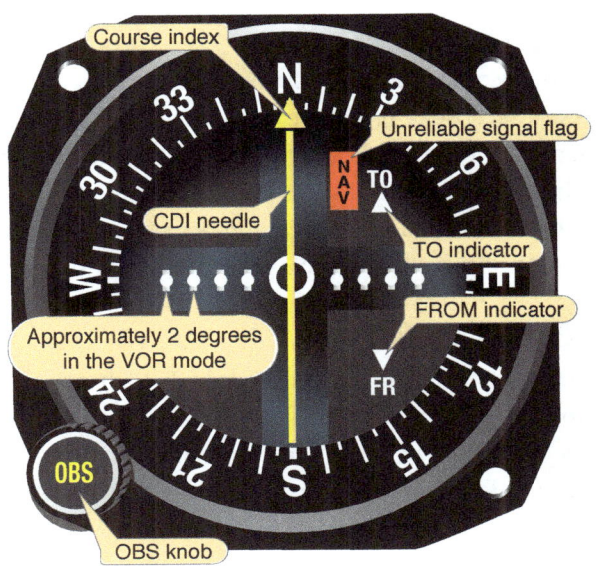

Figure 8-14. VOR indicator.

Unmanned Aerial Systems: The Definitive Guide

AIRCRAFT POSITIONING METHODS

The VOR provides bearing information to the pilot but not distance from the station. There is only one way for a pilot using the VOR to accurately determine an aircraft's position: by obtaining bearing information from two different VORs. By tuning in two different VORs, the pilot can plot a line of position from each VOR. These two lines of position (or radials) can be drawn on a navigation chart, with the aircraft being located at the intersection of the two radials. This is a somewhat cumbersome and inaccurate process.

DME POSITION DETERMINATION

If a pilot wishes to determine an aircraft's location using just one station, a system called distance measuring equipment (DME) must be used. The pilot determines which radial the aircraft is located using the VOR receiver, then uses DME to determine the aircraft's distance from the transmitter.

Figure 8-15. DME receiver/indicator.

TACTICAL AIR NAVIGATION (TACAN)

The VOR-DME system has deficiencies that make it unusable for certain military operations. After an extensive evaluation of the civilian VOR-DME system, the Department of Defense chose to develop an alternative navigation system known as tactical air navigation (TACAN). TACAN is a polar coordinate–based navigation system that provides both bearing and distance information to the pilot using a single transmitter located on the ground. TACAN does not use a passive transmitter on the ground like the VOR but instead operates in much the same way as the DME system.

VORTAC

The FAA and the Department of Defense developed a multi-mode VOR and TACAN based navigation system that is designed such that civilian aircraft use TACAN to provide distance information while still using VOR for azimuth information. Military aircraft are equipped solely with and use the TACAN part of the equipment. This combined navigation aid is known as VORTAC and has become the world wide navigation standard.

In recent years, as various newer navigation systems have come online, the FAA is decommissioning unneeded VOR/VORTAC stations. A skeleton system of VORTACs will remain in operation for the foreseeable future as a potential backup/supplemental navigation system however.

AREA NAVIGATION

When navigating airways using VORTAC, pilot are required to fly from VORTAC to VORTAC until they reach the destination airport. Because of airport location and VORTAC placement restrictions, it is seldom possible to navigate in a straight line from the departure to the destination airport. This forces a pilot to fly a longer distance than necessary. It also creates congestion in the air traffic control system, since every aircraft is forced to navigate along a limited number of airways. In an attempt to alleviate this congestion, a number of systems have been developed to permit pilot to bypass the airway system and navigate directly to the destination airport. These various systems are collectively referred to as area navigation or RNAV.

GLOBAL NAVIGATION SATELLITE SYSTEM

The Global Navigation Satellite System (GNSS) is the accepted term for navigation systems that provide ground-based users with global navigation via space-based satellite systems. GNSS transmitters are typically located on low earth orbit satellites permitting users with fairly small, inexpensive receivers to determine their location in three dimensions (latitude, longitude, and altitude). As long as the transmitters are within the sight line of a number of satellites, the receivers can determine their location within a few meters or even feet.

The Global Positioning System (GPS), is the U.S. GNSS system and is operated by the U.S. Air Force. The Russian GLONASS navigation system is also operational. The European Union is developing a system called Galileo, as are China (Compass), Japan, and India. Due to its accuracy and worldwide availability, GNSS has been designated by ICAO as the future aviation navigation system.

GLOBAL POSITIONING SYSTEM

GPS is a space-based positioning, velocity, and time system composed of a minimum of twenty four satellites in six orbital planes. The satellites operate in circular orbits arranged so that at any one time users worldwide are able to view a minimum of five satellites. GPS operations are based on the concept of ranging and triangulation from a group of satellites in space that act as precise reference points.

A GPS receiver determines location by comparing the travel time of radio signals from multiple satellites. Each satellite transmits a specific code, called a course/acquisition (CA) code that contains information on the satellite's position, an extremely precise GPS system time, clock error, and the accuracy of the transmitted data. The GPS receiver on the aircraft matches each satellite's CA code with an identical code contained in the receiver's database. By comparing the reception time from each satellite, the receiver can calculate its position relative to each satellite. The aircraft GPS receiver then mathematically determines its position by triangulation. Using stored information, the GPS receiver can also compute navigational information such as distance and bearing to a point, ground speed, estimated time enroute, estimated time of arrival, and winds aloft. It does this by using the aircraft's known latitude/longitude, measuring relative movement, and referencing these to a database built into the receiver.

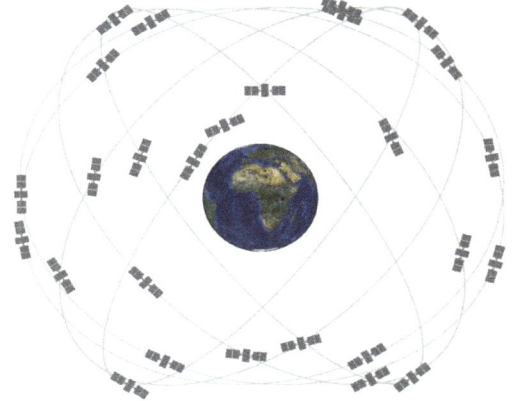

Figure 8-16. GPS satellite constellation.

Figure 8-17. GPS receiver/indicator.

GNSS AUGMENTATION

GNSS signals provide accuracy for enroute and two-dimensional navigation, but they do not provide acceptable vertical or lateral guidance for all weather landings. The standard GNSS signal needs to be augmented to provide this capability. This can be accomplished by using a Satellite Based Augmentation System (SBAS), Ground Based Augmentation System (GBAS), or Aircraft Based Augmentation System (ABAS).

Augmentation provides more accurate lateral guidance during the approach and departure phases of flight and can be used in some enroute environments as well. Augmentation also provides approach with vertical guidance (APV), which offers pilot a positive and stabilized vertical guidance flight path for approach procedures where no current guidance exists.

SATELLITE BASED AUGMENTATION SYSTEMS

SBASs comprise a network of ground reference stations that collect satellite signals and send them to one or more ground processing centers. The centers compare the overall signal inaccuracy from each station and compute a differential correction. This correction is sent to one or more geostationary satellites that transmit the augmentation message to each aircraft.

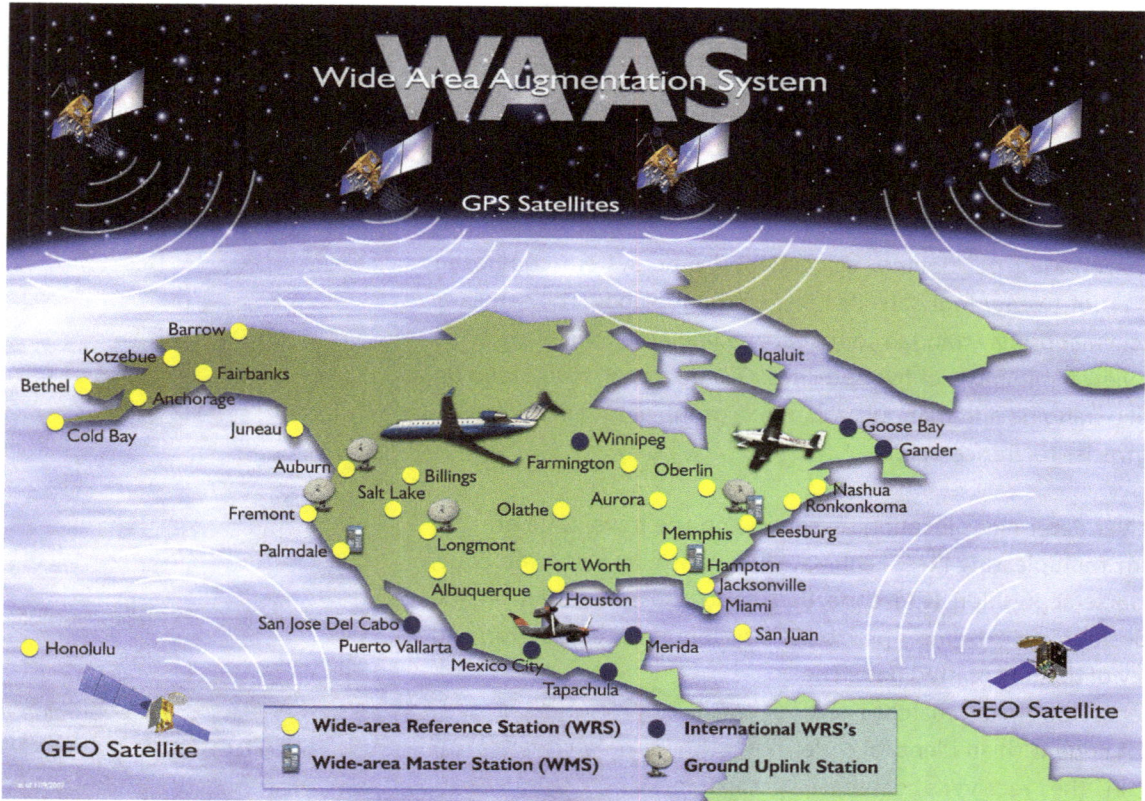

Figure 8-18. Wide Area Augmentation System, a satellite based GPS augmentation system.

There are multiple SBASs being developed and/or in operation. Most operate regionally, over each country's airspace. One currently operational SBAS is the U.S. operated wide area augmentation system (WAAS).

WAAS uses a network of precisely located ground reference stations that monitor transmitted GPS satellite signals. These stations are located throughout the United States (primarily co-located with ARTCCs) as well as in Canada and Mexico. The ground reference stations collect and process error information and send it to the WAAS master station. The master station more or less "averages" the error and develops a correction message that is sent to users via geostationary satellites located above the United States. Using WAAS, GPS signal accuracy is improved from about plus or minus 20 meters to approximately 2 meters both horizontally and vertically.

GROUND-BASED AUGMENTATION SYSTEM

Aircraft using GBAS receive augmentation information directly from a local ground-based transmitter. GBAS is similar to SBAS with the exception that the system error is measured, corrected, and transmitted in only one local geographic area (about 30 nm radius); thereby making the augmentation differential calculation very accurate. The augmentation message is sent only to aircraft in the local area, usually by some form of domestic radio communication.

Aircraft based augmentation systems are still under development, but are designed around the premise of using independent navigation systems onboard each aircraft to augment the GNSS satellite signal.

AIRPORT LAYOUT AND RUNWAY NUMBERING

Runways are referred to by a number between 1 and 36 corresponding to the direction of that runway in relation to magnetic north, rounded to the nearest 10 degrees. For example a runway heading east (90°) would be referred to as runway 9. A runway headed west (270°) would be runway 27, one headed north would be runway 36, while one headed south would be runway 18. Each end of the runway has a different number, 180 degrees opposed to the opposite side.

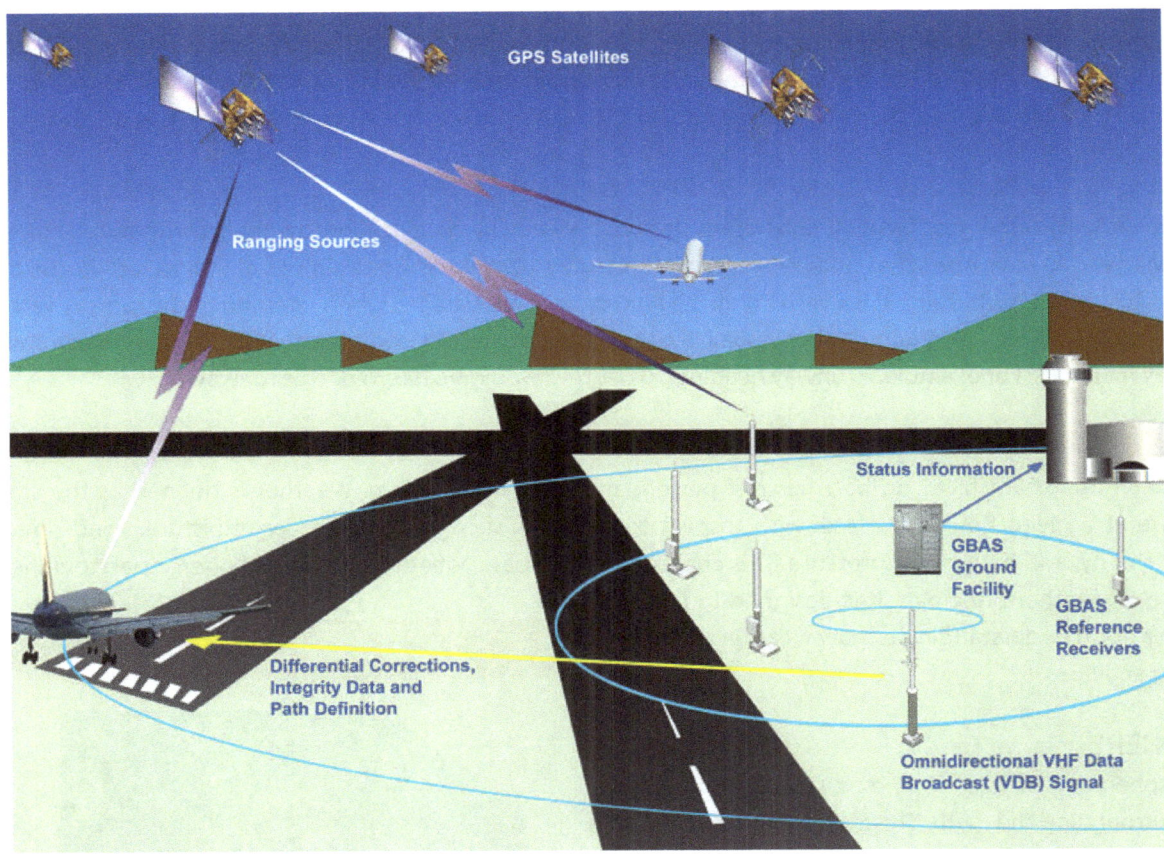

Figure 8-19. GBAS-ground based GPS augmentation system.

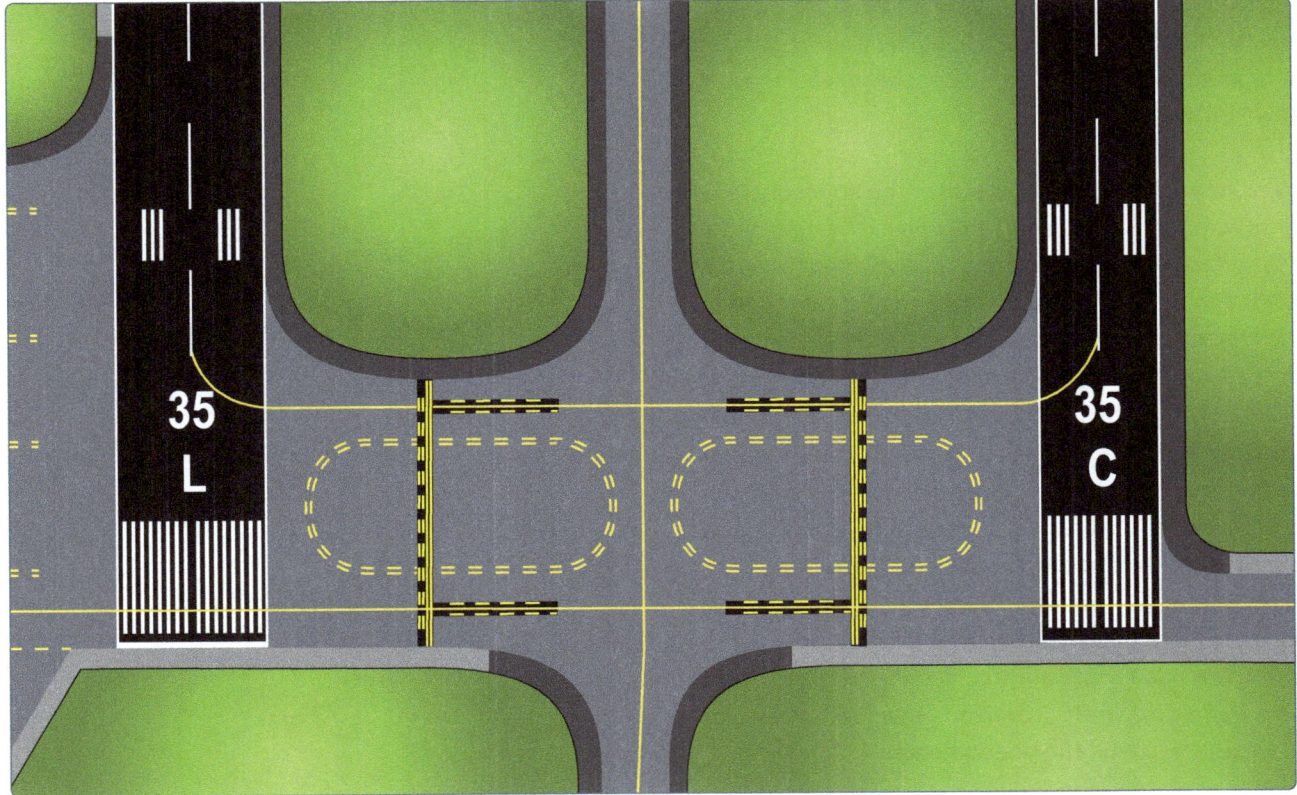

Figure 8-20. Runway markings with parallel left and right surfaces.

Unmanned Aerial Systems: The Definitive Guide 145

If there is more than one runway headed in the same direction each runway is identified by appending an appropriate name (left, right or center) to the runway number. For example, the left most runway headed north would be called runway 35 Left (L). The other northerly runway would be 35R. If there were three runways, the middle one would be called runway 35C (center).

Since there are only three possible variations using this type of runway classification, an airport with four or more parallel runways will need to have one set of runway identifiers shifted by 10 degrees. For example, at Dallas-Fort Worth, this results in runways 36L, 36R, 35L, 35C and 35R, even though all five runways are parallel. When referring to the runway verbally, each digit in the runway name is pronounced individually. In the United States the leading zero is dropped in all communications and runway markings. For example, a runway heading 70 degrees would be referred to as runway 7.

WEATHER

Weather is an important factor in both aircraft performance and flying safety. Weather is defined as the state of the atmosphere at a given time and place, with respect to variables such as temperature, moisture, wind direction and velocity, visibility, and barometric pressure. This chapter explains basic weather theory and offers operators the required knowledge of weather principles. It is designed to help them gain a good understanding of how weather affects daily flying activities.

ATMOSPHERE

The atmosphere is a blanket of air made up of a mixture of gases surrounding the Earth. The atmosphere is about 78 percent nitrogen and 21 percent oxygen, with carbon dioxide and traces of other gases make up the remaining one percent. Air also contains some water vapor, varying from close to zero to about five percent by volume. It is this small amount of water vapor that is responsible for most of what we call weather.

Many factors combine to set the air in the atmosphere in motion, with the primary being the uneven heating of the Earth's surface. As the heat energy is transferred to the air, it upsets any equilibrium, ultimately creating changes in air movement and atmospheric pressure. This movement of air (both vertical and horizontal) is called atmospheric circulation. In general, the Earth (and atmosphere) are warmed by energy radiating from the sun. Warmed air tends to rise which is then replaced by cooler air. Warm air rises because heat causes air molecules to spread apart. As the air expands, it becomes less dense and lighter than the surrounding air, this also cools the air. When air cools, it becomes more dense and heavier than warm air and, as a result, tends to sink and replace the warmer, rising air. This warm air-cold air circulation provides the basis for most weather systems and phenomenon.

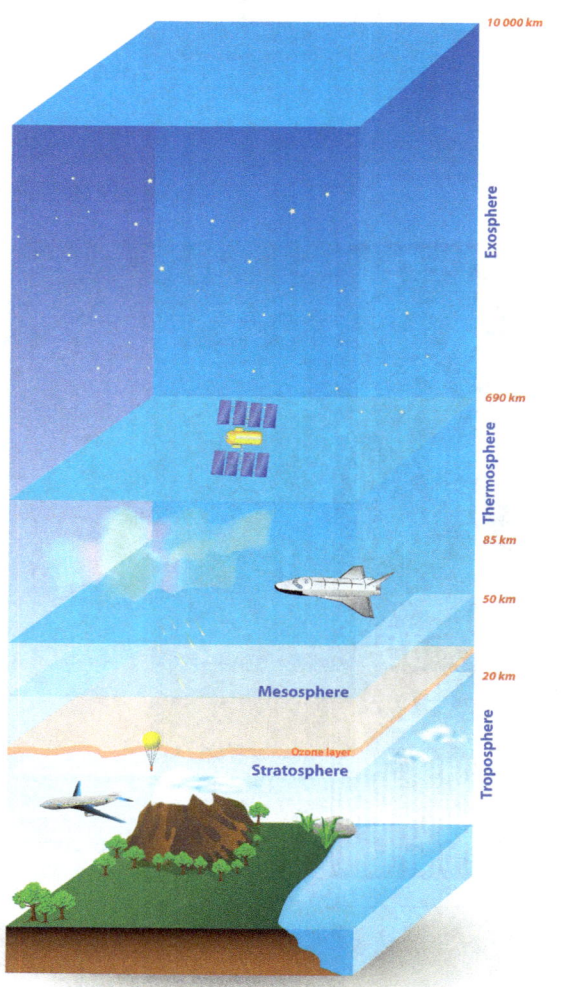

Figure 8-21. The Earth's atmosphere.

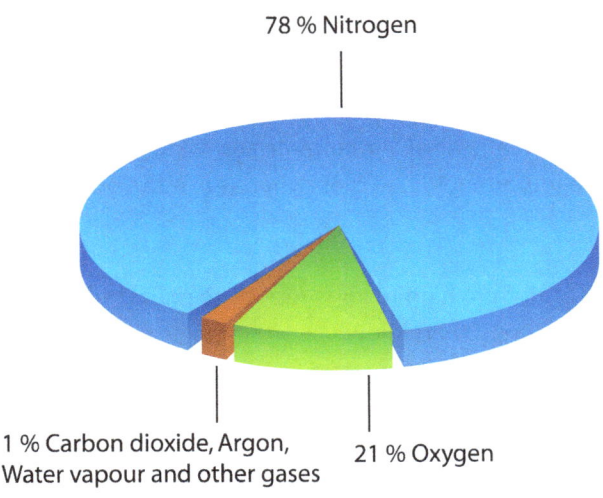

Figure 8-22. Composition of the atmosphere.

Figure 8-23. Global air currents.

Solar heating tends to cause higher temperatures in equatorial areas than near the poles. This causes a north-south circulation as well, with warm equatorial air rising, and then flowing towards the North and South poles. As the warm air flows toward the poles, it cools, becoming denser, and sinks back toward the surface creating a general south to north flow in the northern hemispheres and a corresponding north to south flow in the southern hemisphere.

ATMOSPHERIC PRESSURE

Atmospheric pressure is typically measured in inches of mercury. At sea level in a standard atmosphere, the weight of the atmosphere is 14.7 pounds per square inch. This pressure would support supports a column of mercury 29.92 inches high. Under these conditions, we would state that the barometric pressure was 29.92".

As altitude increases, atmospheric pressure decreases. On average, with every 1,000 feet of increase in altitude, the atmospheric pressure decreases one inch of mercury. As pressure decreases, the air becomes less dense or "thinner." This is the equivalent of being at a higher altitude and is referred to as density altitude (DA). As pressure decreases, DA increases and has a pronounced effect on aircraft performance. Differences in air density caused by changes in temperature result in a change in pressure as well. This, in turn, creates motion in the atmosphere, both vertically and horizontally, in the form of wind currents. It is these air movements which start chain reactions which become weather.

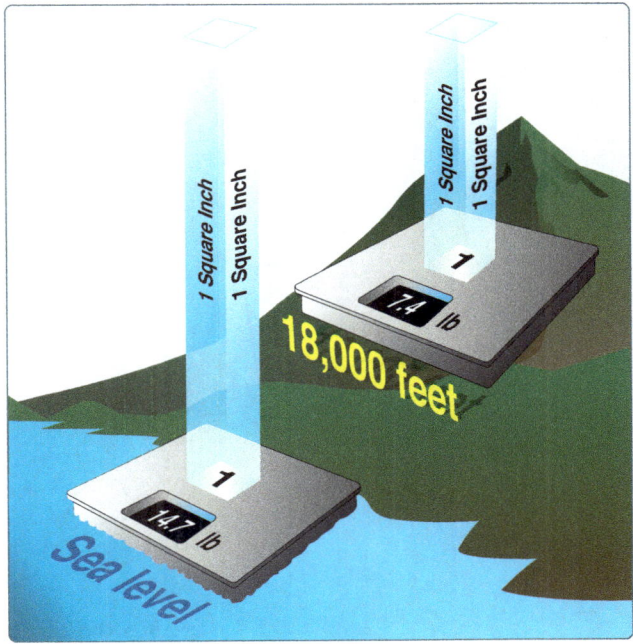

Figure 8-24. Atmospheric pressure.

ALTITUDE AND FLIGHT PERFORMANCE

Altitude affects every aspect of flight. At higher altitudes, with a decreased atmospheric pressure, takeoff and landing distances are increased, as are climb rates. When an aircraft takes off, lift must be developed by the flow of air around the wings. If the air is less dense than standard, more speed will be required to obtain enough lift for takeoff resulting in a longer ground run. An aircraft attempting to take off at an airport situated at 5,000 ft. above sea level might need 50% more takeoff and landing distance than if it were operating at sea level.

WIND AND AIR CURRENTS

Air flows from areas of high pressure into areas of low pressure. Air pressure, temperature changes, and the rotation of the earth (Coriolis force) combine to create two different kinds of air motion in the atmosphere: a vertical movement of ascending and descending currents (up and down drafts) and horizontal air movement (wind). Air currents and winds are important as they affect takeoff, landing, and cruise flight operations but more importantly, it is these changes to the atmospheric circulation that cause changes in the weather.

In the Northern Hemisphere, the rotation of the earth causes the flow of air from high to low pressure to deflect to the right. This tends to produce a clockwise circulation around areas of high pressure. This is known as anticyclonic circulation. The opposite is true of low-pressure areas; the air flows toward a low and is deflected to create a counterclockwise or cyclonic circulation.

High-pressure systems are generally areas of dry, stable, descending air. Good weather is typically associated with high-pressure systems for this reason. Conversely, air flows into a low pressure area to replace rising air. Low-pressure systems tend to be unstable, and usually bring increasing cloudiness and precipitation. While the theory of circulation and wind patterns is accurate for large scale atmospheric circulation, it does not take into account changes to the circulation on a local scale. Local conditions, geological features, and other anomalies can change the wind direction and speed close to the Earth's surface.

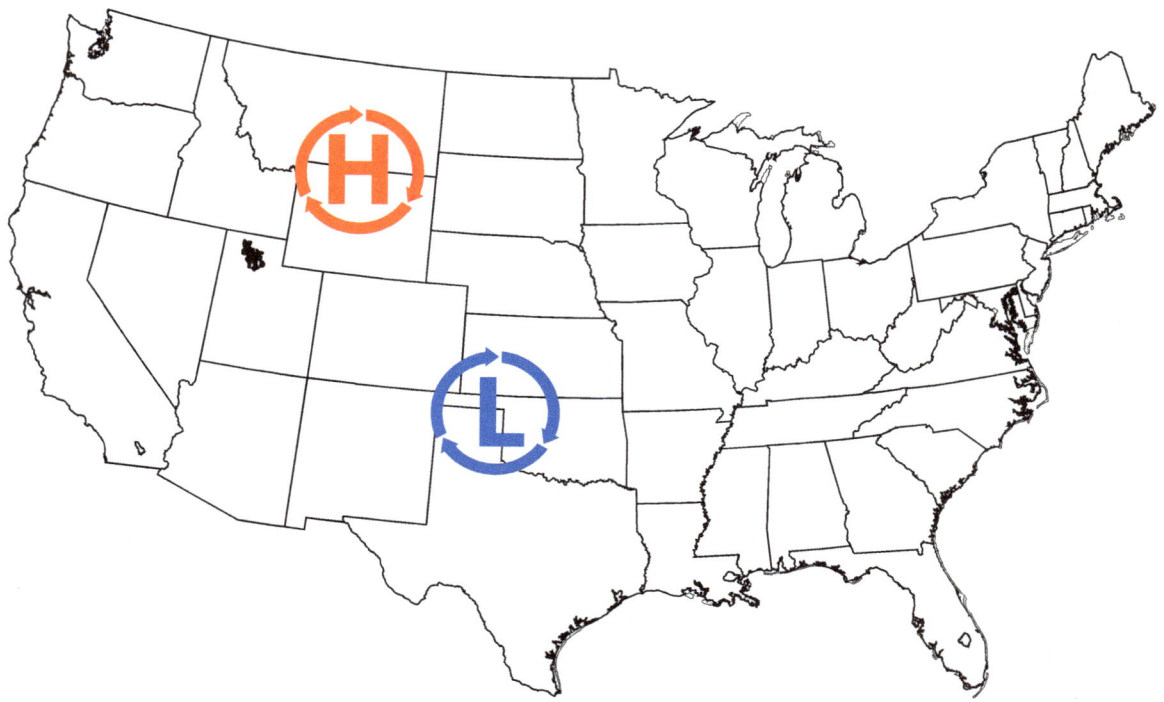

Figure 8-25. Circulation around high and low pressure areas.

CONVECTIVE AIR CURRENTS

Different surfaces radiate heat in varying amounts. Plowed ground, rocks, sand, and barren land both absorb and then give off a large amount of heat. Areas of water, trees, and other vegetation tend to absorb and retain heat as well. Lighter colored areas (such as snow) reflect heat. All of this heat (or lack of) is transmitted to the nearby air. Uneven heating of the air creates small areas of local circulation called convective currents. Convective currents are what cause the bumpy, turbulent air sometimes experienced when flying at lower altitudes during warmer weather. On a low altitude flight over varying surfaces, updrafts are likely to occur over pavement or barren places, and downdrafts often occur over water or expansive areas of vegetation like a group of trees.

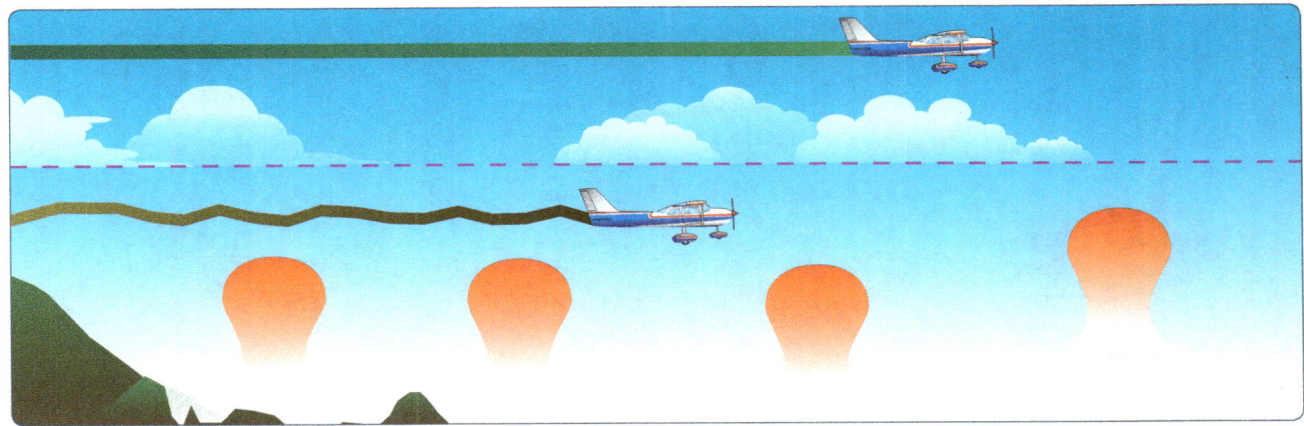

Figure 8-26. Convective turbulence.

Convective currents close to the ground can affect an operator's ability to control the aircraft. For example, on final approach, the rising air from terrain devoid of vegetation sometimes produces a ballooning effect that can cause a UAV to overshoot the intended landing spot. On the other hand, an approach over a large body of water or an area of thick vegetation tends to create a sinking effect that can cause an unwary UAS operator to undershoot and land short.

EFFECT OF OBSTRUCTIONS ON WIND

Obstructions on the ground affect the flow of wind and can be an unseen danger. Ground topography and large buildings can break up the flow of the wind and create wind gusts that change rapidly in direction and speed. These obstructions range from manmade structures like hangars to large natural obstructions, such as mountains, bluffs, or canyons. It is especially important to be vigilant when flying in or out of airports that have large buildings or natural obstructions located near the runway.

The intensity of the turbulence associated with ground obstructions depends on the size of the obstacle and the velocity and direction of the wind. This turbulence can affect the takeoff and landing performance of any aircraft by suddenly dropping due to the turbulence air and being too low to clear nearby obstacles.

This same condition is even more noticeable when flying in mountainous regions. While the wind flows smoothly up the windward side of the mountain and the upward currents help to carry an aircraft over the peak of the mountain, the wind on the leeward side does not act in a similar manner. As the air flows down the leeward side of the mountain, the air follows the contour of the terrain and is increasingly turbulent. This tends to push an aircraft into the ground.

WIND AND PRESSURE REPRESENTATION ON SURFACE WEATHER MAPS

Surface weather maps provide information about fronts, areas of high and low pressure, and surface winds and pressures for each station. This type of weather map allows UAS operators to see the locations of fronts and pressure systems, but more importantly, it depicts the wind and pressure at the surface for each location.

Wind conditions are reported by an arrow attached to the station location circle. The station circle represents the head of the arrow, with the arrow pointing in the direction from which the wind is blowing. Winds are described by the direction from which they blow, thus a northwest wind means that the wind is blowing from the northwest toward the southeast. The speed of the wind is depicted by barbs or pennants placed on the wind line. Each barb represents a speed of ten knots, while half a barb is equal to five knots, and a pennant is equal to 50 knots.

The pressure for each station is recorded on the weather chart and is shown in millibars (mb). Isobars are lines drawn on the chart to depict areas of equal pressure. These lines result in a pattern that reveals the pressure gradient or change in pressure

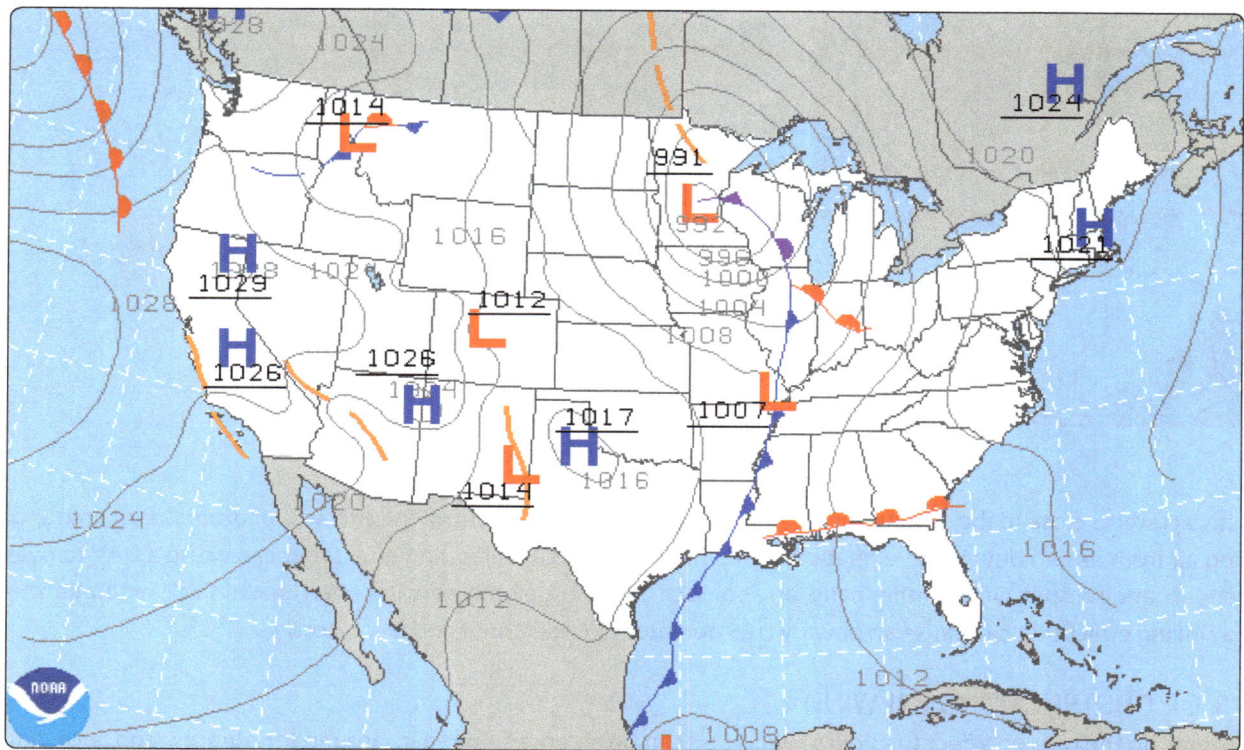

Figure 8-27. Weather map.

over distance. Isobars are similar to contour lines on a topographic map that indicate terrain altitudes and slope steepness. For example, isobars closely spaced indicate a steep wind gradient and strong winds will likely prevail. Shallow gradients, on the other hand, are represented by isobars that are spaced far apart, and are indicative of light winds.

Isobars help identify low and high pressure systems as well as the location of ridges, troughs, and cut-off lows. A high is an area of high pressure surrounded by lower pressure; a low is an area of low pressure surrounded by higher pressure. A ridge is an elongated area of high pressure, and a trough is an elongated area of low pressure.

Isobars furnish valuable information about winds in the first few thousand feet above the surface. Close to the ground, wind direction is modified by the surface and wind speed decreases due to friction with the surface. Generally, the wind a couple of thousand feet above the ground will be from 20° to 40° further to the right than that at the surface and the wind speed will be greater. For example, if there were a wind at the surface from 270 degrees at 10 knots, at 1000 ft. above the ground, the wind might be from 280 degrees at a velocity of 20 knots.

MOISTURE AND TEMPERATURE

The atmosphere, by nature, contains moisture in the form of water vapor. The amount of moisture present in the atmosphere is dependent upon the temperature of the air. Every 20 °F increase in temperature doubles the amount of moisture the air can hold. Conversely, a decrease of 20 °F cuts the capacity in half.

Water is present in the atmosphere in three states: liquid, solid, and gaseous. All three forms can readily change to another, and all are present within the normal temperature ranges of the atmosphere. As water changes from one state to another, an exchange of heat takes place. These changes occur through the processes of evaporation, sublimation, condensation, melting, or freezing. However, water vapor is added into the atmosphere only by the processes of evaporation and sublimation.

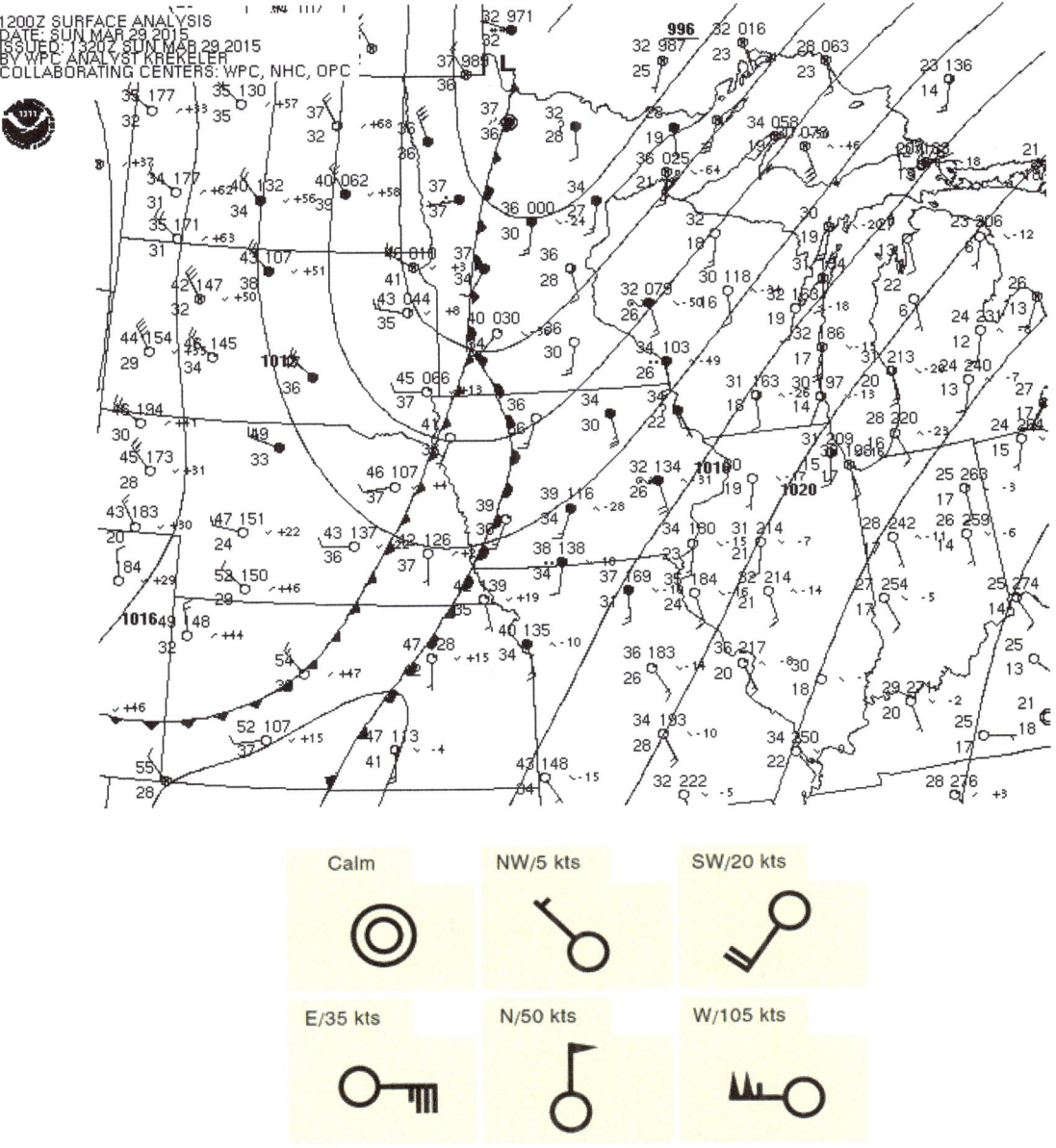

Figure 8-28. Weather chart indicating wind direction and speed, isobars, temperatures and fronts.

RELATIVE HUMIDITY

Humidity refers to the amount of water vapor present in the atmosphere at a given time. Relative humidity is the amount of moisture in the air compared to the total amount of moisture the air could hold at that temperature. For example, if the current relative humidity is 65 percent, the air is holding 65 percent of the total amount of moisture that it is capable of holding at that temperature. While much of the western United States rarely sees days of high humidity, relative humidity readings of 75 to 90 percent are not uncommon in the southern United States during warmer months.

TEMPERATURE/DEW POINT RELATIONSHIP

The relationship between dew point and temperature helps to define the concept of relative humidity. The dew point, given in degrees, is the temperature at which a parcel of air can hold no more moisture. When the temperature of an air mass is reduced to the dew point, the air becomes completely saturated and moisture begins to condense out of the air in the form of fog, dew, frost, clouds, rain, hail, or snow.

Unmanned Aerial Systems: The Definitive Guide

There are four ways by which air can reach the complete saturation point and clouds or fog can form.
1. If warm air moves over a cold surface, the air temperature drops and the air mass will reach the saturation point.
2. The saturation point may be reached when cold air and warm-moist air come into contact with each other.
3. When warmer air cools at night through contact with cooler ground, the air could reach its saturation point.
4. A moist air mass can be lifted or is forced upward in the atmosphere where its own expansion causes it to cool. As air rises, it loses heat energy as it expands. As a result, rising air loses heat rapidly. The rate of temperature decrease is called the "lapse rate". Dry air loses heat at a rate of 3.0° C (5.4° F) for every 1,000 feet of altitude gain. Moist air (fully saturated), loses heat at a rate of 1.5° C (2.7° F) for every 1,000 feet of altitude gain

If moist air is made to rise, clouds often form at the altitude where temperature and dew point reach the same value. When that happens, clouds (or fog) begin to form. When lifted, unsaturated air cools at a rate of 5.4 °F per 1,000 feet and the dew point temperature decreases at a rate of 1 °F per 1,000 feet. This results in a convergence of temperature and dew point at a rate of 4.4 °F. If you were to apply the convergence rate to the reported temperature and dew point, you could determine the height of the cloud base.

For example, if the air temperature is 85 °F at the surface, with a dew point of 71 °F, the difference between the two (the spread) is 14°. If you divide the temperature-dew point spread by the convergence rate of 4.4 °F, and multiply by 1,000 you will be able to estimate the approximate height of the cloud base.

DEW, FROST AND FOG
On cool, calm nights, the temperature of the ground and objects on the surface can cause temperatures of the surrounding air to drop below the dew point. When this occurs, the moisture in the air condenses and deposits itself on the ground, buildings, and other objects. This moisture is known as dew and sometimes can be seen on grass in the morning. If the temperature is below freezing, the moisture is deposited in the form of frost.

Fog is a cloud that begins within 50 feet of the earth's surface. It typically occurs when the temperature of air near the ground is cooled to the air's dew point. At this point, water vapor in the air condenses and becomes visible in the form of fog. Fog is classified according to the manner in which it forms and is dependent upon the current temperature and the amount of water vapor in the air.

CLOUDS
Clouds are visible indicators and are often indicative of future weather. For clouds to form there must be adequate water vapor and condensation nuclei, as well as a method by which the air can be cooled. When the air cools and reaches its saturation point, the invisible water vapor changes into a visible state. Through the processes of deposition (also referred to as sublimation) and condensation, moisture condenses or sublimates onto miniscule particles of matter like dust, salt, and smoke known as condensation nuclei. The nuclei are important because they provide a means for the moisture to change from one state to another.

CLOUD TYPES
Every cloud type is determined by its shape, height, and behavior. Shape can either be horizontally oriented, spread-out clouds, or single clouds with vertical development. These shapes are further classified according to the height of the base of the clouds (above ground level). Behavior generally refers to the type of precipitation that develops. A rain producing cloud usually has a suffix or prefix that uses the work "nimbo or nimbus".

Stratus clouds are generally characterized as more horizontal, layered clouds with a uniform base and thickness with limited vertical development. Cumuliform (or cumulus) clouds are taller, puffier clouds formed by rising thermals. It is possible to combine these two general categories of clouds.

Figure 8-29. Examples of common cloud types.

Low clouds are those that form near the Earth's surface and extend up to 6,500 feet AGL. Typical low clouds include stratus, stratocumulus, and nimbostratus. Fog is classified as a type of low cloud formation. Low clouds typically cause low ceilings and/or visibility.

Middle clouds (alto) extend from around 6,500 ft. AGL up to 20,000 ft.. They can be composed of water, ice crystals, or super-cooled water droplets. Typical middle-level cloud types include altostratus and altocumulus.

High clouds are those with bases above about 20,000 ft. They are usually composed of ice crystals and signify relatively stable air. Typical high-level clouds are cirrus, cirrostratus, and cirrocumulus.

Cumulus clouds with extensive vertical development are either called towering cumulus or cumulonimbus clouds. The base of these clouds form in the low to middle cloud region but the tops can extend well above 50,000 ft.. Towering cumulus clouds indicate areas of instability in the atmosphere, and the air around and inside them is turbulent. Cumulonimbus clouds eventually create rain or thunderstorms. Strong (tall) cumulonimbus clouds contain large amounts of moisture and unstable air, and usually produce hazardous weather phenomena, such as lightning, hail, tornadoes, gusty winds, and wind shear. These extensive vertical clouds can be obscured by other cloud formations and are not always visible from the ground or while in flight. When this happens, these clouds are said to be embedded; hence the term, embedded thunderstorms. Cumulonimbus clouds often form in continuous lines along a front. If they form out ahead of a front they are typically called squall lines.

A thunderstorm cloud has a distinct lifecycle composed of three distinct stages. It begins as a cumulus cloud, in which moisture laden air is lifted. If the atmosphere is relatively moist and sufficient instability is present, the cumulus clouds will continue over time to increase in vertical height. The heat released from the condensing of the moisture into water droplets feeds the cloud and creates continuous, strong updrafts. These updrafts continue until the thunderstorm reaches the mature stage. At this point, drops of moisture, whether rain or ice, finally become too heavy for the updrafts to support and they begin falling in the form of rain or hail.

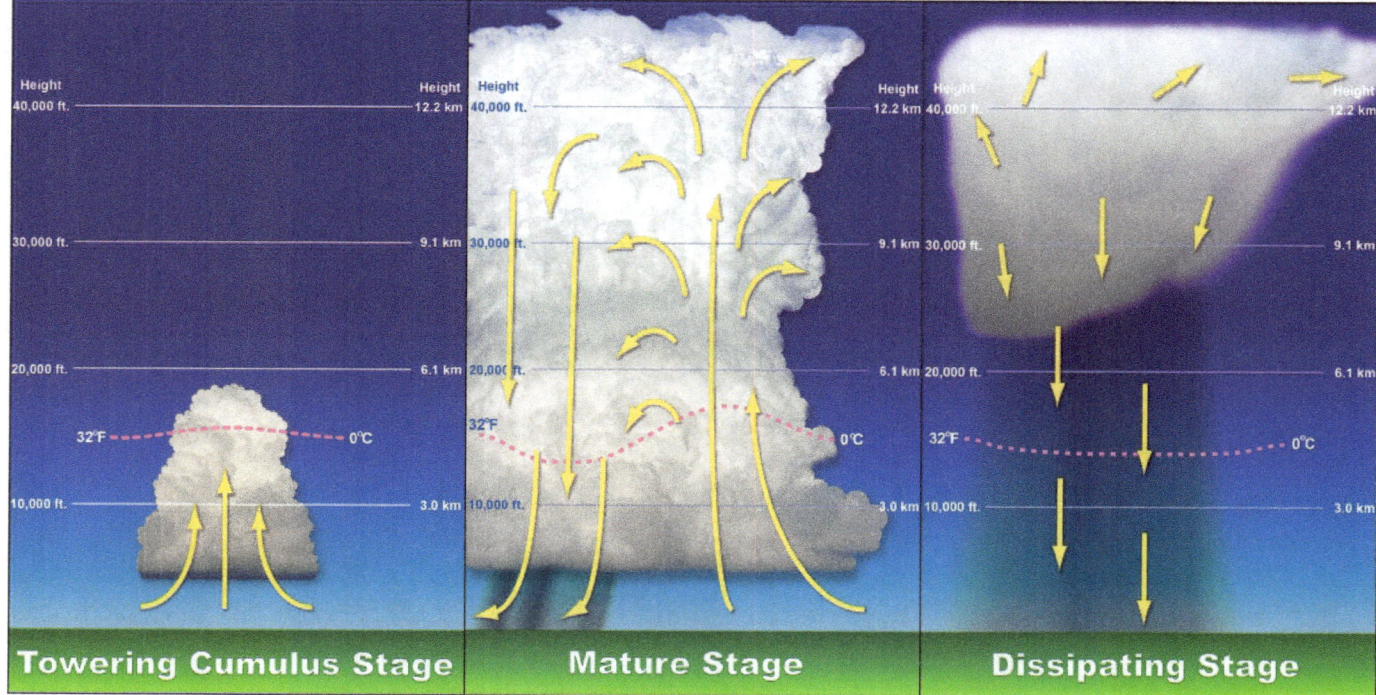

Figure 8-30. Stages of thunderstorm development.

This flow reversal creates a downward motion of the air. Warm, rising air is hit with a burst of cool, precipitation-laden descending air; with strong turbulence created both in and near the cloud. Below the cloud base, the down-rushing air hits the ground and spreads out. Observers up to 10 miles away from the thunderstorm will feel increased surface winds and decreased temperature from this outflow. Directly under the thunderstorm, strong downdrafts, rain, and possibly hail will begin to fall.

Eventually, this downward flow of cold air chokes off the upward flow of warm air, and the thunderstorm begins to dissipate. Significant rain will likely still fall with some strong downdrafts and wind induced turbulence, but the thunderstorm itself is winding down.

Cloud classification can be further broken down into specific cloud types according to the outward appearance and cloud composition.

- Cumulus—heaped or piled clouds
- Stratus—formed in layers
- Cirrus or cirro—ringlets, fibrous clouds, also high level clouds above 20,000 feet
- Castellanus—common base with separate vertical development, castle-like
- Lenticularus—lens shaped, formed over mountains in strong winds
- Nimbo or nimbus—rain-bearing clouds
- Fracto—ragged or broken
- Alto—meaning high, also middle level clouds existing at 5,000 to 20,000 feet

CLOUD COVERAGE

Weather observers report both the altitude of clouds as well as how much of the sky is covered by any given cloud layer. Cloud layers are categorized by how much of the visible horizon is covered by the clouds. A sky condition is called "clear" (CLR) if less than 1/8 of the sky is covered by clouds. "Few" (FEW) indicates 1/8th-2/8ths coverage. "Scattered" (SCT) is used when 3/8ths-4/8ths of the sky is covered. "Broken" (BKN) indicates that 5/8ths to 7/8ths of the sky is covered, while "overcast" (OVC) is used when the entire visible sky (8/8ths) coverage is observed. The cloud "ceiling" is the lowest layer of clouds covering the sky with at least broken or overcast coverage.

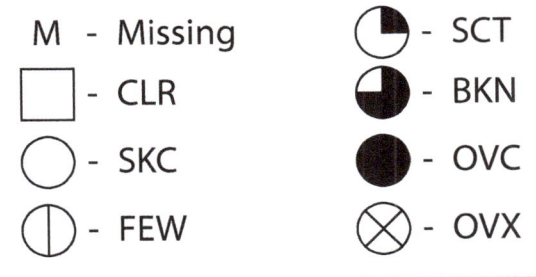

Sky Cover	Contraction
Less than ⅛ (Clear)	SKC, CLR, FEW
⅛–²⁄₈ (Few)	FEW
⅜–⁴⁄₈ (Scattered)	SCT
⅝–⁷⁄₈ (Broken)	BKN
⁸⁄₈ or (Overcast)	OVC

Figure 8-31. Cloud coverage terminology.

VISIBILITY

Closely related to cloud cover and reported ceiling is visibility information. Visibility refers to the greatest horizontal distance at which prominent objects can be viewed with the naked eye. Current visibility is reported in METAR and other aviation weather reports, as well as by automated weather systems. Visibility information, as predicted by meteorologists, is available for operators during a preflight weather briefing.

PRECIPITATION

Precipitation refers to any type of water particles that form in the atmosphere and fall to the ground. Depending on the form of precipitation, it can reduce visibility, add weight to an aircraft, interfere with electronics and radio systems, and affect landing and takeoff performance of an aircraft. Precipitation occurs because water or ice particles in clouds grow in size until the atmosphere can no longer support them. It can occur in several forms as it falls toward the Earth, including drizzle, rain, ice pellets, hail, snow, and ice.

Drizzle is classified as very small water droplets, smaller than 0.02 inches in diameter. Drizzle usually accompanies fog or low stratus clouds. Water droplets of larger size are referred to as rain. Rain that falls through the atmosphere but evaporates prior to striking the ground is known as virga. Freezing rain and freezing drizzle occur when the temperature of the surface is below freezing; the rain freezes on contact with the cooler surface.

If rain falls through a temperature inversion, it may freeze as it passes through the underlying cold air and fall to the ground in the form of ice pellets. Ice pellets are an indication of a temperature inversion and that freezing rain exists at a higher altitude. In the case of hail, freezing water droplets are carried up and down by drafts inside clouds, growing larger in size as they come

Qualifier		Weather Phenomena		
Intensity or Proximity 1	Descriptor 2	Precipitation 3	Obscuration 4	Other 5
− Light	MI Shallow	DZ Drizzle	BR Mist	PO Dust/sand whirls
Moderate (no qualifier)	BC Patches	RA Rain	FG Fog	SQ Squalls
+ Heavy	DR Low drifting	SN Snow	FU Smoke	FC Funnel cloud
VC in the vicinity	BL Blowing	SG Snow grains	DU Dust	+FC Tornado or waterspout
	SH Showers	IC Ice crystals (diamond dust)	SA Sand	SS Sandstorm
	TS Thunderstorms	PL Ice pellets	HZ Haze	DS Dust storm
	FZ Freezing	GR Hail	PY Spray	
	PR Partial	GS Small hail or snow pellets	VA Volcanic ash	
		UP *Unknown precipitation		

The weather groups are constructed by considering columns 1–5 in this table in sequence: intensity, followed by descriptor, followed by weather phenomena (e.g., heavy rain showers(s) is coded as +SHRA).
* Automated stations only

Figure 8-32. Weather phenomenon descriptors and abbreviations.

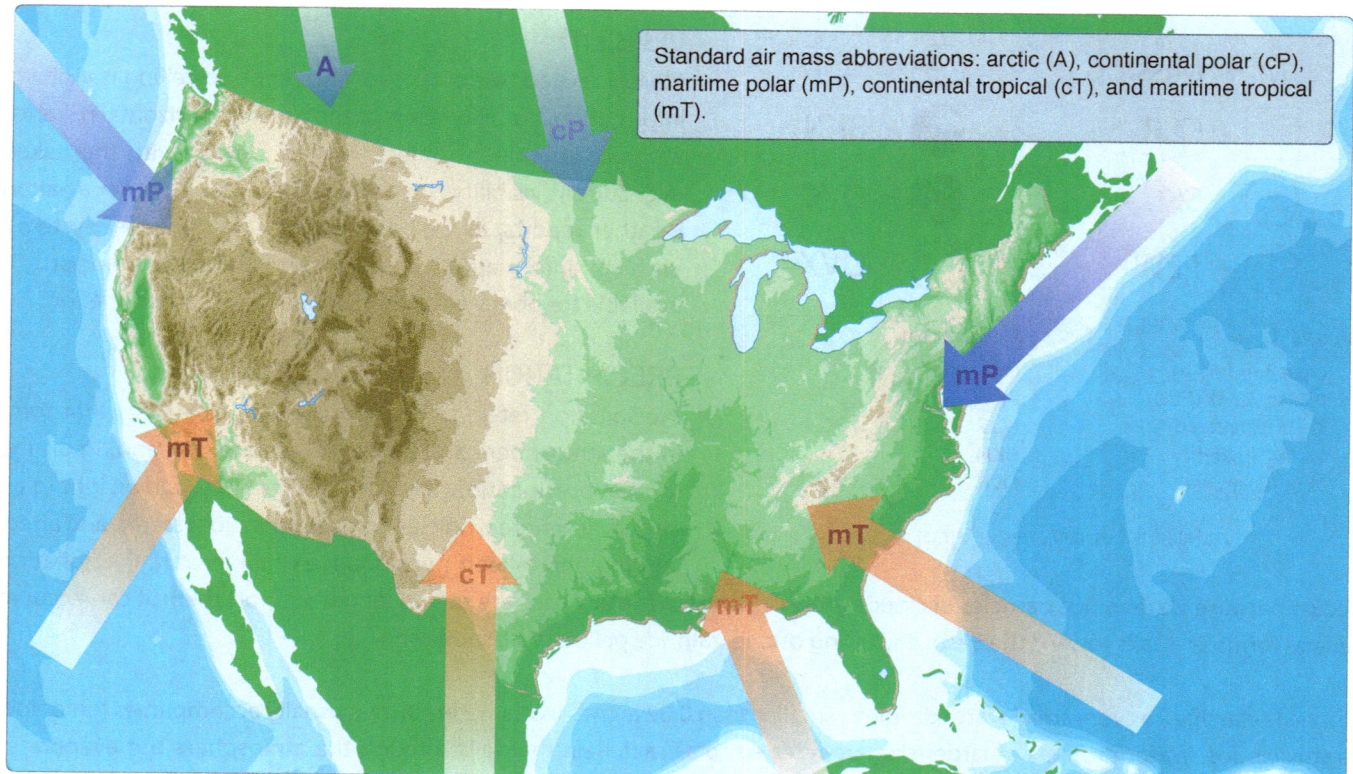

Figure 8-33. Air masses over the United States.

in contact with more moisture. Once the updrafts can no longer hold the freezing water, it falls to the Earth in the form of hail. Hail can be pea sized, or it can grow as large as five inches in diameter, larger than a softball.

Snow is precipitation in the form of ice crystals that falls at a steady rate or in snow showers that begin, change in intensity, and end rapidly. Falling snow also varies in size, being very small grains or large flakes. Snow grains are the equivalent of drizzle in size.

AIR MASSES

Air masses are classified according to the regions where they originate. They are large bodies of air that take on the characteristics of the surrounding area, or source region. A source region is typically an area in which the air remains relatively stagnant for a period of days or longer. During this time of stagnation, the air mass takes on the temperature and moisture characteristics of the source region. Areas of stagnation can be found in Polar Regions, tropical oceans, and dry deserts. Air masses are generally identified as polar or tropical, based on temperature characteristics, and maritime or continental, based on moisture content.

A continental polar air mass forms over a polar region and brings cool, dry air with it. Maritime tropical air masses form over warm tropical waters like the Gulf of Mexico and bring warm, moist air. As the air mass moves from its source region and passes over land or water, the air mass is subjected to the varying conditions of the land or water, and these modify the nature of the air mass.

An air mass passing over a warmer surface is warmed from below, and convective currents form, causing the air to rise. This creates an unstable air mass with good surface visibility. Moist, unstable air causes cumulus clouds, showers, and turbulence to form. Conversely, an air mass passing over a colder surface does not form convective currents, but instead creates a stable air mass with poor surface visibility. The poor surface visibility is due to the fact that smoke, dust, and other particles cannot rise out of the air mass and are instead trapped near the surface. A stable air mass can produce low stratus clouds and fog.

FRONTS

As an air mass moves across bodies of water and land, it eventually comes in contact with another air mass with different characteristics. The boundary layer between two types of air masses is known as a front. An approaching front of any type always means changes to the weather are imminent.

There are four types of fronts, which are named according to the temperature of the advancing air relative to the temperature of the air it is replacing:
- Warm
- Cold
- Stationary
- Occluded

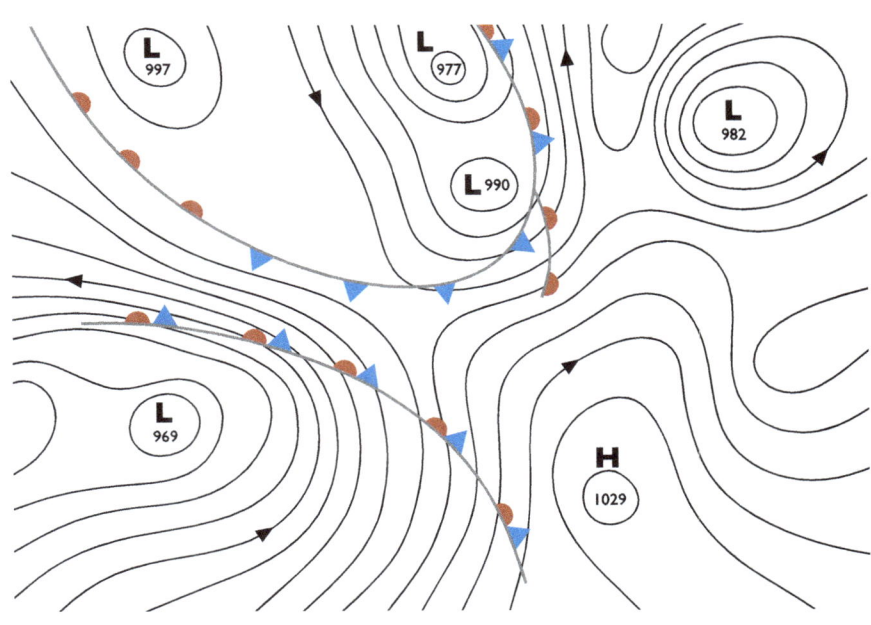

Figure 8-34. Weather fronts.

Symbols for surface fronts and other significant lines shown on the surface analysis chart:
- Warm front (red)
- Cold front (blue)
- Stationary front (red/blue)
- Occluded front (purple)

WARM FRONT

A warm front occurs when a warm mass of air advances and replaces a body of colder air. Warm fronts move slowly, typically 10 to 25 miles per hour (mph). The slope of the advancing front slides over the top of the cooler air and gradually pushes it out of the area. Warm fronts contain warm air that often has very high humidity. As the warm air is lifted, the temperature drops and condensation occurs.

COLD FRONT

A cold front occurs when a mass of cold, dense, and stable air advances and replaces a body of warmer air. Cold fronts move more rapidly than warm fronts, progressing at a rate of 25 to 30 mph. However, extreme cold fronts have been recorded moving at speeds of up to 60 mph. A typical cold front moves in a manner opposite that of a warm front. It is so dense, it stays close to the ground and acts like a snowplow, sliding under the warmer air and forcing the less dense air aloft. The rapidly ascending air causes the temperature to decrease suddenly, forcing the creation of clouds. The type of clouds that form depends on the stability of the warmer air mass. A cold front in the Northern Hemisphere is normally oriented in a northeast to southwest manner and can be several hundred miles long, encompassing a large area of land.

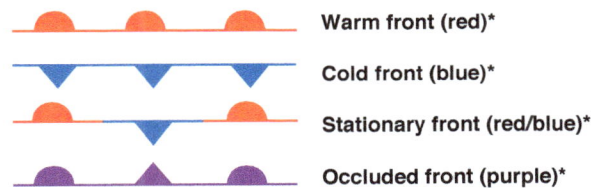

Figure 8-35. Surface front depictions.

Figure 8-36. Warm front.

Prior to the passage of a typical cold front, cirriform or towering cumulus clouds are present, and cumulonimbus clouds are possible. Rain showers and haze are also possible due to the rapid development of clouds. The wind from the south-southwest helps to replace the warm temperatures with the relative colder air. A high dew point and falling barometric pressure are indicative of imminent cold front passage.

As the cold front passes, towering cumulus or cumulonimbus clouds continue to dominate the sky. Depending on the intensity of the cold front, heavy rain showers form and might be accompanied by lightning, thunder, and/or hail. More severe cold fronts can also produce tornadoes. During cold front passage, the visibility is poor, with winds variable and gusty, and the temperature and dew point drop rapidly. A quickly falling barometric pressure bottoms out during frontal passage, and then begins a gradual increase.

Figure 8-37. Cold front.

After frontal passage, the towering cumulus and cumulonimbus clouds begin to dissipate to cumulus clouds with a corresponding decrease in the precipitation. Good visibility eventually prevails with the winds from the west-northwest. Temperatures remain cooler and the barometric pressure continues to rise.

STATIONARY FRONT
When the forces of two air masses are relatively equal, the boundary or front that separates them remains stationary and influences the local weather for days. This front is called a stationary front. The weather associated with a stationary front is typically a mixture that can be found in both warm and cold fronts.

OCCLUDED FRONT
An occluded front occurs when a fast-moving cold front catches up with a slow-moving warm front. As the occluded front approaches, warm front weather prevails, but is immediately followed by cold front weather. There are two types of occluded fronts that can occur, and the temperatures of the colliding frontal systems play a large part in defining the type of front and the resulting weather.

A cold front occlusion occurs when a fast moving cold front is colder than the air ahead of a slow moving warm front. When this occurs, the cold air replaces the cool air and forces the warm front aloft into the atmosphere. Typically, the cold front occlusion creates a mixture of weather found in both warm and cold fronts, providing the air is relatively stable. A warm front occlusion occurs when the air ahead of the warm front is colder than the air of the cold front. When this is the case, the cold front rides up and over the warm front. If the air forced aloft by the warm front occlusion is unstable, the weather is more severe than the weather found in a cold front occlusion. Embedded thunderstorms, rain, and fog are likely to occur.

THUNDERSTORMS
For a thunderstorm to form, the air must have sufficient water vapor, an unstable lapse rate, and an initial lifting action to start the storm process. Some storms occur at random in unstable air, last for only an hour or two, and produce only moderate wind gusts and rainfall. These are known as air mass thunderstorms and are generally a result of surface heating. Steady-state thunderstorms are associated with weather systems. Fronts, converging winds, and troughs aloft force upward motion spawning these storms which often form into squall lines. In the mature stage, updrafts become stronger and last much longer than in air mass storms, hence the name steady state.

SQUALL LINE
A squall line is a narrow band of active thunderstorms. Often it develops on or ahead of a cold front in moist, unstable air, but it may develop in unstable air far removed from any front. It often contains steady-state thunderstorms and presents the single most intense weather hazard to aircraft. It usually forms rapidly, generally reaching maximum intensity during the late afternoon and the first few hours of darkness.

TORNADOES
The most violent thunderstorms draw air into their cloud bases with great vigor. If the incoming air has any initial rotating motion, it often forms an extremely concentrated vortex from the surface well into the cloud. Meteorologists have estimated that winds in such a vortex can exceed 200 knots with pressure inside the vortex quite low. The strong winds gather dust and debris and the low pressure generates a funnel-shaped cloud extending downward from the cumulonimbus base. If the cloud does not reach the surface, it is a funnel cloud; if it touches a land surface, it is a tornado.

Tornadoes occur with both isolated and squall line thunderstorms. Reports for forecasts of tornadoes indicate that atmospheric conditions are favorable for violent turbulence. An aircraft entering a tornado vortex is almost certain to suffer structural damage.

HAIL
Hail competes with turbulence as one of the greatest thunderstorm hazard to aircraft. Super-cooled drops above the freezing level begin to freeze. Once a drop has frozen, other drops latch on and freeze to it, so the hailstone grows—sometimes into a huge ice ball. Large hail occurs with severe thunderstorms with strong updrafts that have built to great heights. Eventually, the hailstones fall, possibly some distance from the storm core. Hail may be encountered in clear air several miles from thunderstorm clouds.

As hailstones fall through air whose temperature is above 0 °C, they begin to melt and precipitation may reach the ground as either hail or rain. Rain at the surface does not mean the absence of hail aloft. Possible hail should be anticipated with any thunderstorm, especially beneath the anvil of a large cumulonimbus. Hailstones larger than one-half inch in diameter can significantly damage an aircraft in a few seconds.

OBSERVATIONS
While weather forecasts are not 100 percent accurate, meteorologists, through careful scientific study and computer modeling, have the ability to predict weather patterns, trends, and characteristics with increasing accuracy. Through a complex system of weather services, government agencies, and independent weather observers, UAS operators and other aviation professionals receive the benefit of this vast knowledge base in the form of up-to-date weather reports and forecasts. These reports and forecasts enable UAS operators to make informed decisions regarding weather and flight safety before and during a flight.

Data gathered from surface and upper altitude observations form the basis of all weather forecasts, advisories, and briefings. There are four types of weather observations: surface, upper air, radar, and satellite.

SURFACE AVIATION WEATHER OBSERVATIONS
Surface aviation weather observations (METARs) are a compilation of elements of the current weather at individual ground stations across the United States. The network is made up of government and privately contracted facilities that provide continuous up-to-date weather information. Automated weather sources, such as the Automated Weather Observing Systems (AWOS), Automated Surface Observing Systems (ASOS), Air Route Traffic Control Center (ARTCC) facilities, as well as other automated facilities, also play a major role in the gathering of surface observations.

Surface observations provide local weather conditions and other relevant information for a radius of five miles of a specific airport. This information includes the type of report, station identifier, date and time, modifier (as required), wind, visibility, runway visual range (RVR), weather phenomena, sky condition, temperature/dew point, altimeter reading, and applicable remarks. The information gathered for the surface observation may be from a person, an automated station, or an automated station that is updated or enhanced by a weather observer. In any form, the surface observation provides valuable information about individual airports around the country. Although the reports cover only a small radius, the UAS operators can generate a good picture of the weather over a wide area when many reporting stations are looked at together.

AVIATION ROUTINE WEATHER REPORT (METAR)

A METAR is an observation of current surface weather reported in a standard international format. METARs are issued hourly unless significant weather changes have occurred. A special METAR (SPECI) can be issued at any interval between routine METAR reports.

This is an example of a METAR report.
METAR KGGG 161753Z AUTO 14021G26 3/4SM +TSRA BR BKN008 OVC012CB 18/17 A2970 RMK PRESFR

A typical METAR report contains the following information in sequential order:
- ***Type of report***—there are two types of METAR reports. The first is the routine METAR report that is transmitted every hour. The second is the aviation selected SPECI. This is a special report that can be given at any time to update the METAR for rapidly changing weather conditions, aircraft mishaps, or other critical information.
- ***Station identifier***—a four-letter code as established by the International Civil Aviation Organization (ICAO). In the 48 contiguous states, a unique three-letter identifier is preceded by the letter "K." For example, Gregg County Airport in Longview, Texas is identified by the letters "KGGG," K being the country designation and GGG being the airport identifier. In other regions of the world, including Alaska and Hawaii, the first two letters of the four-letter ICAO identifier indicate the region, country, or state. Alaska identifiers always begin with the letters "PA" and Hawaii identifiers always begin with the letters "PH."
- ***Date and time of report***—depicted in a six-digit group (161753Z). The first two digits are the date. The last four digits are the time of the METAR, which is always given in coordinated universal time (UTC). A "Z" is appended to the end of the time to denote the time is given in Zulu time (UTC) as opposed to local time.
- ***Modifier***—denotes that the METAR came from an automated source or that the report was corrected. If the notation "AUTO" is listed in the METAR, the report came from an automated source. It also lists "AO1" or "AO2" in the remarks section to indicate the type of precipitation sensors employed at the automated station.
- ***Wind***—reported with five digits (14021) unless the speed is greater than 99 knots, in which case the wind is reported with six digits. The first three digits indicate the direction the true wind is blowing in tens of degrees. If the wind is variable, it is reported as "VRB." The last two digits indicate the speed of the wind in knots unless the wind is greater than 99 knots, in which case it is indicated by three digits. If the winds are gusting, the letter "G" follows the wind speed (G26). After the letter "G," the peak gust recorded is provided. If the wind varies more than 60° and the wind speed is greater than six knots, a separate group of numbers, separated by a "V," will indicate the extremes of the wind directions
- ***Visibility***—the prevailing visibility (¾ SM) is reported in statute miles as denoted by the letters "SM." It is reported in both miles and fractions of miles.
- ***Weather***—can be broken down into two different categories: qualifiers and weather phenomenon (+TSRA BR). First, the qualifiers of intensity, proximity, and the descriptor of the weather will be given. The intensity may be light (-), moderate ( ), or heavy (+). Proximity only depicts weather phenomena that are in the airport vicinity. The notation "VC" indicates a specific weather phenomenon is in the vicinity of five to ten miles from the airport. Descriptors are used to describe certain types of precipitation and obscurations. Weather phenomena may be reported as being precipitation, obscurations, and other phenomena such as squalls or funnel clouds. Descriptions of weather phenomena as they begin or end, and hailstone size are also listed in the remarks sections of the report.

- **Sky condition**—always reported in the sequence of amount, height, and type or indefinite ceiling/ height (vertical visibility) (BKN008 OVC012CB). The heights of the cloud bases are reported with a three-digit number in hundreds of feet AGL. Clouds above 12,000 feet are not detected or reported by an automated station. The types of clouds, specifically towering cumulus (TCU) or cumulonimbus (CB) clouds, are reported with their height. Contractions are used to describe the amount of cloud coverage and obscuring phenomena. The amount of sky coverage is reported in eighths of the sky from horizon to horizon.
- **Temperature and dew point**—the air temperature and dew point are always given in degrees Celsius (C) or (°C 18/17). Temperatures below 0°C are preceded by the letter "M" to indicate minus.
- **Altimeter setting**—reported as inches of mercury ("Hg") in a four-digit number group (A2970). It is always preceded by the letter "A." Rising or falling pressure may also be denoted in the remarks sections as "PRESRR" or "PRESFR" respectively.
- **Remarks**—any additional information that could not be included in the main report.

RADAR OBSERVATIONS

Weather observers use different types of radar to provide information about precipitation, wind, and weather systems. The WSR-88D NEXRAD radar, commonly called Doppler radar, provides in-depth observations that inform surrounding communities of impending weather. FAA terminal Doppler weather radar (TDWR), installed at some major airports around the country, also aids in providing severe weather alerts and warnings to ATC.

SATELLITE OBSERVATIONS

Advancements in satellite technologies has recently allowed for commercial use to include weather uplinks. Through the use of satellite subscription services, individuals are now able to receive satellite transmitted signals that provide near real-time weather information for the North American continent.

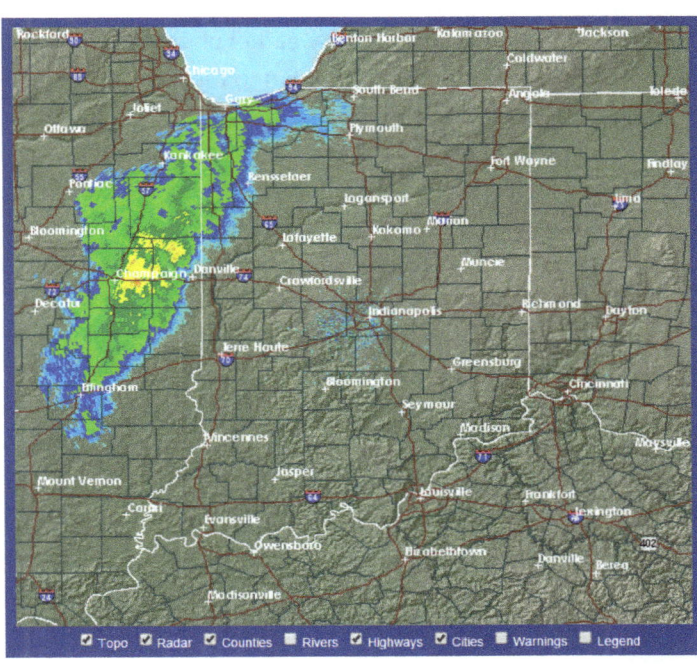

Figure 8-38. Weather radar.

AVIATION FORECASTS

Observed weather condition reports are often used in the creation of forecasts for the same area. A variety of different forecast products are produced and designed to be used in the preflight planning stage. The printed forecasts that UAS operators need to be familiar with are the terminal aerodrome forecast (TAF), aviation area forecast (FA), inflight weather advisories (SIGMET, AIRMET), and the winds and temperatures aloft forecast (FD).

TERMINAL AERODROME FORECASTS (TAF)

A TAF is a report established for the five statute mile radius around an airport. TAF reports are usually issued for larger airports. Each TAF is valid for a 30-hour time period, and is updated four times a day at 0000Z, 0600Z, 1200Z, and 1800Z. The TAF utilizes the same descriptors and abbreviations as used in the METAR report.

Figure 8-39. Satellite observation.

The TAF includes the following information in sequential order:
- *Type of report*—a TAF can be either a routine forecast (TAF) or an amended forecast (TAF AMD).
- *ICAO station identifier*—the station identifier is the same as that used in a METAR.
- *Date and time of origin*—time and date of TAF origination is given in the six-number code with the first two being the date, the last four being the time. Time is always given in UTC as denoted by the Z following the number group.
- *Valid period date and time*—the valid forecast time period is given by a six-digit number group. The first two numbers indicate the date, followed by the two-digit beginning time for the valid period, and the last two digits are the ending time.
- *Forecast wind*—the wind direction and speed forecast are given in a five-digit number group. The first three indicate the direction of the wind in reference to true north. The last two digits state the wind speed in knots as denoted by the letters "KT." Like the METAR, winds greater than 99 knots are given in three digits.
- *Forecast visibility*—given in statute miles and may be in whole numbers or fractions. If the forecast is greater than six miles, it will be coded as "P6SM."
- *Forecast significant weather*—weather phenomena are coded in the TAF reports in the same format as the METAR. If no significant weather is expected during the forecast time period, the denotation "NSW" is included in the "becoming" or "temporary" weather groups.
- *Forecast sky condition*—given in the same manner as the METAR. Only cumulonimbus (CB) clouds are forecast in this portion of the TAF report as opposed to CBs and towering cumulus in the METAR.
- *Forecast change group*—for any significant weather change forecast to occur during the TAF time period, the expected conditions and time period are included in this group. This information may be shown as from (FM), becoming (BECMG), and temporary (TEMPO). "FM" is used when a rapid and significant change, usually within an hour, is expected. "BECMG" is used when a gradual change in the weather is expected over a period of no more than 2 hours. "TEMPO" is used for temporary fluctuations of weather, expected to last less than one hour.
- *Probability forecast*—a given percentage that describes the probability of thunderstorms and precipitation occurring in the coming hours. This forecast is not used for the first 6 hours of the 24-hour forecast.

An example of a TAF would be:
KPIR 111130Z 111212 15012KT P6SM BKN090 TEMPO 1214 5SM BR
FM1500 16015G25KT P6SM SCT040 BKN250 FM0000 14012KT P6SM BKN080 OVC150 PROB40 0004 3SM TSRA BKN030CB
FM0400 1408KT P6SM SCT040 OVC080
TEMPO 0408 3SM TSRA OVC030CB BECMG 0810 32007KT=

This TAF would be translated as:
- Routine TAF for Pierre, South Dakota…on the 11th day of the month, at 1130Z…valid for 24 hours
- From 1200Z on the 11th to 1200Z on the 12th…wind from 150° at 12 knots…visibility greater than 6 sm…broken clouds at 9,000 feet…temporarily, between 1200Z and 1400Z, visibility 5 sm in mist
- From 1500Z winds from 160° at 15 knots, gusting to 25 knots visibility greater than 6 sm…clouds scattered at 4,000 feet and broken at 25,000 feet…from 0000Z wind from 140° at 12 knots…visibility greater than 6 sm…clouds broken at 8,000 feet, overcast at 15,000 feet…between 0000Z and 0400Z, there is 40 percent probability of visibility 3 sm…thunderstorm with moderate rain showers…clouds broken at 3,000 feet with cumulonimbus clouds…
- From 0400Z…winds from 140° at 8 knots…visibility greater than 6 miles…clouds at 4,000 scattered and overcast at 8,000…temporarily between 0400Z and 0800Z…visibility 3 miles…thunderstorms with moderate rain showers…clouds overcast at 3,000 feet with cumulonimbus clouds…becoming between 0800Z and 1000Z…wind from 320° at 7 knots…end of report (=).

AREA FORECASTS

Area forecasts (FA) provides a picture of clouds, general weather conditions, and visual meteorological conditions (VMC) expected over a large area encompassing several states. There are six areas for which area forecasts are published in the contiguous 48 states. Area forecasts are issued three times a day and are valid for 18 hours. This type of forecast gives information vital to en route operations, as well as forecast information for smaller airports that do not have terminal forecasts.

Area forecasts are fairly long and typically disseminated in four sections. The first section, called the header, provides the location identifier of the source of the forecast, the date and time of issuance, the valid forecast time, and the area of coverage.

> For example:
> DFWC FA 120945
> SYNOPSIS AND VFR CLDS/WX
> SYNOPSIS VALID UNTIL 130400
> CLDS/WX VALID UNTIL 122200...OTLK VALID 122200-130400
> OK TX AR LA MS AL AND CSTL WTRS

This example area forecast provides information issued by the Dallas Fort Worth office of the National Weather Service and applies to the region that includes Oklahoma, Texas, Arkansas, Louisiana, Mississippi, and Alabama, as well as a portion of the Gulf coastal waters. It was issued on the 12th day of the month at 0945. The synopsis is valid from the time of issuance until 0400 hours on the 13th. VFR clouds and weather information on this area forecast are valid until 2200 hours on the 12th and the outlook is valid until 0400 hours on the 13th.

The second section of the forecast includes precautionary statements. This section describes IFR conditions, mountain obscurations, and thunderstorm hazards that might occur. Statements made in this section regarding height are given in MSL, and if given otherwise, AGL or ceiling (CIG) will be noted.

> For example:
> SEE AIRMET SIERRA FOR IFR CONDS AND MTN OBSCN.
> TS IMPLY SEV OR GTR TURB SEV ICE LLWS AND IFR CONDS.
> NON MSL HGTS DENOTED BYAGL OR CIG.

The area forecast covers VFR clouds and weather, so the precautionary statement warns that AIRMET Sierra should be referenced for IFR conditions and mountain obscuration. The code TS indicates the possibility of thunderstorms and implies there may be occurrences of severe or greater turbulence, severe icing, low-level wind shear, and IFR conditions. The final line of the precautionary statement alerts the user that heights, for the most part, are MSL. Those that are not MSL will be AGL or CIG.

Section three is the synopsis, which provides a brief summary identifying the location and movement of pressure systems, fronts, and circulation patterns.

> For example:
> SYNOPSIS...LOW PRES TROF 10Z OK/TX PNHDL AREA FCST MOV EWD INTO CNTRL-SWRN OK BY 04Z. WRMFNT 10Z CNTRL OK-SRN AR-NRN MS FCST LIFT NWD INTO NERN OK-NRN AR EXTRM NRN MS BY 04Z.

As of 1000Z, a low pressure trough existed over the Oklahoma and Texas panhandle area, which is forecast to move eastward into central southwestern Oklahoma by 0400Z. A warm front located over central Oklahoma, southern Arkansas, and northern Mississippi at 1000Z is forecast to lift northwestward into northeastern Oklahoma, northern Arkansas, and extreme northern Mississippi by 0400Z.

The last section lists expected sky conditions, visibility, and weather for the next 12 hours and an outlook for the following 6 hours.

```
S CNTRL AND SERN TX
AGL SCT-BKN010. TOPS 030. VIS 3-5SM BR. 14-16Z BECMG AGL SCT030. 19Z AGL SCT050. OTLK…VFR
OK
PNDLAND NW…AGL SCT030 SCT-BKN100. TOPS FL200.
15Z AGL SCT040 SCT100. AFT 20Z SCT TSRA DVLPG.. FEW POSS SEV. CB TOPS FL450.
OTLK…VFR
```

In south central and southeastern Texas, there is a scattered to broken layer of clouds from 1,000 feet AGL with tops at 3,000 feet, visibility is 3 to 5 sm in mist. Between 1400Z and 1600Z, the cloud bases are expected to increase to 3,000 feet AGL. After 1900Z, the cloud bases are expected to continue to increase to 5,000 feet AGL and the outlook is VFR.

In northwestern Oklahoma and panhandle, the clouds are scattered at 3,000 feet with another scattered to broken layer at 10,000 feet AGL, with the tops at 20,000 feet. At 1500 Z, the lowest cloud base is expected to increase to 4,000 feet AGL with a scattered layer at 10,000 feet AGL. After 2000Z, the forecast calls for scattered thunderstorms with rain developing and a few becoming severe; the CB clouds will have tops at flight level 450 or 45,000 feet MSL.

It should be noted that when information is given in the area forecast, locations may be given by states, regions, or specific geological features such as mountain ranges.

WEATHER CHARTS

Weather charts are graphic charts that depict current or forecast weather. They provide an overall picture of the United States and should be used in the beginning stages of flight planning. Typically, weather charts show the movement of major weather systems and fronts. Surface analysis, weather depiction, and radar summary charts are sources of current weather information. Significant weather prognostic charts provide an overall forecast weather picture.

SURFACE ANALYSIS CHART

The surface analysis chart depicts an analysis of the current surface weather. This chart is a computer prepared report that is transmitted every 3 hours and covers the contiguous 48 states and adjacent areas. A surface analysis chart shows the areas of high and low pressure, fronts, temperatures, dew points, wind directions and speeds, local weather, and visual obstructions.

WEATHER DEPICTION CHART

A weather depiction chart details surface conditions as derived from METAR and other surface observations. The weather depiction chart is prepared and transmitted by computer every 3 hours beginning at 0100Z time, and is valid at the time of the plotted data. It is designed to be used for flight planning by giving an overall picture of the weather across the United States.

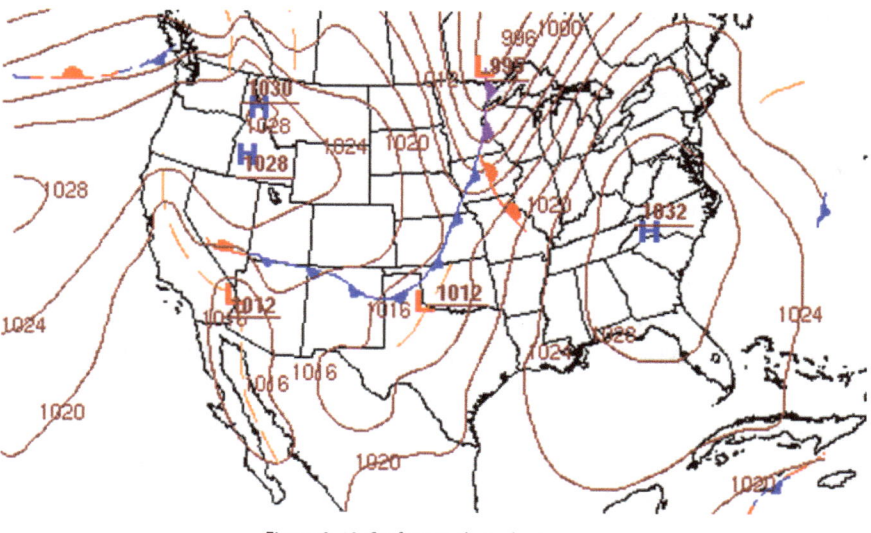

Figure 8-40. Surface analysis chart.

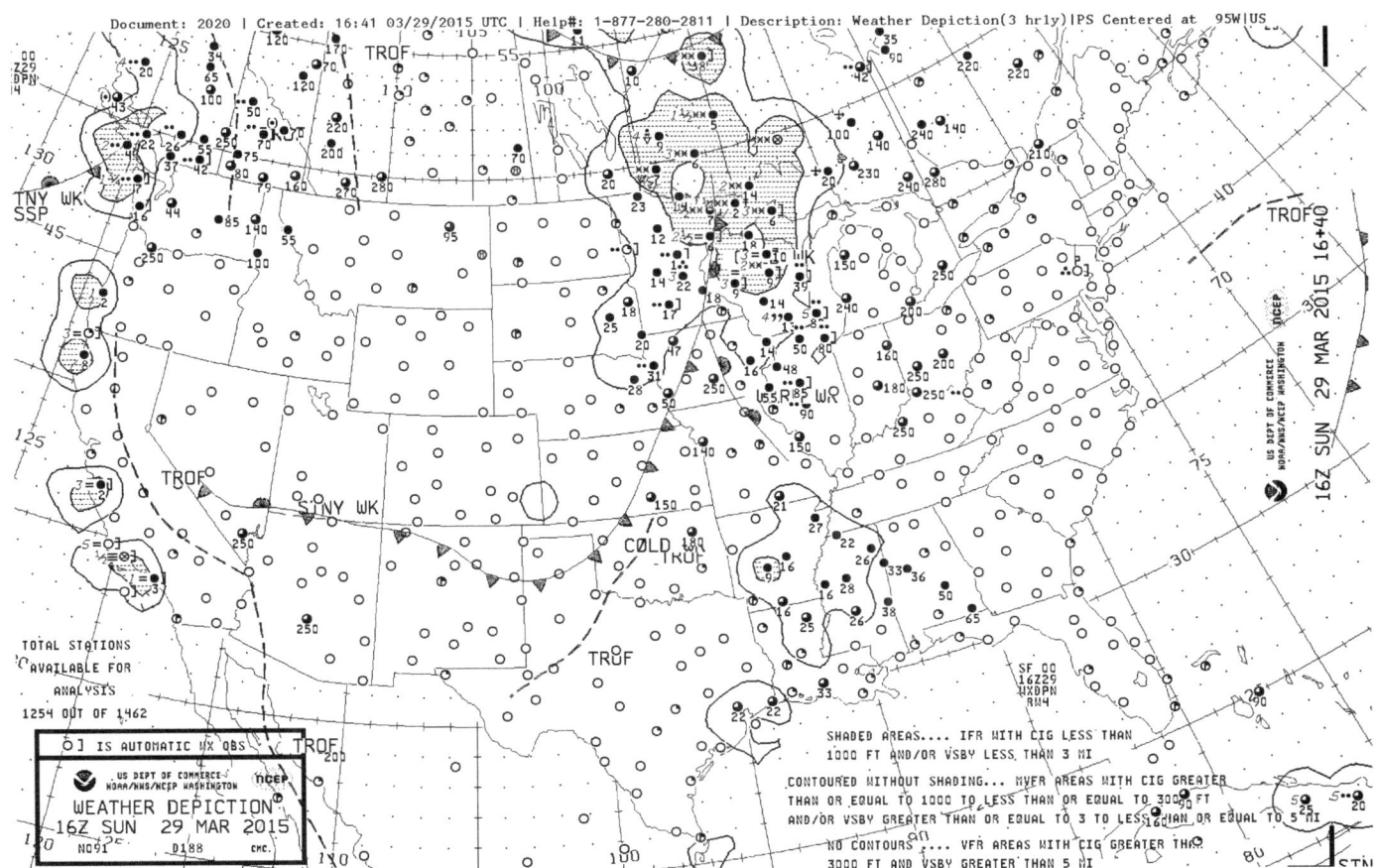

Figure 8-41. Weather depiction chart.

This type of chart typically displays major fronts or areas of high and low pressure. The weather depiction chart also provides a graphic display of IFR, VFR, and MVFR (marginal VFR) weather. Areas of IFR conditions (ceilings less than 1,000 feet and visibility less than three miles) are shown by a hatched area outlined by a smooth line. MVFR regions (ceilings 1,000 to 3,000 feet, visibility 3 to 5 miles) are shown by a non-hatched area outlined by a smooth line. Areas of VFR (no ceiling or ceiling greater than 3,000 feet and visibility greater than five miles) are not outlined.

Weather depiction charts show a modified station model that provides sky conditions in the form of total sky cover, cloud height or ceiling, weather, and obstructions to visibility, but does not include winds or pressure readings like the surface analysis chart. A bracket ( ]) symbol to the right of the station indicates the observation was made by an automated station. A detailed explanation of a station model is depicted in the previous discussion of surface analysis charts.

SIGNIFICANT WEATHER PROGNOSTIC CHARTS

Significant weather prognostic charts are available for low-level significant weather from the surface to FL 240 (24,000 feet), also referred to as the 400 mb level, and high-level significant weather from FL 250 to FL 600 (25,000 to 60,000 feet). The primary concern of this discussion is the low-level significant weather prognostic chart.

The low-level chart comes in two forms: the 12- and 24-hour forecast chart and the 36- and 48-hour surface forecast chart. The first chart is a four-panel chart that includes 12- and 24- hour forecasts for significant weather and surface weather. Charts are issued four times a day at 0000Z, 0600Z, 1200Z, and 1800Z. The valid time for the chart is printed on the lower left corner of each panel.

Chapter 8

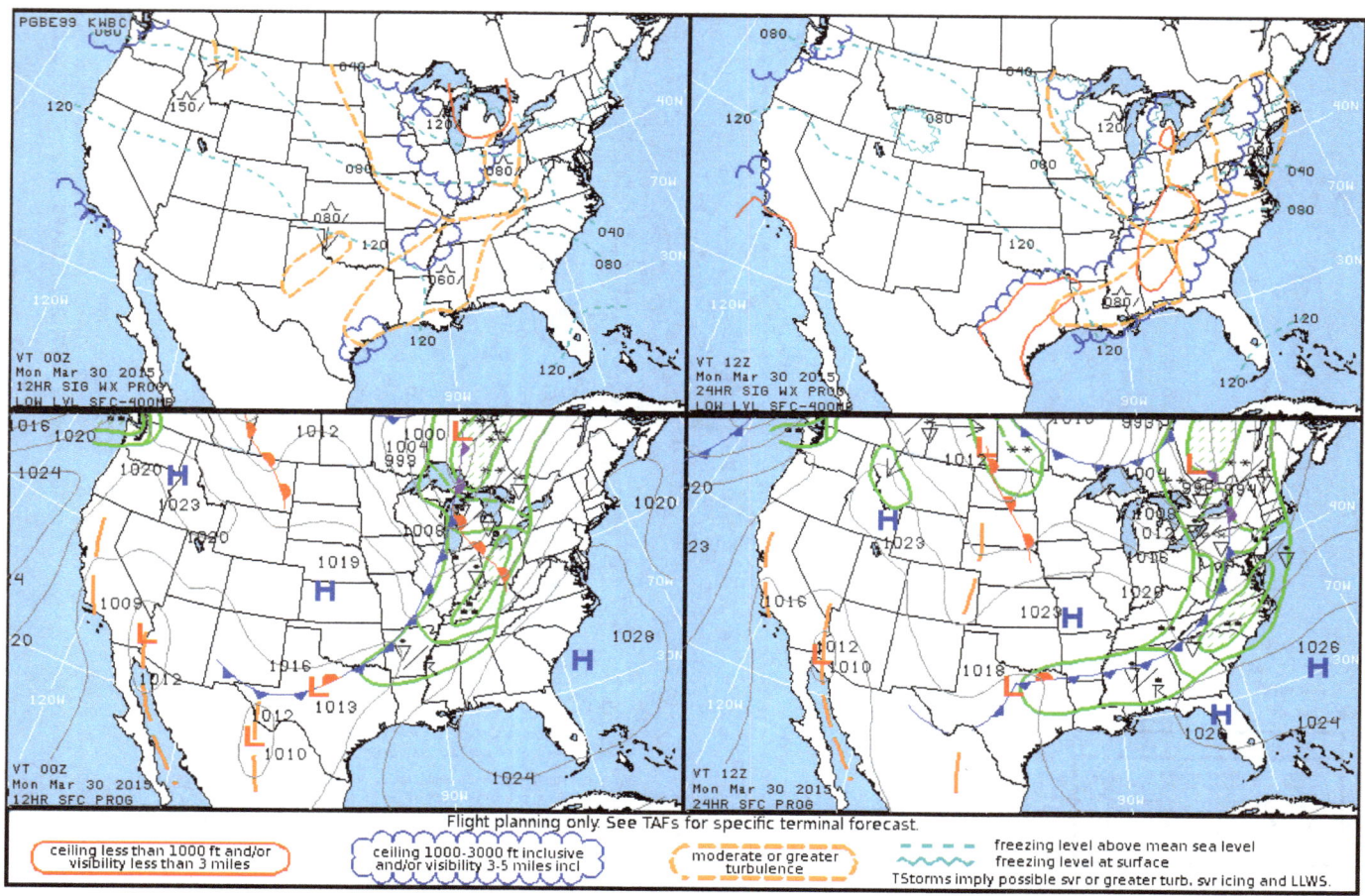

Figure 8-42. Prognostic charts.

CHAPTER 9

FLIGHT OPERATIONS

LOCATION AND ENVIRONMENT

UAS flight operations may occur at prepared locations such as a model aircraft flying field or might require launch and retrieval from an improvised location such as agricultural or forested areas. There are many factors to be considered when planning a UAS mission, regardless of the location selected. An improved runway might be desirable for flight test and system integration to minimize the risk of difficult takeoff and landing efforts. The use of an improvised operating or deployment area will present the most challenges and risks to aircraft, payload, and personnel. In the case of multirotor machines, the length and surface condition of the launch and retrieval area are much less critical, however, buildings, power lines, trees, open water, and impenetrable brush near the operating area can present real challenges to the unmanned operation.

AIRCRAFT LAUNCH AND RECOVERY

Weather conditions play a significant role in the launch and retrieval of UASs. Cool temperatures and a slight headwind are beneficial to creating lift, reducing the ground speed and runway length required, and improving propeller thrust efficiency. Crosswinds, tailwinds, turbulence, or any strong wind will make launch and retrieval problematic. If a runway is available, generally headed into the wind, a conventional tricycle landing gear equipped aircraft may be used. Nose wheel steering, as in manned aircraft, may be needed, although some aircraft are directionally steered using yaw control only, which is not effective until the aircraft has accelerated to a reasonably high airspeed.

Figure 9-1. Catapult for unimproved field takeoff of fixed wing UAV.

Unmanned Aerial Systems: The Definitive Guide

If the aircraft is fairly small or has a light wing loading, a hand launched takeoff may be feasible. Fixed wing aircraft weighing 20 pounds and spanning 10 feet may be hand launched satisfactorily; however, handling and launching an aircraft of this size can prove to be somewhat of an athletic feat. Pusher propeller designs with rear mounted motors should never be hand launched unless safeguards are in place to protect the hand of the person launching. Serious injuries have resulted from this practice.

A catapult launch is another common method used for fixed wing aircraft launches in areas without improved runways or when launching pusher propeller designs. Most operators use a catapult consisting of a band of latex surgical tubing stretched and released to propel the aircraft with a support mechanism, or carriage, traveling along a guide rail. Catapults, once armed with the tubing stretched, can be extremely dangerous to nearby participants and should have precautions and procedures in place to address personnel risk. There are pneumatic catapults commercially available but their cost is prohibitive to all but the most well financed operators.

The car top launch is another option for fixed wing UAVs. During a car launch, the aircrafts powerplant is started, the aircraft is then secured to a release dolly on the roof of a vehicle, the car (and attached aircraft) are accelerated, and then the UAV is released at a predetermined speed. Car launches eliminate the need for runway, catapult, or hand launch but does require a road or road-like surface, a properly equipped vehicle, trained driver, and reliable release mechanism.

AIRCRAFT RETRIEVAL

Getting the aircraft into the air is only half the problem. A means of recovery must be used that is safe, reliable, and predictable. The use of a runway is not always the best option, but does provide the lowest risk recovery method. A runway used for landing needs to be fairly wide and free of obstructions, as well as oriented into the wind.

Many aircraft that are hand launched may be recovered by belly landing on their fuselage underside in a clearing or standing vegetation. This technique has proven successful for years of agricultural imaging operations as there is normally no shortage of standing corn, soybeans, mint, or weeds to provide a soft landing. As many of these aircraft are not equipped with landing gear, the protection of any camera is of primary importance as it is usually located on the bottom of the aircraft or in an open payload bay. This location puts the camera at risk for impact with brush or small rocks in the case of landing in a clear, but unimproved area. Recessing the camera and lens is one strategy that helps to protect the camera. Other methods used in the past include retracting the camera or plastic covers over the camera bay, but both methods have proven unreliable and often present more problems than they solve. In any case, a camera lens cleaning cloth should be kept as part of the ground service equipment as even an ideal landing can foul the lens with dust or plant debris.

Figure 9-2. Capture net for recovering a UAV.

Figure 9-3. Aerial arresting cable for fixed wing UAV recovery.

The use of parachutes is also an option for recovery. Parachute deployment should occur at the lowest practical altitude and airspeed as wind drift can be an issue with the aircraft being easily blown into nearby obstacles. A parachute consumes valuable fuselage interior space and restricts the payload that can be carried. Recovery nets also have a history of use in unmanned aircraft recovery. During a recovery, the aircraft is flown directly into a net that has been stretched between two poles above the ground that will absorb the impact without damage to the aircraft. The main disadvantage of the net recovery method is the skill required to hit a relatively small net. A slight miscalculation of position and/or direction of flight and the aircraft can impact a support pole or miss the net entirely. The snaring cable is a method that has been employed in military UAV operations. In this method, a cable is extended vertically and the aircraft flown into the cable for recovery.

The difficult launch and recovery of fixed wing UAVs has led to the use of helicopter or multirotor aircraft. As these aircraft can land at extremely slow speeds, a launch and retrieval system is seldom necessary. Unfortunately, the vibration, limited payload capability, and short flight durations of most rotorcraft make them a less than perfect alternative to fixed wing UAVs for many applications.

OPERATIONAL CONSIDERATIONS

Regardless of the type of unmanned aircraft in use, a formal set of written operating procedures, tailored to each specific aircraft and type of payload, are necessary if safe and reliable flights are to be conducted. Both comprehensive operating rules and procedures as well as specific, written checklists should be developed and used for each flight.

The actual preparation for any UAS mission should begin several days before ever arriving at the flying field. Preparation for a scheduled flight begins with a review of the mission requirements. Some mission requirements and questions to be asked include:

- Are there mission requirements for specific predicted weather, visibility, or sun position?
- Is the aircraft limited to operations below certain wind velocities or above certain temperatures?
- Can the FAA regulations specifying certain visibility, cloud clearances, and daylight operations be observed?
- Are there specific camera system limitations that will affect the flight?
- What are the regulatory requirements of the flight and have the proper notifications and clearances been obtained?
- Are there any special equipment requirements beyond the standard aircraft, payload, transmitter, and control systems?
- Have all the batteries been cycled, tested, and fully charged?

UAS Operational Checklist

✓ Preflight airframe/motor/prop for damage or wear.
✓ Erect laptop stand and wind direction pole.
✓ Assemble catapult into prevailing wind if used.
✓ Turn laptop on with telemetry USB plug inserted.
✓ Turn manual transmitter on, verify model selected, battery charge, mode switch manual (towards operator).
✓ Plug motor battery in to speed control plug to activate telemetry, GPS search, and motor power. Speed control will arm with tones at this time.
✓ Verify controls move correctly in manual AND autonomous modes.
✓ Range test manual radio with all telemetry powered (video tx) 70 paces, 360 deg.
✓ Open mission planner and verify GPS 3D lock, armed, and HOME identified on flight data HUD screen. Verify no error messages on HUD.
✓ Select and write waypoints from flight planner to autopilot including altitude.
✓ Return to flight data screen in mission planner for flight, again verify GPS 3D lock.
✓ Launch aircraft into prevailing wind, monitor battery capacity on HUD.
✓ Switch from manual to auto mode when safely above ground (about 200′).
✓ If problems occur, select Return-To-Land, (RTL) or Manual mode and land aircraft.
✓ When mission is complete, aircraft has returned, switch to manual mode for landing or parachute trigger.
✓ Retrieve aircraft, remove main motor power.
✓ Shut manual transmitter off.
✓ Shutdown laptop computer.

Figure 9-4. Sample operational checklist.

AUXILIARY EQUIPMENT

Aircraft used in field operations commonly sustain slight damage and/or have some minor problems once transported to the field. In an effort not to cancel any needed flights, yet maintaining the integrity of the vehicle and its systems, the operator must be prepared to make minor field repairs and modifications. A collection of prepared equipment will make it more likely that a successful series of flight missions can be conducted in the field.

Common items that might be needed to conduct operational UAS flights should be packaged together in rugged carrying cases. A "crash box" containing fast setting glues, tape, special tools, extra batteries, extra USB cords, propane soldering iron, solder, heat shrink tubing, lighter, hardware, and extra propellers will prevent cancelling or delaying flights due to small breakages or incidents.

The ground station case should contain items such as a laptop computer, telemetry receiver, video receiver, video screen, video goggles, sun shields, and associated batteries, chargers and/or power inverters (12-110 volts). Labeling various telemetry and transmitter components will help keep those assets organized when deploying multiple aircraft on multiple flights. During flight operations, a single transmitter may be used to control multiple aircraft at various times. This requires careful attention to controller programming and binding protocols.

Electrical power is essential for most UAS operations. If 110 volt ground power is not available, the 12 volt battery of the vehicle used to transport the aircraft and operators to the field site can provide the power for inverters and battery chargers. Be careful to start the vehicle to recharge the battery periodically as it may become excessively drained and not restart, stranding everyone at a remote location. Spare UAV and controller batteries should also be carried. These can be carried in a separate case. It is not recommended to store lithium polymer (lipo) batteries within carrying cases however, as the contents and area surrounding the case may be damaged if the battery ignites or smolders. There are commercially available fire retardant bags, as well as metal bunker type enclosures, for storing and charging lipo batteries. Lithium polymer batteries are also sensitive to overheating and freezing and should not be left in areas where these temperature extremes can occur.

Figure 9-5. Lipo battery safety bag.

An additional carrying case may be necessary during flight test operations, or when investigating system problems. This diagnostic case should contain items such as a tachometer, electrical multi-meter, IR temperature meter, radio spectrum analyzer, vibration meter, and EMI measurement tools. The instruments in this case can be used to measure performance and acquire the necessary information to generate operator's handbooks, aircraft specifications, and checklist limitations of critical system components as well as troubleshoot system problems in the field.

Additional equipment that should be carried to the field site include a first-aid kit, fire extinguisher, two-way radio equipment for ground personnel, and personal items such as sunscreen, sunglasses, charged cellular phone, hats, safety glasses, bug repellant, and sturdy walking shoes. When deployed in remote areas, invariably the aircraft and associated equipment will not always function perfectly and incidents will occur that require attention. Preparedness is essential to a successful day in the field.

Figure 9-6. Ground station with inverter power.

FLIGHT PROFILE AND PAYLOAD PLANNING

Flight profile refers to the path over the ground, and altitude selection, that the aircraft will travel during a flight with a particular payload. Topographical mapping and agricultural flights, with a camera as payload, typically fly grid like patterns at a specific altitude. Flights with air sampling payloads, for example, are often grid like as well, but at varying altitudes to map out a three dimensional column of air.

The autopilot waypoint profiles, as well as altitude or altitudes, will need to be preselected and programmed prior to flight. Careful and controlled visual and telemetry monitoring of the aircraft during the flight via line of sight (LOS) will be necessary to insure it is flying as directed. If the aircraft should deviate from the programmed waypoints, immediate operator intervention will be necessary to successfully recover the aircraft. If the aircraft should go down for any reason during a flight, telemetry data can be viewed to help locate the landing or crash site.

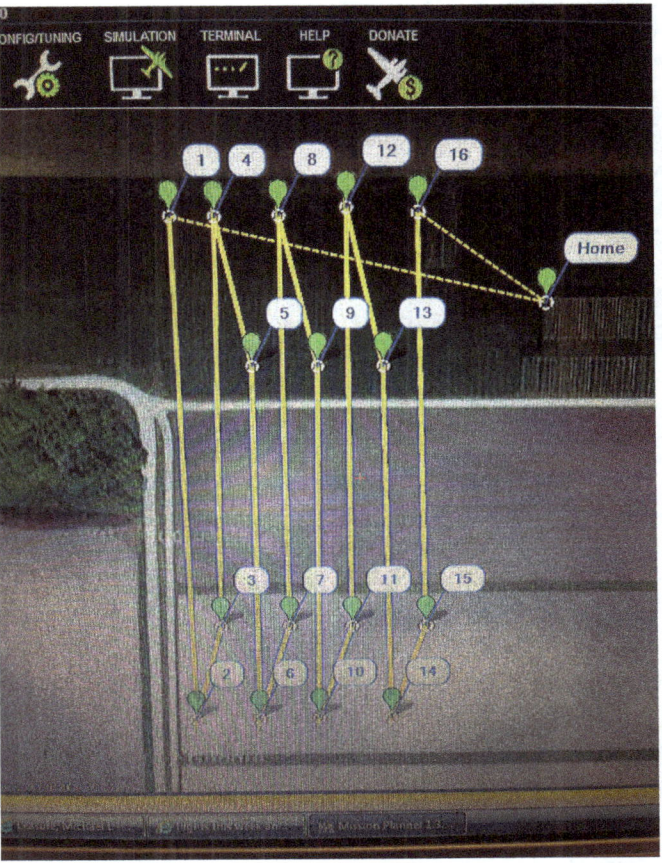

Figure 9-7. Waypoint assignment for agricultural imaging.

POST FLIGHT ANALYSIS

After every flight, whether a test or actual deployment flight, much can be gained by careful measurement and observation, as well as a review of the data. Autopilot telemetry data logs may be downloaded and can be viewed, highlighting important system performance. Batteries need to be recharged and the milliamps required to fully charge the battery should be noted as this information not only allows flight endurance to be more accurately predicted but can also reveal batteries that are beginning to deteriorate. Fuel tanks can refilled, with the amount of fuel used noted, again to be used to predict future flight duration more accurately. The airframe and powerplant should be inspected for anything that has become loose or damaged during the flight. Data should downloaded from the payload and viewed to determine if it is satisfactory or if another flight is needed.

In an effort to detect deteriorating performance in any system it is necessary to establish normal, or baseline, conditions and note any subsequent deviation from that norm. For instance, a higher than normal fuel consumption for a given flight could mean a leak has developed, the carburetor adjustments have changed, the engine is developing a problem, or simply that the programmed altitude of the flight was higher than normal and required more fuel to attain. Careful and methodical attention to detail will help prevent deteriorating conditions from becoming outright mission failures.

FLIGHT AND SYSTEMS TRAINING

Unmanned operator training has unique requirements not found in other areas of flight operations. There are time honored techniques of sharing the skills from instructor to student that have developed in the model aviation community. In recent years, unmanned aircraft training efforts using flight simulators has become popular and effective. Training for systems installation, programming, and testing are also an integral part of any unmanned program. Autonomous flight profiles are only as predictable and stable as the parameters that are programmed into the autopilot. Careful attention to detail, as well as knowledge of the complete flight control system, is essential for successful flight operations.

Figure 9-8. Simulator flight station.

UAS flight simulators have grown in both capability and effectiveness for training unmanned system operators. Modern simulators closely approximate the handling of various aircraft and may be configured to include weather, various scaling of aircraft, selectable propulsion means, and a host of other options. The actual radio transmitter used to control the sUAS when flying actual flights can be used in many cases. A data cord attached, either wirelessly or physically, to both the transmitter and computer is used to communicate with the simulator software.

Two camera views can usually be simulated which is very useful for training student operators. The line of sight view (LOS) replicates what one would see when operating an aircraft remotely from the ground. FPV view is the unobstructed view out the windshield of the aircraft. Both views are highly beneficial for simulating typical conditions of a live video feed or direct observation of the aircraft in flight. The windshield view (FPV) is most interesting as it closely approximates the video feed from the actual camera of a deployed unmanned aircraft.

The graphic presentation of the simulator can be made realistic enough that the operator in training may have difficulty determining whether it is live or simulated. This realistic approximation reduces the inherent challenges associated with transitioning between simulated and actual operations. The better the simulation software replicates actual operations, the better the training. It should be noted that students with computer gaming experience more quickly adapt to FPV view and acquire the ability to maneuver the aircraft successfully in a very short time. If that view is lost however, due to system failure during flight, manual flight control skills will be required to successfully recover the aircraft. These manual flight control skills may take longer for the new operator to develop.

Manual control flight skills are primarily acquired through observing and controlling an actual unmanned aircraft in flight, making small corrections, and noting the effects of those corrections. That being said, the novice UAV operator has neither the ability to visually detect aircraft orientation, nor the skill to quickly and precisely intervene when the aircraft begins to fly off in an unwanted direction, or spiral rapidly towards the ground. Just as in the manned aircraft training environment, it is necessary for the student to attempt flight, begin to see the loss of control, but then have an instructor intervene and regain control. As experience is gained, the instructor intervention becomes less common.

Takeoff and landing training usually follows the successful demonstration of in-flight control. At this point in the training process, unusual flight attitude recovery, flight in windy conditions, as well as flight with failed engines may be introduced to further refine the student's ability to handle aircraft in less than optimum situations.

In early radio control flight training efforts with model aircraft, a single transmitter was handed back and forth from instructor to student. This awkward process resulted in many instructors holding a transmitter, hastily taken from a student, just as the aircraft impacted the ground. A "buddy" or training cord was then introduced into popular use that allowed the instructor to hold a training switch on the master transmitter, allowing the student to manipulate the controls until the switch was released, with the instructor once again assuming control. This system allows a seamless transfer of control of the aircraft from one transmitter to another. The switch action is quick and precise enough to allow successful training in landings and other maneuvers close to the ground.

SYSTEMS TRAINING

The operator's ability to manually fly a UAS is only a portion of the skill set required to become a competent operator. Correct flight control system installation, as well as autopilot programming, is essential to the reliable operation of the aircraft. Although autopilots are capable of completely controlling a flight from takeoff to landing with no manual flight control skills required, they only operate as programmed. Proper programming includes waypoint assignment as well as flight parameter adjustments. The installation of an autonomous system in an actual aircraft can be intimidating to a beginning operator. The many components and associated wiring seems complex. The myriad of flight control parameter options can be intimidating to the beginner as well. It is beneficial to take a measured approach to beginning systems training with the simplest systems used as a starting point.

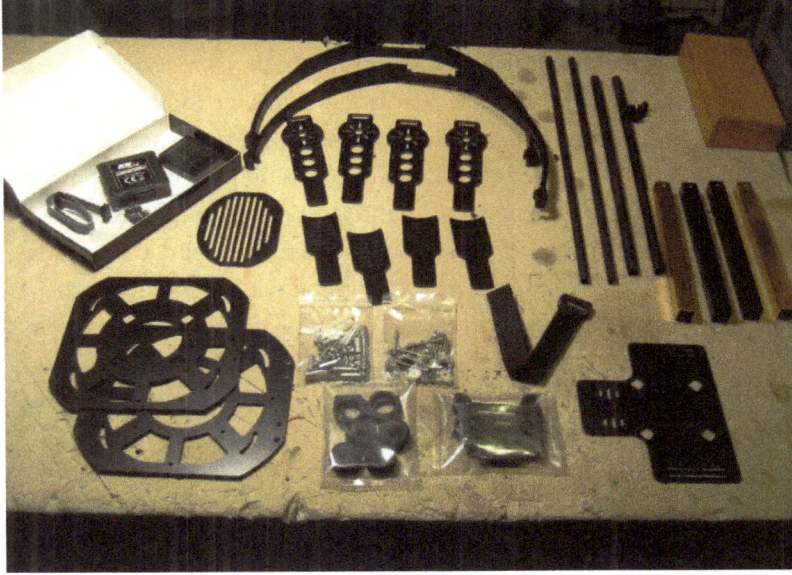

Figure 9-9. Parts of multirotor prior to assembly.

A simple flight stabilization board and manual flight control receiver installation can be used to expose the beginning operator, or technician, to the terminology, components, techniques, and wiring layout of an autopilot system. Telemetry, GPS receivers, waypoint navigation assignment, and payload control can be added as the beginner gains experience. Using a simple flight stabilization board, PID flight control values may be adjusted, and their effects noted directly on aircraft behavior. The initial establishment of motor direction of rotation, and associated propeller rotational requirements, may seem elementary to the seasoned operator but is a new experience for the beginner. Basic skills such as soldering and connector selection can be introduced at this time as well. Battery charging, basic hardware selection, and airframe material type identification are

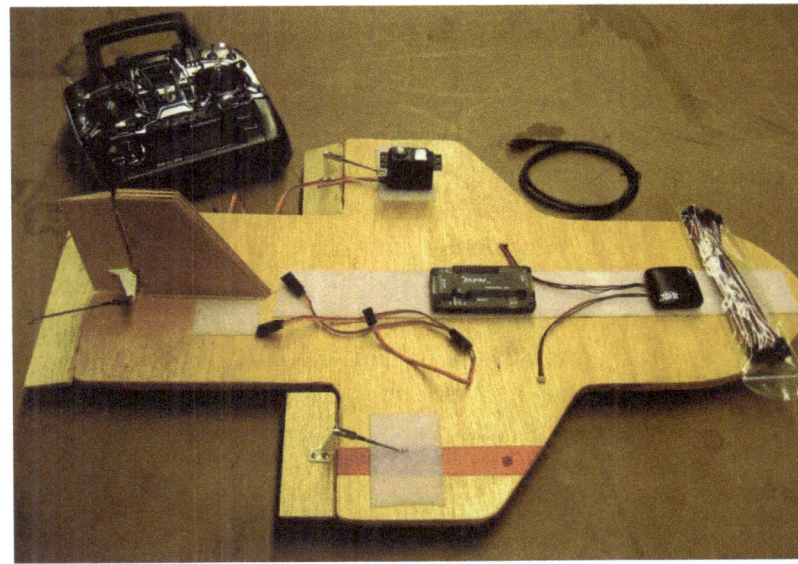

Figure 9-10. Autonomous system trainer mockup board.

all essential skills to be introduced with a basic aircraft system install. Simple repairs, rudimentary fabrication skills, and experience using a computer to research online tutorials must be developed before full autonomous systems can be used.

A simulated autonomous aircraft mockup board has proven useful in teaching basic system installation and programming. It may be beneficial to have several types of boards including flying wing, conventional three axes, and multirotor types as each installation is different in its wiring and programming. The board has all of the components of an installed system. The open layout provides the beginner with a clearer view of the relationship of each component to the others. The mockup board may have all of the more complex system components required of a fully autonomous aircraft without risking such an actual aircraft to beginner's mistakes. Waypoint assignment for a mock autonomous flight can be very revealing at first as the units of altitude selected, or the flight path selected, commonly results in the aircraft being programmed to fly directly into buildings and towers. These mistakes are best made on a non-flying board.

BATTERY MANAGEMENT

Understanding the condition of the batteries powering the various systems of an unmanned aircraft and ground station is essential to safe and reliable flight. Their condition should be methodically monitored by charging and discharging on a regular schedule to detect degrading performance or imminent failure. An 80 percent reduction in capacity below rated, puffing of the battery pack, a distinct chemical odor, or any observed physical damage is cause to discard the pack. Of all the battery types available, the lithium polymer battery has the most demanding service requirements and dangerous failure modes. The charger for a lithium polymer (lipo) battery must be designed and rated specifically for the charging and discharging of this type of battery. Preferably, the charger will have a built in balancing circuit with a connector to the specific lipo pack being charged. Typically a lipo is charged at 1C, meaning 1 times the packs rated capacity. As an example, a 2400 milliamp hour pack would be safely charged at 2.4 amps. The discharge capacity of lipo batteries varies from 15C to over 100C with the high discharge rates being more costly and better suited for extreme amperage discharge installations without overheating and damage.

Figure 9-11. A popular charger designed specifically for lipo battery charge, balance, and discharge

The lipo battery may ignite and burn rapidly, or explode if mishandled. The charging and inspection precautions listed above should prove adequate to keep this from occurring. As a precaution, never leave lipo batteries charging or discharging unattended. There are fire proof charging bunkers and bags designed specifically to contain the flames of an ignited lipo. They are only designed to be used while personnel stand ready to react to a battery emergency. Lipo battery storage for an extended period of time should be done with the battery at 40-50% capacity and in a stable temperature environment near 70 degrees F.

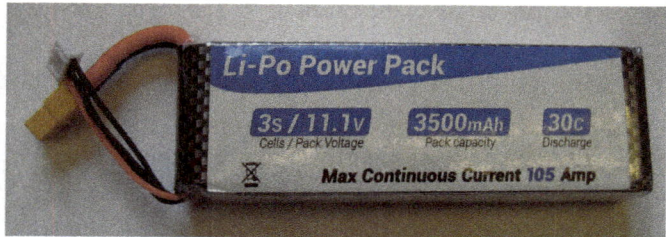

Figure 9-12. A lithium polymer battery pack with voltage and discharge ratings shown.

DOCUMENTS RELEVANT TO PERFORMANCE AND FLIGHT

Manned aircraft operations rely upon several important documents to operate safely and provide guidance for repairs and maintenance. Among those documents are the Pilots Operating Handbook (POH), Weight and Balance forms, Type Certificate Data Sheets or aircraft specifications (TCDS), and the Structural Repair Manual (SRM). FAA mandated Airworthiness Directives (AD), also provide valuable information on correcting known failure possibilities and safety issues on manned aircraft. Manufacturers provide Service Instructions (SI), which provide guidance for maintenance and repair of their particular aircraft. Most small unmanned aircraft currently in use do not have the level of sophisticated performance and operating documentation commonly found in manned aviation. The development of these documents, and the testing and research required for their development, is an important step in the safe integration of unmanned systems in the National Airspace System (NAS).

PILOTS (OPERATORS) OPERATING HANDBOOK

The POH includes all of the information required for the pilot/operator to perform their duties in a safe and informed manner. Aircraft features and instructions for their use are included. Aircraft performance charts, listing such variables as ambient temperature, runway altitude above sea level, and their effect on the specific aircraft's operation, are included. Operator's preflight checklists are included, as well as emergency or unusual aircraft operations checklists. The recommended inspection procedures and checklists are included with notes regarding specific access to parts of the aircraft during inspection. A weight and balance chart is common as well with the limits of the center of gravity and maximum payloads shown.

An unmanned aircraft POH should include items listed above, as well as equipment options and their effect on weight, balance, performance, and handling of the aircraft. In practical use, the observer and operator should work closely together in applying the information in the POH.

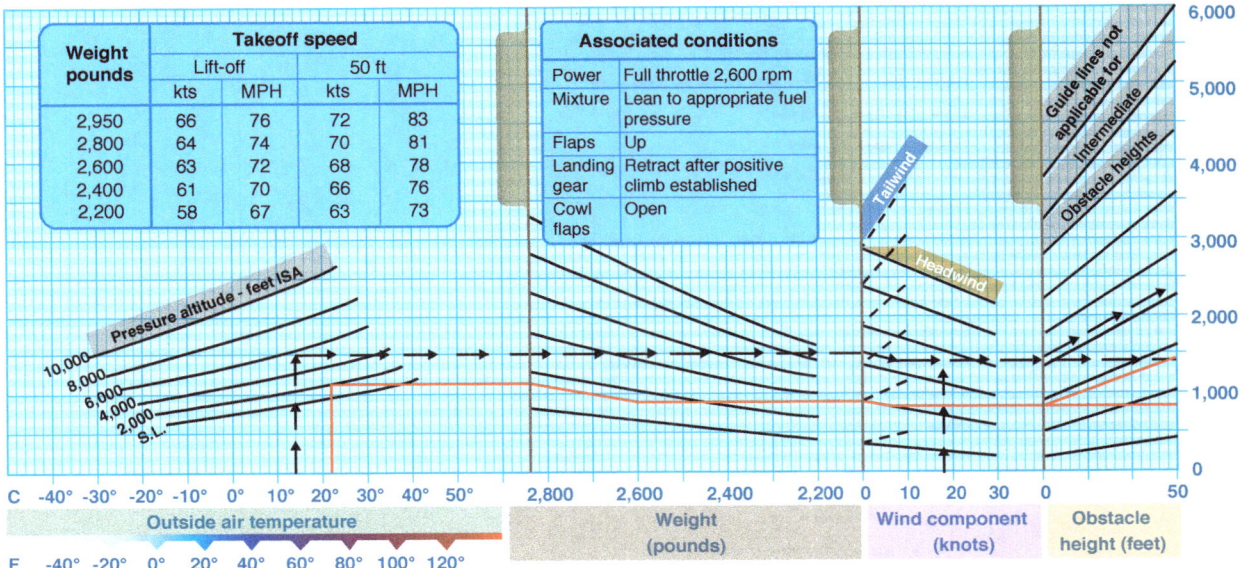

Figure 9-13. Performance charts from POH.

TYPE CERTIFICATE DATA SHEETS

Useful to operator, observer, and technician alike, the TCDS provides all of the official information for the physical dimensions of the aircraft, speed limits and ranges, equipment installed, weight and balance determination methods and limits, as well as propulsion details. The type of fuels, oils, batteries, and sparkplugs, that can be used are included. An unmanned TCDS should include all information necessary to properly maintain and operate the aircraft.

STRUCTURAL REPAIR MANUAL

A structural repair manual is typically produced by the manufacturer of the aircraft and includes all common airframe repair information. Specifics of each typical repair likely to be needed are listed including material types required, adhesives recommended, special fastener types, and determining if repairs have been completed properly through testing. The SRM may not include all possible damage and repair scenarios however. If a repair is needed that is not typical, the manufacturer may be contacted for guidance. The FAA has published an Advisory Circular that lists recommended repair procedures and processes for a wide range of typical construction materials. AC 43-13 is primarily targeted towards manned aircraft repair; however, it contains a wealth of information in such areas as composite, metal, and wood structure repair that are directly applicable to unmanned structures.

WEIGHT AND BALANCE FORMS

All aircraft must balance and weigh within certain limits to achieve safe, controlled flight. The aircraft is physically weighed using scales, and calculations are made to determine where it balances. This balance point is referenced from a designated forward location called the datum. The empty weight of the aircraft is determined by adding the scale values. Test flights are performed to determine the safe operating range of the balance point as well as the maximum weight the aircraft can safely carry. To be safe, a loaded aircraft must not exceed its maximum gross weight, or loaded balance range. The weight and balance form is used prior to an unmanned aircraft flight to determine if it is loaded properly and can operate safely.

```
Type Certificate Data Sheet, Unmanned:                    30-30 UAS, Heavy Lift,
                                                          Leasure
Span – 131 inches
                                                          2014
Chord – 23.375

Length – 110.875

Max gross weight – 55 pounds

Datum – forward tip of nose cone

Center of Gravity (CG ) – 41.5" to 43.33" aft of datum, (25-30% MAC)

Gear – conventional tricycle, steerable nose

Cargo Bay Dimensions – 8 inches wide, 8 inches tall, 21 inches long

Engine – 53cc XYZ, 5.5 horsepower

Propeller - Zinger 20 x 8 Pusher

Fuel – 100 octane with 40:1 oil mix

Fuel tank capacity – 1000cc

Flight Controls – Rudder, Elevator, Throttle, Ailerons, 30 degree Flaps

Radio channels utilized (manual flight) 6

Frequency of transmitter – 2.4Gz. spread spectrum, Turnigy Taranis

Available channels – 16

EMI shielded conduit – full span in wing leading edge, cargo bay

Telemetry bays – each wingtip

NOTES:

Ground Handling - Aircraft to be lifted at spar location of wing, or fuselage only.  Wing leading edge is very fragile

Primary construction materials – Birch plywood, balsa, white pine, fiberglass/epoxy, 6061 aluminum

Covering – TopFlite Monokote

Adhesives – epoxy, aliphatic wood glue, or cyanoacrylate

Power – 12 volt, 7Ah Lead acid sealed battery, charge at 1 Ah rate
```

Figure 9-14. TCDS specifications for unmanned aircraft.

AIRWORTHINESS DIRECTIVES

FAA publishes Airworthiness Directives for manned aircraft that cover events that might make it unsafe to operate an aircraft, part, accessory, or powerplant. The AD provides information about when and how to correct the unsafe condition. This action typically includes required parts inspections, replacements, or repairs as outlined in the AD. Complying with the AD is mandatory and operations may not continue until the AD requirements are met. The AD system is primarily for manned aircraft; however, if an unmanned aircraft utilizes a powerplant or accessory that is certified for use on a manned aircraft as well, the unmanned aircraft would need to comply with the AD.

OPERATOR'S LOGBOOK

The logbook is used to record operator flight time. There is a place to record the date, duration of flight, type of aircraft and equipment used, as well as a notes to record significant aspects of a particular flight. The operator logbook is essential when

AIRWORTHINESS DIRECTIVE

FAA
Aircraft Certification Service

www.faa.gov/aircraft/safety/alerts/
www.gpoaccess.gov/fr/advanced.html

2008-11-18 Cirrus Design Corporation: Amendment 39-15541; Docket No. FAA-2008-0284; Directorate Identifier 2008-CE-006-AD.

Effective Date

(a) This AD becomes effective on July 7, 2008.

Affected ADs

(b) None.

Applicability

(c) This AD applies to Model SR20 airplanes, serial numbers 1005 through 1815, that are certificated in any category.

Unsafe Condition

(d) This AD results from the discovery of engine exhaust fumes in the cabin of Cirrus Design Corporation Model SR20 airplanes. We are issuing this AD to detect and correct leaks in the exhaust system, which could result in exhaust gases leaking into the cabin heating system. This condition could lead to carbon monoxide in the cabin and incapacitation of the pilot.

Figure 9-15. Airworthiness Directive (AD) sample.

documenting experience with various unmanned aircraft types and equipment. It is used in the application for approved operations from the FAA and may provide useful information as to operator competence for insurance, employment, and training credentials. It is best to keep the logbook current by recording flights soon after their conclusion.

SIGNAL SPOOFING

Spoofing is the application of incorrect or very powerful signals in an attempt to interfere with or confuse the sensors of an autonomous system. This is an effort to confuse, degrade, or hijack control of the system. As unmanned operations become

Figure 9-16. Operator's logbook.

more commonplace, and the value of the equipment onboard realized by a larger segment of the population, attempts might be made to interfere with the aircraft's guidance and control systems in order to hijack or steal the aircraft. Another reason to interfere with operations might be a desire to protect one's perceived privacy through inappropriate means.

Military operations require that operators attempt to both attack and defend UAVs by any means available. Privately operated UAVs can be "attacked" as well by "spoofing" or confusing the electronics contained in unmanned systems. Modern UAS systems use GPS, compass, telemetry, and radio or satellite control extensively. Each of these sensor inputs is susceptible to being hijacked, or overpowered, by knowledgeable personnel. A means of defending or hardening systems against this sort of unauthorized control needs to be considered.

ENCRYPTION

One defense for unwanted signals being used against a UAV system is by encrypting the radio links in both the manual control transmitter and telemetry. At the time this book was written, the 2.4Ghz spread spectrum radios used by UAVs are fairly resistant to hacking. The coding/decoding of the unique control signal, as well as the use of frequency hopping, makes this system difficult to interfere with, much less take over control. Telemetry radio signals, however, are not encoded and can be easily overpowered. Research and development on reducing the possibility of unauthorized control of onboard systems against outside interference in both military and civilian applications is ongoing.

A strategy that may be used to protect an autonomous system from spoofing or hijacking is the ability of the system to eliminate external sensor data, if suspected of being illegitimate, and relying upon onboard, self-contained systems for guidance and control, even for short periods. The research in the use of artificial intelligence (AI) to determine if sensor data is legitimate or not, and the ability to manage input from various sensors to determine the most probable correct data is ongoing and shows promise for safer, more reliable autonomous aircraft.

UNMANNED SYSTEMS HUMAN FACTORS AND SAFETY

The FAA has been tasked with the oversight of the national airspace system of the United States. A wealth of information and programs related to aviation human factors and safety for manned aircraft has been developed and is applicable to unmanned operations. One of these resources, a concept FAA has termed "The Dirty Dozen" is one that is very relevant to unmanned operations.

Since unmanned systems still involve operators, technicians, observers, and other support personnel, the human aspect of the safety equation applies to UAV operations, people, and systems as well. The dozen factors affecting safety the FAA has identified are specifically targeted to manned aircraft maintenance technicians; however, UAV operators and others in the system can learn from the concepts presented. A summary of the dozen subject areas related to challenges in human factors related to safety with recommendations for addressing each are shown in Figure 9-17.

Unmanned Aerial Systems: The Definitive Guide

Figure 9-17. The FAA identified "Dirty Dozen" of human factors in safety.

An example of a direct application of the "Dirty Dozen" to unmanned system operation is number 12: Norms. Norms describe expected, yet unwritten, rules of behavior. These norms can be negative in the sense that they are unsafe or produce undesirable risks. For example, when someone's reason for performing a task is that they have always done it that way, this is a response that creates concern and must be examined to determine if it is a negative norm. Norms may be positive as well. The use of a comprehensive checklist prior to each flight of an unmanned aircraft is a positive norm. The checklist is written, but the act of following that checklist is a positive norm.

Another example directly applicable to UAS operations is number 6: Fatigue. Fatigue can affect everyone involved in unmanned system operations. Operators have difficulty multitasking, technicians overlook critical system faults, and observers fail to maintain adequate situational awareness when fatigue sets in. Fatigue may not simply be inadequate sleep or a long day of operations; various common illnesses, medications, and repetitive work can lead to fatigue. The negative risks of fatigue are best alleviated by having others check your performance and be observant of the effects in yourself and others.

In unmanned operations, the effects of fatigue can manifest themselves in forgetting important steps, such as turning on the manual flight transmitter prior to powering up an aircraft, or failing to monitor GPS satellite status prior to launch. Autonomous systems may, or may not, help expose these oversights, but are certainly not to be relied upon in the event of personnel fatigue. The dozen factors are also a reminder that unmanned aviation is a serious endeavor with serious implications for safety and performance from its participants.

CHAPTER 10

REGULATIONS

FEDERAL AVIATION REGULATIONS

The FAA, under the authority of Congress, has the authority to regulate flight in the airspace over the United States. There is some legal dispute as to exactly what is meant by the term "airspace" however. Some view this as all the airspace above both public and private property within the confines of the U.S. Others interpret it to mean the navigable airspace of the United States. In any case, the FAA claims jurisdiction over most UAV flight operations.

By law, any aircraft operation in the national airspace requires a certificated and registered aircraft, a licensed pilot, and operational approval. These requirements are contained in the Federal Aviation Regulations, which are a part of Title 14 of the Code of Federal Regulations (14 CFR). These regulations, commonly referred to as FARs, are broken down into Volumes, Chapters and Parts. There are hundreds of "Parts" that apply to aviators, including UAV operators. It is a complex and interlocking regulatory systems with many different "Parts" applying to different operations. There isn't a single "UAV FAR"; applicable regulations are found in various parts of the FARs. A partial list of the current regulations more likely to be applicable to UAV operations is included below.

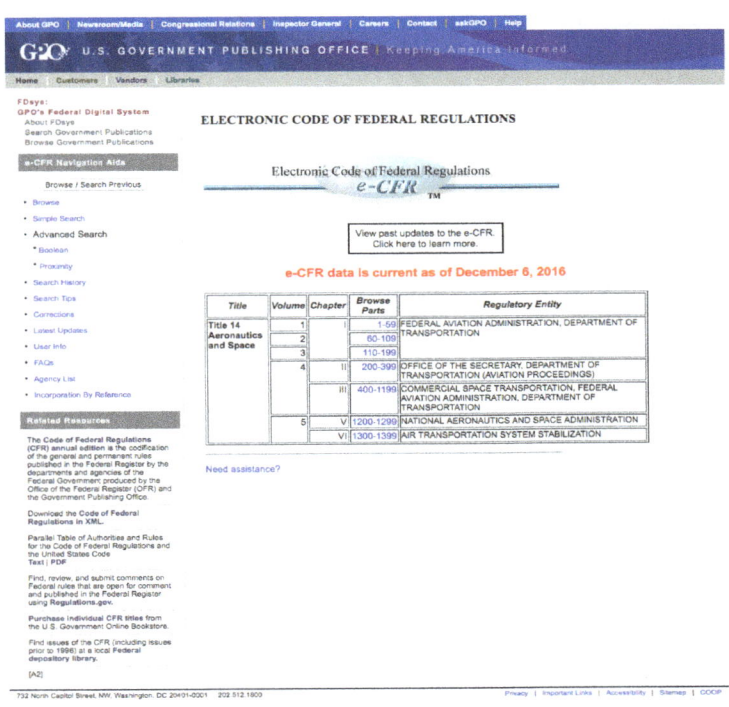

Figure 10-1. Federal Aviation Regulations website.

Subchapter A—Definitions and General Requirements
1 Definitions and Abbreviations
3 General Requirements

Unmanned Aerial Systems: The Definitive Guide

Subchapter B—Procedural Rules
13   Investigative and Enforcement Procedures

Subchapter C—Aircraft
23   Airworthiness Standards: Normal, Utility, Acrobatic, and Commuter Category Airplanes
43   Maintenance, Preventive Maintenance, Rebuilding, and Alteration
45   Identification and Registration Marking
47   Aircraft Registration

Subchapter D—Airmen
61   Certification: Pilots, Flight Instructors, and Ground Instructors
65   Certification: Airmen Other Than Flight Crewmembers
67   Medical Standards and Certification

Subchapter E—Airspace
71   Designation of Class A, B, C, D, and E Airspace Areas;
73   Special Use Airspace

Subchapter F—Air Traffic and General Operating Rules
91   General Operating and Flight Rules
93   Special Air Traffic Rules
139   Certification of Airports

During the spring of 2015, the FAA proposed a new regulation to be designated as FAR Part 107 that is supposed to help define the regulations as they apply to UAV operations. The authors of this book are not lawyers and are in no position to definitively interpret government policy and legal standing for every situation. This chapter will attempt to explain the most recent interpretation of any UAS rules, but anyone flying either a small or micro UAS, either commercially or privately, should consult any and all current, related documents and rules before flying any aircraft in what the FAA might consider regulated airspace.

The proposed regulation, to be known as FAR part 107: Small Unmanned Aircraft Systems, would generally require some level of FAA approval to fly unmanned vehicles; either privately or commercially. The notice of proposed rulemaking actually proposes changes to Far Parts 21, 43, 45, 47, 61, 91, 101, and 183 in addition to the creation of the new FAR. All of these changes are an attempt by the FAA to define the regulations concerning UAV operations. In general, the new regulatory proposal only applies to UAVs that weigh less than 55 pounds. Larger UAVs are still governed by existing manned aircraft regulations.

Anyone who wants to fly any type of aircraft, either piloted or not, in U.S. airspace is required to follow the rules promulgated by the FAA. Some operations such as model or hobby aircraft may be exempted from specific FAA regulations, but still come under the overall purview of the FARs. Small UAVs might be granted some sort of exemption, but even so, must still conform to the applicable FARs.

The FAA currently permits privately owned, hobbyist operated UAV aircraft, flown for recreation purposes only, to be exempted from some FARs so long as the operators conform to model aircraft requirements. Commercial UAS operations are limited and require each operator to have specific operating approval unless they have obtained an exemption. Commercial operators and public entities (such as state and local government agencies, as well as public schools and universities) are required to apply for and receive a Certificate of Authorization (COA) before they can currently conduct flight operations.

As proposed in the new rules, small UASs, flown solely for hobby or recreational reasons typically will not require FAA approval. However, hobbyists are still required to operate their aircraft in accordance with the FAAs model aircraft guidelines as printed in Advisory Circular 91-57; Model Aircraft Operating Standards. Advisory Circulars (AC) are a publication by the FAA that provides guidance for compliance with the FARs. They define acceptable, but not the only, means of accomplishing or showing compliance with the FARs. Technically, Advisory Circulars are neither binding nor regulatory; but they have more or less the effect of standards or regulations.

Congress has exempted model aircraft from the proposed new regulations provided the aircraft are operated "in accordance with a community-based set of safety guidelines and within the programming of a nationwide community-based organization." Advisory Circular 91-57 states that modelers generally are concerned about safety and exercise good judgment when flying model aircraft. However, model aircraft can, at times, pose a hazard to full-scale aircraft in flight and to persons and property on the surface. Compliance with the following standards will help reduce the potential for hazardous operations.

The advisory circular prescribes operating standards that suggest that model aircraft operators should:

1. Select an operating site that is of sufficient distance from populated areas. The selected site should be away from noise sensitive areas such as parks, schools, hospitals, churches, etc. No specific distance is specified in the advisory circular however.
2. Not operate model aircraft in the presence of spectators until the aircraft has been successfully flight tested and proven airworthy.
3. Not fly model aircraft higher than 400 feet above the ground.
    a. When flying aircraft within 3 miles of an airport, operators shall notify the airport operator, or when an air traffic facility is located at the airport, notify the control tower, or flight service station.
4. Give right of way to, and avoid flying in the proximity of, full-scale aircraft. Use observers to help with this task if appropriate.

The FAA Modernization and Reform Act of 2012 has a section related to model aircraft operation which reads as follows.

AC 91-57

DATE June 9, 1981

ADVISORY CIRCULAR

DEPARTMENT OF TRANSPORTATION
Federal Aviation Administration
Washington, D.C.

Subject: MODEL AIRCRAFT OPERATING STANDARDS

1. PURPOSE. This advisory circular outlines, and encourages voluntary compliance with, safety standards for model aircraft operators.

2. BACKGROUND. Modelers, generally, are concerned about safety and do exercise good judgement when flying model aircraft. However, model aircraft can at times pose a hazard to full-scale aircraft in flight and to persons and property on the surface. Compliance with the following standards will help reduce the potential for that hazard and create a good neighbor environment with affected communities and airspace users.

3. OPERATING STANDARDS.

a. Select an operating site that is of sufficient distance from populated areas. The selected site should be away from noise sensitive areas such as parks, schools, hospitals, churches, etc.

b. Do not operate model aircraft in the presence of spectators until the aircraft is successfully flight tested and proven airworthy.

c. Do not fly model aircraft higher than 400 feet above the surface. When flying aircraft within 3 miles of an airport, notify the airport operator, or when an air traffic facility is located at the airport, notify the control tower, or flight service station.

d. Give right of way to, and avoid flying in the proximity of, full-scale aircraft. Use observers to help if possible.

e. Do not hesitate to ask for assistance from any airport traffic control tower or flight service station concerning compliance with these standards.

R. J. VAN VUREN
Director, Air Traffic Service

Initiated by: AAT-220

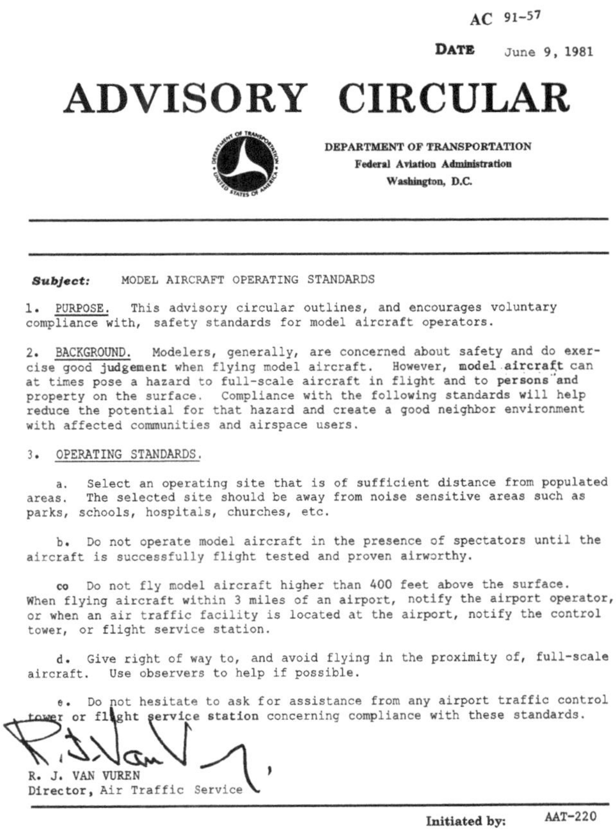

Figure 10-2. Advisory circular 91-57.

SEC. 336. Special Rule for Model Aircraft.

(a) IN GENERAL.—Notwithstanding any other provision of law relating to the incorporation of unmanned aircraft systems into Federal Aviation Administration plans and policies, including this subtitle, the Administrator of the Federal Aviation Administration may not promulgate any rule or regulation regarding a model aircraft, or an aircraft being developed as a model aircraft, if;

1. The aircraft is flown strictly for hobby or recreational use;
2. The aircraft is operated in accordance with a community-based set of safety guidelines and within the programming of a nationwide community-based organization;

The aircraft is limited to not more than 55 pounds unless otherwise certified through a design, construction, inspection, flight test, and operational safety program administered by a community-based organization;

3. The aircraft is operated in a manner that does not interfere with and gives way to any manned aircraft; and
4. When flown within 5 miles of an airport, the operator of the aircraft provides the airport operator and the airport air traffic control tower (when an air traffic facility is located at the airport) with prior notice of the operation (model aircraft operators flying from a permanent location within 5 miles of an airport should establish a mutually-agreed upon operating procedure with the airport operator and the airport air traffic control tower (when an air traffic facility is located at the airport).

In this section, "model aircraft" is defined as a vehicle
- Capable of sustained flight in the atmosphere;
- Flown within visual line of sight of the person operating the aircraft; and
- Flown for hobby or recreational purposes.

The FAA still asserts that the FARs apply to UAS operations, even those covered by the Advisory Circular and the model aircraft rules. In particular, FAR part 91.13 reads:

"No person may operate an aircraft in a careless or reckless manner so as to endanger the life or property of another."

It is under this FARs that the FAA can and has chosen to prosecute UAS operators operating in an unsafe manner.

As currently interpreted, compensation of any sort for any model aircraft use is banned. The FAA claims that the flying of a UAV drone in a manner that is "in furtherance of a business" takes it out of realm of "model aviation". The only way to currently fly a UAS for commercial purposes is to receive either an exemption from the FARs and/or receive a Certificate of Authorization (COA) from the FAA for commercial operations. The interpretation of "in furtherance of business" has been loosely defined but seems to include aerial photography (for pay of any sort), flight instruction or commercial demonstrations. Broadcasting photos or video obtained from a UAV is considered a commercial activity as are operations "for hire". Colleges and universities who charge tuition for UAS classes are currently considered by the FAA to be commercial in nature as well.

PROPOSED NEW UAS RULES

On February 15, 2015, the FAA issued its Notice of Proposed Rulemaking (NPRM), entitled "Operation and Certification of Small Unmanned Aircraft Systems." The proposed rule, which as of the publication date of this text has not been published, would define and permit UAS operations for non-hobbyists, thereby allowing commercial operations under certain conditions. The NPRM is a proposed rule and subject to change before it eventually becomes a federal aviation regulation. The NPRM is not law at this time. The NPRM process can be time consuming, requiring public input and FAA rule modification based on that input. This could easily result in changes to the rule before it is published.

OPERATIONAL REQUIREMENTS

The proposed FAR would permit the commercial operation of UAV so long as the following requirements were met:

VEHICLE REQUIREMENTS

- An FAA airworthiness certification would not be required.
- The total weight of the unmanned aircraft must be less than 55 pounds (25kg).
- The vehicle must be maintained in condition for safe operation and prior to each flight must be inspected to ensure it is in a condition for safe operation.
- Aircraft registration is required in the same manner that applies to all other aircraft.
- Aircraft markings are required in the same manner that applies to all other aircraft, but if aircraft is too small to display markings in standard size, then the aircraft simply needs to display markings in the largest practicable manner.

OPERATOR REQUIREMENTS

- Operators must:
  - Be at least 16 years old.
  - Be vetted by the Transportation Security Administration.
  - Pass an initial aeronautical knowledge test at an FAA-approved knowledge testing center.
  - Obtain an "unmanned aircraft operator certificate" with a "small drone rating," which never expires.
  - Pass a recurrent aeronautical knowledge test every 24 months.
  - Make available to the FAA, upon request, the drone for inspection or testing, and any associated documents/records required to be kept under the proposed rule.
  - Report an accident to the FAA within 10 days of any operation that results in injury or property damage.

OPERATIONAL REQUIREMENTS

Under the proposed rule, UASs:

- Must remain within visual line of sight of the operator or visual observer.
- Must remain close enough to the operator for the operator to be able to see the aircraft with vision unaided by any device other than corrective lenses.
- May not operate over any persons not directly involved in the operation.
- May only be operated from official sunrise to official sunset (local time).
- Must yield the right-of-way to other aircraft, whether manned or unmanned.
- May, but are not required to use a visual observer.
- Cannot satisfy "see-and-avoid" requirements using first person view (FPV) cameras, but FPV but can be used as long as requirement is satisfied in other ways.
- May be flown at a maximum airspeed of 100 mph (87 knots).
- May be flown at a maximum altitude of 500 feet above ground level.
- Must have minimum weather visibility of 3 miles from the UAV control station.
- May not be flown in Class A (18,000 feet & above) airspace.
- May be flown in Class B, C, D and E airspace with ATC permission.
- May be flown in Class G airspace are allowed without ATC permission.
- May not be flown carelessly or recklessly.
- Operations from a moving vehicle or aircraft are not permitted, except from a watercraft on the water.
- Require a preflight inspection before each flight, including specific aircraft and control station systems checks, to ensure the drone is safe for operation.
- May not be flown by a person if he or she knows or has reason to know of any physical or mental condition that would interfere with its safe operation.
- No person may act as an operator or visual observer for more than one unmanned aircraft operation at one time.

MICRODRONE OPTION

The NPRM also appears to propose a "micro drone" option. The FAA states in its NPRM that it is considering the following, with respect to the operation of micro drones:

- A micro drone would weigh no more than 4.4 pounds (2 kilograms).
- It would be made out of frangible materials that break, distort, or yield on impact so as to present a minimal hazard to any person or object that the unmanned aircraft collides with.
- It would not exceed an airspeed of 30 knots.
- It would not travel higher than 400 feet above ground level (AGL).
- It would be flown within visual line of sight; first-person view would not be used during the operation; and the aircraft would not travel farther than 1,500 feet away from the operator.
- The operator would maintain manual control of the flight path of the unmanned aircraft at all times, and the operator would not use automation to control the flight path of the unmanned aircraft.
- Operations would be limited entirely to Class G airspace.
- It would need to maintain a distance of at least 5 nautical miles from any airport.

PROPOSED FARS THAT RELATE TO UAVS

The proposed rules governing commercial UAS operations are listed below. The left hand column is the rule or change as proposed by the FAA in February 2015. The right column is the author's interpretation/explanation of the rule. This could and will likely change prior to becoming an actual FAR. When reading the text, the symbol § is legal shorthand for "part", as in FAR part… the symbol §§ stands for the plural…."parts".

STATE AND LOCAL LAW

States and local governments cannot preempt federal law (FARs) when it comes to the operation of small UASs, but there are a lot of UAV applications that can and will be covered by local and state law. Some of these applications include the use of UAVs by law enforcement, surveillance, wildlife tracking, search and rescue operations, as well as disaster response. Personal and public privacy concerns are also driving this issue. So far, about half of the states have enacted laws that address UAS issues. For example, many states define what is a UAV and limit, or place restriction on, their use by law enforcement. Some state and local law attempts to establish guidelines for the use of UAVs by private citizens as well and provide civil penalties for damages caused by improper use.

Some laws have been enacted that specify when the information obtained from a UAS can be admitted as evidence in any prosecution or civil proceeding within the state. The information can usually be used when it was obtained pursuant to a search warrant, or through a judicially recognized exception to search warrants.

State law has been enacted in some jurisdictions which make it a crime to mount weapons on UAVs, and makes it illegal to interfere with, or gain unauthorized access to, either public or private UAS vehicles. Other laws attempts to define under what conditions, if any, a landowner can bring an action against someone flying a UAV over their property.

Many states are looking into means by which UAVs can be operated while still protecting individual and public privacy. Laws have been written that regulate how law enforcement can obtain and use information gathered from a third (private) party's use of UAS. These laws are also beginning to address if, and when, police can access and use the data collected during routine UAV operations. In some jurisdictions, it is now a misdemeanor if an operator knowingly and intentionally electronically surveys the private property of another without permission. Some state law prohibits taking a photo of a person without their consent for the purpose of distributing it. Some states are considering the use of, and the legal implications and limitations of, using UAVs to enforce traffic laws. Most states define unlawful fishing or hunting with a UAS as well as considering what constitutes "harassment" by UAS.

There will likely be more laws concerning UAVs and their operation enacted over the next few years. The best way to keep up to date is to join a professional UAV association such as AVUSI, monitor professional postings on social media, as well as monitor applicable state law. Most states and some localities place their legal code on the internet where it is available for all to view. Of particular interest, would be the aviation section of the state legal code. It may go by the term aeronautics rather than the more common aviation reference.

FAR 91 AND 101 PROPOSED CHANGES

Proposed Rule or Change	Interpretation
91.1 Applicability.	FAR part 91 is composed of the basic flight rules for manned and unmanned flight including both private and commercial operations
Except as provided in paragraphs (b), (c), and (e) of this section and §§ 91.701 and 91.703, this part prescribes rules governing the operation of aircraft within the United States, including the waters within 3 nautical miles of the U.S. coast.	This part states that the regulation covers flight activities that occur over the land (and water) mass of the U. S. extending outward 3 miles over the ocean. It basically describes the extent of coverage of US law to what is the commonly accepted standard. FAR 91.701 and 91.703 are related to the operation of foreign registered aircraft within the US, and the operation of US registered aircraft outside of the country.
Except as provided in §§ 107.27, 107.47, 107.57, and 107.59 of this chapter, this part does not apply to any aircraft or vehicle governed by part 103 of this chapter, part 107 of this chapter, or subparts B, C, or D of part 101 of this chapter.	These parts refer to particular operator offenses that could get one in trouble with the FAA 107.2. Alcohol or drugs. 107.4. Flight restrictions in the proximity of certain areas designated by notice to airmen. 107.5. Offenses involving alcohol or drugs. 107.5. Refusal to submit to an alcohol test or to furnish test results.
§ 101.1 Applicability. For purposes of this part, a model aircraft is an unmanned aircraft that is: (i) Capable of sustained flight in the atmosphere; (ii) Flown within visual line of sight of the person operating the aircraft; and (iii) Flown for hobby or recreational purposes. **101.41 Applicability.** This subpart prescribes the rules governing the operation of a model aircraft that meets all of the following conditions as set forth in section 336 of Public Law 112-95: (a) The aircraft is flown strictly for hobby or recreational use; (b) The aircraft is operated in accordance with a community-based set of safety guidelines and within the programming of a nationwide community-based organization; (c) The aircraft is limited to not more than 55 pounds unless otherwise certified through a design, construction, inspection, flight test, and operational safety program administered by a community-based organization; (d) The aircraft is operated in a manner that does not interfere with and gives way to any manned aircraft; and FAR part 101.1 defines what is to be considered a "model" aircraft. (e) When flown within 5 miles of an airport, the operator of the aircraft provides the airport operator and the airport air traffic control tower (when an air traffic facility is located at the airport) with prior notice of the operation. (f) § 101.43 Endangering the safety of the National Airspace System. No person may operate model aircraft so as to endanger the safety of the national airspace system.	101.41 describes the general rules that govern the use of a model aircraft. 101.43 states that regardless of the rules, a model aircraft may never be operated in a manner that endangers other aircraft.

FAR PART 107–SMALL UNMANNED AIRCRAFT SYSTEMS-PROPOSED REGULATION

Proposed Rule	Interpretation

Subpart A—General
§ 107.1 Applicability.
(a) Except as provided in paragraph (b) of this section, this part applies to the registration, airman certification, and operation of civil small unmanned aircraft systems within the United States.
(b) This part does not apply to the following:
  (1) Air carrier operations;
  (2) Any aircraft subject to the provisions of part 101 of this chapter;
  (3) Any aircraft conducting an external load operation;
  (4) Any aircraft towing another aircraft or object; or
  (5) Any aircraft that does not meet the criteria specified in § 47.3 of this chapter.
	This proposed rule only applies to non-air carrier UAV operations. It also does NOT apply to operations conducted under FAR part 101 (moored balloons, kites, amateur rockets and unmanned free balloons). It also does not apply to any UAV carrying an external payload or towing some other object. Since there is no current (or proposed) regulation covering these activities, anyone seeking to conduct such an operation would need to apply to the FAA for a Certificate of Authorization (COA).
	
	FAR part 47 is a reference to the aircraft registration requirements and defines what kind of aircraft needs to be registered with the FAA.

§ 107.3 Definitions.
The following definitions apply to this part. If there is a conflict between the definitions of this part and definitions specified in § 1.1 of this chapter, the definitions in this part control for purposes of this part:
  Control station means an interface used by the operator to control the flight path of the small unmanned aircraft. Corrective lenses means spectacles or contact lenses.
  Operator means a person who manipulates the flight controls of a small unmanned aircraft system.
  Small unmanned aircraft means an unmanned aircraft weighing less than 55 pounds including everything that is on board the aircraft.
  Small unmanned aircraft system (small UAS) means a small unmanned aircraft and its associated elements (including communication links and the components that control the small unmanned aircraft) that are required for the safe and efficient operation of the small unmanned aircraft in the national airspace system.
  Unmanned aircraft means an aircraft operated without the possibility of direct human intervention from within or on the aircraft.
  Visual observer means a person who assists the small unmanned aircraft operator to see and avoid other air traffic or objects aloft or on the ground.
	This part defines the terms that will be used later in the regulation. Of particular importance is the definition of the operator, who is the person directly controlling (and ultimately responsible for) the UAS.
	
	The definition of a small unmanned aircraft (less than 55 pounds) is inclusive of everything on board the aircraft at its heaviest during flight. This part also defines the visual observer as an assistant to the operator, and has no actual operations function.

§ 107.5 Falsification, reproduction or alteration.
(a) No person may make or cause to be made—
  (1) Any fraudulent or intentionally false record or report that is required to be made, kept, or used to show compliance with any requirement under this part.
  (2) Any reproduction or alteration, for fraudulent purpose, of any certificate, rating, authorization, record or report under this part.
(b) The commission by any person of an act prohibited under paragraph (a) of this section is a basis for denying an application for certificate, or suspending or revoking the applicable certificate or waiver issued by the Administrator under this part and held by that person.
	If you falsify any required documentation, you could lose your operators certificate and/or be denied the opportunity to obtain one.

Proposed Rule	Interpretation
§ 107.7 Inspection, testing, and demonstration of compliance. (a) An operator or owner of a small unmanned aircraft system must, upon request, make available to the Administrator: 　(1) The operator's unmanned aircraft operator certificate with a small UAS rating; 　(2) The certificate of aircraft registration for the small unmanned aircraft system being operated; and 　(3) Any other document, record, or report required to be kept by an operator or owner of a small unmanned aircraft system under the regulations of this chapter. (b) The operator, visual observer, or owner of a small unmanned aircraft system must, upon request, allow the Administrator to make any test or inspection of the small unmanned aircraft system, the operator, and, if applicable, the visual observer to determine compliance with this part.	At any time, if an employee of the FAA requests to see any certificate (aircraft or operator) or any other required paperwork, the operator must provide it.
§ 107.9 Accident reporting. No later than 10 days after an operation that meets the criteria of either paragraph (a) or (b) of this section, an operator must report to the nearest Federal Aviation Administration Flight Standards District Office any operation of the small unmanned aircraft that involves the following: (a) Any injury to any person; or (b) Damage to any property, other than the small unmanned aircraft.	An accident is defined as any incident that injures any person; or damages any property, other than the small unmanned aircraft. If an accident occurs, it must be reported to the appropriate local FAA office (known as a Flight Standards District Office or FSDO) within 10 days.
Subpart B—Operating Rules **§ 107.11 Applicability.** This subpart applies to the operation of all civil small unmanned aircraft systems to which this part applies.	Any aircraft that is covered under FAR part 107 must be flown in accordance with the following rules.
§ 107.13 Registration, certification, and airworthiness directives No person may operate a civil small unmanned aircraft system for purposes of flight unless: (a) That person has an unmanned aircraft operator certificate with a small UAS rating issued pursuant to Subpart C of this part and satisfies the requirements of § 107.65; (b) The small unmanned aircraft being operated has been registered with the FAA pursuant to subpart D of this part; (c) The small unmanned aircraft being operated displays its registration number in the manner specified in subpart D of this part; and (d) The owner or operator of the small unmanned aircraft system complies with all applicable airworthiness directives..	Any aircraft that comes under the jurisdiction of FAR part 107 must be operated by someone with an FAA issued unmanned operator certificate with at least a small UAS rating. At present, that certificate and rating do not exist, but will be created by the FAA if this regulation goes into force. It appears that additional ratings (such as "large") are a possibility, but are not explicitly addressed in this NPRM. Any UAS operated under this part must be registered with the FAA and must display its assigned registration number. If the manufacturer of the UAS issues an airworthiness directive (which is a mandatory modification to the vehicle), it must be complied with to remain airworthy.
§ 107.15 Civil small unmanned aircraft system airworthiness. (a) No person may operate a civil small unmanned aircraft system unless it is in a condition for safe operation. This condition must be determined during the preflight check required under § 107.49 of this part. (b) The operator must discontinue the flight when he or she knows or has reason to know that continuing the flight would pose a hazard to other aircraft, people, or property.	It is the UAS operator's responsibility to insure that the aircraft is airworthy at all times. The aircraft must be checked prior to each flight (pre-flight check). If at any time during operations, the operator believes the aircraft may be unairworthy, the flight must be discontinued.
§ 107.17 Medical condition. No person may act as an operator or visual observer if he or she knows or has reason to know that he or she has a physical or mental condition that would interfere with the safe operation of a small unmanned aircraft system.	Although the operator does not need to hold an FAA issued medical certificate, if the operator knows (or should know) about a medical deficiency that would interfere with safely operating a UAV, they are no longer able to legally operate a UAV under this part.

Proposed Rule	Interpretation
§ 107.19 Responsibility of the operator. (a) The operator is directly responsible for, and is the final authority as to the operation of the small unmanned aircraft system. (b) The operator must ensure that the small unmanned aircraft will pose no undue hazard to other aircraft, people, or property in the event of a loss of control of the aircraft for any reason.	The UAV has to be operated at all times so as not to pose a danger to people or property. If the vehicle is operated in an unsafe manner, or becomes unsafe it is the responsibility of and fault of the aircraft operator.
§ 107.21 Maintenance and inspection. An operator must: (a) Maintain the system in a condition for safe operation; and (b) Inspect the small unmanned aircraft system prior to flight to determine that the system it is in a condition for safe operation.	It is the operator's responsibility to maintain and inspect the aircraft for airworthiness.
§ 107.23 Hazardous operation. No person may: (a) Operate a small unmanned aircraft system in a careless or reckless manner so as to endanger the life or property of another; or (b) Allow an object to be dropped from a small unmanned aircraft if such action endangers the life or property of another.	If the UAV is ever operated in a manner that is careless or reckless, it is the operators fault. Items can be dropped from a UAV, but only if the dropping of such items does not endanger others or their property. This rule is similar to FAR 91.13 that prohibits careless and reckless operation of pilot aircraft.
§ 107.25 Operation from a moving vehicle or aircraft. No person may operate a small unmanned aircraft system - (a) From a moving aircraft; or (b) From a moving vehicle unless that vehicle is moving on water.	The only places(s) that an operator can operate from is a stationary position, or on a boat. An operator cannot control a UAV from a moving vehicle such as a car, plane, train, etc.
§ 107.27 Alcohol or drugs. A person acting as an operator or as a visual observer must comply with the provisions of §§ 91.17 and 91.19 of this chapter.	FAR parts 91.17 and 91.19 specify that a pilot (operator) cannot control an aircraft within 8 hours after the consumption of any alcoholic beverage or while under the influence of alcohol. They also cannot operate a UAV while using any drug that affects the person's faculties in any way contrary to safety. Upon the request of any law enforcement officer, an operator must submit to a test to indicate the alcohol concentration in the blood or breath. FAR part 91.19 expressly prohibits the carrying by any aircraft (including UAVS) of any narcotic drugs, marihuana, and depressant or stimulant drugs or substances as defined in federal or state statutes unless so authorized by federal or state statute or by any federal or state agency.
§ 107.29 Daylight operation. No person may operate a small unmanned aircraft system except between the hours of official sunrise and sunset.	UAV operations governed by FAR part 107 can only be conducted during daylight hours. Sunrise and sunset are defined as the times when the upper edge of the disk of the Sun is on the horizon, atmospheric conditions are assumed to be average, and the location is in a level region on the Earth's surface. Official sunrise and sunset times are published by the U. S. Naval Observatory and are available from many sources.

Proposed Rule

§ 107.31 Visual line of sight aircraft operation.
With vision that is unaided by any device other than corrective lenses, the operator or visual observer must be able to see the unmanned aircraft throughout the entire flight in order to:
(a) Know the unmanned aircraft's location;
(b) Determine the unmanned aircraft's attitude, altitude, and direction;
(c) Observe the airspace for other air traffic or hazards; and
(d) Determine that the unmanned aircraft does not endanger the life or property of another.

§ 107.33 Visual observer.
If a visual observer is used during the aircraft operation, all of the following requirements must be met:
(a) The operator and the visual observer must maintain effective communication with each other at all times.
(b) The operator must ensure that the visual observer is able to see the unmanned aircraft in the manner specified in §§ 107.31 and 107.37.
(c) At all times during flight, the small unmanned aircraft must remain close enough to the operator for the operator to be capable of seeing the aircraft with vision unaided by any device other than corrective lenses.
(d) The operator and the visual observer must coordinate to do the following:
  (1) Scan the airspace where the small unmanned aircraft is operating for any potential collision hazard; and
  (2) Maintain awareness of the position of the small unmanned aircraft through direct visual observation.

§ 107.35 Operation of multiple small unmanned aircraft systems.
A person may not act as an operator or visual observer in the operation of more than one unmanned aircraft system at the same time.

§ 107.37 Operation near aircraft; right-of-way rules.
(a) Each operator must maintain awareness so as to see and avoid other aircraft and vehicles and must yield the right-of-way to all aircraft, airborne vehicles, and launch and reentry vehicles.
  (1) In order to maintain awareness so as to see other aircraft and vehicles, either the operator or a visual observer must, at each point of the small unmanned aircraft's flight, satisfy the criteria specified in § 107.31.
  (2) Yielding the right-of-way means that the small unmanned aircraft must give way to the aircraft or vehicle and may not pass over, under, or ahead of it unless well clear.
(b) No person may operate a small unmanned aircraft so close to another aircraft as to create a collision hazard.

§ 107.39 Operation over people.
No person may operate a small unmanned aircraft over a human being who is:
(a) Not directly participating in the operation of the small unmanned aircraft; or
(b) Not located under a covered structure that can provide reasonable protection from a falling small unmanned aircraft.

Interpretation

The operator must keep the vehicle in sight at all times, unaided by any assistive device such as binoculars, cameras, etc. and is responsible for the safety of the vehicle.

If you are using a visual observer, they must maintain real-time verbal communications with the operator at all times. Cell phone or other time delayed systems are not acceptable.
The visual observer can assist the operator in all functions, but cannot and is not responsible for the vehicle.

An operator or visual observer can only control or work with one UAV at a time.

The operator can never let the UAV get close enough to people or to other vehicles so as to create the possibility of a collision hazard. It is up to the UAV operator to cede right of way to any other nearby vehicle. This means that the UAV must get out of the way, it cannot pass under or over the other aircraft.

The operator cannot ever let the UAV operate over any human beings who are not part of the aircraft operation unless those people are in a covered structure strong enough to provide substantial protection from the UAV if it were to hit the structure.

Unmanned Aerial Systems: The Definitive Guide

Proposed Rule	Interpretation
§ 107.41 Operation in certain airspace. (a) A small unmanned aircraft may not operate in Class A airspace. (b) A small unmanned aircraft may not operate in Class B, Class C, or Class D airspace or within the lateral boundaries of the surface area of Class E airspace designated for an airport unless the operator has prior authorization from the Air Traffic Control (ATC) facility having jurisdiction	Small UAVs may NEVER fly in class A airspace. If the operator gets permission from the controlling facility (usually a control tower or TRACON), the UAV can operate in class B, C, D or E airspace. This does not authorize the UAV to operate at an altitude higher than 500' agl however.
§ 107.45 Operation in prohibited or restricted areas. No person may operate a small unmanned aircraft in prohibited or restricted areas unless that person has permission from the using or controlling agency, as appropriate.	Similar to the previous paragraph, a UAV may not operate in airspace designated as restricted or prohibited unless permission has been granted by the controlling agency.
§ 107.47 Flight restrictions in the proximity of certain areas designated by notice to airmen. No person may operate a small unmanned aircraft in areas designated in a Notice to Airmen under §§ 91.137 through 91.145, or § 99.7 of this chapter, unless authorized by: (a) Air Traffic Control (ATC); or (b) A Certificate of Waiver or Authorization issued by the FAA.	If the airspace has been temporarily restricted by the issuance of a NOTAM, a UAV cannot be operated within that airspace unless permission has been granted by the controlling agency or the operator has a COA that permits such operation.
§ 107.49 Preflight familiarization, inspection, and actions for aircraft operation. (a) Prior to flight, the operator must: (1) Assess the operating environment, considering risks to persons and property in the immediate vicinity both on the surface and in the air. This assessment must include: (i) Local weather conditions; (ii) Local airspace and any flight restrictions; (iii) The location of persons and property on the surface; and (iv) Other ground hazards. (2) Ensure that all persons involved in the small unmanned aircraft operation receive a briefing that includes operating conditions, emergency procedures, contingency procedures, roles and responsibilities, and potential hazards; (3) Ensure that all links between ground station and the small unmanned aircraft are working properly; and (4) If the small unmanned aircraft is powered, ensure that there is enough available power for the small unmanned aircraft system to operate for the intended operational time and to operate after that for at least five minutes. (b) Each person involved in the operation must perform the duties assigned by the operator.	UAVs cannot be operated unless the operator performs a preflight inspection prior to EVERY flight. Every preflight must include ALL of the items listed in paragraph 107.49. Every UAV flight must be planned such that when the aircraft returns to base, it has a power reserve of at least 5 minutes.
§ 107.51 Operating limitations for small unmanned aircraft. An operator must comply with all of the following operating limitations when operating a small unmanned aircraft system: (a) The airspeed of the small unmanned aircraft may not exceed 87 knots (100 miles per hour) calibrated airspeed at full power in level flight; (b) The altitude of the small unmanned aircraft cannot be higher than 500 feet (150 meters) above ground level; (c) The minimum flight visibility, as observed from the location of the ground control station must be no less than 3 statute miles (5 kilometers); and (d) The minimum distance of the small unmanned aircraft from clouds must be no less than: (1) 500 feet (150 meters) below the cloud; and (2) 2,000 feet (600 meters) horizontally away from the cloud.	UAVs operated under part 107 cannot be designed or operated such that they could exceed 87 knots of airspeed in level flight. The UAV shall never be operated at an altitude above 500' agl. The operator must be able to see at least 3 statute miles in every direction during UAV operations. Anytime a UAV is operated in the vicinity of clouds, the UAV itself must remain clear of the clouds and at least, 500 feet below the cloud; and at least 2,000 feet horizontal distance away from the cloud. If the cloud ceiling is 500 feet or less, a UAV would not be legally able to fly and remain below the cloud level.

Proposed Rule

Subpart C—Operator Certification
§ 107.53 Applicability.
This subpart prescribes the requirements for issuing an unmanned aircraft operator certificate with a small UAS rating.

§ 107.57 Offenses involving alcohol or drugs.
(a) A conviction for the violation of any Federal or State statute relating to the growing, processing, manufacture, sale, disposition, possession, transportation, or importation of narcotic drugs, marijuana, or depressant or stimulant drugs or substances is grounds for:
   (1) Denial of an application for an unmanned aircraft operator certificate with a small UAS rating for a period of up to 1 year after the date of final conviction; or
   (2) Suspension or revocation of an unmanned aircraft operator certificate with a small UAS rating.
(b) Committing an act prohibited by § 91.17(a) or § 91.19(a) of this chapter is grounds for:
   (1) Denial of an application for an unmanned aircraft operator certificate with a small UAS rating for a period of up to 1 year after the date of that act; or
   (2) Suspension or revocation of an unmanned aircraft operator certificate with a small UAS rating.

§ 107.59 Refusal to submit to an alcohol test or to furnish test results.
A refusal to submit to a test to indicate the percentage by weight of alcohol in the blood, when requested by a law enforcement officer in accordance with § 91.17(c) of this chapter, or a refusal to furnish or authorize the release of the test results requested by the Administrator in accordance with § 91.17(c) or (d) of this chapter, is grounds for:
(a) Denial of an application for an unmanned aircraft operator certificate with a small UAS rating for a period of up to 1 year after the date of that refusal; or
(b) Suspension or revocation of an unmanned aircraft operator certificate with a small UAS rating.

§ 107.61 Eligibility.
Subject to the provisions of §§ 107.57 and 107.59, in order to be eligible for an unmanned aircraft operator certificate with a small UAS rating under this subpart, a person must:
(a) Be at least 17 years of age;
(b) Be able to read, speak, write, and understand the English language. If the applicant is unable to meet one of these requirements due to medical reasons, the FAA may place such operating limitations on that applicant's certificate as are necessary for the safe operation of the small unmanned aircraft;
(c) Pass an initial aeronautical knowledge test covering the areas of knowledge specified in § 107.73(a); and
(d) Not know or have reason to know that he or she has a physical or mental condition that would interfere with the safe operation of a small unmanned aircraft system.

Interpretation

Subpart C is dedicated to the requirements necessary to obtain and hold an unmanned aircraft operator certificate with a small UAS rating.

If an operator is convicted for violating most state and/or federal alcohol or drug laws, they may have their certificate revoked by the FAA.

Anyone convicted will need to wait a year before applying or reapplying for a certificate.

If you refuse to submit to an alcohol test when requested by a duly certified law enforcement officer, your operator's certificate may be revoked for up to one year. This applies even if the drug and/or alcohol violation had nothing to do with the operation of a UAV.

To be eligible for a unmanned aircraft operator certificate with a small UAS rating, you must be at least 17 years old, be conversant in English, not have any physical or medical issues and must pass an initial aeronautical knowledge test.

Proposed Rule	Interpretation
§ 107.63 Issuance of an unmanned aircraft operator certificate with a small UAS rating. An applicant for an unmanned aircraft operator certificate with a small UAS rating under this subpart must make the application in a form and manner acceptable to the Administrator. (a) The application must include: 　(1) An airman knowledge test report showing that the applicant passed an initial aeronautical knowledge test, or recurrent aeronautical knowledge test for those individuals that satisfy the requirements of §107.75; and 　(2) A certification signed by the applicant stating that the applicant does not know or have reason to know that he or she has a physical or mental condition that would interfere with the safe operation of a small unmanned aircraft system. (b) The application must be submitted to a Flight Standards District Office, a designated pilot examiner, an airman certification representative for a pilot school, a certified flight instructor, or other person authorized by the Administrator. The person accepting the application submission must verify the identity of the applicant in a manner acceptable to the Administrator.	To actually obtain an unmanned aircraft operator certificate with a small UAS rating, you must fill out and take both an application and the aeronautical knowledge test report to an FAA office or one of the additional individuals who can issue the actual certificate.
§ 107.65 Aeronautical knowledge recency. A person may not operate a small unmanned aircraft system unless that person has completed one of the following, within the previous 24 calendar months: (a) Passed an initial aeronautical knowledge test covering the areas of knowledge specified in § 107.73(a); or (b) Passed a recurrent aeronautical knowledge test covering the areas of knowledge specified in § 107.73(b).	Even after you have been issued an operators certificate, you must have either passed the initial aeronautical knowledge test, or passed a recurrent aeronautical knowledge test within the last 24 months.
§ 107.67 Knowledge tests: General procedures and passing grades. (a) Knowledge tests prescribed by or under this part are given at times and places, and by persons designated by the Administrator. (b) An applicant for a knowledge test must have proper identification at the time of application that contains the applicant's: 　(1) Photograph; 　(2) Signature; 　(3) Date of birth, which shows the applicant meets or will meet the age requirements of this part for the certificate sought before the expiration date of the airman knowledge test report; and 　(4) If the permanent mailing address is a post office box number, then the applicant must provide a current residential address. (c) The minimum passing grade for the knowledge test will be specified by the Administrator.	These tests will be offered (likely by private vendors) at a number of locations. You need to provide basic identification to take the test. The FAA will state what the passing grade will be, but it is usually a 70%.

Proposed Rule

§ 107.69 Knowledge tests: Cheating or other unauthorized conduct.
(a) An applicant for a knowledge test may not:
   (1) Copy or intentionally remove any knowledge test;
   (2) Give to another applicant or receive from another applicant any part or copy of a knowledge test;
   (3) Give assistance on, or receive assistance on, a knowledge test during the period that test is being given;
   (4) Take any part of a knowledge test on behalf of another person;
   (5) Be represented by, or represent, another person for a knowledge test;
   (6) Use any material or aid during the period that the test is being given, unless specifically authorized to do so by the Administrator; and
   (7) Intentionally cause, assist, or participate in any act prohibited by this paragraph.
(b) An applicant who the Administrator finds has committed an act prohibited by paragraph (a) of this section is prohibited, for 1 year after the date of committing that act, from:
   (1) Applying for any certificate, rating, or authorization issued under this chapter; and
   (2) Applying for and taking any test under this chapter.
(c) Any certificate or rating held by an applicant may be suspended or revoked if the Administrator finds that person has committed an act prohibited by paragraph (a) of this section.

§ 107.71 Retesting after failure.
An applicant for a knowledge test who fails that test may not reapply for the test for 14 calendar days after failing the test.

§ 107.73 Initial and recurrent knowledge tests.
(a) An initial aeronautical knowledge test covers the following areas of knowledge:
   (1) Applicable regulations relating to small unmanned aircraft system rating privileges, limitations, and flight operation;
   (2) Airspace classification and operating requirements, obstacle clearance requirements, and flight restrictions affecting small unmanned aircraft operation;
   (3) Official sources of weather and effects of weather on small unmanned aircraft performance;
   (4) Small unmanned aircraft system loading and performance;
   (5) Emergency procedures;
   (6) Crew resource management;
   (7) Radio communication procedures;
   (8) Determining the performance of small unmanned aircraft;
   (9) Physiological effects of drugs and alcohol; (10) Aeronautical decision-making and judgment; and
   (11) Airport operations.
(b) A recurrent aeronautical knowledge test covers the following areas of knowledge:
   (1) Applicable regulations relating to small unmanned aircraft system rating privileges, limitations, and flight operation;
   (2) Airspace classification and operating requirements, obstacle clearance requirements, and flight restrictions affecting small unmanned aircraft operation;
   (3) Official sources of weather;
   (4) Emergency procedures;
   (5) Crew resource management;
   (6) Aeronautical decision-making and judgment; and
   (7) Airport operations.

Interpretation

If you cheat on the test, or help someone else cheat, you could have your operator certificate revoked (if you already hold one) and/or be ineligible to seek an operators certificate for up to one year.

If you take the test and fail, you have to wait 14 days before you can re-take the exam.

The tests, both initial and recurrent, will cover applicable UAS regulations, airspace issues, weather, SUAS loading and performance, emergency procedures, crew resource management, radio communication, effect of drugs and alcohol, aeronautical decision-making and judgment, and airport operations.

Proposed Rule	Interpretation

§ 107.75 Military pilots or former military pilots.
(a) <u>General</u>. Except for a person who has been removed from unmanned aircraft flying status for lack of proficiency or because of a disciplinary action involving any aircraft operation, a U.S. military unmanned aircraft pilot or operator or former U.S. military unmanned aircraft pilot or operator who meets the requirements of this section may apply, on the basis of his or her U.S. military unmanned aircraft pilot or operator qualifications, for an unmanned aircraft operator certificate with small UAS rating issued under this part.
(b) <u>Military unmanned aircraft pilots or operators and former military unmanned aircraft pilots or operators in the U.S. Armed Forces</u>. A person who qualifies as a U.S. military unmanned aircraft pilot or operator or former U.S. military unmanned aircraft pilot or operator may apply for an unmanned aircraft operator certificate with a small UAS rating if that person;
  (1) Passes a recurrent aeronautical knowledge test covering the areas of knowledge specified in § 107.73(b); and
  (2) Presents evidentiary documents that show:
    (i) The person's status in the U.S. Armed Forces;
    (ii) That the person is or was a U.S. military unmanned aircraft pilot or operator.
	Military UAS pilots or operators may be exempt from some of the initial certification requirements and might be issued an FAA operators certificate partially based upon their experience.

§ 107.77 Change of name or address.
(a) Change of Name. An application to change the name on a certificate issued under this subpart must be accompanied by the applicant's:
  (1) Operator certificate; and
  (2) A copy of the marriage license, court order, or other document verifying the name change.
(b) The documents in paragraph (a) of this section will be returned to the applicant after inspection.
(c) Change of address. The holder of an unmanned aircraft operator certificate issued under this subpart who has made a change in permanent mailing address may not, after 30 days from that date, exercise the privileges of the certificate unless the holder has notified the FAA of the change in address using one of the following methods:
  (1) By letter to the FAA Airman Certification Branch, P.O. Box 25082, Oklahoma City, OK 73125 providing the new permanent mailing address, or if the permanent mailing address includes a post office box number, then the holder's current residential address; or
  (2) By using the FAA website portal at www.faa.gov providing the new permanent mailing address, or if the permanent mailing address includes a post office box number, then the holder's current residential address.
	If you change your name and/or address, you have to notify the FAA.

§ 107.79 Voluntary surrender of certificate. (a) The holder of a certificate issued under this subpart may voluntarily surrender it for cancellation. (b) Any request made under paragraph (a) of this section must include the following signed statement or its equivalent: "I voluntarily surrender my unmanned aircraft operator certificate with a small UAS rating for cancellation. This request is made for my own reasons, with full knowledge that my certificate will not be reissued to me unless I again complete the requirements specified in §§ 107.61 and 107.63."	If, for some reason, you wish to voluntarily surrender your operator's certificate back to the FAA, you may do so.

Proposed Rule	Interpretation
Subpart D—Small Unmanned Aircraft Registration and Identification. **§ 107.87 Applicability.** This subpart prescribes the rules governing the registration and identification of all civil small unmanned aircraft to which this part applies.	Subpart D describes the aircraft registration and identification requirements for small UASs.
§ 107.89 Registration and identification. (a) All small unmanned aircraft must be registered in accordance with part 47 of this chapter. (b) All small unmanned aircraft must display their nationality and registration marks in accordance with the requirements of subpart C of part 45 of this chapter.	This part requires all small UASs to be registered with the FAA. It also requires the FAA identification number to be displayed on the UAS in a manner that will be determined later and explained in FAR part 45.

FUTURE TRENDS AND TECHNOLOGY

Civilian unmanned aerial systems owe much of their past advancements to the military sector. The unprecedented investment of time and money by world governments has produced systems that would have been the substance of science fiction only a few years prior. Advancements in related civilian technologies such as smart phone components, batteries, and camera systems have also played a role in the level of technology we see today.

The future of UAS holds many exciting possibilities as well. Advancements in power systems, larger and more capable aircraft, collision avoidance, airspace integration, artificial intelligence, and operational deployment strategies will shape the next generation of unmanned flight. Just as past developments in motors, batteries, computer miniaturization, and advanced composite structures have yielded the state of the art unmanned aircraft of today, the systems of tomorrow will be the product of advancing technologies and proven reliability in multiple areas.

POWER SYSTEMS

Power systems of UAVs are key to extended flight duration and increased payload capacity. Current electrically powered systems are primarily limited by onboard battery capacity at the time of takeoff. Possible future alternatives to this limitation include midair refueling via lasers and/or solar panel based recovery of lost power. Solar panels may be integrated into the structure of the UAV in such as way as to provide dual functionality as both structural skin as well as a power source, saving the weight of additional structure or systems. Electric "refueling" stations (both ground based and airborne) are currently under development that would allow UAVs to descend onto a charge station autonomously, recharge the onboard battery, and continue to operate.

Fuel cell technology, as well as experimental battery technology, shows promise in extending flight times and payload capacities. Fueled propulsion is also undergoing changes as engines are now being developed specifically for unmanned aircraft. These engines are optimized for the altitude and mission profiles needed by UAVs instead of being adapted from existing manned aircraft or other ground based engines. As the market for unmanned engines expands, new powerplant technology will see increasing investment. Alternative fuels are being developed as well, with bio-based and forms of diesel

Unmanned Aerial Systems: The Definitive Guide

fuel showing promise. Various rotary, piston, and turbine engines are currently in development that promise increased efficiency, less maintenance, and increased power over existing powerplants.

LARGER AIRCRAFT

Much of the market for small unmanned systems of today is being driven by the FAA requirement for line of site operations below 500 feet AGL. This limitation makes larger, more capable aircraft undesirable in our current regulatory environment. Much of the agricultural surveying, mapping, and aerial spray application missions would be better served by larger aircraft, than the regulations seem to permit. This limitation illustrates how advances in one area of unmanned systems can have a profound effect on others. The raising of the altitude restriction or removal of the line of sight requirement, due to advances in collision avoidance technology, could usher in a whole new class of larger and more capable aircraft.

The technology currently exists for using these larger airframes as they are nothing more than manned aircraft reconfigured, or larger aircraft designed from scratch, to be operated autonomously. There will likely be an active market for retrofitting existing manned airframes with autonomous control systems. The most efficient airframes would be newly designed and manufactured specifically for unmanned operation, however, this is costly and time consuming compared to retrofitting existing airframes. Modern airliners are already equipped with autonomous systems that can be enhanced for true pilotless operations. Aircraft of this size might open the door to unmanned cargo and/or passenger services, as well as a host of other applications requiring the lifting and speed potential of their size.

COLLISION AVOIDANCE

The issue of traffic separation and collision avoidance has been at the forefront of the concerns with unmanned aircraft, and rightfully so. The current means of collision avoidance has been accomplished by isolating manned and unmanned aircraft from one another as well as using see and avoid strategies. A system of active collision avoidance, using onboard receivers and transmitters, has been in development for years and does show promise for eventually eliminating need for line of sight and altitude restrictions. This system requires all aircraft in a given area (both manned and unmanned) to be equipped with the necessary equipment. As this equipment becomes smaller, and more affordable, the possibility of providing automated separation of aircraft becomes a possibility.

Another strategy being developed for separation is the use of onboard cameras with high-speed computer processing of the video images to detect and avoid potential collision threats. This system does not rely on external radio signals at all and can provide a measure of autonomy in environments not conducive to reliable radio operation. It is likely that in the foreseeable future, human observation, either directly or through remote video, paired with onboard computing systems will all work together to provide for airspace integration.

REGULATIONS

As the agency tasked with the safety of the National Airspace System, the FAA has taken a cautious approach to integrating and regulating unmanned operations. This incremental approach has opened the door to the future reduction of restrictions as technology, as well as operating procedures, has become more reliable and proven. Power systems, airframe structures, radio links, autopilots, and every other component of UAS have, and will continue to have, failures. It is the management of these failures that is the key to safety. Manned aviation has a rich history of addressing safety concerns and much can be gained from utilizing this experience, adapting it to the needs of UAS.

Typically, the aviation system has been made safer through personnel education, certification, demonstrated ability, recurrent training, aircraft preventative maintenance, approved operating procedures, and regulatory oversight. If UAS adapt this approach with more community experience in safe operations and measured safety failures investigated and mitigated along the way, the regulations will likely become less restrictive. For example, the operation of agricultural UAVs often occur in remote, rural areas with little possibility of personal injury or property damage. This type of operation might logically be the first to experiment with less restrictive regulations. If the new regulations were proven to provide an acceptable level of safety, they could be expanded for use in more populated areas. Likewise, as specific technologies develops a proven record of safety and reliability, they might also be integrated into an approved system.

FUTURE APPLICATIONS AND DEPLOYMENT

New applications are found for unmanned aerial systems every day. The future is as wide open for the application of this technology as the dreams and ideas of the people seeking to solve the problems facing mankind from the simplest to the most profound. With each new advance in technology comes a whole host of new possibilities for unmanned operations. The primary areas of development at this time are in precision agriculture, scientific study of our planet and atmosphere, as well as surveillance and data gathering and emergency response.

The use of UAVs in precision agriculture takes many forms. The aerial imaging component utilizes very sensitive hyper-spectral cameras to provide plant health evaluation and yield prediction. Insect damage can be detected as well as areas needing infusions of water or fertilizers. The images can be used to model rain runoff and develop topography maps. Other areas of future development are in precision, autonomy, and application of herbicides and pesticides. Detectors are in development that can trigger sprays from slow moving rotorcraft applying them in limited quantities to individual weeds or insects as needed. The current process of broadcasting large amounts of spray over an entire field is not only costly and environmentally unsound, but wasteful as well. The use of UAVs for agricultural applications will be much more environmentally sensitive.

Future developments in scientific measurement include increased data gathering flights into extreme weather, development of wildlife management strategies based on data gathered from unmanned aircraft, and measurement of atmospheric conditions such as radiation and carbon monoxide levels at various altitudes. Finally, various government agencies have shown interest in unmanned technology for emergency response, surveillance, crime scene reconstruction and analysis, as well as supporting common tasks such as traffic management and search and rescue efforts.

The regulatory environment in the United States has, thus far, hindered much of the implementation of this technology. But as the operating environment for UASs matures, the applications listed will expand rapidly and new applications will emerge that have yet not been thought of.

ARTIFICIAL INTELLIGENCE

Artificial Intelligence (AI) development is at the forefront of technology for future autonomous aircraft. The ability of a machine to learn, adapt to change, and make successful autonomous decisions is the foundation of any AI system. Currently, some autopilots use a "learn" function for determining compass deviation over a given operational area. This function does improve compass accuracy and performance, but is a simplistic and crude form of AI at best. True AI is dynamic, evolving, and problem solving, and based on external sensors and stimuli to create unique changes in system performance to achieve goals.

Advanced AI systems are currently in development as researchers study how humans make decisions, how to emulate that process in a machine, and how to avoid the pitfalls of human error, yet retain the creative aspect of problem solving. There are many applications of this science and technology to unmanned aerial systems. Military operators have an obvious interest in AI technology, but civilian opportunities for enhanced safety, operating autonomy, and collision avoidance are also very real.

SUMMARY OF TRENDS

When predicting the future of unmanned flight, it is helpful to determine the strengths and limitations of both technological and human-based systems. Autonomous flight controllers operate with precision measured in millimeters and can operate as long as power can be maintained. With proper maintenance and replacement intervals measured in years, a UAVs performance should not measurably degrade over time. This is important when considering the effect of long duration flight on humans as compared to autonomous systems.

The pilot of a manned aircraft will eventually fall victim to fatigue, distraction, thirst and other factors that impact their decision making and control precision. Even when considering relatively short duration flights, a human pilot is only capable of the degree of precision that their mental condition and training allow. Many unmanned operators have viewed in awe the precision flight of their aircraft once released from manual flight control and switched to autonomous, stabilized flight. A flight controller does not consider the stresses of life, the past, the future, or any other distracting concepts beyond the precision control of the aircraft in flight. It does not become impatient or bored. The flight controller does not require an atmosphere of very narrow temperatures, pressures, oxygen levels, or visible light to operate effectively.

The flight controller, however will fly where it is told and how it is told, not deviating from its programming. This rigidity can be a weakness of autonomous systems however. This weakness is being progressively mitigated with artificial intelligence strategies. Human operators have their strengths and weaknesses as well. A human excels at taking in various sensory data, processing the changing information, considering alternative actions, and then choosing a course of action based upon those changes. This process can be accomplished in real time, and can be very rapid as the situation dictates. The decision making process used by humans has weaknesses and faults but is superior to any available artificial substitute so far. When considering the future of unmanned flight, the best applications will likely be those that capitalize on the strengths of both the autonomous and the human systems, while reducing the liabilities of each.

FIGURES AND ATTRIBUTION

Figure #	Copyrights and Attribution	Identifier
Chapter 1		
Title Image	Creative Commons, Richard Unten	https://goo.gl/su8v3A
1-1	Creative Commons	http://goo.gl/wM11q6
1-2	Creative Commons	https://goo.gl/rg5Rr0
1-3	Copyright "Keith Tarrier/Shutterstock"	Image ID:169823552
1-4	Creative Commons	https://goo.gl/Q9ddbx
1-5	Public Domain	http://goo.gl/sKDC02
1-6	Public Domain	http://goo.gl/hq6hFf
1-7	Creative Commons	https://goo.gl/vGEs4h
Chapter 2		
Title Image	Creative Commons, The National Guard	https://goo.gl/vPtknd
2-1	Michael Leasure	-
2-2	Michael Leasure	-
2-3	Michael Leasure	-
2-4	Michael Leasure	-
2-5	Copyright "Glocatskiy/Shutterstock"	184391279
2-6	Creative Commons	https://goo.gl/w63Zcl
2-7	Public Domain	https://goo.gl/BCC8Ox
2-8	Public Domain – US Air Force	http://goo.gl/WQyV6K
2-9	Michael Leasure	-
2-10	Creative Commons	http://goo.gl/wqGLV0
2-11	Michael Leasure	-
2-12	eAcademicBooks LLC	-
2-13	Federal Aviation Administration	H-8083-30, fig. 3-53
2-14	Federal Aviation Administration	H-8083-31. fig. 2-5
2-15	Federal Aviation Administration	H-8083-25B, fig. 5-3
2-16	Federal Aviation Administration	H-8083-31, fig. 2-6
2-17	eAcademicBooks LLC	-
2-18	Federal Aviation Administration	H-80803-31, fig.2-14
2-19	Federal Aviation Administration	H-8083-25B, fig. 5-44
2-20	Federal Aviation Administration	Helicopter. Fig.2-1
2-21	Federal Aviation Administration	H-8083-25B, fig. 5-63
2-22	Federal Aviation Administration	H-8083-25B, fig.5-18
2-23	Public Domain	-
2-24	Federal Aviation Administration	Helicopter. Fig.2-31

FIGURES AND ATTRIBUTION

2-25	Federal Aviation Administration	Helicopter. Fig.2-25
2-26	Copyright "Cat Design/Shutterstock"	-
2-27	Copyright "Cat Design/Shutterstock"	-
2-28	Federal Aviation Administration	H-8083-31, fig. 1-14
2-29	Federal Aviation Administration	H-8083-31, fig. 1-15
2-30	Federal Aviation Administration	H-8083-31, fig. 1-16, 17
2-31	Copyright "Aaron Kohr/Shutterstock"	728016
2-32	Michael Leasure	-
Chapter 3		
Title Image	Creative Commons, TobiX	http://bit.ly/1D9uTsD
3-1	Federal Aviation Administration	Helicopter, fig. 1-13
3-2	Copyright "Tyler Olson/Shutterstock"	155139986
3-3	Copyright "J. Lekavicius/Shutterstock"	231301714
3-4	Copyright "J. Lekavicius/Shutterstock"	231300418
3-5	Michael Leasure	-
3-6	Michael Leasure	-
3-7	Copyright "Netopaek/Shutterstock"	244709503
3-8	Copyright "Maksym Sukhenko/Shutterstock" Copyright "Ben44/Shutterstock"	211627321 235062292
3-9	Copyright "Chaiyapruk Chanwatthana/Shutterstock"	245474098
3-10	Copyright "Tanaphongpict/Shutterstock"	153889946
3-11	Federal Aviation Administration	H-8083-31 fig. 7-2
3-12	Michael Nolan	-
3-13	Michael Nolan	-
3-14	Michael Nolan	-
3-15	Michael Nolan	-
3-16	Michael Leasure	-
3-17	Federal Aviation Administration	H-8083-31 fig. 7-24
3-18	Michael Nolan	-
3-19	Michael Leasure	-
3-20	Michael Leasure	-
3-21	Michael Leasure	-
3-22	Michael Leasure	-
3-23	Michael Leasure	-
3-24	Federal Aviation Administration	H-8083-31 fig. 1-19, 20
3-25	Federal Aviation Administration	H-8083-31 fig. 1-22
3-26	Federal Aviation Administration	H-8083-31 fig. 4-192

FIGURES AND ATTRIBUTION

3-27	Federal Aviation Administration	H-8083-31 fig. 1-47
3-28	Michael Leasure	-
3-29	Michael Leasure	-
3-30	Michael Leasure	-
Chapter 4		
Title Image	Copyright "Keellla/Shutterstock"	205876582
4-1	Copyright "Designua/Shutterstock"	165219182
4-2	Copyright "gualtiero boffi/Shutterstock"	226217089
4-3	Copyright "Fouad A. Saad/Shutterstock"	176121545
4-4	Copyright "Fouad A. Saad /Shutterstock"	176121554
4-5	Copyright "Fouad A. Saad /Shutterstock"	236457343
4-6	Copyright "ridjam/Shutterstock"	232715125
4-7	Copyright "udaix/Shutterstock"	83923882
4-8	Copyright "petrmalinak/Shutterstock"	221733370
4-9	Copyright "Natykach Nataliia/Shutterstock"	106154837
4-10	Copyright "Petar Ivanov Ishmiriev/Shutterstock"	48014110
4-11	Copyright "photoiconix/Shutterstock"	167013374
4-12	Copyright "Mrs_ya/Shutterstock" Copyright "AkeSak/Shutterstock"	255309286 and 159420245
4-13	Copyright "Oleksandr Kovalchuk/Shutterstock"	228396937
4-14	Copyright "Oleksandr Kovalchuk/Shutterstock"	97648400
4-15	Copyright "Maksim Chaikou/Shutterstock"	34703947
4-16	Copyright "Oleksandr Kostiuchenko/Shutterstock"	78039646
4-17	Federal Aviation Administration	H-8083-31, fig.9-22,23
4-18	Copyright "hsagencia/Shutterstock" Copyright "Krasowit/Shutterstock"	88795630 111089144
4-19	Copyright "Prasolov Alexei /Shutterstock"	254908306
4-20	Copyright "The Len/Shutterstock"	257528644
4-21	Federal Aviation Administration	H-8083-31 V2, fig.10-10
4-22	Federal Aviation Administration	H-8083-31 V2, fig.10-12
4-23	Federal Aviation Administration	H-8083-31 V2, fig.10-11
4-24	Copyright "finallast /Shutterstock"	197288234
4-25	Copyright "Olga Gabay/Shutterstock"	84208927
4-26	Federal Aviation Administration	H-8083-31 V2, fig.10-21
4-27	Federal Aviation Administration	H-8083-31 V2, fig.10-22
4-28	Copyright "Geir Olav Lyngfjell/Shutterstock"	34650691
4-28A	Federal Aviation Administration	H-8083-31 V2, fig. 10-24
4-28B	Michael Leasure	-
4-29	Copyright "Ivsanmas/Shutterstock"	106408973
4-30	Federal Aviation Administration	H-8083-31 V2, Fig. 10-31, 32
4-31	Federal Aviation Administration	H-8083-31 V2, fig.10-42

Attributes

FIGURES AND ATTRIBUTION

4-32	Federal Aviation Administration	H-8083-31 V2, fig.10-60
4-33	Federal Aviation Administration	H-8083-31 V2, fig.10-63,64
4-34	Federal Aviation Administration	H-8083-31 V2, fig.10-73
4-35	Copyright "Jason Winter/Shutterstock"	153724628
4-36	Copyright "Jason Winter/Shutterstock"	153724628
4-37	Copyright "Designua/Shutterstock"	205382488
4-38	Federal Aviation Administration	H-8083-31 V2, fig.10-75
4-39	Copyright "snapinadil/Shutterstock"	188577731
4-40	Copyright "Designua/Shutterstock"	209336125
4-41	Copyright "Art Konovalov/Shutterstock"	221280358
4-42	Michael Leasure	-
4-43	Michael Leasure	-
4-44	Michael Leasure	-
4-45	Michael Leasure	-
4-46	Federal Aviation Administration	H-8083-31 V2, fig. 11-94
4-47	Icom America Inc	-
4-48	Copyright "Piotr Adamowicz/Shutterstock"	227183014
4-49	Copyright "chris kolaczan/Shutterstock"	133397462
4-50	Copyright "Scott T. O'Donnell/Shutterstock"	670653
4-51	Copyright "Designua/Shutterstock"	173109830
4-52	Federal Aviation Administration	http://goo.gl/iulR9A
4-53	Federal Aviation Administration	http://goo.gl/fGo2tC
Chapter 5		
Title Image	Creative Commons, Victor Camilo	https://goo.gl/VKE9GQ
5-1	Federal Aviation Administration	H-8083-32, fig. 1-35
5-2	Federal Aviation Administration	H-8083-32, fig. 1-36
5-3	Federal Aviation Administration	H-8083-32, fig. 1-37
5-4	Michael Leasure	-
5-5	Federal Aviation Administration	H-8083-32, fig. 1-38
5-6	Public Domain	http://goo.gl/TbjWwi
5-7	Federal Aviation Administration	H-8083-32, fig. 1-43
5-8	Michael Leasure	-
5-9	Michael Leasure	-
5-10	Michael Leasure	-
5-11	Michael Leasure	-
5-12	Michael Leasure	-
5-13	Michael Leasure	-
5-14	eAcademicBooks LLC	-
5-15	Michael Leasure	-
5-16	-	-

FIGURES AND ATTRIBUTION

Chapter 6

Title Image	Copyright "funkyfrogstock/Shutterstock"	166504457
6-1	Creative Commons, Juhan Sonin	https://goo.gl/1OkdPd
6-2	Creative Commons	https://goo.gl/Kp23Me
6-3	Michael Leasure	-
6-4	Creative Commons	https://goo.gl/VRncwm
6-5	Michael Leasure	-
6-6	Michael Leasure	-
6-7	Michael Leasure	-
6-8	Copyright "lucadp/Shutterstock"	256454941
6-9	Michael Leasure	-
6-10	Michael Leasure	-
6-11	Public Domain	http://goo.gl/TSucfo
6-12	Copyright "Tyler Olson/Shutterstock"	153853328
6-13	Creative Commons	https://goo.gl/g8Y0w9
6-14	Michael Leasure	-
6-15	Michael Leasure	-
6-16	Michael Leasure	-
6-17	Michael Leasure	-
6-18	Parrot	https://goo.gl/jZwbC0
6-19	Creative Commons	http://goo.gl/ciNy1y
6-20	Creative Commons	http://goo.gl/l964t2

Chapter 7

Title Image	Creative Commons, Richard Unten	https://goo.gl/h6Qbt4
7-1	Michael Leasure	-
7-2	University of Nebraska	-
7-3	Michael Leasure	-
7-4	Michael Leasure	-
7-5	Michael Leasure	-
7-6	Creative Commons, Ville Hyvönen	https://goo.gl/nmOCTH

Chapter 8

Title Image	Creative Commons, Richard Unten	https://goo.gl/GUdhMz
8-1	Federal Aviation Administration	https://goo.gl/LSmhuX
8-2	Michael Nolan	-
8-3	Michael Nolan	-
8-4	Michael Nolan	-
8-5	Michael Nolan	-
8-6	Michael Nolan	-
8-7	Michael Nolan	-
8-8	Michael Nolan	-

FIGURES AND ATTRIBUTION

8-9	Michael Nolan	-
8-10	Michael Nolan	-
8-11	Michael Nolan	-
8-12	Michael Nolan	-
8-13	Copyright "Scott T. O'Donnell/Shutterstock"	670653
8-14	Federal Aviation Administration	http://goo.gl/ZsMQjF
8-15	eAcademicBooks LLC	-
8-16	Copyright "Designua/Shutterstock"	173109830
8-17	GARMIN	-
8-18	Federal Aviation Administration	http://www.nstb.tc.faa.gov/images/Waaspic.jpg
8-19	Federal Aviation Administration	http://goo.gl/ditYei
8-20	Federal Aviation Administration	H-8083-25B, fig 14-16
8-21	Copyright "Designua/Shutterstock"	137935010
8-22	Copyright "imagedb.com/Shutterstock"	155679464
8-23	Federal Aviation Administration	H-8083-25B, fig 12-3
8-24	Federal Aviation Administration	H-8083-25B, fig. 12-4
8-25	Copyright "John T Takai/Shutterstock" Copyright "bolera/Shutterstock"	67912702 271236713
8-26	Federal Aviation Administration	H-8083-25B, fig 12-12
8-27	FAA PHAK	H-8083-25B fig. 13-10
8-28	Public Domain-National Weather Servic. (chart) Federal Aviation Administration (wind barb explanation)	Chart: NWS FAA: Wind barb explanation
8-29	Copyright "Maksym Darakchi/Shutterstock"	222279142
8-30	Public Domain	http://goo.gl/O8zdCW
8-31	Federal Aviation Administration	H-8083-25B, fig 13-6
8-32	Federal Aviation Administration	H-8083-25B fig. 13-5
8-33	Federal Aviation Administration	H-8083-25B fig. 12-23
8-34	Copyright "Robert Adrian Hillman/Shutterstock"	89099830
8-35	Federal Aviation Administration	H-8083-25B fig. 12-24
8-36	Copyright "Designua/Shutterstock"	209215186
8-37	Copyright "Designua/Shutterstock"	209215186
8-38	Public Domain-National Weather Service	-
8-39	Public Domain-National Weather Service	-
8-40	Public Domain-National Weather Service	-
8-41	Public Domain-National Weather Service	-
8-42	Public Domain-National Weather Service	-
Chapter 9		
Chapter 9 Title	Creative Commons, Dennis Jarvis	https://goo.gl/GaT3hR
9-1	Michael Leasure	-
9-2	Public Domain	http://goo.gl/RaXoNN

FIGURES AND ATTRIBUTION

9-3	Public Domain	http://goo.gl/AHW4Bl
9-4	Michael Leasure	-
9-5	Michael Leasure	-
9-6	Michael Leasure	-
9-7	Michael Leasure	-
9-8	Michael Nolan	-
9-9	Michael Leasure	-
9-10	Michael Leasure	-
9-11	Michael Leasure	-
9-12	Michael Leasure	-
9-13	Federal Aviation Administration	H-8083-25B fig. 11-23
9-14	Michael Leasure	-
9-15	Federal Aviation Administration	-
9-16	Creative Commons	http://goo.gl/2IG35B
9-17A, B	https://www.faasafety.gov/files/gslac/library/documents/2	Dirty dozen
Chapter 10		
Title Image	Public Domain	https://goo.gl/YSBu9h
10-1	Public Domain	http://goo.gl/1rpnwj
10-2	Public Domain	http://goo.gl/BGQp1L
Chapter 11		
Title Image	Creative Commons, Steve Rainwater	https://goo.gl/e6vKcX

INDEX

A

Accelerometers	78
Acoustic Payloads	120
Adhesives	36
ADS-B	92
Aerodynamics and Flight Controls	18
Aeronautical Charting	129
Aerospace Materials and their Properties	35
Aircraft Identification	140
Aircraft Launch and Recovery	167
Aircraft Loads and Stress	28
Aircraft Retrieval	168
Aircraft Speeds	139
Aircraft Stability and Control	24
Aircraft Structural Concepts	33
Aircraft Structures, Damage and Repair	52
Aircraft Structures, Materials, and Repair	33
Aircraft Weight	121
Airfoils and Lift	19
Airfoil Shapes	20
Air Masses	156
Airport Layout and Runway Numbering	144
Air Sampling Payloads	119
Airspace	127
Airspace Classes and Navigational Charts	128
Airspace Operations	127
Airspeed Indicators	76
Air Traffic Control Facilities	129
Air Traffic Control Facilities	140
Airways, Routes, and Navigation Aid Descriptions	140
Airworthiness Directives	176
Alert Areas	136
Altimeters and Altitude	74
Altimeter Settings	139
Altitude and Flight Performance	147
Altitudes	137
Analog and Digital Signals	81
Antenna Wiring	86
Area Forecasts	163
Area Navigation	142
Area of a Circle	99
Artificial Intelligence	201
Assisted Manual Control	108
ATC Services in Different Airspace Classes	131
Atmosphere	146
Atmospheric Pressure	147
Attitude Indicators	80
Autonomous Flight Control	109
Autonomous Testing	114
Autopilot Installation	113
Auxiliary Equipment	169
Aviation Forecasts	161
Aviation Navigation Systems	89
Aviation Routine Weather Report (METAR)	160
Axes of Motion of an Aircraft	23

B

Basic Electricity	59
Battery Management	174
Blind Rivets	40
Bluetooth	89
Build, Modify or Readymade	18

C

Calculating an Aircraft's CG	123
Carbon and/or Graphite Fiber	45
Center of Gravity	122
Center of Gravity Calculation	123
Chemical	62
Circuit Protection Devices	65
Circuits	67
Class F and G Airspace	133
Classification of Metal Damage	42
Cloud Coverage	154
Clouds	152
Cloud Types	152
Cloverleaf Antenna	86
Cold Front	157
Collision Avoidance	200
Combined Radar Approach Control and Tower with Radar	131
Commonly Used Unmanned Aircraft Antennas	85
Communication and Navigation Systems	81
Communications Systems	137
Composite Repair Techniques	50
Composite Structural Damage	48
Composite Structures	44
Compound Stresses	35
Compression	35
Compression Ratio	99
Compression Stroke and Ignition	96

Index

Conductors and Insulators ... 60
Controlled Firing Areas ... 136
Control Systems ... 107
Convective Air Currents ... 148
Current ... 59

D

Data Logging ... 111
DC Flight Restricted Zone and Special Flight Rules Area ... 135
Dew, Frost and Fog ... 152
Diesel Cycle Engines ... 97
Diesel Engine Fuel ... 97
Dipole Antenna ... 86
Direct and Alternating Current ... 64
Direction Indicating Instruments ... 80
DME Position Determination ... 142
Documents Relevant to Performance and Flight ... 174
Dual Purpose Flight Control Surfaces ... 56

E

Effect of Obstructions on Wind ... 149
Effects of Weight ... 121
Electrical Energy Production ... 61
Electrical Temperature Measuring Indicators ... 80
Electricity, Electrical, Communications and Navigation Systems ... 59
Electric Motor Power Ratings and Selection ... 104
Electric Motor Propulsion Characteristics ... 102
Electronic Speed Control (ESC) ... 102
Encryption ... 177
Engine Power and Efficiency Calculations ... 98
Enroute air traffic control ... 131
Exhaust Stroke ... 96
Exhaust Valve ... 96

F

Fabric ... 56
Fabric Coverings ... 37
Failsafe Systems ... 112
Federal Aviation Regulations ... 181
Firmware ... 112
First Person View (FPV) ... 115
Flight and Systems Training ... 171
Flight Control ... 107
Flight Controller ... 27
Flight Control Surfaces ... 55
Flight Operations ... 167
Flight Profile and Payload Planning ... 171

Flight Service Stations ... 131
Foam Core Structures ... 47
Forces Acting On an Aircraft ... 18
Four-Stroke or Four-Cycle Engine ... 94
Fronts ... 157
Fuel Cells ... 63
Fueled Engine Maintenance ... 105
Fuselage ... 30
Fuselage ... 52
Future Applications and Deployment ... 201
Future Trends and Technology ... 199

G

Gas Turbine Engine Characteristics ... 100
Gas Turbine Types and Operation ... 100
Global Navigation Satellite System ... 90
Global Navigation Satellite System ... 142
Global Positioning System ... 90
Global Positioning System ... 143
GNSS Augmentation ... 90
GNSS Augmentation ... 143
Ground-Based Augmentation System ... 91
Ground-Based Augmentation System ... 144
Gyro Stabilization ... 119

H

Hail ... 159
Headings ... 139
Helicopter Structure ... 57
Horsepower ... 98
Hybrid Designs and Airships ... 16

I

IFR Flight in Controlled Airspace (Class A, B, C, D, and E) ... 128
IFR Flight in Uncontrolled Airspace (Class G) ... 129
Inrunner versus Outrunner Motors ... 103
Inspection of Composite Materials ... 49
Instrument Charts ... 129
Instrument Classifications ... 69
Instrument Components ... 69
Instrument Operating Principles ... 69
Instrument Systems ... 69
Intake Stroke ... 95
Internal Combustion Engine Terminology ... 94
Internal Combustion-Reciprocating Engines ... 93
Internet Wi-Fi ... 87
Introduction to Designs ... 13

Introduction to Unmanned Aerial Systems 9

K
KV or kV Motor Rating 104

L
Laminates 44
Landing Gear 56
Larger Aircraft 200
Location and Environment 167
Logic Circuits 68

M
Manual Flight Control 107
Materials 44
Matrix Materials 45
Mechanical Balancing 125
Mechanical Generators 64
Mechanical Motion Indicators 77
Metal Airframe Inspection 40
Metallic Structural Materials 38
MicroDrone Option 185
Military Operations Area 136
Military Training Routes 136
Mission Driven Design 13
Mobile Phone Technology 88
Moisture and Temperature 150
Monocoque Type 30
Motors 67
Multiple Stresses 29
Multirotor Stability 27

N
Nondestructive Inspection, Composites 49
Non-Electric Temperature Indicators 79
Numbers 137

O
Observations 159
Occluded Front 158
Operational Considerations 169
Operational Requirements 184
Operational Requirements 185
Operator requirements 185
Operator's Logbook 176

P
Patch Antenna 86
Payload Installation 117
Payload Integration 118
Payload Mounting Systems 118
Pilots (Operators) Operating Handbook 174
Piston Displacement 98
Pitot-Static Systems 73
Platform Selection 14
Post Flight Analysis 171
Power 61
Powerplant Inspection and Maintenance 105
Powerplant Selection 17
Powerplant Theory and Operation 93
Power Stroke 96
Power Systems 199
Precipitation 155
Pre-Impregnated Products 46
Preparation for the Application of Adhesives 36
Prepreg Composites 51
Pressure 61
Pressure Measuring Instruments 72
Pressure Switches 72
Prohibited Areas 134
Propellers and Rotorcraft 22
Proposed FARs that relate to UAVs 186
Proposed New UAS Rules 184

R
Radar Observations 161
Radio Communication 82
Radio Phraseology 137
Radio Wave Creation and Transmission 83
Reciprocating Engine Operation 93
Regulations 181
Regulations 200
Relative Humidity 151
Resistance 60
Restricted Areas 134
Rotorcraft Advantages and Disadvantages 15
Rotorcraft Stability 124

S
Sandwich Structures 47
Satellite Based Augmentation Systems 91
Satellite Based Augmentation Systems 143
Satellite Observations 161
Sectional Charts 129
Semiconductors 67

Index

Semimonocoque Type	31
Sensors and Payloads	117
Shear	35
Signal Spoofing	177
Significant Weather Prognostic Charts	165
Skew-Planar Wheel Antenna	86
Solar Energy	64
Solid State Magnetometers	80
Special flight rules areas	135
Special Stability Issues	125
Special Use Airspace	133
Specific Platform Advantages and Disadvantages	14
Speed and Distance Measurements	76
Squall Line	159
Stability and Balance	124
Stall Warning and Angle of Attack Indicators	78
Standard Pronunciation	137
State and Local Law	186
Stationary Front	158
Stress Considerations in Repair	29
Stresses in Structural Repairs	34
Structural Fasteners	39
Structural Repair Manual	175
Summary of Trends	201
Surface Analysis Chart	164
Surface Aviation Weather Observations	159
Switches	66
Switch Types	66
Systems Training	173

T

Tactical Air Navigation (TACAN)	89
Tactical Air Navigation (TACAN)	142
Telemetry	111
Temperature/Dew Point Relationship	151
Temperature Measuring Instruments	79
Temporary Flight Restrictions	134
Tension	35
Terminal Aerodrome Forecasts (TAF)	161
Terminal Radar Approach Control (TRACON)	130
Test Flight and Flight Test	115
Thermal Electricity Generation	64
Thunderstorms	158
Time	138
Tornadoes	159
Torque Compensation	25
Transceivers	87

Truss Type	30
Two-Stroke Engines	97
Type Certificate Data Sheets	175
Types of Composite Fibrous Materials	45
Types of Electric Motors	102
Types of Metallic Damage and Defects	41
Types of Pressure	71

U

UAS and VFR Flight in Controlled Airspace (Class A, B, C, D, and E)	128
UAS and VFR Flight in Uncontrolled Airspace (Class G)	129
Unconventional Payloads	120
Unique Forces Acting on the Helicopter	24
Unmanned Aerial Vehicle Design and Construction	13
Unmanned Multirotor Aerodynamics	26
Unmanned Systems Human Factors and Safety	177

V

Valve Timing	95
Vehicle Requirements	184
VHF Omnidirectional Range (VOR)	141
Visibility	155
VOR	89
VORTAC	142

W

Warm Front	157
Warning Area	135
Watt-Motor Comparison	104
Weather	146
Weather Charts	164
Weather Depiction Chart	164
Weight and Balance	121
Weight and Balance Forms	175
Weight Limitations	122
Wet Layup Process	46
Wind and Air Currents	148
Wind and Pressure Representation on Surface Weather Maps	149
Wind Direction and Velocity	139
Wing Configurations	21
Wing Ribs	31
Wings	53
Wing Skin	32
Wing Spars	31
Wooden Structures	35
Work	98

WORKBOOK

CHAPTER 1 - INTRODUCTION TO UNMANNED AERIAL SYSTEMS

SECTION A
Chapter Review and Study Aid Questions:

1. The country of _____ was the first to routinely use a large model aircraft equipped with a camera for military surveillance.
    a. Pakistan
    b. India
    c. Israel
    d. United States

2. _____ developed a rudimentary unmanned aircraft to fly explosives toward enemy cities during WW2.
    a. Germany
    b. Japan
    c. Russia
    d. United States

3. The Dennyplane was developed and widely used for _____.
    a. surveillance
    b. aerial photography
    c. remote sensing of agricultural fields
    d. surface-to-air gunnery practice

4. UAS is a term used by the FAA to describe an unmanned aerial vehicle and _____.
    a. the operator of the controls
    b. all necessary systems associated with the vehicle
    c. the observer of the vehicle
    d. UAS is not a term used by FAA

5. Prior to the Wright brother's flights at Kitty Hawk, unmanned flight was virtually unknown.
    a. True
    b. False

6. The development of _____ contributed to the widespread availability, and use, of small civilian unmanned aircraft.
    a. heavy fuel engines
    b. miniaturized computer processing capability
    c. composite structures
    d. both b and c

Unmanned Aerial Systems: The Definitive Guide

7. FAA Advisory Circular 91-57A addresses _____.
   a. commercial multirotor design
   b. commercial fixed wing design
   c. recreational model aircraft
   d. pilot certification and licensing

8. What is the maximum recommended operating altitude for a recreational rotorcraft?
   a. 00 feet above ground level
   b. 500 feet above mean sea level
   c. 400 feet above mean sea level
   d. 400 feet above ground level

9. What is the maximum weight allowed for a recreational fixed wing aircraft?
   a. 55 pounds
   b. 55 kilos
   c. 4.5 pounds
   d. 15.5 kilos

10. A manned aircraft must remain 500 feet from any person, vessel, _____, or vehicle, except for the purpose of takeoff and landing.
    a. tree
    b. power line
    c. structure
    d. cannot be determined

11. The ability to see a live video feed on the ground from an operating unmanned aircraft is commonly referred to as _____.
    a. GPS
    b. OWL
    c. ADS-B
    d. FPV

12. The primary purpose of unmanned system education is _____.
    a. safety
    b. competent repair technicians
    c. competent operators
    d. efficient observers

SECTION B

Knowledge Application and Demonstration Questions:

1. An operator wishes to research the history of unmanned flight for a presentation to a local civic organization. The keywords to describe early unmanned systems might include?
2. An unmanned aircraft designer, seeking to minimize the weight of their proposed design, would study the strength characteristics of what modern materials?
3. Advice from the FAA on the operation of recreational model aircraft would be found in what document?
4. A group of recreational model aircraft flyers are proposing to build an operating area with a small runway 6 miles from an active manned airport. The airport manager asks, "What is the maximum altitude the models will be flying, and how much can they weigh"? Your answer is:
5. An unmanned aircraft operator wishes to have a view from their aircraft as if they were seated inside the cockpit. This may be accomplished with a camera system that provides what type of view?

CHAPTER 2 – UNMANNED AERIAL VEHICLE DESIGN AND CONSTRUCTION

SECTION A
Chapter Review and Study Aid Questions:

1. Manned and unmanned aircraft share common _____.
    a. structural materials
    b. propulsion systems
    c. control systems
    d. all of the above *(circled)*

2. The primary factor that shapes the design of an unmanned aircraft is the _____.
    a. materials availability
    b. mission, or use *(circled)*
    c. propulsion type
    d. control surface type and material

3. The ability of a multirotor unmanned aircraft to _____ is its primary distinguishing performance characteristic.
    a. hover as well as takeoff and land vertically *(circled)*
    b. lift large payloads
    c. remain aloft for extended periods
    d. cannot be determined

4. The fixed wing unmanned aircraft can fly for periods with its propulsion system off.
    a. True *(circled)*
    b. False

5. A _____ is needed for a fixed wing unmanned aircraft to takeoff and land.
    a. hand launch
    b. retrieval net
    c. catapult
    d. runway *(circled)*

6. The natural stability of a multirotor in flight is one of its many advantages.
    a. False *(circled)*
    b. True

7. If the thrust from the propulsion system of a fixed wing unmanned aircraft is lost, the aircraft _____.
    a. may also be lost due to lack of control
    b. will descend with little chance of landing
    c. may be stopped and control regained
    d. may glide to a controlled landing *(circled)*

Unmanned Aerial Systems: The Definitive Guide

Workbook

8. When vibration sensitive payloads are carried by an unmanned aircraft, the _____ is the best choice to reduce the vibration.
   a. *(fixed wing aircraft)*
   b. helicopter
   c. multirotor
   d. cannot be determined

9. A three motor multirotor does not provide enough thrust for flight.
   a. True
   b. *(False)*

10. The _____ of a multirotor unmanned aircraft is essential to controlled flight.
    a. empennage
    b. flight control surfaces
    c. variable pitch rotor blades
    d. *(flight control board)*

11. A tilt rotor unmanned aircraft _____.
    a. does not exist
    b. has not been fully developed
    c. *(uses rotors for vertical lift and forward thrust)*
    d. cannot be determined

12. A _____ is an unmanned airship that is tethered to the ground.
    a. balloon
    b. aeroelastic blimp
    c. dirigible
    d. *(aerostat)*

13. A liquid fuel powered unmanned aircraft will commonly place the engine _____ to minimize the effects of the vibration, interference, and the exhaust plume of the engine.
    a. in the front
    b. in the middle
    c. on the wing
    d. *(to the rear)*

14. A flying wing unmanned aircraft will commonly use _____ for flight control.
    a. elevators
    b. ailerons
    c. ruddervators
    d. *(elevons)*

15. In the balanced flight on an unmanned aircraft weight opposes _____ and thrust opposes _____.
    a. thrust, gravity
    b. thrust, drag
    c. lift, gravity
    d. *(lift, drag)*

16. Aircraft lift always acts perpendicular to _____.
    a. relative wing
    b. **relative wind**
    c. drag and gravity
    d. weight and thrust

17. The _____ of the wing is the term used to describe the effect of the upper and lower curvature.
    a. caster
    b. control offset
    c. wing root
    d. **mean camber**

18. Increasing the angle of attack of a wing increases _____.
    a. lift
    b. drag
    c. the pitching moment of inertia
    d. **both a and b**

19. The turbulent detachment of the air at high angles of attack is called _____.
    a. **stall**
    b. under camber
    c. oscillation
    d. lateral lift

20. The creation of lift requires higher _____ on the top of the wing airfoil.
    a. air pressure
    b. **air speed**
    c. air density
    d. cannot be determined

21. A long, narrow wing has a high _____.
    a. **aspect ratio**
    b. aspect ration
    c. profile drag
    d. angle of attack

22. An unmanned, fixed wing aircraft, without ailerons would require _____ for stable flight.
    a. low pressure
    b. pitching stabilization
    c. **dihedral**
    d. elevons

Workbook

23. A _____ produces lift in a horizontal direction.
    a. wing
    b. empennage
    c. motor
    (d.) propeller

24. _____ must always remain in front of the center of lift for stable flight.
    a. Motors
    b. Thrust
    c. Gravity
    (d.) Center of gravity

25. The effect of the center of gravity of an aircraft being too far to the rear in relationship to the center of lift is _____.
    a. pitch stability and roll instability
    (b.) pitch instability and difficult control
    c. roll instability with yaw stability
    d. cannot be determined

26. The three axes of rotation of an aircraft are _____, _____, _____.
    (a.) roll, pitch, yaw
    b. roll, pitch, lateral
    c. gravity, drag, thrust
    d. gravity, lift, thrust

27. An aircraft _____ about its longitudinal axis.
    a. pitches
    b. yaws
    (c.) rolls
    d. oscillates

28. An aircraft _____ about its lateral axis.
    (a.) pitches
    b. yaws
    c. rolls
    d. oscillates

29. The rudder of a fixed wing aircraft controls _____.
    a. roll
    b. pitch
    (c.) yaw
    d. cannot be determined

30. _____ is the ability of the aircraft to be directed along a desired flight path.
    a. Stability
    b. **Controllability**
    c. Maneuverability
    d. Maintainability

31. A helicopter uses the _____ for both thrust and lift.
    a. propeller
    b. elevator
    c. engine
    d. **rotor**

32. The _____ of a helicopter acts as a source of lift, and as a primary flight control.
    a. wing
    b. motor
    c. tail
    d. **rotor**

33. When the tip plane of a helicopter rotor is angled upward at the rear, _____ flight occurs.
    a. backward
    b. **forward**
    c. vertical
    d. stationary

34. Multirotor and helicopter aircraft are different from conventional fixed winged aircraft in that they can _____ sideways in flight without turning in the direction of motion.
    a. deflect
    b. pitch
    c. roll
    d. **slide**

35. A _____ counteracts the main rotor torque that would otherwise yaw a helicopter.
    a. **tail boom**
    b. cyclic control
    c. rotor path pitch plane
    d. tail rotor

36. An unmanned multirotor uses _____ to ascend without pitch, yaw, or roll changes.
    a. motor speed increase
    b. rotor pitch
    c. thrust increase
    d. **both a and c**

37. Yaw control of an unmanned multirotor primarily uses _____ to rotate the aircraft.
    a. thrust
    (b.) torque
    c. lift
    d. drag

38. Helicopters and fixed wing aircraft may be _____, multirotors cannot.
    a. computer numerically controlled
    b. electric powered
    c. flown in reverse
    (d.) flown without computer stability systems

39. The _____ of a multirotor requires all motors to be decelerated.
    a. ascent
    b. climb
    c. control
    (d.) descent

40. An "X" quadcopter with the forward left motor designated as M1, and the forward right motor designated as M2, with a clockwise rotating propeller mounted on M1, will decelerate motors _____ and _____ to yaw to the left.
    (a.) M2, M4
    b. M1
    c. M1, M3
    d. Cannot be determined

41. A "X" quadcopter with forward left motor designated as M1, and the forward right motor designated M2, with a clockwise rotating propeller mounted on M1, will decelerate motors _____ and _____ to yaw to the right.
    a. M2, M4
    b. M4
    c. M2
    (d.) M1, M3

42. An "X" quadcopter with forward left motor designated as M1, and the forward right motor designated M2, with a clockwise rotating propeller on M1, will accelerate motors _____ and _____ to pitch forward.
    a. M1, M3
    b. M2, M4
    c. M2, M3
    (d.) M3, M4

43. An "X" quadcopter with forward left motor designated as M1, and forward right motor designated as M2, with a counter clockwise rotating propeller on M1, will accelerate motors _____ and _____ to pitch rearward.
    (a.) M1, M2
    b. M2, M4
    c. M2, M3
    d. M3, M4

44. Unmanned aircraft designate the left and right sides as viewed from the rear.
    a. True
    b. False

45. A helicopter is directed to slide to the right. This will require the tip path plane of the rotor to _____ on the left side.
    a. lower
    b. rise
    c. both a and b
    d. cannot be determined

46. The flight control board of a multirotor adjusts motor speed through _____.
    a. an electronic speed control
    b. a servo and pushrod
    c. adjusting gain settings in flight
    d. cannot be determined

47. A flight control board with no GPS or compass inputs cannot be _____.
    a. absolute
    b. mean adjusted
    c. geostationary
    d. calibrated easily

48. Stress analysis is the evaluation of the _____ to determine stress types and levels.
    a. operator
    b. pilot
    c. airframe
    d. both a and b

49. Stress is an _____ force, and strain is an _____ resistance to deformation.
    a. internal, external
    b. unusual, internal
    c. unavoidable, unusual
    d. external, internal

50. Bending forces exhibit tension and _____.
    a. shear
    b. torsion
    c. compression
    d. cannot be determined

51. Tensile strength of materials is measured in _____.
    a. pounds per square inch or psi
    b. cubic centimeters
    c. square inches
    d. tensiotons

52. The top skin of an aircraft wing in flight is loaded primarily in _____.
    a. tension
    b. bending
    c. compression ✓
    d. torsion

53. The top skin of an aircraft wing while on the ground is loaded primarily in _____.
    a. compression
    b. torsion
    c. bending
    d. tension ✓

54. A truss type of fuselage structure relies upon the strength of the _____ for the majority of the flight and landing loads.
    a. skin covering
    b. stringers
    c. bulkheads
    d. internal structure ✓

55. A monocoque type fuselage structure relies upon the strength of the _____.
    a. skin covering ✓
    b. internal structure
    c. empennage
    d. wing spar

56. Repairs to the skin of what type of unmanned structure are the most critical?
    a. truss
    b. fabric covering
    c. monocoque ✓
    d. cannot be determined

57. The loads placed upon the wing skin in flight are transferred to what other components within the airframe?
    a. bulkheads, formers
    b. trusses and covering
    c. stringers and formers
    d. spars and ribs ✓

58. The skin repair of the _____ type structure is the most critical as it carries the majority of the flight loads.
    a. truss
    b. rib
    c. spar
    d. monocoque ✓

59. The balsa sheeting of a foam core UAV wing is an example of a _____ type structure.
    a. truss
    b. semimonocoque ✓
    c. monocoque
    d. cannot be determined

SECTION B
Knowledge Application and Demonstration Questions:

1. An unmanned systems designer wishes to investigate all available propulsion possibilities for their new aircraft design. What segments of aviation would provide this information?
2. A mission to perform precision agricultural imaging requires an aircraft that can fly for 1 hour and lift 8 pounds. A further mission requirement is that the aircraft be able to land safely in the event of propulsion power, or limited flight control failures. What is the best choice of aircraft design for this mission?
3. The primary purpose of placing an internal combustion engine at the rear of an unmanned aircraft design would be _____.
4. Elevons are selected as a means of controlling the pitch and roll of an unmanned aircraft. When a right turn is desired, what position will the left elevon control surface be in relation to the wing chord line?
5. A truss type fuselage structure is involved in a minor crash that bends a longeron on the aft fuselage. The skin covering the longeron is damaged as well. A repair is performed to the skin but the longeron is left bent. Is this a structural strength concern for the aircraft? Why?

Workbook

CHAPTER 3 - AIRCRAFT STRUCTURES, MATERIALS, AND REPAIR

SECTION A
Chapter Review and Study Aid Questions:

1. The rotors of a helicopter are considered to be part of the _____.
    a. fuselage
    b. tail boom
    c. propulsion system
    d. **airframe** ✓

2. The _____ of a fixed wing, conventional aircraft contains the elevator and rudder controls and mounting points.
    a. **empennage** ✓
    b. tail cone
    c. fuselage
    d. vertical stabilizer

3. Two examples of modern composite materials are _____ and _____.
    a. steel, aluminum
    b. steel, wood
    c. **aramid, carbon** ✓
    d. aramid, wood

4. A scratch or gouge in the surface of a highly stressed piece of metal often causes a stress concentration and can lead to failure of the part.
    a. False
    b. **True** ✓

5. An unmanned aircraft structural repair is considered adequate when it restores the original strength and _____.
    a. rigidity
    b. torsion
    c. **aerodynamic characteristics** ✓
    d. weight of materials before and after the repair

6. In regards to compressive strength, which structural member is stronger?
    a. a member with holes drilled in it for lightening
    b. **a member with no holes** ✓
    c. a member with loosely fitting fasteners
    d. cannot be determined

7. Shear stress in aircraft repair is primarily concerned with _____.
    a. **fastener installation** ✓
    b. rigidity of the damaged structure
    c. ductility of the structure
    d. aluminum sheetmetal in compression

8. Laminated wood may be identified by its grain running in what direction?
   a. perpendicular with each layer
   b. horizontal
   c. parallel in each member
   d. wood is never laminated in unmanned structures

9. Aircraft plywood is a series of thin wood veneers glued together with the grain of each veneer oriented 90 degrees, or perpendicular.
   a. True
   b. False

10. Aircraft wood must not have any _____ present.
    a. growth rings
    b. small knots
    c. decay
    d. grain

11. _____ failure is the crushing of the wood fibers perpendicular to the grain.
    a. Mineral streak
    b. Knot
    c. Grain
    d. Compression

12. A type of adhesive that is gap filling is the close contact type.
    a. True
    b. False

13. A type of glue application where the adhesive is applied to one side only is _____?
    a. single spread
    b. one spread
    c. monoplique
    d. Glue is always applied to two sides.

14. The time after the glue is applied but before the part is assembled or clamped, is referred to as _____.
    a. pot life
    b. mixing time
    c. open assembly time
    d. closed assembly time

15. _____ glue is a common wood glue that is waterproof when dry.
    a. Aliphatic resin
    b. Epoxy chromate
    c. Lacquer
    d. Enamel

16. Cyanoacrylate (CA) adhesive is often used for field repairs due to its rapid curing properties.
    a. **True**
    b. False

17. Wax is often applied to wood prior to gluing to act as a bond enhancer.
    a. True
    b. **False**

18. Nails and staples provide gluing pressure only and may be _____ after the glue cures.
    a. varnished
    b. left to provide additional strength
    c. **removed**
    d. cannot be determined

19. Plastic films on light unmanned aircraft are tightened by _____.
    a. dope sealers
    b. stretching
    c. adhesive glue
    d. **heat application**

20. Aluminum clad is _____ for corrosion resistance.
    a. epoxy bonded aluminum alloy
    b. **pure aluminum bonded to an alloy core**
    c. alloy aluminum bonded to a core of pure aluminum
    d. a heat treating process

21. 2024 aluminum alloy is the softest alloy and commonly used as a cladding.
    a. True
    b. **False**

22. _____ aluminum alloy is used for the manufacture of propeller blades.
    a. 1100
    b. 2024
    c. 3303
    d. **2025**

23. Heat treatment and _____ working are used to form aircraft aluminum.
    a. **cold**
    b. rolled
    c. hammer
    d. press

24. Rivets used in unmanned structures are divided into two main categories including blind and _____.
    a. non-blind
    b. solidified
    c. bucked
    d. **solid shank**

25. Rivets should not be installed where _____ loads are present.
    a. altitude
    b. flight
    c. **tension** ✓
    d. shear

26. Unmanned aircraft structural rivets are removed by _____.
    a. shearing
    b. punching
    c. pressing
    d. **drilling** ✓

27. What is the preferred rivet to use on the first third of a wing chord, upper surface, where minimum airflow disruption is desirable?
    a. universal head
    b. **countersunk head** ✓
    c. brazed head
    d. cannot be determined

28. A _____ must be used to install a blind rivet.
    a. rivet hammer
    b. bucking bar
    c. squeezer
    d. **puller** ✓

29. Corrosion in unmanned aircraft aluminum structures _____.
    a. is not a concern due to the extra material thickness available
    b. is a common form of paint damage
    c. is not an issue due to the alloys used in construction
    d. **must be prevented as structural strength may be degraded** ✓

30. When is a blind rivet required in an aluminum aircraft structure?
    a. when a smooth, aerodynamic fastener is required
    b. **when access to only one side of a structure is available** ✓
    c. when maximum strength is required
    d. when access to both sides of a structure is available

31. A working rivet is one that performs as designed.
    a. True
    b. **False** ✓

32. Aircraft structural damage may extend well beyond the visual indications of distorted skin and should be investigated thoroughly for further internal damage.
    a. **True** ✓
    b. False

33. A small, thin section of metal extending beyond a regular surface, usually located at a corner or on the edge of a hole, describes what type of metal damage?
    a. brinelling
    b. burnishing
    c. galling
    d. burr

34. The loss of metal from the surface, by chemical or electrochemical action, that is removed by chemical or mechanical means.
    a. burr
    b. burnishing
    c. corrosion
    d. corruption

35. A breakdown (or build-up) of metal surfaces, due to excessive friction between two parts having relative motion. Particles of the softer metal are torn loose and welded to the harder metal.
    a. galling
    b. cracking
    c. gouging
    d. denting

36. A deeper tear or break in metal surface than a scratch that may show discoloration from temperature produced by friction.
    a. scratching
    b. brinelling
    c. chattering
    d. score

37. Why is negligible damage to an unmanned structure not serious enough for repair?
    a. It results in only minor structural weakening.
    b. It is cosmetic only, but may extend into internal members.
    c. It is time consuming to correct and therefore seldom repaired.
    d. It is minor damage with no structural weakening.

38. Negligible or minor damage should be _____.
    a. monitored and inspected routinely
    b. repaired immediately by grounding the aircraft
    c. covered with adhesive tape
    d. disregarded

39. Damage repairable by patching must _____ the damaged area and provide lost structural support.
    a. bridge
    b. underpin
    c. undercut
    d. cannot be determined

Unmanned Aerial Systems: The Definitive Guide

40. _____ are especially important in regard to repair design and performance as they are primary load carrying members of the structure
    a. Ribs
    b. Stringers
    c. Spars ✓
    d. Fairings

41. Welding is the _____ of base metals and filler rod to form a solid structural seam.
    a. gluing
    b. fusing ✓
    c. fastening
    d. hardening

42. Spot welding differs from many other types as it does not require _____.
    a. fusing
    b. pressure
    c. filler rod ✓
    d. heat

43. Gas welding and electric arc welding differ in what primary way?
    a. Gas welding uses little heat and no filler rod.
    b. Electric arc welding uses little heat and no filler rod.
    c. Gas welding is not used.
    d. The source of the heat for melting the metal. ✓

44. Brazing and soldering differ from welding in what primary way?
    a. the method of heat generation
    b. in the materials thickness
    c. they do not melt the base metals ✓
    d. they are electric insulators

45. Composite structures use fibers supported by _____ to create structural materials.
    a. matrix ✓
    b. fastener
    c. isotropic
    d. anisotropic

46. Fiber orientation in a composite structure helps the structure _____.
    a. resist corrosion
    b. bond to finishing paint
    c. support loads imposed in various directions
    d. eliminate the requirement for matrix materials ✓

47. _____ has advantages over other composite materials in that it is generally inexpensive, has a relatively high chemical and galvanic corrosion resistance, and is electrically resistive.
    a. Carbon
    b. Aramid
    (c.) Boron
    d. Fiberglass

48. Carbon and graphite fibers are based on the hexagonal internal molecular structure.
    (a.) True
    b. False

49. _____ fibers are very stiff and strong, three to ten times stiffer than glass fibers.
    a. Boron
    b. Elastomer
    c. Aramid
    (d.) Carbon

50. Thermoset matrix materials may be heated and reshaped many times.
    a. True
    (b.) False

51. _____ matrix materials may be heated and reshaped many times.
    (a.) Thermoplastic
    b. Thermoset
    c. Thermoelastic
    d. Thermos

52. Epoxy resin is a form of _____ matrix material
    a. thermoplastic
    (b.) thermoset
    c. thermoelastic
    d. thermos

53. What describes the method of heat forming plastic over a mold for such items as nonstructural fairings on unmanned aircraft?
    a. blow molding
    b. male plug
    c. tooling
    (d.) vacuum forming

54. Which matrix material type is liquid when forming and then hardens into a permanent structure through chemical reaction?
    (a.) thermoset
    b. thermoplastic
    c. thermos
    d. exothermic

55. Preimpregnated composite structures may contain which reinforcing fibers?
    a. carbon
    b. aramid
    c. fiberglass
    d. all of the above

56. How must preimpregnated fibers be stored prior to use?
    a. at room temperature
    b. at 300 degrees F
    c. at 0 degrees F
    d. cannot be determined

57. Wet layup differs from prepreg layup in what significant way?
    a. Wet layup uses only epoxy resins.
    b. Wet layup uses liquid resin to saturate the reinforcing fibers.
    c. Prepreg uses liquid resin to saturate the reinforcing fibers.
    d. Prepreg and wet layup do not differ in any significant way.

58. Sandwich type composite construction requires _____.
    a. sand for forming
    b. fiberous core reinforcement
    c. a core faced on both sides with laminated sheets
    d. prepreg layup combined with wet layup to form a sandwich

59. _____ is the primary structural benefit of honeycomb structural composites.
    a. Bending
    b. Repair ability
    c. Resistance to impact
    d. Stiffness

60. _____ is a common core material used in honeycomb composite structures.
    a. Titanium
    b. Brass
    c. Paper
    d. Wax

61. _____ has very good fire-resistant properties and is relatively very low density, but also has low strength properties.
    a. Styrofoam
    b. Phenolic foam
    c. ABS
    d. EOE foam

62. Polypropylene can be shaped with a hot wire and is compatible with most adhesives and epoxy resins but cannot be used with polyester resins.
    a. True
    b. False

63. Another name for Polymethacrylimide foam is _____.
    a. rohacell ✓
    b. ABS
    c. PMC
    d. poly

64. When used as a core material, balsa wood is constructed with the face laminates _____ to the grain of the wood.
    a. parallel
    b. opposite
    c. perpendicular ✓
    d. alternated

65. A delaminated matrix is a more serious form of composite damage requiring repair.
    a. True ✓
    b. False

66. Delaminations and debonds of a composite structure, when loaded in _____ may fail catastrophically.
    a. tension
    b. shear
    c. torsion
    d. compression ✓

67. Ultraviolet (UV) light can affect the strength of composite materials.
    a. True ✓
    b. False

68. Visual and _____ are the most simple and common types of composite structural inspection.
    a. tap testing ✓
    b. ultrasonic
    c. eddy current
    d. magnetic particle

69. _____ inspection has proven useful in detecting subsurface delaminations and debonds not readily discernible with simpler inspection methods.
    a. Eddy current
    b. Tap testing
    c. Ultrasonic ✓
    d. Hypersonic

70. Composite structural fabrication and repair processes use vacuum bags to _____.
    a. apply pressure to structures during curing of the matrix
    b. hold repair laminates in place during matrix cure
    c. hold heat blankets and caul plates in place during matrix cure
    d. all of the above ✓

Workbook

71. Bleeder ply materials used during vacuum bagging _____.
    a. absorb excess fibers
    b. allow air to enter the repair for lightness
    c. absorb excess matrix material *(circled)*
    d. are not used during vacuum bagging

72. Heat is often applied to composite structures during fabrication or repair to slow curing of the matrix for better fiber saturation.
    a. True
    b. False *(circled)*

73. Unmanned airframes may be constructed entirely of foam with reinforcements only used at points such as spar joiners and landing gear attach points.
    a. True *(circled)*
    b. False

74. What term best describes a wing that is braced entirely on the inside?
    a. strutted
    b. braced
    c. delta
    d. cantilever *(circled)*

75. What flight control surface is hinged at the rear of the horizontal stabilizer?
    a. rudder
    b. elevator *(circled)*
    c. aileron
    d. elevon

76. A ruddervator combines the action of an elevator and rudder. In order to yaw to the left, the left ruddervator surface will move up or down?
    a. up
    b. down *(circled)*
    c. cannot be determined
    d. both a and b

77. _____ landing gear most often includes a steerable nosewheel.
    a. Conventional
    b. Tricycle *(circled)*
    c. Composite
    d. Helicopter

78. The primary operational challenge with the conventional gear is that the _____ is located behind the main landing gear location.
    a. tailwheel *(circled)*
    b. center of lift
    c. nosewheel
    d. center of gravity

SECTION B
Knowledge Application and Demonstration Questions:

1. The design team of a large unmanned aircraft is tasked with creating a repair manual for the aircraft. A good source of information and examples of standard structural repairs could be obtained from what source?
2. An unmanned aircraft design team is debating the advantages and disadvantages of various landing gear configurations. They have narrowed their choice to conventional and tricycle gear configurations. What are the advantages and disadvantages of each type?
3. A fairing is needed to cover the electronics installation of a quadcopter for use in rain and snow conditions. The fairing must be light, easily formed, and moisture resistant. What are some choices for materials and fabrication in this situation?
4. FAA recommends welding as a repair method for steel tube aircraft structures. Why can't brazing be substituted in this case?
5. The loads imposed on the composite landing gear leg of a large unmanned system are primarily vertical during landing. The orientation of the fibers in this case should be?

Workbook

CHAPTER 4 – ELECTRICITY, ELECTRICAL, COMMUNICATIONS AND NAVIGATION SYSTEMS

SECTION A
Chapter Review and Study Aid Questions:

1. Electricity is the flow of _____ through a conductor such as a copper wire.
    a. atoms
    b. power
    c. protons
    d. electrons

2. _____ is the total amount of electron flow in an electrical circuit.
    a. Voltage
    b. Current
    c. Power
    d. Resistance

3. Voltage is best described as an electromotive force, or pressure.
    a. True
    b. False

4. The greater the _____ the less amperage will flow.
    a. resistance
    b. voltage
    c. conductor area
    d. cannot be determined

5. An insulator has what primary characteristic as related to electron flow?
    a. It enhances electron flow.
    b. It increases voltage.
    c. It increases amperage.
    d. It resists electron flow.

6. The length and diameter of wire used in an unmanned aircraft power system will have a direct effect upon _____.
    a. voltage
    b. insulation properties
    c. resistance
    d. cannot be determined

7. A main wire to the power distribution board of an unmanned multirotor begins to heat up during use. This will _____ resistance in the wire.
    a. increase
    b. decrease
    c. have no effect upon the
    d. cannot be determined

8. A 12 volt battery is supplying 30 amps to a circuit. This is how many watts of power?
    a. 12
    b. 30
    c. 360
    d. 2.5

9. An electric motor is rated at 900 watts maximum power. Approximately how many amps is this if the battery to be used is rated at 16 volts?
    a. 34
    b. 69
    c. 14400
    d. none of the above

10. An 11.1 volt lithium polymer battery rated at 2400 milliamp hours will supply how many amps for one hour?
    a. 4.8
    b. 2400
    c. 1
    d. 2.4

11. A 3 cell lithium polymer battery rated at 2400 milliamp hours will supply how many amps for one half hour?
    a. 4.8
    b. 2400
    c. 1
    d. 2.4

12. A lithium polymer 4 cell battery rated at 3600 milliamp hours is powering a motor consuming 14.4 amps. How many minutes will the battery last to full depletion?
    a. 900
    b. 80
    c. 3.36
    d. 15

13. Pressure generation of electricity is known as _____ generation.
    a. piezoelectric
    b. pizoelastic
    c. piezoresistive
    d. piezotropic

14. Wet cell batteries use what materials to generate electricity?
    a. conductive, insulator
    b. electrolyte, resistor
    c. electrolyte, two different metals
    d. two different metals, insulator

15. A battery described as a secondary cell may be _____.
    a. used and discarded
    b. the second in a series of batteries
    c. used as a backup power source
    d. recharged

16. What percentage of a batteries capacity may be lost before it is considered unusable in UAS applications?
    a. 80%
    b. 20%
    c. 10%
    d. cannot be determined

17. What is a battery cycle?
    a. one complete discharge, recharge
    b. a method of recharging
    c. recharging a primary cell
    d. cannot be determined

18. What factor below will reduce a batteries useful life?
    a. properly charging and discharging
    b. storing in a properly charged state
    c. storing in a discharged state
    d. periodically adding electrolyte to a wet cell type

19. A dry type battery is typically not _____.
    a. useful for unmanned applications
    b. recharged
    c. useful until charged with acid
    d. yet available and is in development

20. Fuel cells are joined together in _____ to increase their useful power.
    a. series
    b. chains
    c. rows
    d. parallel

21. What is the term used for electricity generated by two dissimilar metals when heated?
    a. piezoelectric
    b. heat release
    c. wet cell
    d. thermocouple

22. Solar panels absorb _____ to produce usable electric power.
    a. neutrons
    b. photons
    c. electrons
    d. neurons

23. What is the term for a device to create electrical energy by rotating a coil of wire within a magnetic field?
    a. battery
    b. solar array
    c. generator
    d. secondary cell

24. Direct electrical current (DC) is produced by _____ and alternating current (AC) by _____.
    a. primary cell, secondary cell
    b. batteries, solar panels
    c. fuel cells, solar panels
    d. generators, alternators

25. Alternating current devices may be smaller and lighter than comparable direct current devices.
    a. True
    b. False

26. What is a device for protecting electrical systems from excess amperage?
    a. fuse
    b. circuit breaker
    c. alternator
    d. both a and b

27. Excess amperage in an unprotected electrical circuit, beyond the level the circuit was designed to carry, may cause _____.
    a. decreased charge levels to the battery
    b. decreased performance of motors
    c. damaging heat and fire
    d. no problems as this is a safety feature

28. What type of switch controls one circuit and has both on and off positions?
    a. SPDT
    b. DPST
    c. SPST
    d. cannot be determined

29. A single switch is used in a circuit that is 12 volts and controls two circuits. How much amperage will flow through the switch?
    a. 24 amps
    b. 12 amps
    c. 1 amp
    d. cannot be determined

30. What type of switch would be commonly used on a starter motor circuit of a piston engine?
    a. simple toggle
    b. knife
    c. momentary toggle
    d. mercury

31. Six lead acid battery cells at 2 volts each are wired in series. This will produce how many volts?
    a. 6 volts
    b. 12 volts
    c. 24 volts
    d. 3 volts

32. Six lead acid battery cells at 2 volts each are wired in parallel. This will produce how many volts?
    a. 6 volts
    b. 2 volts
    c. 24 volts
    d. 3 volts

33. A diode is used to control electrical flow in what way?
    a. reverses the flow
    b. series circuit
    c. parallel circuit
    d. blocks flow in one direction and allows flow in another

34. An _____ is a form of diode that provides usable light.
    a. EMP
    b. RFI
    c. EMI
    d. LED

35. In most modern logic circuits, thousands, if not millions of diode like functions have been placed on one small chip called a _____.
    a. microcircuit
    b. microarray
    c. diode array
    d. microprocessor

36. Logic circuits use what type of diode based system to provide useful computer calculations and operations?
    a. yes, no
    b. true, false
    c. 1,0
    d. all of the above

37. Sense and _____ are the basic components of all unmanned aircraft instrumentation systems.
    a. avoid
    b. interrupt
    c. display
    d. log

Unmanned Aerial Systems: The Definitive Guide

38. An altimeter would be an example of what type of general instrument classification?
    a. flight
    b. propulsion
    c. attitude
    d. navigation

39. An airspeed indicator would be an example of what type of general instrument classification?
    a. flight
    b. propulsion
    c. attitude
    d. navigation

40. A magnetic compass would be an example of what type of general instrument classification?
    a. flight
    b. propulsion
    c. attitude
    d. navigation

41. A _____ senses pressure changes and will uncoil (open) or retract (close) in response to those changes.
    a. bourbon tube
    b. bourdon tube
    c. bellows
    d. airspeed indicator

42. Pressure sensing aircraft instrument mechanisms include _____, and _____.
    a. bellows, cams
    b. bellows, needles
    c. diaphragm, bellows
    d. diaphragm, cams

43. _____ sensors, used in most modern aviation applications, typically utilize either varying electrical output, or resistance changes, when pressure changes are applied.
    a. Solid-state
    b. Hydro-mechanical
    c. Mechanical
    d. Hydro-electric

44. Absolute pressure is a measurement comparing the measured force to that created in a total vacuum.
    a. True
    b. False

45. Standard day pressure used for aeronautical purposes is _____ inches of mercury.
    a. 30
    b. 29.92
    c. 1
    d. a variable value measured in

46. _____ is the difference between the pressure to be measured and the ambient atmospheric pressure.
    a. Absolute
    b. Altitude
    c. Gauge
    d. Differential

47. An aircraft's airspeed indicator is a/an _____ pressure gauge.
    a. absolute
    b. gauge
    c. differential
    d. atmospheric

48. An aircraft engine manifold pressure gauge is reading slightly below atmospheric pressure. The engine is _____.
    a. at idle
    b. off
    c. at full throttle
    d. cannot be determined

49. EPR compares the pressure of the engines exhaust to the pressure of the ram air at the inlet of the _____ engine.
    a. reciprocating piston
    b. electric
    c. diesel
    d. gas turbine

50. It is a preferred arrangement in aircraft to place a sealed fuel quantity or flow sensing mechanism in the fuel tank itself and send a signal to a remotely located indicator. This is to prevent _____.
    a. lengthy runs of fuel lines and risk of leaks
    b. accurate fuel sensing information
    c. fuel vaporization
    d. fuel starvation

51. A hydraulic system that turns the pump off at a predetermined pressure would utilize what type of switch?
    a. rotary
    b. SPDT
    c. momentary pushbutton
    d. pressure

52. A vertical speed indicator is a type of _____ instrument.
    a. absolute
    b. ambient
    c. pitot static
    d. remote

53. Where is the best location for the installation of a pitot tube on an unmanned aircraft?
    a. inside the engine cowl in calm air
    b. on the leading edge forward of the wing
    c. in mildly turbulent airflow
    d. on the tail facing aft

54. When studying altimeters it is important to know that as altitude increases, air pressure _____.
    a. increases
    b. decreases
    c. remains the same
    d. decreases but then increase again gradually

55. Accurate altitude sensing is important in unmanned operations due to the need for terrain avoidance and accurate reporting to air traffic control as well as insuring the aircraft is above approved minimum altitudes.
    a. True
    b. False

56. Altimeters can be adjusted to read altitude above ground level. This is accomplished by adjusting the pressure compensation such that the altimeter indicates an altitude of zero feet while _____.
    a. on the ground prior to takeoff
    b. below 1000 feet
    c. above 1000 feet
    d. in the air once cruising altitude is reached

57. What unit of distance is the standard in United States aeronautics?
    a. statute mile
    b. kilometer
    c. greenwich mean mile
    d. nautical mile

58. What is known as true airspeed or TAS, would be the same as calibrated airspeed if the flight occurred when _____ day conditions exist.
    a. normal
    b. standard
    c. cold
    d. regular

59. The ground speed of an unmanned aircraft will be primarily dependent upon what factor?
    a. regular day temperature
    b. regular day pressure
    c. wind speed
    d. airspeed

60. Stall warning systems sense the aircraft's _____ and alert the operator when the safe value is exceeded.
    a. dihedral angle
    b. approach speed
    c. departure speed
    d. angle of attack

61. The glass face of a magnetic compass allows the numbers on the rotating float to be referenced against a vertical lubber line.
    a. True
    b. False

62. Solid state magnetometers have no moving parts and are extremely accurate. Tiny layered structures react to _____ on a molecular level.
    a. magnetism
    b. reactance
    c. inductance
    d. angular change

63. Accelerometers are used to generate the _____ display of an unmanned aircraft.
    a. altitude
    b. airspeed
    c. attitude
    d. amplitude

64. A significant advantage of digital transmission over analog is the control of _____.
    a. noise
    b. frequency
    c. gradient shift
    d. wavelength

65. The wavelength of a radio transmission is the actual distance from one wave peak to another as viewed on an/. _____.
    a. VOM
    b. radio screen
    c. HUD
    d. oscilloscope

66. The radio waves that follow the curvature of the earth from transmitter to receiver are referred to as _____.
    a. reflex waves
    b. ground waves or surface waves
    c. atmospheric sky waves
    d. earth or terrain waves

67. High frequency radio waves travel _____ and may bounce off of the earth's ionosphere.
    a. at the speed of sound
    b. greater distances than other waves
    c. in a straight line
    d. in a curved line following the earth's curvature

68. High frequency radio waves are limited to line of sight transmission and reception.
    a. True
    b. False

69. FM radio stations carry _____ information on their carrier waves than AM stations.
    a. less
    b. about the same
    c. more
    d. no more

70. Demodulation is the process of removing the original information from the radio carrier wave.
    a. True
    b. False

71. An antenna _____ the length of a received signals wavelength is the most resonant meaning that it is able to maximize voltage and current creation.
    a. two thirds
    b. a full value of
    c. along
    d. half

72. The skew-planar wheel type antenna is a form of circular cloverleaf with _____ lobes offset 90 degrees from one another.
    a. 2
    b. 3
    c. 4
    d. 6

73. The primary disadvantage of any cloverleaf style antennae is they are neither compact nor aerodynamic.
    a. True
    b. False

74. The _____ is a linear antenna requiring that both the transmitter and receiver be aligned either vertically or horizontally for best signal reception.
    a. dipole
    b. cloverleaf
    c. skew-planar
    d. patch

75. Transmitters and receivers must be connected to their antennas via conductive wire. What is this wire called?
    a. multi-strand
    b. flex
    c. coaxial
    d. biaxial

76. What primary disadvantage must be considered when utilizing a ground based patch antenna receiver?
    a. Patch antennas are very short range.
    b. Patch antennas must be aligned vertically or horizontally.
    c. Patch antennas are directional and must be pointed with their face to the UAV.
    d. Patch antennas have no inherent disadvantages.

77. The shielding of a coaxial cable is electrically _____.
    a. active
    b. grounded
    c. charged
    d. neutral

78. A _____ is a communication radio that transmits and receives.
    a. omnidirectional
    b. bidirectional
    c. transceiver
    d. dipolor

79. Wi-Fi routers are high frequency radios. This high frequency allows them to carry more data on the carrier.
    a. True
    b. False

80. Wi-Fi _____ can be added to a system to overcome difficulties of interference and limited useful range.
    a. range dividers
    b. range multipliers
    c. duplexers
    d. range extenders

81. Mobile "cellular" phones are limited by what two factors regarding range and reception?
    a. line of sight, power output
    b. line of sight, communication protocol
    c. size, antenna orientation
    d. they are not limited

82. The Global Navigation Satellite System is another term for the satellites of the United States providing global positioning system (GPS) data.
    a. True
    b. False

83. GPS data may be used to determine location in _____ dimensions on the earth with multiple satellites visible to the receiver onboard an unmanned aircraft.
    a. 1
    b. 2
    c. 3
    d. 4

84. _____ is/are used by the GPS receiver to pinpoint its location.
    a. Quadrangles
    b. Numerators
    c. Triangulation
    d. Algorithms

85. A ground based augmentation system uses satellite signals, as well as ground transmitters, to improve the accuracy of navigational systems.
    a. True
    b. False

86. _____ is a promising GPS based technology for collision avoidance that uses radio transmitters and receivers on each aircraft to display location and direction of all aircraft in a geographical area.
    a. UDS-A
    b. ABS-D
    c. ADB-S
    d. ADS-B

SECTION B
Knowledge Application and Demonstration Questions:

1. An unmanned aircraft has onboard systems powered by electricity. The secondary batteries are to be recharged in flight. The options available to recharge them would include _____?
2. Unlike manned aircraft, instruments and indicators onboard an unmanned aircraft must show their results on a ground station display. An airspeed indicator could use what sources of information to provide this data to the ground station display?
3. A cinematographer wants to increase the range of their video downlink display system. It is decided that a patch antenna on a tripod would be a good choice. What limitations does this solution present?
4. A researcher is creating a very precise map of an agricultural field using a rotorcraft equipped with a GPS guided autopilot and a camera that "tags" each image with its precise location. A series of GPS transmitters are mounted on tripods to increase the accuracy of the system. What manned aircraft solution does this most closely replicate?
5. An unmanned flight is occurring well inside class D airspace with an operational control tower. The operator wishes to communicate with the tower during the flight. What is their best option for maintaining 2 way radio contact?

CHAPTER 5 – POWERPLANT THEORY AND OPERATION

SECTION A
Chapter Review and Study Aid Questions:

1. Unmanned aircraft may be powered by what types of propulsion systems?
    a. turbine, reciprocating piston, electric
    b. electric and reciprocating piston only
    c. turbine and electric only
    d. fueled and turbine only

2. The four strokes of an internal combustion engine are _____, _____, _____, _____.
    a. intake, compression, ignition, exhaust
    b. intake, compression, power, exhaust
    c. intake, compression, ignition, power
    d. exhaust, ignition, intake, compression

3. In a liquid fueled UAV engine, the fuel is vaporized, compressed, and burnt which converts _____ energy into _____ energy.
    a. heat, latent
    b. mechanical, power
    c. heat, mechanical
    d. air, thrust

4. What component is primarily responsible for allowing spent combustion gases to exit the cylinder during the exhaust stroke?
    a. piston
    b. crankshaft
    c. head
    d. valve

5. What valve is open during the compression of the fuel air mixture?
    a. intake
    b. exhaust
    c. rotary
    d. none

6. Cylinder _____ is the interior diameter of the cylinder.
    a. boar
    b. bore
    c. combustion chamber
    d. piston diameter

7. TDC is an engine term used to represent the upper most travel of the piston.
    a. True
    b. False

8. The ignition event of a four stroke engine will occur a certain number of degrees before top dead center.
    a. True
    b. False

9. The four stroke reciprocating engine rotates _____ degrees between ignition events.
    a. 720
    b. 360
    c. 180
    d. cannot be determined

10. The time that both the intake and exhaust valves are open is called valve _____.
    a. lag
    b. lead
    c. drop
    d. overlap

11. How many degrees of crankshaft rotation are required to complete one cycle of a two stroke engine?
    a. 720
    b. 360
    c. 180
    d. 0

12. The lubrication of most two stroke engines is accomplished by _____.
    a. synthetic additives
    b. mixing fuel with alcohol
    c. mixing fuel with oil
    d. adding oil to crankcase

13. What is commonly required to optimize two stroke engine and propeller operating speeds respectively?
    a. propeller hub dampeners
    b. engine governors
    c. reduction system
    d. engine deduction systems

14. A type of compression ignition engine is the diesel which uses a properly timed spark ignition system to produce useful power.
    a. True
    b. False

15. The concept of horsepower is based on the work done by an actual horse in a certain period of time. The time factor is derived from what parameter in an unmanned propulsion system?
    a. torque
    b. moment arm
    c. rpm
    d. btu

16. UAV horsepower may be compared to electrical power using what unit of measure?
    a. volt
    b. amp
    c. watt
    d. they do not compare

17. The term used to describe the volume of an aircraft engine cylinder at BDC vs. TDC is _____.
    a. displacement
    b. compression factor
    c. compression ratio
    d. compression displacement

18. Gas turbine engine parts do not reciprocate but rather turn in one direction continuously. This has a great effect on _____ and _____.
    a. thrust, heat
    b. thrust, pressure
    c. vibration, engine life
    d. fuel economy, exhaust temperature

19. What type of unmanned operations will most benefit from the use of turbofan propulsion?
    a. turboshaft
    b. sea level operations
    c. turboprop
    d. high altitude

20. The _____ extracts energy within the gas turbine engine to drive the compressor.
    a. accessory section
    b. mainshaft
    c. combustion can
    d. turbine section

21. What form of UAV propulsion has an advantage of no exhaust emissions?
    a. gas turbine
    b. electric
    c. electronic
    d. electro-dynamic

22. Brushless electric motors are _____ % efficient compared to brushed motors at 75-80 % efficiency.
    a. 85-90
    b. nearly 100
    c. 90-100
    d. they cannot be compared by efficiency

23. What is one primary disadvantage of brushed DC motors in unmanned aircraft applications?
    a. exhaust emissions
    b. EMI, RFI interference
    c. EMP interference
    d. vibration

24. Electric motors used in UAV aircraft can be identified by the number of motor input wires as to their being brushed or brushless.
    a. True
    b. False

25. A/An _____ greatly simplifies the selection of electronic speed control functions such as soft start or braking.
    a. beep and tone card
    b. programming card
    c. manufacturer's manual
    d. online APP

26. The outrunner style electric motor is especially suited to _____.
    a. low rpm, high torque
    b. high rpm, low torque
    c. ducted fan unmanned aircraft
    d. small propellers

27. The location of the _____ determines if a UAV motor is described as inrunner or outrunner in design.
    a. stator
    b. permanent magnets
    c. commutator
    d. coil windings

28. KV is the measured rpm of an unloaded electric motor with 1 _____ applied.
    a. watt
    b. amp
    c. volt
    d. farad

29. Low KV rated electric motors will turn _____ propellers _____.
    a. smaller, slower
    b. larger, slower
    c. smaller, faster
    d. larger. faster

30. UAV powerplant maintenance and inspection is especially important as vibration, heat, wear, and stress have detrimental effects upon the powerplant.
    a. False
    b. True

SECTION B
Knowledge Application and Demonstration Questions:

1. A designer of unmanned aircraft has set low vibration as a top priority in the selection of their propulsion system. What options are available to them from lowest to highest concerning vibration?
2. An experimental rotorcraft UAS utilizes ducted fan propulsion on each of its 8 arms. The motor selected to optimize performance would have a Kv rating that is _____?
3. A recreational model aircraft pilot wishes to eliminate the spur gear reduction system between their motor and propeller. They would select what type of electric motor to achieve similar performance?
4. A student is writing a report on four stroke reciprocating engines and they want to list some specifications of the engine. How would they determine the number of spark events in one minute for a particular engine?
5. A company wishes to do high altitude surveillance of the highway system surrounding a major city. The unmanned aircraft is to remain aloft for 8 hours at an altitude of 30,000 feet. The propulsion system selected for this mission would most likely be what type?

Workbook

CHAPTER 6 – FLIGHT CONTROL

SECTION A
Chapter Review and Study Aid Questions:

1. The method of unmanned flight that relies upon an operator only to control the aircraft is called _____.
    a. manual ✓
    b. assisted manual
    c. autonomous
    d. operator assisted

2. The stabilized flight of an unmanned aircraft to a predetermined waypoint, with no operator input is considered _____.
    a. assisted manual
    b. automatic
    c. manual
    d. autonomous ✓

3. Controlled flight by reference to a video downlink camera is called FPV and is a form of _____ unmanned flight.
    a. manual
    b. assisted manual ✓
    c. autonomous
    d. operator enhanced

4. A mode 2 manual flight transmitter has the yaw control _____.
    a. on the right stick
    b. on a rotary switch
    c. on a 3 position aux switch
    d. on the left stick ✓

5. A mode 2 manual flight transmitter controls down pitch _____.
    a. by pushing the left stick towards the top of the transmitter
    b. by pushing the right stick towards the top of the transmitter ✓
    c. by pulling the right stick towards the bottom of the transmitter
    d. by pulling the left stick towards the bottom of the transmitter

6. Flight mode selection is normally accomplished by _____ on a manual flight transmitter.
    a. moving the sticks
    b. cycling the on/off switch
    c. moving various toggle or rotary switches ✓
    d. releasing the trainer switch

7. A _____ is the muscle to move the control surface of a UAV.
    a. receiver
    b. transmitter
    c. battery
    d. servo motor ✓

8. When a control stick is moved a small amount and this results in a small control surface movement this is called _____ control.
   a. **proportional** ✓
   b. proper
   c. assisted manual
   d. pulse

9. One transmitter may use only one frequency in the 72 MHz band. This limitation was eliminated with 2.4GHz spread spectrum technology.
   a. **True** ✓
   b. False

10. The operation of matching one receiver to one transmitter utilizing spread spectrum frequency control is referred to as _____.
    a. matching
    b. setting
    c. controlling
    d. **binding** ✓

11. A piezo gyroscope is a device to stabilize one _____ of an unmanned aircraft.
    a. **axis** ✓
    b. wing
    c. tail
    d. fuselage

12. If the operator of an unmanned aircraft with a piezo gyro installed wants to initiate a right roll they would _____.
    a. release the transmitter sticks
    b. **move the aileron stick to the right** ✓
    c. command the gyro to initiate a right turn
    d. cannot be determined

13. An unmanned aircraft autopilot system is installed between the _____ and the _____.
    a. battery, receiver
    b. receiver, transmitter
    c. servos, battery
    d. **receiver, servos** ✓

14. Autopilot systems are sensitive to temperatures and should be allowed to stabilize with their outside environment for best accuracy and control.
    a. **True** ✓
    b. False

15. Return to launch is an autopilot mode that automatically returns the aircraft to the point of takeoff in some systems. This feature requires _____.
    a. **a functioning GPS**
    b. sonar
    c. radar
    d. cannot be determined

16. If RTL is initiated with a large tree between the operator and the aircraft, the aircraft will avoid the tree using GPS, compass, and barometric information sensors.
    a. True
    b. **False**

17. Return to launch relies upon GPS and compass sensors to provide stabilized flight back to the point of takeoff. If RTL is not functioning what are the operator's options?
    a. descend in place using manual flight control
    b. attempt to return using manual, or assisted manual, flight control
    c. establish visual orientation and attempt a return flight manually
    d. **all of the above**

18. Telemetry is a unidirectional downlink that provides the information to generate a heads up display on a ground station only.
    a. True
    b. **False**

19. Telemetry radios in unmanned aircraft are selected with frequencies _____ the manual flight controller.
    a. the same as
    b. conflicting with
    c. **different than**
    d. telemetry does not use radio frequencies

20. What is an example of typical telemetry based information routinely displayed on the HUD.
    a. servo position
    b. battery position
    c. **aircraft attitude**
    d. magnetic interference

21. What is the term used to describe the ability of an unmanned aircraft autopilot to record flight data?
    a. flight data recorder
    b. data transfer
    c. data telemetry
    d. **data logging**

22. An example of an autonomous failsafe would be the unmanned aircraft circling in place after losing the telemetry radio signal for 20 seconds.
    a. **True**
    b. False

23. A _____ is an example of a failsafe mechanical system.
    a. servo motor
    b. receiver
    c. transmitter
    d. parachute

24. The _____ must be changed when installing an autopilot from a multirotor to a fixed wing aircraft.
    a. motors
    b. batteries
    c. firmware
    d. sensor package

25. The tuning of PID values is a method of _____ for the autopilot.
    a. failsafe installation
    b. installation tuning
    c. sensor installation
    d. connector installation

26. PID vales are adjusted in what direction to increase the authority and control of the autopilot.
    a. lower values
    b. relative values
    c. higher values
    d. cannot be determined

27. Vibration directly affects what internal components of the autopilot?
    a. initial measurement units
    b. GPS module
    c. compass module
    d. inertial measurement units

28. A wire leading from the motor to the power system battery of an unmanned aircraft may introduce what unwanted condition?
    a. compass declination
    b. radio frequency interference
    c. electromagnetic interference
    d. power separation

29. The magnetometer of an unmanned aircraft autopilot installation may be protected from interference by metallic shielding and physically locating the compass away from sources of onboard magnetism.
    a. False
    b. True

30. When testing a new autopilot installation, what direction should the left aileron move when the aircraft is manually rolled to the right in autonomous mode?
    a. down
    b. neutral
    c. up
    d. cannot be determined

31. _____ is/are used to test the correct autonomous function of a multirotor aircraft prior to flight.
    a. Special gauges
    b. Magnetometers
    c. Deviation
    d. Motor rpm

32. When in stability control mode, the _____ motors of a quadcopter should accelerate when the front of the aircraft is lowered by a wind gust.
    a. M2, M3
    b. M1, M4
    c. front
    d. rear

33. _____ is the initial flight of an unmanned vehicle and may reveal serious weaknesses in the design or installed systems.
    a. Test flight
    b. Flight line
    c. Over flight
    d. Flight test

34. The data logging capability is very important in the flight test phase of an unmanned aircraft.
    a. True
    b. False

35. The _____ GHz band has the best overall performance for first person viewer flight operations using video transmitters.
    a. 2.4
    b. 72
    c. 433
    d. 5.8

36. An/A _____ must be used when flying FPV for situational awareness and collision avoidance with manned aircraft.
    a. tether
    b. observer
    c. operator
    d. communication radio

SECTION B
Knowledge Application and Demonstration Questions:

1. A manned aircraft is approaching the area where you are operating solely by reference to the video display within a pair of FPV goggles. Your observer tells you about the approaching aircraft. How should you respond?
2. The HUD display is showing a bad compass health warning when the electric motor is throttled beyond mid position. What can be done about this issue?
3. When autonomous flight is selected on a fixed wing aircraft, the wings begin to roll left and right aggressively. What programming features of the autopilot will correct this problem?
4. The designer and flight test technician of an unmanned aircraft wish to determine the position of the elevator servo in relation to airspeed and pitch angle. This information may be obtained from what location?
5. A manual flight control receiver of a UAS is operating on 2.4Ghz. A data researcher wants to install a camera system that transmits video to the ground. What is your advice regarding frequency selection?

CHAPTER 7 – SENSORS AND PAYLOAD

SECTION A
Chapter Review and Study Aid Questions:

1. When integrating a payload on an unmanned aircraft, what are the 3 primary concerns?
    a. weight, emissions, vibration
    b. cost, weight, EMI
    c. cost, weight, vibration
    d. weight, EMI, emissions

2. The weight of the payload will determine the size and lifting capability of the UAV required.
    a. True
    b. False

3. UAV vibration can be an issue with sensitive payloads. One way to reduce vibration is to _____.
    a. use vibration absorbing mounts
    b. select a fixed wing design with electric propulsion
    c. select a multirotor aircraft
    d. both a and b

4. Radio emissions from a particular payload communicating information to the ground will have the most potential effect upon the UAV's _____.
    a. propulsion system
    b. weight and balance
    c. guidance and stability systems
    d. cannot be determined

5. Reciprocating piston engines on unmanned aircraft are especially difficult to integrate in regards to _____.
    a. vibration and weight
    b. vibration and duration
    c. exhaust emissions and weight
    d. vibration and EMI, RFI emissions

6. If a payload is sensitive to electromagnetic interference _____ may be used.
    a. magnets
    b. shielding
    c. refraction
    d. reflection

7. Locating the autopilot and magnetometer as far from the UAV _____ as possible will help reduce EMI.
    a. engine
    b. tail
    c. GPS
    d. center of gravity

Unmanned Aerial Systems: The Definitive Guide

Workbook

8. _____ of the payload must be considered when integrating into a UAV airframe.
    a. Mounting permanence
    b. Accessibility
    c. Accountability
    d. Manufacturer

9. The rotation of a payload about any or all of the three axes of movement is provided by a _____.
    a. vibration isolator
    b. pivot
    c. sling
    d. gimbal

10. When a camera payload is mounted to a rotorcraft, the _____ function may be provided by the aircraft itself.
    a. macro
    b. flash
    c. pan
    d. zoom

11. A _____ gimbal system uses motion and acceleration sensors, much like an autopilot, to level the camera despite UAV axes changes.
    a. fixed
    b. removable
    c. temporary
    d. stabilized

12. One limitation of the servo actuated camera gimbal is the _____.
    a. cost
    b. output arm travel
    c. motor rotation
    d. power required

13. Payloads that sample air often require a _____ for accurate sampling.
    a. battery
    b. remote inlet
    c. gasoline engine
    d. rotorcraft

14. Two examples of acoustic payload applications would include _____ and _____.
    a. surveillance, water sampling
    b. transmitting, absorbing
    c. surveillance, natural events
    d. water sampling, absorbing

15. The brushless gimbal is so named for its resistance to fouling and binding by plants during unimproved field deployment.
    a. True
    b. False

16. The static load of an unmanned aircraft is _____ than the dynamic load.
    a. less
    b. greater
    c. wider
    d. narrower

17. A 60 degree bank of a fixed wing aircraft will _____ the G loading.
    a. half
    b. third
    c. reduce
    d. double

18. A fixed wing UAV weighing 54 pounds enters a coordinated 60 degree bank to the left. What will be the weight supported by the airframe in this example?
    a. cannot be determined
    b. 27 pounds
    c. 108 pounds
    d. 120 pounds

19. An unmanned aircraft is weighed without gasoline onboard. Is this a possible scenario regarding the weight and balance required for controlled flight?
    a. no
    b. yes
    c. cannot be determined

20. The effect of a heavily loaded UAV is _____.
    a. increased climb rate
    b. higher landing speed
    c. longer takeoff distance
    d. both b and c

21. If the center of gravity of a UAV is moved aft, the resulting effect on flight control is that the _____.
    a. roll will become more sensitive
    b. roll will become less sensitive
    c. pitch control will become less sensitive
    d. pitch control will become more sensitive

22. The center of gravity of a fixed wing aircraft travels along the _____ axis.
    a. lateral
    b. vertical
    c. horizontal
    d. longitudinal

23. In center of gravity calculations for unmanned aircraft _____.
    a. weight minus moment equals arm
    b. weight multiplied by arm equals moment
    c. total weight plus arm equals moment
    d. moment minus arm equals weight

24. Rotorcrafts are more or less sensitive to lateral balance than fixed wing aircraft?
    a. more
    b. less
    c. cannot be determined

25. The empty weight of an unmanned aircraft is defined as all weight except _____ weight.
    a. battery and systems
    b. fuel and payload
    c. fuel and tare
    d. battery and motor

26. The longitudinal center of gravity is calculated and a point established along the _____.
    a. lateral axis
    b. vertical axis
    c. yaw axis
    d. mean aerodynamic chord

27. Total moment divided by _____ is used to determine the center of gravity of an unmanned aircraft.
    a. total arm
    b. arm divided by two
    c. total weight
    d. cannot be determined

28. The _____ is a vertical reference line. Items added to the left will have a negative arm and items to the right will have a positive arm.
    a. buttock line
    b. station line
    c. ballast
    d. datum

29. What material is commonly used for ballast in UAV center of gravity modifications?
    a. water
    b. fuel
    c. lead
    d. electrolyte

30. If a UAV is weighed and the following results obtained, what is the resulting CG?
    Nose wheel = 20 pounds at +2 inches
    Right main wheel = 53 pounds at +42 inches
    Left main wheel = 52 pounds at +42 inches
    a. 35.6 inches aft of datum or just ahead of the main wheels
    b. 35.6 inches aft of datum or just behind the main wheels
    c. 35.6 feet
    d. .028 inches

31. An unmanned rotorcraft's center of lift is normally located at the center shaft of the main rotor.
    a. True
    b. False

32. An unmanned rotorcraft is leveled prior to weighing _____.
    a. full of fuel and payload
    b. empty fuel with no payload
    c. both laterally and longitudinally
    d. all of the above

33. The _____ location determines the arm value when weighing unmanned aircraft.
    a. nose
    b. fuel tank
    c. vernier scale
    d. station

34. Dynamic stability can be either _____ and has a great impact upon UAV controllability, stability, and maneuverability.
    a. upper, neutral, or lower
    b. positive, neutral, or negative
    c. greater, lesser, or the same
    d. is not a form of stability

SECTION B
Knowledge Application and Demonstration Questions:

1. An unmanned, fixed wing aircraft is being used for agricultural imaging. The flight of the aircraft must pass up and down the field with the camera pointed directly down, and not yawed with the aircraft to compensate for cross winds. The solution to this problem would be?
2. A new unmanned rotorcraft is found to be unbalanced along the lateral axis. The best solution to this problem would be to add or subtract weight in what location?
3. In horizontal flight the elevator of an unmanned, fixed wing aircraft is deflected upward for a moment by the servo and then returned to neutral. The aircraft has negative pitch stability. The resulting effect will be?
4. The video feed from the gimbal mounted camera of a rotorcraft is distorted by vibration. The solution to this issue would be?
5. An unmanned aircraft is nearing the end of its flight and runs out of fuel. The result is an overly sensitive pitch response with a crash when attempting to land. The fuel tank is located in the aircraft nose. What happened in this scenario and what can be done to prevent recurrence?

Workbook

CHAPTER 8 – AIRSPACE OPERATIONS

SECTION A
Chapter Review and Study Aid Questions:

1. Knowledge of the national airspace system is as important to manned aircraft pilots as it is to unmanned operators for the purpose of safety.
    a. True
    b. False

2. Active control of aircraft, in regards to airspace, is _____.
    a. manual flight control
    b. autonomous flight control
    c. being in contact with an air traffic control facility
    d. only used in unmanned aircraft

3. When operating under instrument flight rules in manned aircraft (IFR) you must contact the appropriate control tower to receive a clearance to land.
    a. True
    b. False

4. VFR stands for _____.
    a. vertical flight regime
    b. various flight requirements
    c. vertical flight rules
    d. visual flight rules

5. Uncontrolled airspace is airspace that individuals must provide their own _____ primarily by see and avoid techniques.
    a. separation
    b. landing area
    c. aircraft
    d. landing clearance

6. Positive controlled airspace differs from uncontrolled in what significant way?
    a. All aircraft use visual flight rules for separation.
    b. All aircraft are separated by air traffic control.
    c. Only instrument flight rule aircraft may enter positive airspace.
    d. Only visual flight rule aircraft may enter positive airspace.

7. Class _____ is the most restrictive airspace and class _____ the least restrictive.
    a. B,G
    b. A,G
    c. D,E
    d. C,D

8. Sectional charts are scaled to _____ and provide the unmanned operator with vital airspace information.
    a. 2 miles to the inch
    b. 8 miles to the inch
    c. 2 cm to the kilometer
    d. 8 cm to the kilometer

9. A sectional chart will depict restricted airspace in what way?
    a. yellow border
    b. red border
    c. capital letter R
    d. capital letter P

10. UAS and VFR flight are not permitted in class _____ airspace at or above 18,000 feet.
    a. B
    b. A
    c. G
    d. D

11. Class B airspace may allow UAS operations at the discretion of the _____.
    a. ATC personnel
    b. operator
    c. observer
    d. pilot

12. Class C airspace normally surrounds less busy airports and extends from the surface to approximately _____ feet, depending upon the facility.
    a. 3000
    b. 2000
    c. 1000
    d. 4000

13. All control towers are required to have operational radar and provide aircraft separation within their established airspace boundaries.
    a. True
    b. False

14. If an unmanned aircraft takes off and lands outside of controlled airspace there is no need to contact ATC prior to flight.
    a. True
    b. False

15. Who is responsible for contacting ATC prior to operating an unmanned aircraft in class B airspace?
    a. ATC
    b. FAA
    c. UAS operator
    d. cannot be determined

16. Class F airspace begins at 700 feet and extends upward to _____ feet.
    a. 18,000
    b. 2500
    c. 700
    d. cannot be determined

17. The airspace above the White House is designated as _____.
    a. B
    b. A
    c. Prohibited
    d. Restricted

18. A temporary restricted area or TFR serves as a temporary _____.
    a. prohibited area
    b. restricted area
    c. class B airspace
    d. class E airspace

19. A notice to airmen, or NOTAM, advises _____ of special, temporary, airspace changes or other situations regarding air safety.
    a. unmanned operators
    b. ATC
    c. manned aircraft pilots
    d. all of the above

20. How is 18,000 feet above mean sea level expressed in aviation documents?
    a. FL 18
    b. FL 18 MSL
    c. FL 18 AGL
    d. FL 180

21. A military operating area or MOA contains military aircraft operations of what potential nature?
    a. aerobatic training
    b. flight training
    c. maneuvers for simulated ground attack
    d. all of the above

22. Aircraft flying VFR are prohibited from flying in active MOA airspace.
    a. True
    b. False
    c. cannot be determined

23. How are military controlled firing areas depicted on sectional charts?
    a. magenta lines
    b. blue lines
    c. letter P
    d. they are not depicted

24. Radio communications with ATC are standardized, when expressing the number 11 in singular format, an unmanned operator would say _____.
    a. "eleven"
    b. one 11 one
    c. one one
    d. even

25. The UAS call letters N778U would be expressed as _____ when communicating with ATC.
    a. Nova seven seven ate you
    b. November seven seventy eight you
    c. November seven seven eight Uniform
    d. En seven hundred seventy eight Uw

26. All altitudes used in the ATC system, except cloud heights, is _____.
    a. MSL
    b. AGL
    c. 29.99
    d. 59 degrees

27. UTC, or uncoordinated universal time, is the time based on a clock in Greenwich, England at the corner of prime and meridian streets.
    a. True
    b. False

28. The proper terms to describe universal time versus local time would be _____ and local.
    a. zeum
    b. zulo
    c. zumu
    d. zulu

29. When receiving information from an ATC facility regarding wind, the statement "wind one eight zero at one five" would indicate _____.
    a. a north wind at 5 mph
    b. south wind at 15 mph
    c. north wind at 15 knots
    d. south wind at 15 knots

30. A _____ and VHF Omnidirectional Range (VOR) station must be used together when navigating by reference to only one VOR station.
    a. DFE
    b. GPS
    c. TRACON
    d. DME

31. GNSS transmitters are typically located on low earth orbit satellites and provide the primary information for what form of navigation?
    a. VORTAC
    b. WAS
    c. VOR
    d. GPS

32. GNSS signals must be _____ to provide the necessary accuracy for precision, automated, landings and takeoffs.
    a. shielded
    b. adapted
    c. augmented
    d. encrypted

33. Improving the accuracy of GPS navigation may be accomplished with ground, satellite, and potentially aircraft based stations.
    a. True
    b. False

34. Runway 27 is oriented so unmanned aircraft would be taking off and landing while facing _____.
    a. north
    b. northwest
    c. east
    d. west

35. Runway 9 is oriented so unmanned aircraft would be taking off and landing while facing _____.
    a. east
    b. north
    c. southeast
    d. southwest

36. What primary elements in the atmosphere are responsible for weather?
    a. nitrogen, oxygen
    b. humidity, UV radiation
    c. water vapor, uneven heating
    d. carbon, nitrogen

37. Standard day barometric pressure at sea level is _____.
    a. 29.92 psi
    b. 14.7 inches of mercury
    c. 29.92 inches of mercury
    d. not easily determined

38. Atmospheric temperature and pressure comprise the elements of what aeronautical concept?
    a. pressure altitude
    b. weather
    c. inversion
    d. density altitude

39. Wind currents are primarily created by what differences in the atmosphere?
    a. pressure
    b. humidity
    c. temperature
    d. oxygen

40. A high density altitude will have what effect upon UAV performance?
    a. reduced
    b. increased
    c. remains constant
    d. increased lift

41. Air flows from areas of _____ pressure to areas of _____ pressure resulting in the phenomenon we describe as wind.
    a. low, high
    b. high, low
    c. low, low
    d. water, land

42. Another way to describe an anti-cyclonic circulation is _____.
    a. a low pressure area
    b. hurricane
    c. cloud formation
    d. high pressure area

43. As viewed from a satellite, a high pressure area will rotate clockwise.
    a. True
    b. False

44. Areas of low pressure will rotate _____ as viewed from above.
    a. clockwise
    b. counter clockwise
    c. vertically
    d. North to South

45. A high pressure zone is moving from west to east across the middle of the United States, the unmanned operator can expect winds from a _____ direction on the back, or trailing side, of the air mass.
    a. southerly
    b. northerly
    c. easterly
    d. cannot be determined

46. Convective air currents are created by _____.
    a. melting ice caps
    b. ocean tide
    c. moon phase
    d. uneven heating

47. An unmanned aircraft on landing approach must transverse a large parking lot and then a grassy field immediately prior to landing. The likely effect these terrain features will provide on a sunny day is _____.
    a. an initial descent, then ascent on approach
    b. an initial ascent, then descent on approach
    c. a steady approach with little vertical displacement
    d. a strong vertical displacement after touch down

48. Mountains have the same effect upon unmanned aircraft flight as trees and other obstructions in that air will _____ on the windward side and _____ on the leeward side.
    a. descend, ascend
    b. ascend, descend
    c. drop, climb
    d. increase in temperature, decrease in temperature

49. A line of trees along the runway will have the most effect on unmanned aircraft operations if the operating area is windward, or leeward of the trees?
    a. windward
    b. no effect
    c. leeward
    d. cannot be determined

50. When atmospheric isobars are very tightly represented on a weather map, this would indicate to the unmanned operator that _____.
    a. the wind will be light
    b. the wind will be from the North
    c. the wind will be variable
    d. the wind will be strong

51. Areas of calm wind are represented in what way on a weather map?
    a. dashed line
    b. circle with three slashes
    c. line with three slashes
    d. circle within a circle

52. Relative humidity is the amount of water vapor in the air in the form of rain.
    a. True
    b. False

53. Relative humidity is the amount of water vapor in the air as compared to what the air is capable of holding and is expressed as a percentage.
    a. True
    b. False

54. Visibility is likely to be restricted in the atmosphere by _____ relative humidity and this may affect the unmanned operator's ability to see and avoid other aircraft.
    a. lower
    b. higher
    c. colder
    d. isotropic

55. As dew point and atmospheric temperature become closer together, what weather phenomenon is likely to occur?
    a. high pressure area
    b. tornado
    c. fog
    d. low pressure area

56. _____ activity in the atmosphere produces updrafts and downdrafts and may make the control of an unmanned aircraft difficult.
    a. Cloud
    b. Convective
    c. Barometric pressure
    d. Isobaric

57. A rain producing cloud usually has a suffix or prefix that uses the word "nimbo or nimbus".
    a. True
    b. False

58. Typical high level clouds are cirrus, cirrostratus, and cirrocumulus.
    a. True
    b. False

59. What is the name for a cloud type that forms in layers?
    a. cummulis
    b. cirrus
    c. stratus
    d. lenticular

60. The term for a cloud layer that is less than overcast is _____.
    a. broken
    b. scattered
    c. fracto
    d. nimbus

61. Horizontal surface visibility is primarily important to the unmanned operator for _____.
    a. reliable autonomous operation
    b. unobstructed radio transmissions
    c. condensation on sensitive electronics
    d. safety in see and avoid flight

62. An air mass is formed when air that has been stagnant in a region begins to move. These may be _____ or _____ depending upon their origin.
    a. warm and moist, cold and dry
    b. isobaric, isotropic
    c. convective, conductive
    d. cannot be determined

63. What is the term used to describe the boundary layer between two different masses of air?
    a. cyclone
    b. tsunami
    c. tropical depression
    d. front

64. An advancing cold front will _____ when it encounters a warm air mass.
    a. wedge under and push the warm air upward
    b. wedge over and suppress the warm air
    c. form an inversion with cold air on top
    d. be deflected and dissipate

65. A nearby towering cumulonimbus cloud is a concern to the unmanned operator for what reason?
    a. It signals the stagnation of a warm front with very high temperatures possible.
    b. It signals that the air mass is extremely stable and will not produce adequate lift.
    c. It signals a steady weather pattern with light drizzle and fog possible.
    d. It signals the possible presence of extreme weather with heavy rain and turbulence.

66. Surface _____ provide local weather conditions and other relevant information for a radius of five miles of a specific airport.
    a. anemometers
    b. observations
    c. conduction
    d. augmentations

67. This METAR pilot weather report - METAR KGGG 161753Z AUTO 14021G26 3/4SM +TSRA BR BKN008 OVC012CB 18/17 A2970 RMK PRESFR indicates the wind is:
    a. 161 degrees, at 53 knots
    b. 297 degrees at 0 mph
    c. 18 degrees at 17 knots
    d. 140 degrees at 21 knots gusting to 26

68. Surface visibility in weather reports is expressed in statute or nautical miles?
    a. statute
    b. nautical
    c. cannot be determined
    d. none of the above

69. As expressed in a METAR, the altimeter setting of A2991 would be _____?
    a. 29.92 psi
    b. Absolute 2991
    c. 29.91 in. hg.
    d. The above expression is not an altimeter setting.

70. Real time weather depictions in the cockpit derive their information from _____?
    a. augmented ground stations
    b. AWOS
    c. NORAD
    d. satellites

71. The weather depiction chart is prepared and transmitted by computer every 3 hours beginning at 0100Z time.
    a. True
    b. False

SECTION B
Knowledge Application and Demonstration Questions:

1. An unmanned test flight is being planned 24 hours in advance. The weather forecast shows an approaching high pressure area that will be centered over the proposed flight area at the time of the flight. The winds are predicted to be calm. As the operator makes their own assessment, is this a forecast that makes sense?
2. An unmanned aircraft is planning a flight at FL19. Who must be contacted to enter this airspace?
3. A wind is blowing from 270 at 18. A row of trees on the left side of runway 36 will have what effect on the landing?
4. An unmanned operator is in contact with ATC using a two way radio. The tower says descend to 200 and turn heading 145 for collision avoidance with a crop duster arriving for fuel at the towered airport. The operator will respond in what way?
5. The temperature and dew point are predicted to be very close together when planning for an early morning data acquisition flight. The UAS operator can expect what type of weather?

CHAPTER 9 – FLIGHT OPERATIONS

SECTION A
Chapter Review and Study Aid Questions:

1. When operating unmanned aircraft from unimproved areas, the best weather conditions regarding performance would be _____.
    a. hot with light and variable winds
    b. cool with light and variable winds
    c. cool with light, steady winds
    d. hot with strong winds

2. Ground handling, regarding directional control, of tricycle landing gear equipped UAV is usually accomplished with a _____ but may also include _____.
    a. steerable nose gear, rudder
    b. steerable tailwheel, rudder
    c. rudder, ailerons
    d. rudder, elevator

3. The takeoff of a fixed wing UAV from an unimproved surface may be accomplished with _____.
    a. a catapult
    b. a properly equipped automobile
    c. hand launch
    d. all of the above

4. Recessing the camera and lens within the cargo bay is one strategy that helps to protect the camera during landing of a UAV in rough areas.
    a. True
    b. False

5. What is the biggest risk when using a parachute for routine UAV recovery?
    a. increased descent rate
    b. wind drift
    c. decreased descent rate
    d. material selection

6. A catapult accelerates the unmanned aircraft to what speed for takeoff?
    a. stall speed
    b. 50 knots
    c. flying speed
    d. Vne

7. The propulsion force of an inexpensive catapult is provided by what means?
    a. drag weight
    b. centrifugal force
    c. guide rail
    d. latex tubing or bungee

Unmanned Aerial Systems: The Definitive Guide

8. The actual preparation for any UAS mission should begin several days before ever arriving at the flying field.
   a. **True**
   b. False

9. A _____ is an essential part of safe and reliable UAS operations.
   a. flashlight
   b. variometer
   c. **checklist**
   d. fast setting glue

10. What item in the unmanned system ground station receives the radio telemetry signal and displays the information for reference?
    a. video monitor
    b. inverter
    c. **laptop computer**
    d. generator

11. Where should lithium polymer batteries be stored and recharged when conducting operations from remote areas?
    a. inside the UAV
    b. inside the ground station case
    c. inside the tools and equipment case
    d. **in specially designed bags and bunkers**

12. What tool or equipment would be typically stored in a diagnostic case?
    a. flashlight
    b. fast setting epoxy
    c. **tachometer**
    d. video monitor

13. A device to convert 12 volt vehicle power to 110 volt power for laptops and camera chargers is the _____.
    a. reverser
    b. charger
    c. **inverter**
    d. alternator

14. If the UAV begins to obviously deviate from a preprogrammed flight path while in autonomous mode, the best action to take is _____.
    a. trust the autopilot to land in place
    b. **regain manual flight control**
    c. select camera tilt
    d. continue monitoring beyond line of sight

15. Telemetry logs are useful for reviewing a flight for performance, failures, required adjustments, and autopilot accuracy.
    a. **True**
    b. False

16. Review of data logs can be used to determine such things as takeoff speed, cruise speed, and any onboard magnetic interference.
    a. **True**
    b. False

17. What may be determined by observing the amount of charge required to recharge onboard batteries after an unmanned flight?
    a. battery condition
    b. approximate duration
    c. capacity consumed
    d. **all of the above**

18. Flight simulators offer little resemblance to real world unmanned flight and are seldom used for this reason.
    a. True
    b. **False**

19. What piece of equipment has been popular to train operators in manual flight control.
    a. system inverter
    b. patch antenna
    c. **training cord**
    d. piezo gyro

20. What two flight simulator views are most useful for training unmanned operators?
    a. **LOS, FPV**
    b. ADF, GPS
    c. manual, assisted manual
    d. ground, sky

21. What reduction in measured battery capacity will require replacement when used in unmanned aircraft?
    a. **20%**
    b. 80%
    c. 40-50%
    d. cannot be determined

22. A 4400 mah lithium polymer battery pack powering an unmanned multirotor would be charged at what rate?
    a. **4.4 amps**
    b. 1C
    c. 4400 mah
    d. all of the above

23. A lithium polymer battery is rated at a 60 C discharge rate and has a nominal voltage of 11.1 volts. What is the maximum safe discharge available?
    a. 666 amps
    b. 6.66 amps
    c. 66.6 volts
    d. **cannot be determined**

24. Never leave lithium polymer batteries unattended while charging.
    - (a.) True
    - b. False

25. The _____ would contain UAV performance charts and data necessary for safe operations.
    - a. SRM
    - (b.) POH
    - c. W&B
    - d. TCDS

26. An unmanned aircraft would be flight tested in order to generate the data for what documents?
    - (a.) POH, TCDS
    - b. SRM, DME
    - c. certificates, registration
    - d. license, registration

27. The pilot of an unmanned aircraft is referred to as a/an _____ by the FAA.
    - a. pilot
    - b. observer
    - (c.) operator
    - d. technician

28. Information for calculating empty weight center of gravity would be found in the _____ of an unmanned aircraft.
    - a. Hdop
    - b. SRM
    - (c.) TCDS
    - d. logbook

29. FAA publishes _____ for the purpose of correcting unsafe conditions in aircraft.
    - a. service alerts
    - b. service instructions
    - (c.) airworthiness directive
    - d. airworthiness certificates

30. The use of incorrect or over powering signals to confuse or take control of an unmanned system is called _____.
    - (a.) spoofing
    - b. sparking
    - c. encryption
    - d. phase shifting

31. One method of protecting unmanned systems from interference from outside sources is by _____ the signals used to control the vehicle.
    a. spoofing
    b. enclosing
    c. blocking
    d. **encrypting**

32. Complacency and lack of understanding are just two examples of the human factors FAA refers to as the "dirty dozen".
    a. **True**
    b. False

SECTION B
Knowledge Application and Demonstration Questions:

1. Would a higher, or lower altitude be best for parachute deployment as a form of unmanned landing recovery and why?
2. A fixed wing agricultural imaging UAS must get airborne without an improved runway. What are the options for accomplishing this?
3. A new operator is uncomfortable flying the aircraft chosen by a team of researchers to carry their very expensive camera package. How can this operator become familiar with the flight characteristics of the aircraft without risking a crash?
4. A large unmanned aircraft is utilizing a Lycoming engine removed from a certified manned aircraft. An Airworthiness Directive is issued against the engine by FAA. What must the owner of the unmanned aircraft do?
5. Charging and discharging lithium polymer batteries within the unmanned aircraft may result in what?

Workbook

CHAPTER 10 - REGULATIONS

SECTION A
Chapter Review and Study Aid Questions:

1. How are federal air regulations organized?
    a. title, chapter, paragraph
    b. in numerical order
    c. volumes, chapters, parts
    d. alphabetically

2. The primary organization that oversees the regulation of the navigable airspace of the United States is the _____.
    a. NOAA
    b. JAAR
    c. NSF
    d. FAA

3. What is the FAA part number under which most UAS specific regulations are contained?
    a. 102
    b. 135
    c. 147
    d. 107

4. An advisory circular (AC) such as AC 91-57A, published by the FAA, is not legally binding as a regulation.
    a. True
    b. False

5. What is the primary difference between recreational model flight and commercial UAS operations?
    a. Commercial operations are recreational only.
    b. Commercial UAVs weigh more than 55 pounds.
    c. Commercial UAVs are operated above 400 feet AGL.
    d. Recreational operations are of a hobby nature for fun.

6. Aerial photographs, taken for use in the sale of a home, are considered _____.
    a. commercial operations
    b. hobby nature
    c. recreational
    d. outside of the regulatory requirements

7. Receiving class credit to fly an unmanned rotorcraft for university research is _____.
    a. recreational
    b. hobbyist
    c. commercial
    d. exempt

8. Model aircraft operations may utilize autonomous systems as long as it is for hobby or recreational purposes.
   a. True
   b. False

9. A large multirotor carrying a life vest is used to recover a stranded swimmer from a river. The pilot is a paid employee of the rescue company. This would be an example of _____.
   a. hobby use
   b. humanitarian operations which are exempted from any regulations
   c. commercial operations
   d. police and fire applications which are exempt from all regulation

10. An operator flying a fixed wing aircraft, using FPV technology, records aerial video of their farm field and home. This is considered to be what type of operations?
    a. recreational
    b. commercial
    c. humanitarian
    d. public use

11. An unmanned aircraft equipped with an autopilot, telemetry, a camera, and parachute recovery system is flown to produce a 3D map for an architectural company. This is what type of operation?
    a. hobby/recreational
    b. public use
    c. commercial
    d. humanitarian

12. Model aircraft operators, that fly for recreational purposes only, are excluded from all advisory or regulatory compliance.
    a. True
    b. False

13. The introduction of new legislation by the FAA will often take the form of an NPRM and provide a/an _____ for public input.
    a. exemption
    b. COA
    c. comment period
    d. volume

14. AC 91-57A does not apply if an unmanned aircraft is operated _____.
    a. within the United States
    b. over water
    c. commercially
    d. as a hobbyist

15. Under the regulations for UAS, a micro drone would weigh no more than _____.
    a. 55 pounds
    b. 55 kilos
    c. .55 pounds
    d. 2.2 pounds (1 kilogram)

16. A local ordinance prohibits the use of unmanned aircraft in city parks. This ordinance may be disregarded by an unmanned pilot as the FAA has jurisdiction over all airspace.
    a. True
    b. False

17. Unmanned aircraft, flown for recreational purposes only, may be operated over spectators as they are not regulated by the FAA.
    a. True
    b. False

18. Many local communities have restricted the use of unmanned systems for gathering data that may be considered a/an _____.
    a. invasion of privacy
    b. crop analysis
    c. source of public information
    d. all of the above

SECTION B
Knowledge Application and Demonstration Questions:

1. What are the factors in the flight of an unmanned aircraft that determines if it is recreational or commercial according to the FAA?
2. If you were asked by a local model aircraft flying club to fly your unmanned system, that you routinely use for commercially photographing real estate, what factors would determine if this was a commercial flight or recreational?
3. You are asked to acquire aerial images of a marathon foot race ending in the boundaries of a local park. What entities may have restrictions, regulations, or requirements for operating in this park?
4. What restriction regarding time of day is addressed in the part 107 regulations?
5. A remote pilot's license must be renewed, where would you locate the time interval for this renewal?

Workbook

CHAPTER 11 – FUTURE TRENDS AND TECHNOLOGY

SECTION A
Chapter Review and Study Aid Questions:

1. The modern unmanned system has a rich history in _____ investment of time and money to produce the technology available today.
    a. private sector
    b. university
    c. business
    d. government

2. The propulsion battery recharging developments showing the most promise at this time are _____.
    a. liquid fueled generators
    b. hydrogen fuel catalyst
    c. solar and laser in air, and ground charging stations
    d. in air battery chargers with cycling capability

3. A _____ panel that also forms the skin surface of the wing on a UAV is a form of integrated structure.
    a. fiberglass
    b. carbon
    c. boron
    d. solar

4. A large unmanned aircraft, with greater capabilities, is primarily limited by current _____ regulations.
    a. autopilot
    b. fuel capacity
    c. battery capacity
    d. line of sight (VLOS)

5. Modern airliners and corporate aircraft have autopilot systems installed that could be enhanced for pilotless, autonomous flight.
    a. True
    b. False

6. The primary limitation of line of sight operations is adequate _____ technology.
    a. autonomous landing
    b. FPV range
    c. battery
    d. collision avoidance

7. The use of an unmanned aircraft to apply pesticides to very tightly defined areas is an example of _____.
    a. autonomous limitations
    b. artificial intelligence (AI)
    c. precision agriculture
    d. precision industrial control

Unmanned Aerial Systems: The Definitive Guide

8. The primary limitation of current AI systems is their inability to process changing information in order to make autonomous decisions in real time.
    a. True
    b. False

9. Future unmanned systems will seek to _____.
    a. minimize human and machine advantages
    b. maximize human and machine advantages
    c. minimize human and machine limitations
    d. both b and c

SECTION B
Knowledge Application and Demonstration Questions:

1. Unmanned aircraft guidance technology has progressed to the point of fully autonomous, out of sight flight operations. What limitations make this a technical reality but not a practical one for civilian operators?
2. Describe an integrated UAS structure and give examples.
3. Artificial Intelligence is being pursued as a goal for unmanned aircraft for what reasons.
4. Development of a new unmanned aircraft design, with a full load of autonomous and data systems could cost millions of dollars. What are some practical solutions to this cost?
5. One of the most promising areas of unmanned system applications is in precision agriculture. How will this technology benefit humanity?

WORKBOOK ANSWER KEY

CHAPTER 1 ANSWERS:

SECTION A
1. c
2. a
3. d
4. b
5. b
6. d
7. c
8. d
9. a
10. c
11. d
12. a

SECTION B
1. UAV, UAS, drone, RPV, pilotless, unmanned, Dennyplane, Scout, Firebee, Kettering bug.
2. Composite materials.
3. AC91-57A.
4. 400 feet AGL, 55 pounds.
5. First Person View or FPV.

CHAPTER 2 ANSWERS:

SECTION A
1. d
2. b
3. a
4. a
5. d
6. a
7. d
8. a
9. b
10. d
11. c
12. d
13. d
14. d
15. d
16. b
17. d
18. d
19. a
20. b
21. a
22. c
23. d
24. d
25. b
26. a
27. c
28. a
29. c
30. b
31. d
32. d
33. b
34. d
35. a
36. d
37. b
38. d
39. d
40. a
41. d
42. d
43. a
44. a
45. b
46. a
47. c
48. c
49. a
50. c
51. a
52. c
53. d
54. d
55. a
56. c
57. d
58. d
59. b

SECTION B
1. Manned and unmanned segments of aviation.
2. Fixed wing aircraft.
3. To prevent the exhaust plume from interfering with onboard sensors and cameras.
4. Angled downward.
5. Yes, truss type structures rely upon the strength integrity of the internal structure.

CHAPTER 3 ANSWERS:

SECTION A

1. d	17. b	33. d	49. d	65. a
2. a	18. c	34. c	50. b	66. d
3. c	19. d	35. a	51. a	67. a
4. b	20. b	36. d	52. b	68. a
5. c	21. b	37. d	53. d	69. c
6. b	22. d	38. a	54. a	70. d
7. a	23. a	39. a	55. d	71. c
8. c	24. d	40. c	56. c	72. b
9. a	25. c	41. b	57. b	73. a
10. c	26. d	42. c	58. c	74. d
11. d	27. b	43. d	59. d	75. b
12. b	28. d	44. c	60. c	76. b
13. a	29. d	45. a	61. b	77. b
14. c	30. b	46. c	62. a	78. d
15. a	31. b	47. d	63. a	
16. a	32. a	48. a	64. c	

SECTION B

1. FAA, specifically advisory circular AC43-13.
2. Tricycle gear provides the most stability for takeoff and landing. Conventional, or tailwheel, configurations are lighter and provide more propeller clearance but are more unstable on the ground.
3. Vacuum formed thermoplastics, lightweight fiberglass cloth saturated with epoxy matrix and cured in a mold, preimpregnated fiberglass cloth formed over a mold and vacuum bagged.
4. Brazing does not fuse the base metals and does not provide the structural strength of welding.
5. Unidirectional from the mounting point on the fuselage to the axle.

CHAPTER 4 ANSWERS:

SECTION A

1. d	16. b	31. b	46. c	61. a
2. b	17. a	32. b	47. c	62. a
3. a	18. c	33. d	48. c	63. c
4. a	19. b	34. d	49. d	64. a
5. d	20. a	35. d	50. a	65. d
6. c	21. d	36. d	51. d	66. b
7. a	22. b	37. c	52. c	67. c
8. c	23. c	38. a	53. b	68. a
9. d	24. d	39. a	54. b	69. c
10. b	25. a	40. d	55. b	70. a
11. a	26. d	41. b	56. a	71. d
12. d	27. c	42. b	57. d	72. c
13. a	28. c	43. a	58. b	73. a
14. c	29. d	44. a	59. c	74. a
15. d	30. c	45. b	60. d	75. c

76. c	79. a	82. a	85. a	
77. b	80. d	83. c	86. d	
78. c	81. a	84. c		

SECTION B
1. Generator, alternator, solar panel.
2. Pitot static pressure, GPS, IMU, or a combination of these.
3. Patch antennas are directional and the flat face would need to be positioned towards the operating UAS at all times.
4. GBAS or ground based augmentation system.
5. Portable transceiver capable of transmitting and receiving appropriate tower radio frequencies.

CHAPTER 5 ANSWERS:

SECTION A
1. a	7. a	13. c	19. d	25. b
2. b	8. a	14. b	20. d	26. a
3. c	9. a	15. c	21. b	27. b
4. d	10. d	16. c	22. a	28. c
5. d	11. b	17. c	23. b	29. b
6. b	12. c	18. c	24. a	30. b

SECTION B
1. Electric, turbine, reciprocating piston.
2. relatively high.
3. Brushless outrunner.
4. Revolutions per minute divided by 2.
5. Turbine.

CHAPTER 6 ANSWERS:

SECTION A
1. a	9. a	17. d	25. b	33. a
2. d	10. d	18. b	26. c	34. a
3. b	11. a	19. c	27. d	35. d
4. d	12. b	20. c	28. c	36. b
5. b	13. d	21. d	29. b	
6. c	14. a	22. a	30. a	
7. d	15. a	23. d	31. d	
8. a	16. b	24. c	32. c	

SECTION B
1. Remove the goggles, establish manual flight control, descend, and return to launch (RTL).
2. The compass or power leads to the motor may be shielded to prevent EMI.
3. Aileron (roll) PID gain tuning within the parameters.
4. Data logging function of the autopilot.
5. Any frequency may be used that does not interfere with the manual flight receiver or other essential flight control systems including telemetry.

CHAPTER 7 ANSWERS:

SECTION A

1. a	8. b	15. b	22. d	29. c
2. a	9. d	16. a	23. b	30. a
3. d	10. c	17. d	24. a	31. a
4. c	11. d	18. c	25. b	32. c
5. d	12. b	19. b	26. d	33. d
6. b	13. b	20. d	27. c	34. b
7. a	14. c	21. d	28. d	

SECTION B

1. Mount the camera in a stabilized gimbal.
2. Remove weight from the heavy arm. If that cannot be accomplished, weight should be added to the light arm as far from the vertical axis as practical.
3. The aircraft will pitch upward, and continue pitching more upward, until a down elevator command is given. It will then pitch downward at an ever increasing rate. This is a very difficult plane to control.
4. Vibration isolate the gimbal from the airframe using rubber, silicone, or other means and retest.
5. The aircraft center of gravity progressively moved aft during the flight as the fuel was burned. This resulted in neutral to negative pitch stability. Weight can be moved forward within the aircraft to eliminate this problem.

CHAPTER 8 ANSWERS:

SECTION A

1. a	16. d	31. d	46. d	61. d
2. c	17. d	32. c	47. b	62. a
3. a	18. b	33. a	48. b	63. d
4. .	19. d	34. d	49. c	64. a
5. a	20. b	35. a	50. d	65. d
6. b	21. d	36. c	51. d	66. b
7. .	22. b	37. c	52. b	67. d
8. b	23. d	38. d	53. a	68. a
9. c	24. c	39. a	54. b	69. c
10. a	25. c	40. a	55. c	70. d
11. a	26. a	41. b	56. b	71. a
12. d	27. b	42. d	57. a	
13. b	28. d	43. a	58. a	
14. a	29. d	44. b	59. c	
15. c	30. d	45. a	60. a	

SECTION B

1. Yes.
2. ATC.
3. The air will be turbulent, possibly descending, and will require a crab angle to the left to align with the runway.
4. The operator will acknowledge receiving the directions, descend to 200 feet, and turn to the southeast.
5. low visibility, fog, and possible flight delay due to cloud ceilings and visible moisture.

CHAPTER 9 ANSWERS:

SECTION A

1. c	8. a	15. a	22. a	29. c
2. a	9. c	16. a	23. d	30. a
3. d	10. c	17. d	24. a	31. d
4. a	11. d	18. b	25. b	32. a
5. b	12. c	19. c	26. a	
6. c	13. c	20. a	27. c	
7. d	14. b	21. a	28. c	

SECTION B

1. Lower so that wind drift can be minimized and better control of the landing location exercised.
2. Catapult, car top launch, hand launch.
3. A flight simulator with a similar aircraft selected or the use of a training cord from the transmitter of a more experienced operator.
4. Read and comply with the instructions contained within the AD.
5. Fire and loss of the aircraft and systems with possible destruction of the ground vehicle.

CHAPTER 10 ANSWERS:

SECTION A

1. c	5. d	9. c	13. c	17. b
2. d	6. a	10. a	14. d	18. a
3. d	7. c	11. c	15. c	
4. a	8. a	12. b	16. b	

SECTION B

1. Receiving money, compensation, or furtherance of business for the flight is commercial. Flying for fun is recreational.
2. Whether you were paid or compensated in any way. Free use of the flying field when a fee exists is compensation.
3. Federal, state, and local authorities.
4. No night flights permitted.
5. Part 107.

CHAPTER 11 ANSWERS:

SECTION A
1. d
2. c
3. d
4. d
5. a
6. d
7. c
8. a
9. d

SECTION B
1. FAA regulations and insufficient collision avoidance systems when operating outside of see and avoid profiles.
2. An integrated structure is one that replaces the structure of an airframe with a material that performs two or more functions. The wing skins of an aircraft being used as a solar panel, or radio antenna, are two examples.
3. AI will reduce operator workload, allow flight with limited outside sensor input, and assist the operator in gathering and prioritizing data.
4. Modifying existing airframes with the equipment for unmanned flight, developing several smaller systems that work together (swarming), and pursuing automated manufacturing of large volumes of systems to bring per unit costs down.
5. Lower volumes of pesticides and herbicides applied with better control and effect, large scale crop monitoring for stressors such as drought, fungus, bugs, and damage. The study of genetic characteristics from aerial imaging with the goal of increased yields and targeting of specific, beneficial, genetic traits.